THE
LITERATURE
BOOK

THE
LITERATURE
BOOK

DK LONDON

SENIOR EDITOR
Sam Atkinson

SENIOR ART EDITOR
Gillian Andrews

ART EDITOR
Saffron Stocker

MANAGING EDITOR
Gareth Jones

MANAGING ART EDITOR
Lee Griffiths

ART DIRECTOR
Karen Self

ASSOCIATE PUBLISHING DIRECTOR
Liz Wheeler

PUBLISHING DIRECTOR
Jonathan Metcalf

JACKET DESIGNER
Natalie Godwin

JACKET EDITOR
Claire Gell

JACKET DESIGN DEVELOPMENT MANAGER
Sophia MTT

SENIOR PRODUCER, PRE-PRODUCTION
Tony Phipps

PRODUCER, PRE-PRODUCTION
Nadine King

SENIOR PRODUCERS
Mandy Innes, Rita Sinha

ILLUSTRATIONS
James Graham

DK DELHI

JACKET DESIGNER
Dhirendra Singh

SENIOR DTP DESIGNER
Harish Aggarwal

MANAGING JACKETS EDITOR
Saloni Singh

original styling by
STUDIO8 DESIGN

produced for DK by
COBALT ID

ART EDITORS
Darren Bland, Paul Reid

EDITORS
Richard Gilbert, Diana Loxley,
Kirsty Seymour-Ure, Marek Walisiewicz,
Christopher Westhorp

First published in Great Britain in
2016 by Dorling Kindersley Limited,
80 Strand, London, WC2R 0RL

4 6 8 10 9 7 5 3
005 - 274739 - March/2016

Copyright © 2016
Dorling Kindersley Limited
A Penguin Random House Company

A CIP catalogue record for this book is available
from the British Library.

ISBN: 978-0-2410-1546-9

Printed and bound in China

A WORLD OF IDEAS:
SEE ALL THERE IS TO KNOW

www.dk.com

CONTRIBUTORS

JAMES CANTON, CONSULTANT EDITOR

Our consultant and co-author James Canton
is a lecturer in literature at the University
of Essex, England, where he teaches the
MA "Wild Writing: Literature and the
Environment". His published work includes
*From Cairo to Baghdad: British Travellers in
Arabia* (2011) and *Out of Essex: Re-Imagining
a Literary Landscape* (2013), which explores
the ties between our landscapes and our
selves, delving into the natural world and
its wonders. He is currently writing a tale
about a journey across Britain's wildest
lands on the trail of prehistoric worlds.

HELEN CLEARY

A non-fiction writer and editor, Helen Cleary
studied English literature at Cambridge
University, England. She went on to complete
the prestigious creative writing MA at the
University of East Anglia, where she was
taught by W G Sebald and Lorna Sage. Helen
is a published writer of poetry and short fiction
as well as non-fiction.

ANN KRAMER

A writer and historian, Ann Kramer worked
for various publishers, including DK, before
becoming a full-time writer. Over the years
she has written numerous books for the
general reader on subjects ranging from
art, literature, and the humanities through
to women's history. Having a deep love of
books and literature, Ann has also taught
adult literacy and literature classes.

ROBIN LAXBY

A freelance editor and writer, Robin Laxby has a degree in English from Oxford University, England, and has worked as a publishing director in London. He has reviewed fiction for *The Good Book Guide* and has published five books of poetry since 1985. The Society of Authors recently awarded him a grant to complete a 30,000-word prose poem.

DIANA LOXLEY

Diana Loxley is a freelance editor and writer, and a former managing editor of a publishing company in London, England. She has a doctorate in literature from the University of Essex. Her published works include an analysis of colonial and imperial ideology in various key texts of 19th-century fiction.

ESTHER RIPLEY

Esther Ripley has a first-class degree in literature with psychology and has worked for many years as a journalist, education magazine editor, book reviewer, and short-story competition judge. A former managing editor at DK, she has written books for children and now writes on a range of cultural subjects.

MEGAN TODD

A senior lecturer in social science at the University of Central Lancashire, England, Megan Todd has a degree in English literature from the University of Aberdeen, Scotland. She taught English literature at a grammar school in Cumbria and completed a Masters in gender studies at Newcastle University, with a focus on women's writing.

HILA SHACHAR

A Lecturer in English literature at De Montfort University, England, and writer for The Australian Ballet, Hila Shachar has a doctorate in English literature from The University of Western Australia. She has published widely on literature and film, including her *New York Times* featured book, *Cultural Afterlives and Screen Adaptations of Classic Literature* (2012). She is also the author of several studies on the adaptation of literary works, feminism in literature, and popular and classic fiction. She is currently writing a monograph on literary biopics, examining the screen adaptation of the figure of the author.

ALEX VALENTE

A researcher at the University of East Anglia, England, literary translator, and writer, Alex Valente has contributed to the *Oxford Companion to Children's Literature* (2015), the *Cultures of Comics Work* (2016), and several smaller poetry and prose publications, in both Italian and English. He has also taught first-year English literature modules at the University of East Anglia.

BRUNO VINCENT

As a former bookseller, then a book editor, and now a freelance writer, Bruno Vincent has spent his entire working life around books and the written word. He is the author of ten titles, including two *Sunday Times* top ten bestsellers and two volumes of Dickensian Gothic horror stories for children.

NICK WALTON

Nick Walton is Shakespeare Courses Development Manager at the Shakespeare Birthplace Trust in Stratford-upon-Avon, England. He has written introductory material for the Penguin editions of *Timon of Athens* and *Love's Labour's Lost*, and is co-author of *The Shakespeare Wallbook*. He is also a contributor to DK's *The Shakespeare Book* in the Big Ideas series.

MARCUS WEEKS

Marcus Weeks studied music, philosophy, and musical instrument technology, and had a varied career, first as a teacher of English as a foreign language, then a musician, art-gallery manager, and instrument restorer before becoming a full-time writer. He has written and contributed to numerous books on the humanities, arts, and popular sciences aimed at making big ideas accessible and attractive, including many titles in DK's Big Ideas' series.

PENNY WOOLLARD

A Theatre Studies administrator at the University of Essex, England, Penny Woollard has a doctorate in literature, from the same university, entitled "Derek Walcott's Americas: the USA and the Caribbean". She has lectured on Walcott and has also taught US literature at Essex university.

6

CONTENTS

10 INTRODUCTION

HEROES AND LEGENDS
3000 BCE–1300 CE

20 **Only the gods dwell forever in sunlight**
The Epic of Gilgamesh

21 **To nourish oneself on ancient virtue induces perseverance**
Book of Changes, attributed to King Wen of Zhou

22 **What is this crime I am planning, O Krishna?**
Mahabharata, attributed to Vyasa

26 **Sing, O goddess, the anger of Achilles**
Iliad, attributed to Homer

34 **How dreadful knowledge of the truth can be when there's no help in truth!**
Oedipus the King, Sophocles

40 **The gates of hell are open night and day; smooth the descent, and easy is the way**
Aeneid, Virgil

42 **Fate will unwind as it must**
Beowulf

44 **So Scheherazade began...**
One Thousand and One Nights

46 **Since life is but a dream, why toil to no avail?**
Quan Tangshi

47 **Real things in the darkness seem no realer than dreams**
The Tale of Genji, Murasaki Shikibu

48 **A man should suffer greatly for his Lord**
The Song of Roland

49 **Tandaradei, sweetly sang the nightingale**
"Under the Linden Tree", Walther von der Vogelweide

50 **He who dares not follow love's command errs greatly**
Lancelot, the Knight of the Cart, Chrétien de Troyes

52 **Let another's wound be my warning**
Njal's Saga

54 **Further reading**

RENAISSANCE TO ENLIGHTENMENT
1300–1800

62 **I found myself within a shadowed forest**
The Divine Comedy, Dante Alighieri

66 **We three will swear brotherhood and unity of aims and sentiments**
Romance of the Three Kingdoms, Luo Guanzhong

68 **Turn over the leef and chese another tale**
The Canterbury Tales, Geoffrey Chaucer

72 **Laughter's the property of man. Live joyfully**
Gargantua and Pantagruel, François Rabelais

74 **As it did to this flower, the doom of age will blight your beauty**
Les Amours de Cassandre, Pierre de Ronsard

75 **He that loves pleasure must for pleasure fall**
Doctor Faustus, Christopher Marlowe

76 **Every man is the child of his own deeds**
Don Quixote, Miguel de Cervantes

82 **One man in his time plays many parts**
First Folio, William Shakespeare

90 **To esteem everything is to esteem nothing**
The Misanthrope, Molière

91 **But at my back I always hear Time's winged chariot hurrying near**
Miscellaneous Poems, Andrew Marvell

92 **Sadly, I part from you; like a clam torn from its shell, I go, and autumn too**
The Narrow Road to the Interior, Matsuo Bashō

93 **None will hinder and none be hindered on the journey to the mountain of death**
The Love Suicides at Sonezaki, Chikamatsu Monzaemon

94 I was born in the Year 1632, in the City of York, of a good family
Robinson Crusoe, Daniel Defoe

96 If this is the best of all possible worlds, what are the others?
Candide, Voltaire

98 I have courage enough to walk through hell barefoot
The Robbers, Friedrich Schiller

100 There is nothing more difficult in love than expressing in writing what one does not feel
Les Liaisons dangereuses, Pierre Choderlos de Laclos

102 Further reading

ROMANTICISM AND THE RISE OF THE NOVEL
1800–1855

110 Poetry is the breath and the finer spirit of all knowledge
Lyrical Ballads, William Wordsworth and Samuel Taylor Coleridge

111 Nothing is more wonderful, nothing more fantastic than real life
Nachtstücke, E T A Hoffmann

112 Man errs, till he has ceased to strive
Faust, Johann Wolfgang von Goethe

116 Once upon a time...
Children's and Household Tales, Brothers Grimm

118 For what do we live, but to make sport for our neighbours, and laugh at them in our turn?
Pride and Prejudice, Jane Austen

120 Who shall conceive the horrors of my secret toil
Frankenstein, Mary Shelley

122 All for one, one for all
The Three Musketeers, Alexandre Dumas

124 But happiness I never aimed for, it is a stranger to my soul
Eugene Onegin, Alexander Pushkin

125 Let your soul stand cool and composed before a million universes
Leaves of Grass, Walt Whitman

126 You have seen how a man was made a slave; you shall see how a slave was made a man
Narrative of the Life of Frederick Douglass, Frederick Douglass

128 I am no bird; and no net ensnares me
Jane Eyre, Charlotte Brontë

132 I cannot live without my life! I cannot live without my soul!
Wuthering Heights, Emily Brontë

138 There is no folly of the beast of the Earth which is not infinitely outdone by the madness of men
Moby-Dick, Herman Melville

146 All partings foreshadow the great final one
Bleak House, Charles Dickens

150 Further reading

DEPICTING REAL LIFE
1855–1900

158 Boredom, quiet as the spider, was spinning its web in the shadowy places of her heart
Madame Bovary, Gustave Flaubert

164 I too am a child of this land; I too grew up amid this scenery
The Guarani, José de Alencar

165 The poet is a kinsman in the clouds
Les Fleurs du mal, Charles Baudelaire

166 Not being heard is no reason for silence
Les Misérables, Victor Hugo

168 Curiouser and curiouser!
Alice's Adventures in Wonderland, Lewis Carroll

172 Pain and suffering are always inevitable for a large intelligence and a deep heart
Crime and Punishment, Fyodor Dostoyevsky

178 To describe directly the life of humanity or even of a single nation, appears impossible
War and Peace, Leo Tolstoy

182 It is a narrow mind which cannot look at a subject from various points of view
Middlemarch, George Eliot

184 We may brave human laws, but we cannot resist natural ones
Twenty Thousand Leagues Under the Sea, Jules Verne

185 In Sweden all we do is to celebrate jubilees
The Red Room, August Strindberg

186 She is written in a foreign tongue
The Portrait of a Lady, Henry James

188 Human beings can be awful cruel to one another
The Adventures of Huckleberry Finn, Mark Twain

190 He simply wanted to go down the mine again, to suffer and to struggle
Germinal, Émile Zola

192 The evening sun was now ugly to her, like a great inflamed wound in the sky
Tess of the d'Urbervilles, Thomas Hardy

194 The only way to get rid of a temptation is to yield to it
The Picture of Dorian Gray, Oscar Wilde

195 There are things old and new which must not be contemplated by men's eyes
Dracula, Bram Stoker

196 One of the dark places of the earth
Heart of Darkness, Joseph Conrad

198 Further reading

BREAKING WITH TRADITION
1900–1945

208 The world is full of obvious things which nobody by any chance ever observes
The Hound of the Baskervilles, Arthur Conan Doyle

209 I am a cat. As yet I have no name. I've no idea where I was born
I Am a Cat, Natsume Sōseki

210 Gregor Samsa found himself, in his bed, transformed into a monstrous vermin
Metamorphosis, Franz Kafka

212 Dulce et decorum est pro patria mori
Poems, Wilfred Owen

213 Ragtime literature which flouts traditional rhythms
The Waste Land, T S Eliot

214 The heaventree of stars hung with humid nightblue fruit
Ulysses, James Joyce

222 When I was young I, too, had many dreams
Call to Arms, Lu Xun

223 Love gives naught but itself and takes naught but from itself
The Prophet, Kahlil Gibran

224 Criticism marks the origin of progress and enlightenment
The Magic Mountain, Thomas Mann

228 Like moths among the whisperings and the champagne and the stars
The Great Gatsby, F Scott Fitzgerald

234 The old world must crumble. Awake, wind of dawn!
Berlin Alexanderplatz, Alfred Döblin

235 Ships at a distance have every man's wish on board
Their Eyes Were Watching God, Zora Neale Hurston

236 Dead men are heavier than broken hearts
The Big Sleep, Raymond Chandler

238 It is such a secret place, the land of tears
The Little Prince, Antoine de Saint-Exupéry

240 Further reading

POST-WAR WRITING
1945–1970

250 BIG BROTHER IS WATCHING YOU
Nineteen Eighty-Four, George Orwell

256 I'm seventeen now, and sometimes I act like I'm about thirteen
The Catcher in the Rye, J D Salinger

258 Death is a gang-boss aus Deutschland
Poppy and Memory, Paul Celan

259 I am invisible, understand, simply because people refuse to see me
Invisible Man, Ralph Ellison

260 Lolita, light of my life, fire of my loins. My sin, my soul
Lolita, Vladimir Nabokov

262 He leaves no stone unturned, and no maggot lonely
Waiting for Godot, Samuel Beckett

263 It is impossible to touch eternity with one hand and life with the other
The Temple of the Golden Pavilion, Yukio Mishima

264 He was beat – the root, the soul of beatific
On the Road, Jack Kerouac

266 What is good among one people is an abomination with others
Things Fall Apart, Chinua Achebe

270 Even wallpaper has a better memory than human beings
The Tin Drum, Günter Grass

272 I think there's just one kind of folks. Folks.
To Kill a Mockingbird, Harper Lee

274 Nothing is lost if one has the courage to proclaim that all is lost and we must begin anew
Hopscotch, Julio Cortázar

276 He had decided to live forever or die in the attempt
Catch-22, Joseph Heller

277 Everyday miracles and the living past
Death of a Naturalist, Seamus Heaney

278 There's got to be something wrong with us. To do what we did
In Cold Blood, Truman Capote

280 Ending at every moment but never ending its ending
One Hundred Years of Solitude, Gabriel García Márquez

286 Further reading

CONTEMPORARY LITERATURE
1970–PRESENT

296 Our history is an aggregate of last moments
Gravity's Rainbow, Thomas Pynchon

298 You are about to begin reading Italo Calvino's new novel
If on a Winter's Night a Traveller, Italo Calvino

300 To understand just one life you have to swallow the world
Midnight's Children, Salman Rushdie

306 Freeing yourself was one thing; claiming ownership of that freed self was another
Beloved, Toni Morrison

310 Heaven and Earth were in turmoil
Red Sorghum, Mo Yan

311 You could not tell a story like this. A story like this you could only feel
Oscar and Lucinda, Peter Carey

312 A historical vision, the outcome of a multicultural commitment
Omeros, Derek Walcott

313 I felt lethal, on the verge of frenzy
American Psycho, Bret Easton Ellis

314 Quietly they moved down the calm and sacred river
A Suitable Boy, Vikram Seth

318 It's a very Greek idea, and a profound one. Beauty is terror
The Secret History, Donna Tartt

319 What we see before us is just one tiny part of the world
The Wind-Up Bird Chronicle, Haruki Murakami

320 Perhaps only in a world of the blind will things be what they truly are
Blindness, José Saramago

322 English is an unfit medium for the truth of South Africa
Disgrace, J M Coetzee

324 Every moment happens twice: inside and outside, and they are two different histories
White Teeth, Zadie Smith

326 The best way of keeping a secret is to pretend there isn't one
The Blind Assassin, Margaret Atwood

328 There was something his family wanted to forget
The Corrections, Jonathan Franzen

330 It all stems from the same nightmare, the one we created together
The Guest, Hwang Sok-yong

331 I regret that it takes a life to learn how to live
Extremely Loud and Incredibly Close, Jonathan Safran Foer

332 Further reading

340 GLOSSARY
344 INDEX
352 ACKNOWLEDGMENTS

INTRODU

CTION

Storytelling is as old as humanity itself. The tradition of capturing the events and beliefs of communities reaches back to a time when humans first sat by a fire and told tales. History was preserved in the form of legends and mythologies that were passed down from one generation to the next, and offered answers to the mysteries of the universe and its creation.

Written accounts emerged at the same time as ancient civilizations, but at first the invention of writing met simple, prosaic functions – for example to record transactions between traders or tally quantities of goods. The thousands of cuneiform clay tablets discovered at Ugarit in Syria reveal the already complex

I begin with writing the first sentence – and trusting to Almighty God for the second.
Laurence Sterne

nature of the written form by 1500 BCE. Writing soon evolved from a means of providing trading information, to preserving the oral histories that were integral to every culture and their customs, ideas, morals, and social structures. This led to the first examples of written literature, in the epic stories of Mesopotamia, India, and ancient Greece, and the more philosophical and historical texts of ancient China. As John Steinbeck so succinctly put it in his Nobel Prize acceptance speech in 1962: "Literature is as old as speech. It grew out of human need for it, and it has not changed except to become more needed."

Miss Bingley of Jane Austen's *Pride and Prejudice* may have been talking fatuously when she declared: "How much sooner one tires of anything than of a book!", but this sentiment rings true for many of us. Despite the almost limitless diversions that face readers today, literature continues to satisfy a spiritual or psychological need, and open readers' minds to the world and its extraordinary variety. There are works penned hundreds of years ago that continue to enchant and amuse to this day; complex postmodern texts that can be challenging in the extreme, yet still hold us in their grip; and

new novels that feel so fresh that they read as if words have only just been invented.

Defining literature
Although the simple definition of "literature" is "anything that is written down", the word has become primarily associated with works of fiction, drama, and poetry, and weighted with the impossible-to-quantify distinction of merit and superiority. These values are intrinsic to the canon of literature drawn upon for academic study and appreciation that has been evolving since the middle of the 19th century. The term "canon" was borrowed from the ecclesiastical canons of authorized religious texts. The literary canon – a collection of works commonly agreed to be of exceptional quality – was formed almost entirely from familiar works of western European literature.

Since the mid-20th century, cultural and literary theorists have done much to destabilize the canon by disputing the authority of these lists of the works of "dead, white Europeans". The idea of a perceived canon of "great works" still stands as a useful framework, but rather than the term being used to define the same set of titles, it evolves with each new generation, which

re-examines the ideology and power structures that underpin the selections of previous generations, and questions why certain other works were excluded. Arguably, studying how literature is created and testing its place in the canon may help to make us better readers. In the same spirit, this book features many titles that are traditionally regarded as "great works", but explores their place in the wider story of literature, and within a richer mix of writing drawn from around the globe. They sit alongside newer texts that empower some of the voices that were silenced over the centuries by social constructs such as colonialism and patriarchy, and Europe's dominance over literature.

Choosing books

This book takes a chronological journey through literature, using more than a hundred books as waymarks along the route. It also takes a global approach, exploring literary texts from a wide range of different cultures that many readers may not have encountered previously.

The Literature Book's chosen works are either exemplars of a particular writing style or technique, or represent a group or movement that took a new direction, which was then adopted by other contemporary writers or expanded upon by future generations. The works are arranged chronologically to highlight the emergence of literary innovations against the social and political backdrop of their times. For example, during the 17th and 18th century, French literature evolved from Molière's neoclassical comedies of manners into Voltaire's satirical undermining of Enlightenment optimism, and later into a savage depiction of decadent French aristocracy shown in Pierre Choderlos de Laclos' *Les Liaisons Dangereuses*, published in the lead-up to the French Revolution. These changes in literature inevitably overlap as writers pioneered techniques that

Some books leave us free and some books make us free.
Ralph Waldo Emerson

took time to enter the mainstream, while others continued literary traditions from previous eras.

Lists are always contentious; arguably the hundred or so books chosen here could be replaced with a hundred others, many times over. They are not presented as a definitive list of "must reads"; instead each work is framed by a focus or context that is supported by a timeline of related literary milestones and events. Cross-references link to works of a similar type, or that have influenced or been influenced by the book under discussion, while more than 200 titles are listed for further reading, exploring the literary landscape of each period in greater detail.

The story of literature

Around 4,000 years ago, the first stories to be written down came in the form of poems such as Mesopotamia's *The Epic of Gilgamesh* and India's *Mahabharata*, which were based on oral traditions. Rhyme, rhythm, and metre were essential aids to memory in songs and oral accounts, so it is unsurprising that the first texts made use of familiar poetic devices. Many early written texts were religious, and sacred texts such as the Bible and the Qur'an tell »

the stories of early histories, and have influenced writing for centuries. The form of literature that became Greek drama used a narrative ballad-like form and introduced characters with individual voices, choruses of commentary, and the distinct categories of comedy and tragedy that continue to be used today. The collections of stories that make up the Arabic *One Thousand and One Nights* have multiple origins, but this prose fiction, written in plain speech, makes use of techniques that eventually became a mainstay in modern novels, such as framing (which introduces stories within the framework of another story), foreshadowing, and the inclusion of repetitive themes.

Although the vast medieval era was studded with secular highlights such as the Anglo-Saxon *Beowulf* and tales of chivalric romance, it was dominated in the West by religious texts in Latin and Greek. During the Renaissance, the joint energies of new philosophical investigation and sheer invention opened the door to literary innovation. The driving force behind the Renaissance was the production of new translations of ancient Greek and Roman texts which freed scholars from the dogma of the church. A humanist programme of education which incorporated philosophy, grammar, history, and languages was built on the wisdom of the ancients. The Bible was translated into vernacular speech, enabling Christians to commune directly with their God. Gutenberg's printing press brought books into the lives of ordinary people, and authors such as Geoffrey Chaucer and Giovanni Boccaccio made everyday life the subject of literature. By the early 17th century, Miguel de Cervantes and Daniel Defoe had given the world what many scholars consider to be the first novels, and the First Folio of Shakespeare's plays was published.

The rise of the novel
Drama and poetry continued to evolve as the novel rose inexorably in importance, and by the end

A word after a word after a word is power.
Margaret Atwood

of the 18th century the novel had become a major form of literary expression.

Just as artists are described in terms of movements such as Baroque and Rococo, so literary history is defined by authors united by a particular style, technique, or location. The Romantic movement, characterized by stories driven by the emotions of idiosyncratic heroes, rather than plot and action, had its roots in the German Sturm und Drang movement. Meanwhile, in England, the Romantic poets testified to the power of nature to heal the human soul, and similar themes were taken up by the New England Transcendentalists. The word "genre" was increasingly applied to fiction's subsets – for example, novels in the Gothic genre. In the 19th century, Romanticism was superseded by a new form of social realism, played out in the drawing rooms of Jane Austen's English middle and upper classes, and Gustave Flaubert's provincial French towns, but used increasingly to depict the harsh lives of the poor. Fyodor Dostoyevsky described his novel *Crime and Punishment* as "fantasy realism", and the dark interior monologues of the murderer Raskolnikov have the elements of a psychological thriller. Over the years,

fiction has diversified into multiple genres and subgenres, which today include everything from dystopian novels to fictional autobiography and Holocaust writing.

Alongside the growth of the novel, the vocabulary of literature expanded to describe styles of writing: for example, "epistolary" novels were written in the form of letters; and "Bildungsroman" and "picaresque" denoted coming-of-age tales. The language used within literature was developing too, and novels in the vernacular voice broadened the scope of national literature with writers such as Harriet Beecher Stowe and Mark Twain capturing the diversity of the people of the USA.

In the early 20th century, Western society was revolutionized by industrial and technological advances, new artistic movements, and scientific developments. Within two decades, a generation of young men had been wasted in World War I. A perfect storm of literary experimentation followed, as Modernist writers searched for inventive stylistic features such as stream-of-consciousness writing, and wrote fragmented narratives representing the anguish and alienation of their changing world. After a brief period of literary optimism and experimentation, the world was again thrown into turmoil as World War II began, and the production of literature slowed as many writers became involved in the war effort, and produced propaganda or reported from the front rather than writing literature.

The global explosion

After two brutal global wars, the world was ready for change, and literature was central to the counterculture in the West of the 1950s and '60s. Postmodernist writers and theorists focused on the artifice of writing, demanding more of the reader than simply engaging with a realist narrative. Novels now had fractured or non-linear timespans, unreliable narrators, episodes of magical realism, and multiple-choice endings. During this period, the West, and in particular writing in English, also loosened its grip on world culture. Postcolonial writing emerged in countries such as Nigeria, South Africa, and India, and authors such as Gabriel García Márquez helped raise the status of a group of South American writers of extraordinary creativity.

Modern literature now sings with the previously unheard voices of feminists, Civil Rights campaigners, gay people, black and Native Americans, and immigrants. There is a healthy meritocratic blurring of distinction between classic and popular fiction. Global publishing, independent and internet publishing, global literature courses, national and international book prizes, and the growing number of works published in translation are bringing Australian, Canadian, South African, Indian, Caribbean, and modern Chinese novels, among others, to a world audience. This vast library of global literature has become both a reminder of shared connections worldwide and a celebration of difference. ∎

Reading is the sole means by which we slip, involuntarily, often helplessly, into another's skin, another's voice, another's soul.
Joyce Carol Oates

HEROES
LEGEND
3000 BCE—
1300 CE

AND
S

The earliest known texts, in the Sumerian language, are **written on tablets in Abu Salabikh**, southern Mesopotamia.

c.2600 BCE

King Wen of Zhou writes a commentary on **an ancient method of divination**, which is later expanded into the *Book of Changes* (the *Yijing* or *I Ching*).

12TH–11TH CENTURY BCE

The **ancient Greek epic poems** *Iliad* and *Odyssey*, ascribed to Homer, are written.

c.8TH CENTURY BCE

The adoption of a **democratic constitution** by the Greek city state of Athens ushers in the classical era.

508 BCE

FROM 2100 BCE

The Epic of Gilgamesh is one of the **world's earliest examples of written literature**.

9TH–4TH CENTURIES BCE

The great Sanskrit epic poems *Mahabharata* and *Ramayana* are **composed** in ancient India.

551–479 BCE

The Chinese philosopher Kong Fuzi (Confucius) is active teaching and **compiling the Five Classics**.

5TH CENTURY BCE

The tragedians **Aeschylus, Euripides, and Sophocles** compete for the title of greatest dramatist of Athens.

Systems of writing were first used as a means of recording administrative and commercial transactions. Gradually, these systems became more advanced, preserving ancient wisdom, historical records, and religious ceremonies, all of which had previously been memorized and were passed down orally. Throughout the world's early civilizations, in Mesopotamia, China, India, and Greece, the written canon of literature first emerged as history and mythology.

The form that this earliest literature took was a long narrative poem, known as an epic, which focuses on the legends surrounding a great warrior or leader, and his battles to protect his people from their enemies and the forces of evil. The combination of historical events and mythical adventures, told in a metrical verse form, explained the people's cultural inheritance in an exciting and memorable way.

Tales of gods and men

The first known epics, which include the various versions of *The Epic of Gilgamesh*, and the great Sanskrit epics *Mahabharata* and *Ramayana*, often tell of the origin of a civilization, or a defining moment in its early history. Seen through the exploits of a heroic individual or a ruling family, these epics also explained the involvement of the gods, often contrasting their powers with the frailties of human heroes. This was a theme that also appeared in the later epics ascribed to Homer. His heroes Achilles and Odysseus are depicted not only as noble warriors in the Trojan War that established ancient Greece as a great power, but also as very human characters confronting both fate and their own weaknesses. Later, as Greek influence declined, Roman poets developed their own Latin version of the form, even borrowing the story of the Trojan War, as Virgil did in the *Aeneid*, to produce an epic of the beginning of Rome. The scale and depth of Homer's epics, and their poetic structure, provided the foundation on which Western literature is built.

Greek drama

Another product of the tradition of storytelling in ancient Greece was drama, which developed from recounting a narrative to acting out the part of a character and thereby bringing the tale to life. Gradually,

The *shi* tradition of Chinese poetry reaches its **high point during the Tang dynasty**, in works by poets such as Li Bai and Du Fu.

Virgil writes his masterpiece, and probably the best known Latin epic poem, the *Aeneid*.

Nordic settlers on the island of Iceland establish **a general assembly known as the Althing** for their new commonwealth.

In **the "Golden Age" of Islamic culture**, classical Arabic poetry flourishes and the *One Thousand and One Nights* are collected for the first time.

In *Lancelot, the Knight of the Cart*, Chrétien de Troyes introduces **the idea of chivalric romance** in the context of the Arthurian legends.

29–19 BCE   **618–907 CE**   **930**   **c.8TH–13TH CENTURIES**   **c.1175–81**

5TH CENTURY CE   **868**   **8TH–11TH CENTURY**   **11TH CENTURY**

The poet **Kalidasa writes the Sanskrit epics** *Raghuvamsha* and *Kumarasambhava*, and the play *Abhijnanashakuntala*.

The **earliest known printed book** – a Buddhist text, the *Diamond Sutra* – is produced in China using block printing.

The Anglo-Saxon epic *Beowulf* is composed, the **oldest surviving epic poem in Old English**.

Murasaki Shikibu's *The Tale of Genji* and Sei Shōnagon's *The Pillow Book* use **life in Japan's Heian Court** as their backdrop.

---

this dramatic storytelling became more sophisticated, and by the time Athens was established as a democratic nation-state, the theatre was an integral part of its culture, with dramatists such as Aeschylus, Euripides, and Sophocles producing tragedies and comedies which attracted audiences of thousands.

From Europe to Asia

In northern Europe oral storytelling prevailed, and the tales of these cultures were not written down until around the 8th century. The earliest known complete Anglo-Saxon epic, *Beowulf*, relates history and mythology preserved by the Scandinavian ancestors of the English. The later Icelandic sagas also drew from the Norse legends. Meanwhile, in mainland Europe the nobility were entertained by

professional poets. Some poets took their subject matter from the mythology of ancient Greece and Rome, while the troubadours of southern France chose stirring stories of Charlemagne and his men in battle with the Islamic Moors and Saracens. The *trouvères* of northern France, in contrast, recited lyrical and passionate tales of chivalry and courtly love about the reign of the legendary King Arthur of Britain.

Further east, during the "Golden Age" of Islamic culture in the late medieval period when scholarship was held in high esteem, epic narrative tales such as those in the *One Thousand and One Nights* were valued for their capacity to entertain, although poetry was considered to be the highest form of literature. In ancient China, too,

heroic legends were considered more a form of folklore than literature, and the first written texts to be accorded the status of classics were those that preserved the history, customs, and philosophy of the culture. Along with these factual texts, however, was a collection of odes that provided a model for Chinese poetry for centuries, reaching its high point under the emperors of the Tang dynasty.

In the 11th century, Japan, which had been dominated by Chinese culture, produced its own distinctive literature in the Japanese language. Fictional prose accounts of life in the Heian court developed from the ancient chronicles of the ruling dynasties, anticipating the emergence of the novel in Europe. ∎

ONLY THE GODS DWELL FOREVER IN SUNLIGHT
THE EPIC OF GILGAMESH (FROM 2100 BCE)

Writing first appeared in Mesopotamia at the beginning of what is now known as the Bronze Age (c.3300–1200 BCE). Cuneiform symbols, originally devised as a means of recording commercial transactions, had evolved from numerals into representations of sounds, which offered a means of writing down the Sumerian and Akkadian languages.

Among the fragments of texts discovered in 1853 by the Assyrian archaeologist Hormuzd Rassan are tablets inscribed with tales of the legendary King Gilgamesh of Uruk, which are some of the earliest examples of written literature. The stories had probably been passed down orally in a form that combined history and mythology.

From tyrant to hero

The Epic of Gilgamesh, as the collected tales are known, tells how the oppressive ruler of the Mesopotamian city of Uruk is taught a lesson, and goes on to become a local hero. To punish

Gilgamesh for his arrogance, the gods send the "wild man" Enkidu, formed from clay, to torment him. After a fight, however, they become friends, and embark on a series of monster-slaying adventures. Angered by this turn of events, the gods sentence Enkidu to death. Gilgamesh is distraught at the loss of his companion, but also becomes aware of his own mortality. The second half of the tale tells of Gilgamesh's quest for the secret of eternal life and of his return to Uruk – still a mortal, but a wiser man and more noble ruler. ∎

The life that you seek you never will find.
The Epic of Gilgamesh

See also: *Mahabharata* 22–25 ▪ *Iliad* 26–33 ▪ *Beowulf* 42–43 ▪ *Njal's Saga* 52–53

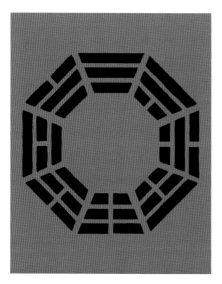

TO NOURISH ONESELF ON ANCIENT VIRTUE INDUCES PERSEVERANCE
BOOK OF CHANGES (12TH–11TH CENTURY BCE), ATTRIBUTED TO KING WEN OF ZHOU

IN CONTEXT

FOCUS
The Five Classics

BEFORE
c.29th century BCE Fu Xi, China's mythical first emperor, devises a method of divination with trigrams, the basis for a Chinese writing system.

AFTER
c.500 BCE The original *Book of Rites*, describing Chinese rituals and ceremonies, is compiled, traditionally thought to be the work of Confucius.

2nd century BCE A Confucian canon of writing begins with the so-called Five Classics.

136 BCE Emperor Wu of Han describes the *Zhou yi* as the foremost of the classics, and titles it *Book of Changes*.

960–1279 CE During the Song era, scholar Zhu Xi includes the Four Books, each of which appeared before 300 BCE, in the canon of Confucian literature alongside the Five Classics.

The *Book of Changes* is about divination; it is a kind of oracle. The original method of divination from which it evolved is attributed to the legendary emperor Fu Xi, and was formalized by King Wen of Zhou (1152–1056 BCE) in a text known as the *Zhou yi*. The "King Wen sequence" describes 64 hexagrams, possible combinations of numbers obtained by casting yarrow stalks or coins, each associated with a certain situation or circumstance, to which Wen offered judgements. Later scholars added comments in the "Ten Wings", including the Great Commentary, which together with the *Zhou yi* became known as the *Book of Changes* (*Yijing* or *I Ching*, as it is still often called).

The book is often referred to as one of the Five Classics, with the *Book of Documents* (*Shujing*), *Spring and Autumn Annals* (*Chunqiu*), *Book of Rites* (*Liji*), and *Book of Odes* (*Shijing*). These Classics are believed to have been compiled by Kong Fuzi (traditional dates 551–479 BCE), who is better known in the West as Confucius. Kong Fuzi's moral and political philosophy was adopted as the official ideology of China during the 3rd century BCE.

Much later, in around the 12th century, shorter writings – either ascribed to Confucius or said to have been inspired by his teachings – were grouped into the Four Books of Confucianism.

A source of wisdom

The Five Classics and Four Books were the main point of reference for Confucianism as a state ideology. The *Book of Changes* seems an odd fit for rational Confucianism, but it was thought to be a source of great wisdom. It complemented the volumes of Confucian philosophy, history, etiquette, and poetry as a book to be consulted not only for its prophetic ability, but also as a model of wise counsel, describing what the "superior man" should do in various situations, and it has remained a source of wisdom in China (and beyond) to the present day. ∎

See also: *Quan Tangshi* 46 ▪ *Romance of the Three Kingdoms* 66–67 ▪ *The Narrow Road to the Interior* 92

WHAT IS THIS CRIME I AM PLANNING, O KRISHNA?

MAHABHARATA (9TH–4TH CENTURIES BCE), ATTRIBUTED TO VYASA

IN CONTEXT

FOCUS
The great Sanskrit epics

BEFORE
3rd millennium BCE Vyasa writes the original version of the *Mahabharata*, in which he appears as a character.

c.1700–500 BCE The Vedas (the Rig Veda, Yajur Veda, Sama Veda and Atharva Veda) are composed in Sanskrit, and together constitute the first of the Hindu scriptures.

AFTER
c.5th–4th century BCE According to tradition, Valmiki writes the *Ramayana*, using the *sloka* (meaning "song") which becomes the standard Sanskrit verse form.

c.250 BCE–1000 CE A canon of Hindu texts known as the Puranas develops. It includes the genealogy of the deities and narratives of cosmology.

The epic poetry of the Indian subcontinent is among the oldest known literature, and it emerged from a long oral tradition of storytelling and reciting. As with other ancient literature, the tales are a mixture of mythology, legends, and historical events, which developed over centuries and were eventually written down.

In addition to this epic poetry, ancient Indian writing includes the Vedas, which are the central sacred texts of Brahminical Hinduism, recorded from around the middle of the 2nd millennium BCE. The Vedas and the poetry were written in Sanskrit, which was regarded as the common literary language of

See also: *The Epic of Gilgamesh* 20 ▪ *Iliad* 26–33 ▪ *One Thousand and One Nights* 44–45 ▪ *Ramayana* 55 ▪ *The Canterbury Tales* 68–71 ▪ *Midnight's Children* 300–05 ▪ *A Suitable Boy* 314–17

Poets have told it before,
poets are telling it now,
other poets shall tell this
history on earth in the future.
Mahabharata

ancient India, and is the language from which many Indo-European languages evolved.

Up to the 1st century CE, Sanskrit literature was dominated by the Vedas and two great epic poems: the *Mahabharata* and the *Ramayana*. Although the *Ramayana* contains historical narrative, mythology, and folktales, it appears to be an original work by a single poet, and is traditionally attributed to the sage Valmiki. In contrast, the *Mahabharata*, the better known and much longer of the two, has a more complex provenance, which suggests a long period of evolution.

A gift of Vishnu
The *Mahabharata* probably first took shape in the 9th century BCE and only reached its final form in around the 4th century BCE. The work is very long and comprises more than 100,000 verse couplets, known as *shloka*, divided into 18 books, or *parvas*. As well as recounting the story of two warring families, it tells of their history, and that of India and the Hindu religion that is integral to it. At the outset, the narrator of the first book,

the *Adi Parva* ("The Book of the Beginning"), explains: "Whatever is here, is found elsewhere. But what is not here, is nowhere else."

According to tradition, and as described in its opening section, the *Mahabharata* was written by a poet and wise man called Vyasa. Said to have lived in the 3rd millennium BCE, Vyasa was an avatar (incarnation) of the Hindu god Vishnu. The narrator of the greater part of the epic is Vyasa's disciple Vaisampayana, but two other people also narrate sections: a minstrel-sage, Ugrasrava Sauti, and a courtier, Sanjaya.

Vaisampayana explains how Vyasa dictated the entire story to the elephant-headed god Ganesha in a single sitting. Subsequently, many years later, Vaisampayana's story takes its final form as the *Mahabharata* when it is retold by Sauti to a meeting of Hindu sages,

as described in the *Adi Parva*. This complicated nesting of frame narratives probably reflects the existence of different historical versions of the story before it took the shape we know today.

It is also typical of the way in which the historical, mythological, and religious intertwine throughout the *Mahabharata*. Although the central plot concerns the split in the ruling Bharata family of northern India, and the ensuing battle at Kurukshetra and its aftermath, the story is given a mythical dimension by the introduction of the character Krishna, another avatar of Vishnu. There are also numerous subplots, and several philosophical and »

The sage Vyasa dictates the epic *Mahabharata*, which means "Great Story of the Bharata", referring to a ruling family of northern India. The scribe is elephant-headed god Ganesha.

religious digressions, one of which, the *Bhagavad Gita*, has become important in its own right. The epic explores themes of family ties and conflict, duty and courage, fate and choice, and presents them in a series of allegories to explain the elements of *dharma*, a complex concept of "correct conduct".

Family divisions

After its explanatory preamble, the *Mahabharata* proper describes how the ruling clan of the Kuru becomes divided into two rival families, the Kaurava and the Pandava. These are the descendants of two princes, the blind Dhritarashtra and his brother Pandu. The enmity begins when Dhritarashtra is denied the throne because of his disability. Pandu becomes king instead, but a curse prevents him from fathering children. The gods, however, impregnate his wife and the line of Pandava seems safe. But the 100 sons of Dhritarashtra feel that they have a claim to the kingdom, and after Yudhishtira, the eldest Pandava, is crowned, they trick him into losing everything in a game of dice. In disgrace, the Pandavas are sent into exile.

Some years later, the five Pandava brothers return to claim the throne, and so starts the series

> Man is not the master of destiny, but a wooden doll that is strung on a string.
> **Mahabharata**

of battles at Kurukshetra. The second son of Pandu, Arjuna, goes into war with his cousin and close companion Krishna as his charioteer, but only reluctantly joins the fight after Krishna persuades him that it is his duty to fight for what is right. The war turns out to be a bloodbath, in which almost all the Kauravas are slaughtered; the few who survive take their revenge on the Pandava troops by murdering them in their sleep. Only the five brothers survive the massacre, and they ensure the Kauravas are wiped out completely.

Yudhishtira becomes king again, but the victory is hollow and the poem goes on to detail the war's awful aftermath. Krishna, or at least this particular incarnation of Vishnu, is accidentally killed, and the Pandavas begin their long, dangerous journey to heaven. Only at the very end are the brothers reunited, and reconciled with their cousins the Kauravas, in the spiritual world.

Moral dilemmas

Dharma is a recurrent theme in the *Mahabharata*, both in terms of how this notion applies to each of us in every situation, and of how it is a difficult path to follow, because of human weaknesses and the

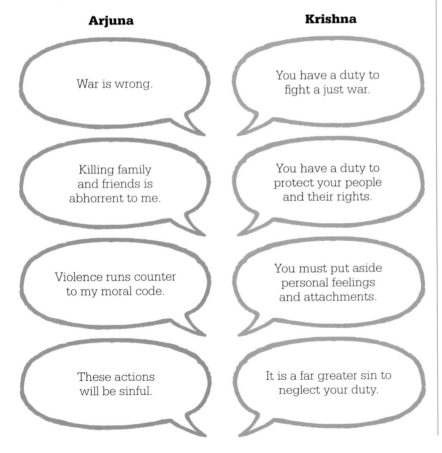

Arjuna's desire to behave in accordance with *dharma* causes him to waver before acting, but his charioteer Krishna guides him on the path of correct conduct.

Arjuna	Krishna
War is wrong.	You have a duty to fight a just war.
Killing family and friends is abhorrent to me.	You have a duty to protect your people and their rights.
Violence runs counter to my moral code.	You must put aside personal feelings and attachments.
These actions will be sinful.	It is a far greater sin to neglect your duty.

Dhritarashtra reaches out blindly for his wife Gandhari, who has bound her eyes to share his darkened world. Bad actions in a previous life meant his disability was a consequence of *karma*.

force of fate. As Kripa – one of the Kauravas – says in the tenth book, *Sauptika Parva* ("The Book of the Sleeping Warriors"), "There are two forces: fate and human effort – all men depend on and are bound by these, there is nothing else". What is right and wrong is seldom clear, and it is by reconciling conflicting interests such as love and duty that we can achieve liberation from the cycle of life, death, and rebirth.

In each of the *Mahabharata's* episodes human strengths and weaknesses are contrasted, and the battle between right and wrong, writ large in the devastating war between the Kauravas and the Pandavas, is shown to be complex, subtle, and ultimately destructive. While most of the poem shows its characters dealing with moral dilemmas in their human affairs, in the final sections, and especially after the death of Krishna, we see

them facing up to their spiritual fate. The story ends, after much tragedy and conflict, with the protagonists achieving eternal bliss, but also with the warning that the human struggles continue here on Earth.

Cultural keystone

The *Mahabharata's* wide-ranging storyline and subject matter, built on favourite mythological and historical stories with a moral and religious message, have ensured the epic's popularity up to the present day. Such was its success that for several centuries only the *Ramayana* could rival its claim to be the great Sanskrit epic. While it cannot match the *Mahabharata* for sheer scope and excitement, the *Ramayana* is more consistent and elegantly poetic, and together the two inspired a school of Sanskrit epic poetry that flourished from the 1st to the 7th centuries CE. As sources of Hindu wisdom and Indian history and mythology, the great epics enjoy a cultural value in India comparable with Homer's *Iliad* and *Odyssey* in the West. ∎

The *Bhagavad Gita*

At the heart of the epic *Mahabharata* is the war at Kurukshetra, beginning with the sixth book, which includes a section now known as the *Bhagavad Gita*, the "Song of the Blessed". Prior to battle, Arjuna, the Pandava prince, recognizes members of his family in the opposing Kaurava army, and lays down his bow. But his cousin and companion Krishna reminds him of his duty to fight this just war. The philosophical dialogue between them is described in the 700-verse *Bhagavad Gita*, which has become an important Hindu scripture in its own right, explaining such concepts as *dharma* (right conduct), *karma* (intentions and outcomes), and *moksha* (liberation from the cycle of death and rebirth). Although Krishna's counsel is specific to Arjuna's duty to fight, the battleground setting can be interpreted as a metaphor for the opposing forces of good and evil in general, and Arjuna's crisis of conscience as representing the choices we all must make.

When the Gods deal defeat to a person, they first take his mind away, so that he sees things wrongly.
Mahabharata

SING, O GODDESS, THE ANGER OF ACHILLES

ILIAD (c.8TH CENTURY BCE), ATTRIBUTED TO HOMER

IN CONTEXT

FOCUS
The Greek epic

KEY DATES
From 2100 BCE Versions of the first known written literature, *The Epic of Gilgamesh*, appear in the Sumerian language.

9th century BCE The epic *Mahabharata* emerges in India.

AFTER
c.8th century BCE Attributed to Homer, the epic *Odyssey* continues the story of a leading figure in the *Iliad*, Odysseus.

c.700 BCE At roughly the same time as the final versions of the Homeric epics take shape, Hesiod writes the *Theogony* ("Birth of the Gods"), a poem that describes the creation of the world and the mythology of the ancient Greek gods.

1st century BCE The Greek epic poems provide a model for Roman poets such as Horace, Virgil, and Ovid.

Epics are narrative poems that recount the story of a hero who represents a particular culture. They chronicle his quests and ordeals, and account for the hero's choices and motives, so helping to establish and codify the moral principles of a society.

Epics were among the earliest forms of literature in many cultures around the world. These popular stories were initially told orally, and over time were embellished, reinterpreted, formalized, and finally written down, often laying the foundation's of a culture's literary history. Epics usually contained many characters and genealogies, and were long and complex in structure. They were probably learned by rote in a repetitive poetic metre, or recited to a musical accompaniment, as it is far easier to memorize verse than prose. Indeed, the word "epic" itself is derived from the ancient Greek word *epos*, meaning both "story" and "poem".

The Trojan War
In ancient Greece many epic tales were told about the Trojan War – a conflict between the Achaeans

Drink deep of battle.
Iliad

(an alliance of the Greek states) and the city of Troy. The first and most famous of these accounts were the *Iliad* and *Odyssey*, both attributed to a single author, known as Homer. Historians concede that these epics were inspired by actual events – sporadic wars between Greece and Troy did occur some five centuries before the works were written – but their characters and plots are works of the imagination. However, the Greeks of Homer's era would have believed these stories to be true accounts of the heroism of their ancestors.

The Greeks began to write down their epics around the 8th century BCE. Like the spoken tales on which they were based, they

Homer lived in a time before realistic portraiture. This bust is based on images of the writer that appeared only in the 2nd century BCE.

The Homeric question

The two great ancient Greek epics, the *Iliad* and the *Odyssey*, are traditionally ascribed to the poet Homer – yet little is known about him. Since the time of the Greek historian Herodotus in the 5th century BCE, widely differing suggestions have been made for Homer's dates of birth and death, place of origin, and other details of his life. Classical scholars refer to "the Homeric question", which includes a number of related issues. Who is Homer – did he ever exist, and if so when? Was Homer the sole author of the epics, or one of a number of authors? Did the author or authors of the work originate them, or simply make a written record of poems that had been passed down orally through the generations?

Many scholars argue that the epics evolved from an oral tradition and were refined and embroidered upon by multiple poets in several versions. Solid evidence is lacking and the Homeric question is yet to be answered definitively.

See also: *The Epic of Gilgamesh* 20 ▪ *Oedipus the King* 34–39 ▪ *Aeneid* 40–41 ▪ *Beowulf* 42–43 ▪ *Odyssey* 54 ▪ *Theogony* 54 ▪ *Metamorphoses* 55–56 ▪ *Digenis Akritas* 56 ▪ *The Tale of Igor's Campaign* 57 ▪ *Ulysses* 214–21

The Greeks and Trojans were helped or hindered by the gods, who used the conflict to fight their own battles. Hera, Athena, and Poseidon were aligned with the Greeks, while Apollo, Aphrodite, and Artemis supported the Trojans. Zeus remained largely neutral.

The Gods

Zeus
king of
the gods

Hera
queen of
the gods

Athena
goddess of
wisdom

Poseidon
god of
the sea

Apollo
god of
the sun

Aphrodite
goddess
of love

Artemis
goddess of
the moon

The Achaeans (Greeks)

Agamemnon
king of
Mycenae

Achilles
Greece's greatest
warrior

Patroclus
companion of
Achilles

Menelaus
king of
Sparta

Odysseus
commander, and
king of Ithaca

The Trojans

Priam
king of
Troy

Hector
son of
Priam

Paris
brother of
Hector

Helen
wife of
Menelaus

Aeneas
a son of
Aphrodite

took the form of narrative poems. These Greek epics have a regular metre – each line is comprised of six basic rhythmic units, and each of these units contains one long and two short syllables. This metre is known as dactylic hexameter, or more commonly, "epic metre". Variations on this basic rhythmic pattern give the flexibility needed for poetic composition.

A tale of gods and men

The *Iliad* is a sophisticated piece of storytelling. It relates the tale of the war in Ilium (Troy) from the perspective of one character in particular – Achilles. Parts of the story of the war are told in flashback, or in prophecies of the future. Woven into this storyline are subplots and insights into the lives of the protagonists.

How much of this complexity can be credited to Homer, and how much is a result of refinement and embroidering over previous generations, is impossible to tell. The result is a work that combines history, legend, and mythology, while offering the essential ingredients of good storytelling – adventure and human drama – that make it a compelling read.

The *Iliad* is massive, both in its length and its narrative scope (it is, after all, where we get the idea of things being on an "epic" scale), consisting of over 15,000 lines of verse, divided into 24 books. Rather than simply telling the tale chronologically, Homer grabs the reader's attention by using a device common to many epics. This is to drop the reader straight into the thick of the action,

or *in media res* ("the middle of the thing") as described by the Roman poet, Horace. Homer's account starts in the final year of the conflict, which has already been »

Troy was believed for many years to be a mythical city. However, archaeologists now agree that excavations in Anatolia, Turkey, have revealed the Troy of Homer's *Iliad*.

raging for nine years. Homer digresses to explain some of the background to the events he is describing, but he assumes much prior knowledge about the causes of the conflict, which contemporary readers would have known well.

Origins of the war

The roots of the Trojan War can be found in events that occurred at the wedding of the sea-nymph Thetis to the Greek hero Peleus, who was a companion to the hero Hercules. The celebrations were attended by may gods and godesses, including Hera, Athena, and Aphrodite. An argument broke out between the three goddesses, each of whom claimed to be the most beautiful. To resolve the dispute, Zeus asked Paris, the son of King Priam of Troy, to judge a beauty contest between them. Aphrodite offered Paris a bribe – the hand of Helen of Troy, the most beautiful woman in the world. Unfortunately, Helen was already married to Menelaus, brother of King Agamemnon of Mycenae, a Greek state. The subsequent abduction of Helen by Paris triggered the conflict.

Readers join the narrative when Agamemnon's Achaean forces are fighting to recapture Helen. The book's opening, "Sing, O Goddess, the anger of Achilles" sets the scene,

Victory passes back and forth between men.
Iliad

preparing the reader for a story of war, but also implies that this is a tale of personal vengeance – and alludes to the involvement of the gods. The history of the war runs in parallel with Achilles' story, and his sense of honour and valour mirrors that of the Greek nation itself.

The power of anger

Anger is a predominant theme in the *Iliad*, manifested in the war itself and as a motivation for the actions of the individual characters. There is the righteous anger of Agamemnon and Menelaus over the kidnapping of Helen, but also the wrath that drives Achilles and makes him such a fearsome warrior, provoked again and again by events in the story. His anger is not directed solely at the Trojans, nor even restricted to human foes; at one point he is so enraged he fights the river god Xanthus.

Underlying the wrath of Achilles is a sense of honour and nobility which, like that of the Greek people, is offended by disrespect and injustice, but is sometimes directed

When Paris is asked who is the "fairest" goddess, Hera tries to bribe him with empire, Athena with glory, and Aphrodite promises him Helen, the world's most beautiful woman.

inwards as he struggles with the conflicts that arise between duty, destiny, ambition, and loyalty.

At the beginning of the *Iliad*, Achilles becomes enraged by King Agamemnon, the Greek commander, who has taken for himself Briseis – a woman who had been given to Achilles as a prize of war. Unable to vent his anger towards the king directly, Achilles withdraws to his tent, refusing to fight any more. Only the death in action of his close friend, Patroclus, at the hands of Hector, the eldest son of King Priam and the hero of the Trojans, brings him back into battle, more violently than ever, by giving him a focus for his anger.

A tale of two heroes

Hector is, like Achilles, a military leader. He is considered the noblest and mightiest of the Trojan warriors. But his character and motivation stand in contrast to those of Achilles, highlighting two very different attitudes to war.

Achilles is driven by an inner rage, but also the nobler motives of defending the honour of his king and country, and ultimately avenging the killing of Patroclus, his comrade-in-arms. Hector fights out of loyalty – to Troy, of course, but also to his family. As well as being protective of his younger brother, Paris, whose abduction of Helen has caused the war, he is loyal to his father, Priam, who is portrayed as a wise and benevolent king. Achilles is the professional soldier, with few family ties, and Hector the reluctant but fierce fighter, defending home and family rather than honour.

Homer portrays both men as noble, but not without their flaws. Their characteristics and situations are metaphors for the contrasting values of society and those of the individual, and those of duty and responsibility compared with loyalty and love. Neither side is wholly right or wrong, but in this war one must emerge victorious. Even though both heroes ultimately die in the conflict – Achilles slays Hector, and is himself killed by a fatal arrow in his heel – it is the heroism personified by Achilles that wins out over Hector's bonds of kinship. Ultimately, the *Iliad* affirms that there is glory in warfare, and that honourable reasons exist for fighting.

Destiny and the gods

Homer knew that his readers – the Greeks – were aware of the outcome of the story because if Troy had won the war, there would have been no Greek civilization. The Greeks were destined to win, and to reinforce this inevitability, Homer makes reference to many prophecies throughout the *Iliad*, and to the role of fate and the gods in deciding the war's outcome.

To the ancient Greeks, the gods were immortals who had dominion over certain realms or possessed

Among all creatures that breathe on earth and crawl on it there is not anywhere a thing more dismal than man is.
Iliad

certain powers; they were not the omnipotent deities of later beliefs. Occasionally they interacted with humans, but generally left them to their own devices. In the *Iliad*, however, several of the gods had vested interests that led them to become involved in the Trojan War from time to time. The war had, after all, been triggered by the abduction of Helen, the daughter »

Community-minded, Hector is a family man who tries to avert wider bloodshed.

Dependable, Hector leads his men bravely, bonded by ancestral loyalty.

Moderate in mood, Hector is fallible and weakens in the final confrontation.

The warriors Hector and Achilles have contrasting personalities and motivations, which provide recurrent themes in Homer's examination of the heroic ideal.

Individualistic, Achilles is absorbed in his own thirst for glory.

Unpredictable, Achilles is indifferent to others and obsessed with honour.

Hot tempered and prone to rage, Achilles thrives in the violence of battle.

> I have gone through
> what no other mortal on
> earth has gone through;
> I put my lips to the hands
> of the man who has
> killed my children.
> **Iliad**

of Zeus and Leda. Paris had seized Helen in collusion with Aphrodite, so sides had already been taken on Mount Olympus, the home of the gods. There were also other connections between the gods and the mortals: Thetis, for example, was not only a sea nymph but also the mother of Achilles.

Such allegiances prompted the gods to intervene in human affairs, protecting their favourites from harm, and making life difficult for their enemies. Apollo in particular is fiercely anti-Greek, and causes them trouble on several occasions. For example, when Patroclus goes into battle disguised as Achilles, by wearing Achilles' famously protective armour, Apollo contrives to dislodge it, allowing Hector to kill him. Incensed by the death of his best friend, Achilles vows vengeance. And again the gods intervene: his immortal mother Thetis presents him with a new suit of divine armour, specially forged by the god Hephaestus.

The need humans have for such protection underlines the difference between them and the gods – their mortality. Heroes go to war knowing they face death, but reconcile themselves with the knowledge that all humans must eventually die. The characters are not only mortal, but their creations are impermanent. They know that the war will have more than human casualties, because one nation must be destroyed – and even the victorious civilization will come to an end one day. Homer sometimes overtly states this fact by citing prophecies of the future for both the *Iliad*'s main characters and for Troy, but it is implicit that this is the common fate of mankind – the destiny of every society. What lives on, however, is the glory of the heroes and their great deeds, recounted in the stories passed down through the ages.

Beyond the conflict

After war, bloodshed, and fury, Homer's epic ends with peace and reconciliation. In perhaps the most memorably moving scene of the poem, the elderly King Priam visits Achilles and pleads for the return of the body of Hector, his son. Achilles is moved by the old man's plea, and a temporary truce is called to give the Trojans time for an appropriate funeral, and this

Priam kisses Achilles' hand, and asks him to take pity and surrender the body of his son Hector, whom Achilles has killed in battle. Achilles displays empathy with Priam's grief.

also lays Achilles' rage to rest. But despite this apparently peaceful ending, we know that this calm will be short-lived. The battle will resume, Troy will fall, and at some point Achilles will die. The story is not over yet.

Indeed, Homer's second epic poem, the *Odyssey*, ties up some of the loose ends by following the fortunes of another of the Greek heroes, Odysseus (known to the Romans as Ulysses), as he makes his way home to Ithaca from Troy after the war. In the *Odyssey*, the hero recounts the eventual destruction of Troy, and the death of Achilles, but this is very much background to the story of his own arduous journey.

Western cornerstone

It is almost impossible to overstate the impact of the *Iliad* and the *Odyssey* on the literature of ancient Greece and Rome, and therefore the whole of Western literature. They were not simply the first literary works in Europe, but monumental examples that firmly laid the foundations of the epic genre.

Homer's expert use of complex and highly visual similes gave his poetry unprecedented depth, and his mastery of dactylic hexameter provided an inspirational musicality to his verse. The metre used by Homer was adopted for subsequent epic poetry in Greek as well as in Latin, and the hybrid dialect he used became the recognized Greek of literature.

Perhaps most significantly of all, Homer turned an oral tradition of stories about folk heroes into a literary form – the epic. He also set out the characteristics of that form; for example, that the main narrative should follow the hero's quest or journey, and that this should be set against a historical backdrop, with

multiple interweaving or episodic plots. Homer also set the standard for the subtext of the epic, where personal and social values often stand in opposition.

The *Iliad* and the *Odyssey* inspired a number of Greek poets to write epics on similar themes, but they also influenced the new form of drama that developed in the classical period. While Homer was popular reading in ancient Greece, the *Iliad* and *Odyssey* were standard texts in ancient Rome,

Zeus knows, no doubt, and every immortal too which fighter is doomed to end all this in death.
Iliad

The *Odyssey* details the death of the hero Achilles. He is killed by an arrow fired by Paris, which is guided to the one vulnerable spot of Achilles' body – his heel – by the god Apollo.

inspiring poets to develop a distinctive Latin epic poetry. This reached its height in Virgil's *Aeneid*, which as well as being a homage to Homer took as its starting point the fall of Troy.

Eternally influential

Reverence for the Homeric epics did not end in classical times. Homer's works were widely read and studied in the Middle Ages and their stories have been retold countless times in different forms.

Homer's ancient poems can be considered the antecedents of medieval sagas, as well as the novel. Since the beginning of the 20th century, other forms of mass-audience storytelling – from movies to television series – have followed the epic model, and are deeply indebted to Homer for their structure and cultural relevance. ■

HOW DREADFUL KNOWLEDGE OF THE TRUTH CAN BE WHEN THERE'S NO HELP IN TRUTH!

OEDIPUS THE KING (c.429 BCE), SOPHOCLES

IN CONTEXT

FOCUS
Classical Greek drama

BEFORE
c.7th century BCE
Dithyrambs, song and dance
entertainments by a chorus,
are performed in honour of
Dionysus in Delos and Athens.

c.532 BCE Thespis, considered
to be the first actor, appears on
stage playing a role in a drama.

c.500 BCE Pratinas introduces
satyr plays – a satirical genre.

458 BCE Aeschylus's *Oresteia*,
the only trilogy of the classical
period to have survived intact,
is first performed in Athens.

431 BCE Euripides' *Medea*
introduces a realism that
shocks audiences.

AFTER
423 BCE Aristophanes' comedy
The Clouds satirizes the social
scene in Athens, and in
particular Socrates.

With the revolt that
overthrew the last
tyrant king in 510 BCE,
and the establishment of a form of
democracy, the city-state of Athens
ushered in the era of classical
Greece. For two centuries, Athens
was not only a centre of political
power in the region, but also a
hotbed of intellectual activity that
fostered an extraordinary flowering
of philosophy, literary culture, and
art, which was to have a profound
influence on the development of
Western civilization.

Classical Greek culture was
dominated by the achievements
of Athenian thinkers, artists, and
writers, who developed aesthetic
values of clarity, form, and balance –
principles that were epitomized by
classical architecture. A human-
centred view also influenced the
development of a comparatively
new literary art form, drama,
which evolved from religious
performances by a chorus in
honour of the god Dionysus.

The birth of drama
By the beginning of the classical
era, religious performances had
changed from essentially musical

Delphi's theatre has three spaces:
the stage, the orchestra or chorus
(in front), and the amphitheatre.
It was built in the 4th century BCE
and could seat about 5,000 people.

ceremonies to something more like
drama as we know it today, with
the addition of actors to play the
parts of the characters in a story,
rather than simply narrating.

This new form of entertainment
was enormously popular, and
formed the focal point of an annual
festival of Dionysia, which was held
over several days in a custom-built
open-air theatre that attracted
audiences of up to 15,000 people.

Sophocles

Sophocles was born (c.496 BCE) in
Colonus, near Athens. He showed
an early aptitude for music, and
through this became interested in
the art of drama, encouraged and
perhaps trained by the innovative
tragedian Aeschylus. With his first
entry in the Dionysia theatre
contest in 468 BCE, he won first
prize from the reigning champion
Aeschylus, and he soon became
the most celebrated tragedian of
his generation. In all, he wrote
more than 120 plays, of which only
a handful have survived intact.
Sophocles was also a respected
member of Athens society, and
was appointed as a treasurer in
Pericles' government and later
as a military commander. He
married twice, and both his son
Iophon and grandson Sophocles
followed in his footsteps as
playwrights. Shortly before his
death in 406 BCE, he finished
his final play, *Oedipus at
Colonus*, which was produced
posthumously by his grandson.

Other key works

c.441 BCE *Antigone*
c.429 BCE *Oedipus the King*
c.409 BCE *Electra*

See also: *Iliad* 26–33 ▪ *Aeneid* 40–41 ▪ *Odyssey* 54 ▪ *Oresteia* 54–55 ▪ *Medea* 55 ▪ *Wasps* 55 ▪
First Folio 82–89 ▪ *The Misanthrope* 90

Writers submitted work to be performed at the festival, in the form of a trilogy of tragedies followed by a comic play, and competed for prestigious prizes.

Three dramatists dominated the prizewinners' list for much of the 5th century BCE: Aeschylus (c.525/524–c.456/455 BCE), Euripides (c.484–406 BCE), and Sophocles (c.496–406 BCE). Their contribution, which amounted to several hundred plays, set a definitive standard for the art of tragedy. Aeschylus, as the earliest of the three great tragedians, is generally considered the innovator, initiating many of the conventions associated with the form. He is credited with expanding the number of actors in his plays, and having them interact in dialogue, which introduced the idea of dramatic conflict. Where formerly the chorus had presented the action of the drama, the actors now took centre stage, and the chorus took on the role of setting the scene and commenting on the actions of the characters.

The move towards a greater realism was sustained by Euripides, who further reduced the role of the chorus, and presented more three-dimensional characters with more complex interaction.

Breaking with convention

Of the three great dramatists, it is Sophocles whose tragedies have come to be regarded as the high point of classical Greek drama. Sadly, only seven of the 123 tragedies he wrote have survived, but of these perhaps the finest is *Oedipus the King*.

The play was one of three written by Sophocles about the mythical king of Thebes (the others

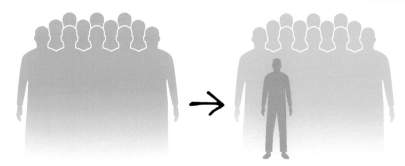

The development of Greek tragedy

The chorus presented the tragedies, narrating the action; even in later times, the chorus always set the scene and gave the characters' internal thoughts, which could not be acted on stage.

The protagonist, introduced by Thespis, performed the part of the main tragic character, thus initiating the birth of acting.

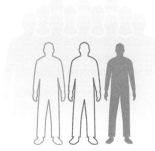

The tritagonist, a third actor introduced by Sophocles, took on the role of adversary, while the deuteragonist became a support role for the protagonist, such as an aide or advisor.

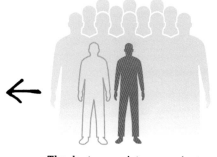

The deuteragonist, a second actor introduced by Aeschylus, usually performed the role of the antagonist in the drama. Characters could now interact in dialogue, introducing the idea of dramatic conflict.

being *Oedipus at Colonus* and *Antigone*), known collectively as the Theban plays. Breaking with the convention of presenting tragedies in trilogies established by Aeschylus, Sophocles conceived each of these as a separate entity, and they were written and produced several years apart and out of chronological order.

In *Oedipus the King* (often referred to instead by its Latinized title *Oedipus Rex*), Sophocles created what is now regarded as the epitome of classical Athenian tragedy. The play follows the established formal structure: a prologue, followed by the introduction of characters and the unfolding of plot through » a series of episodes interspersed with commentary from the chorus, leading to a choral *exodus*, or conclusion. Within this framework, Sophocles uses his own innovation of a third actor to widen the variety of character interaction and enable a more complex plot, creating the psychological tensions synonymous with the word "drama" today.

Typically, a tragedy of this sort was the story of a hero suffering a misfortune that leads to his undoing, traditionally at the hands of the gods or fate. As classical tragedy developed, however, the hero's reversal of fortune was increasingly portrayed as the result of a frailty or fault in the character of the protagonist – the "fatal flaw". In *Oedipus the King* both fate and character play their part in the tragic events. The character of Oedipus is also far from black and white. At the beginning of the play he appears as the respected ruler of Thebes, to whom the people turn to rid them of a curse, but as the plot unfolds his unwitting involvement in the curse is revealed.

The greatest griefs are those we cause ourselves.
Oedipus the King

This revelation contributes to the atmosphere of foreboding that was a characteristic of the best classical tragedies. The sense of doom arose from the fact that many of these stories were already well known, as that of Oedipus must have been. Such a situation creates tragic irony, when the audience is aware of a character's fate and witnesses his unsuspecting progress towards inevitable doom. In *Oedipus the King*, Sophocles ratchets up this atmosphere of inevitability by introducing various references to prophecies that were made many

years before, which both Oedipus and his wife Jocasta have ignored. The story is not so much about the events that lead to Oedipus's downfall, as about the events that prompt revelations of the significance of his past actions.

Tragedy foretold

The chain of events begins with Thebes stricken by plague. When consulted, the oracle at Delphi says that the plague will abate when the murderer of Laius, the former king of Thebes and previous husband of Jocasta, is found. Oedipus seeks the advice of the blind prophet Tiresias to find the killer. This puts Tiresias in a difficult position because, although blind, he can see what Oedipus cannot: that Oedipus himself is the unwitting murderer, and advises him to let the matter rest. But Oedipus demands the truth, and then furiously refuses to believe the prophet's accusation, while Tiresias further reveals that the killer will turn out to be the son of his own wife. A rattled Oedipus recalls a visit to Delphi as a youth, where he had gone to determine his true parentage, having overheard that he had been adopted. Instead, the oracle told him that he would murder his father and marry his mother – so he had fled, journeying towards Thebes. On his way to the city, he had met and killed an older man who barred his way.

The significance of this is not lost on the audience, especially when Sophocles introduces Jocasta, Oedipus's wife and the widow of Laius, who comforts Oedipus by arguing that prophecies are untrue;

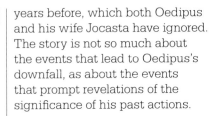

An ancient house-mosaic depicts masks used in tragedies. Actors often wore masks, some with exaggerated expressions, to help convey the character they were representing.

Aristophanes' comedy *Wealth* (*Ploutus* in Greek), performed here by modern actors, is a gentle satire that focuses on life – and the distribution of wealth – in Athens.

there was a prophecy that Laius would be killed by his son, she says, when he was slain by bandits.

This information makes clear to the audience that the prophecy given to Oedipus has been self-fulfilling; it prompted him to leave home and set in motion the events that led to his unconsciously killing his own father Laius and becoming king of Thebes in his place, with his own mother Jocasta as his wife.

The climax is reached as things become clear to Oedipus. He reacts by blinding himself. The chorus, which has throughout the tragedy expressed the inner thoughts and feelings that could not be expressed by the characters

themselves, closes the drama by repeating to an empty stage that "no man should be considered fortunate until he is dead".

The Western tradition

Oedipus the King gained immediate approval with Athenian audiences, and was hailed by Aristotle as probably the finest of all classical Greek tragedies. Sophocles' skilful handling of a complex plot, dealing with themes of free will and determinacy, and the fatal flaw of a noble character, not only set a benchmark for classical drama, but also formed the basis of the subsequent Western tradition of drama.

Following their deaths, there were no Greek tragedians of the same stature as Aeschylus, Euripides, and Sophocles. Drama continued to be a central part of Athenian cultural life, but the plaudits were more often given to the producer or actors than the writer himself. The comedies of Aristophanes (c.450–c.388 BCE) also helped to fill the void left by the absence of great tragedy, and gradually popular taste grew for less serious drama.

Even today, however, the tragedies of the classical Greek period remain significant, not least for their psychological exploration of character, which Freud and Jung used in their theories of the unconscious, drives, and repressed emotion. The surviving works of the Athenian tragedians, and *Oedipus the King* in particular, were revived during the Enlightenment, and have been performed regularly ever since, with their themes and stories reinterpreted by many writers. ∎

Why should anyone in this world be afraid, Since Fate rules us and nothing can be foreseen? A man should live only for the present day.
Oedipus the King

Aristotle's *Poetics* c.335 BCE

Aristotle (384–322 BCE) held the tragedians in high regard, and his *Poetics* is a treatise on the art of tragedy. He saw tragedy as a *mimesis* (an imitation) of an action, one that should arouse pity and fear. These emotions are given a *katharsis*, a purging, by the unfolding of the drama.

The quality of such a tragedy is determined by six elements: plot, character, thought, diction, spectacle, and melody. The plot must be a "unity of action", with a beginning, middle, and end.

At least one of the characters should undergo a change in fortune, through fate, a flaw in character, or a blend of the two. Next in importance is thought, by which he means the themes, and the moral message, of the play. This is followed by diction, the language, such as the use of metaphors, and the actor's delivery. The spectacle (scenery and stage effects) and melody (from the chorus) should be integral to the plot and enhance the portrayal of character.

THE GATES OF HELL ARE OPEN NIGHT AND DAY; SMOOTH THE DESCENT, AND EASY IS THE WAY

AENEID (29–19 BCE), VIRGIL

IN CONTEXT

FOCUS
Literature of the Roman world

BEFORE
3rd century BCE Gnaeus Naevius writes epic poems and dramas based on Greek models, but in Latin and about Roman mythology and history.

c.200 BCE Quintus Ennius's epic *Annals* tells the history of Rome following the fall of Troy.

c.80 BCE Cicero's oratory as a lawyer marks the beginning of the "Golden Age" of Latin literature, which lasts until the death of Ovid in 17 or 18 CE.

AFTER
1st century BCE Horace's poetry includes the *Odes*, the *Satires*, and the *Epodes*.

c.8 CE Ovid's narrative poem *Metamorphoses* is published.

2nd century Apuleius writes the irreverent *Metamorphoses*, also known as *The Golden Ass*.

Rome began to replace Greece as the dominant Mediterranean power from around the 3rd century BCE, and it is from that time that the first literature in Latin appeared. The influence of Greek culture on ancient Rome was enormous to begin with, and a recognizable Roman literary culture emerged only slowly. Although Roman writers were writing in Latin, they produced poetry, drama, and histories firmly in the Greek mould until around 80 BCE when the statesman, orator, writer, and poet Cicero inspired the beginning of a "Golden Age" of Latin literature, which established the style and forms of a distinct Roman tradition.

Roots of empire

The so-called Golden Age straddled Rome's evolution from Republic to Empire. This transformation, which involved the turmoil of civil wars, was reflected in a shift from the historical and rhetorical writings of Cicero, Sallust, and Varro, to the poetic works of Horace, Ovid, and Virgil, especially during the reign of Emperor Augustus from 27 BCE.

Virgil

Publius Vergilius Maro was born in 70 BCE in Mantua, northern Italy. He spent much of his early life in this part of the Roman Republic, and wrote his poems of rustic life, the *Eclogues*, there. Virgil's next major work, the *Georgics*, was dedicated to his patron, the statesman Gaius Maecenas. Virgil also befriended Octavian, who was to become Emperor Augustus, and established himself in Rome as a poet alongside Horace and Ovid. He began work on his magnum opus, the *Aeneid*, in around 29 BCE, encouraged by Octavian, and continued writing and revising it until his death from fever in 19 BCE. It is said that on his deathbed Virgil asked that the *Aeneid* be destroyed, possibly because of his disappointment with Augustus's reign, but it was published posthumously on the orders of the emperor.

Other key works

c.44–38 BCE *Eclogues*
29 BCE *Georgics*

See also: *Iliad* 26–33 ▪ *Metamorphoses* 55–56 ▪ *The Golden Ass* 56 ▪ *The Divine Comedy* 62–65 ▪ *Paradise Lost* 103

Endure the hardships
of your present state,
Live, and reserve
yourselves for better fate.
Aeneid

Acknowledged during his lifetime as Rome's leading literary figure, Virgil wrote a number of poetic works, but it is for his epic *Aeneid* that he achieved lasting respect. His story of the ancestry of Rome was possibly commissioned by Emperor Augustus, and the rising tide of pride in the new imperial era no doubt played some part in the patriotic poem's success.

Despite its nationalistic theme, the *Aeneid* has its roots in Greek literature, and especially Homer's *Iliad* and *Odyssey*, on which it is largely modelled, sharing the same regular poetic metre, or classical "epic metre". The 12 books of the *Aeneid* recount the journey of Aeneas from his home in Troy to Italy, and the war in Latium (the land of the Latins), which ultimately led to the foundation of Rome.

A Homeric achievement

Aeneas was already known as a character in the *Iliad*, but Virgil's continuation of his story neatly connects the legends of Troy with those of Rome, and in particular the virtues of the hero with traditional Roman values.

Aeneas's travels in the Mediterranean

1 Troy: Flees the city with others, including his father King Anchises, and his wife's shade tells him to find the land of the Tiber.

4 Crete: Has a dream in which the gods appear to him and reveal that the land of his forefathers that he seeks is in distant Italy.

5 Strophades islands: Survives attack when taken off course to the home of the Harpies, who prophesy that a famine lies ahead in Italy.

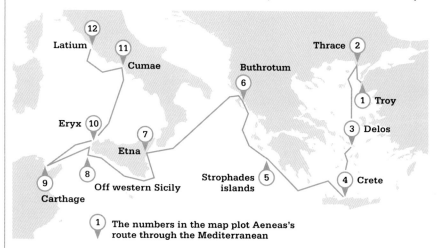

① The numbers in the map plot Aeneas's route through the Mediterranean

9 Carthage: Meets and falls in love with Queen Dido, and only leaves her because the gods persuade him he must resume his journey.

11 Cumae: Is guided by the prophetic Sibyl to the underworld, where he talks to spirits and the future Rome is revealed to him.

12 Latium: Welcomed here at the mouth of the River Tiber by King Latinus who offers his daughter Princess Lavinia in marriage.

Virgil begins the poem "Arma virumque cano …" ("I sing of arms and a man …"), stating his themes in a similar way to the *Iliad* ("Sing, O goddess, the anger of Achilles, son of Peleus …"), and takes up Aeneas's story on his way to Italy as he is forced by a storm to land in Carthage. Here, he tells Queen Dido of the sack of Troy. Feigning retreat, the Greeks had hidden offshore and left behind a vast, wheeled wooden horse. The Trojans were persuaded by a Greek agent that the horse was under Athene's protection and would make Troy impregnable. At night, after the Trojans had taken it within the walls, a select band of warriors emerged and opened the gates for the returned Greek army.

Throughout the epic, Virgil emphasizes Aenas's *pietas*, his virtue and duty, which is steered by fate and the intervention of the gods, taking him from his home to his destiny in Latium.

The *Aeneid* not only secured Virgil's reputation as a distinctly Roman writer, but went on to become probably the most respected work in Latin. Virgil was revered as a writer throughout the Middle Ages, and appears as the guide in Dante's *Divine Comedy*. Stories from the *Aeneid* have been retold continuously since it first appeared, and the idea of danger represented by the "Trojan horse" – "Beware of Greeks bearing gifts" – has entered popular culture. ▪

FATE WILL UNWIND AS IT MUST

BEOWULF (8TH–11TH CENTURY)

IN CONTEXT

FOCUS
Anglo-Saxon literature

BEFORE
7th century CE Caedmon, a shepherd-turned-monk at Whitby Abbey, writes a hymn that is the first-known example of a poem in Old English.

c.8th century CE Fragments of runic inscription carved on the Ruthwell Cross – now in Scotland but once part of the kingdom of Northumbria – are lines from a poem now known as "The Dream of the Rood", which blends warrior imagery with the Crucifixion story.

AFTER
c.1000 The epic poem *Waldere* is transcribed. Only two fragments have survived, but they offer insights into the Anglo-Saxon warrior ideal.

10th century Benedictine monks compile an anthology of Anglo-Saxon poetry now known as the Exeter Book.

lthough academic opinions differ about the exact date *Beowulf* was written, it is the earliest Anglo-Saxon epic poem to survive in its entirety. It is told in the language now known as Old English, or Anglo-Saxon, which developed from the Germanic languages brought over to Britain by Scandinavian invaders, and remained the common language until the Norman Conquest in 1066.

Old English was widely spoken in England and southern Scotland from the 5th century, but written literature in the vernacular only

Each of us must expect an end of living in this world; let him who may win glory before death: for that is best at last for the departed warrior.
Beowulf

emerged gradually. During the 7th century, Britain underwent conversion to Christianity. Latin was the language of the literate classes, and used in the Christian monasteries and abbeys where manuscripts were created. But by the reign of King Alfred (reigned 871–899), Old English translations of Christian Latin texts were appearing alongside original texts.

An oral tradition
It is likely that *Beowulf* dates from between the 8th and early 11th centuries, because it appears to have been written from a Christian perspective, in spite of its pagan subject matter. It is not clear whether *Beowulf* was composed by the person or persons who wrote the original manuscript, or whether this was a transcription of an older poem. There was an Anglo-Saxon oral tradition of storytelling by reciters of poetry known as "scops", mentioned in several Old English texts including *Beowulf*, and it is possible that the poem had been passed down orally many years before it was recorded.

Like its language, the poem's story has its roots in Scandinavia, and deals with the legends of the

See also: *The Epic of Gilgamesh* 20 ▪ *Mahabharata* 22–25 ▪ *Iliad* 26–33 ▪ *Aeneid* 40–41 ▪ *Lancelot, the Knight of the Cart* 50–51 ▪ *Njal's Saga* 52–53 ▪ *Cantar de Mio Cid* 56–57 ▪ *The Divine Comedy* 62–65 ▪ *The Lord of the Rings* 287

people there, including several historical figures from around 500 CE. It tells of the life and exploits of a Geatish warrior, Beowulf, who comes to the aid of Hrothgar, king of the Danes, to rid the land of the monster Grendel and then Grendel's mother. Beowulf progresses from a brash young adventurer to become a respected king of the Geats, following Hrothgar's advice to "Incline not to arrogance, famous warrior!". His final battle is to save his own people from a dragon.

Both epic and elegy

As well as the story of a monster-slaying hero, and the battle of good and evil, the poem deals with themes of loyalty and brotherly love, the ephemeral quality of life, and the danger of pride and arrogance in the face of humanity's inevitable doom. The English writer and scholar J R R Tolkien argued that *Beowulf* is as much an elegy as an epic, mournful as well as heroic; not just a lament for the death of the eponymous hero, but also a nostalgic elegy for a dying way of life, and of our struggles against fate.

Although the manuscript of *Beowulf* was preserved in the late 10th- or early 11th-century Nowell Codex, it was regarded as simply a historical artefact until the 19th century, when the first translations into modern English were made. Not until the 20th century, largely due to Tolkien's championing of the work, was its literary merit recognized. *Beowulf* has now been translated countless times into many languages, and as well as its popularity in its own right, the poem has influenced much recent fantasy literature. ∎

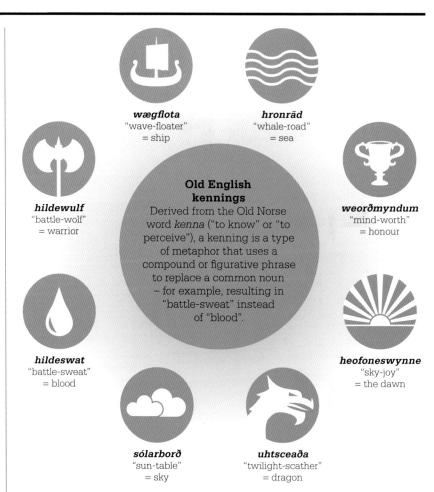

wægflota
"wave-floater"
= ship

hronrād
"whale-road"
= sea

hildewulf
"battle-wolf"
= warrior

Old English kennings
Derived from the Old Norse word *kenna* ("to know" or "to perceive"), a kenning is a type of metaphor that uses a compound or figurative phrase to replace a common noun – for example, resulting in "battle-sweat" instead of "blood".

weorðmyndum
"mind-worth"
= honour

hildeswat
"battle-sweat"
= blood

heofoneswynne
"sky-joy"
= the dawn

sólarborð
"sun-table"
= sky

uhtsceaða
"twilight-scather"
= dragon

Poetry in Old English

Beowulf is in the form of an epic poem – 3,182 lines long – in a declamatory (forcefully expressed) style and using idiosyncratic Anglo-Saxon poetic devices.

Most strikingly, unlike the rhyme schemes of modern verse, Old English poetry is typically written in a form of alliterative verse. Each line is divided into two halves, which are linked not by the rhyming of the ends of words, but by the similar sounds of the beginnings of words or syllables. The two halves of each line are often divided by a caesura, or pause, effectively marking them as an alliterative couplet. Another feature is a metaphorical device known as a kenning: a figurative compound word in place of a less poetic single word, such as *hildenaedre* ("battle-serpent") for "arrow".

Devices such as these pose problems for the translator into modern languages, especially given the richness of allusion in Old English.

SO SCHEHERAZADE BEGAN...
ONE THOUSAND AND ONE NIGHTS
(c.8TH–15TH CENTURY)

IN CONTEXT

FOCUS
Early Arabic literature

BEFORE
610–632 According to Islamic belief, the Qur'an (Arabic for "Recitation") is revealed to Muhammad by God.

8th century A collection of seven pre-Islamic poems, some dating to the 6th century, are written in gold on linen, and are said to have been put up on the walls of the Kaaba at Mecca. They are known as *Al-Mu'allaqat* ("hung poems").

AFTER
c.990–1008 Badi' al-Zamān al-Hamadāni writes *Maqamat* ("assemblies"), a collection of stories in rhymed prose that relate the encounters of the witty Abul-Fath al-Iskanderi.

13th century *The Story of Bayad and Riyad*, a romance about the love of a merchant's son for a foreign court lady, is written in Islamic Andalusia.

A cross the Arab world there is a long tradition of storytelling, with folktales passed down orally through many generations. However, from the 8th century onwards, with the rise of flourishing urban centres and a sophisticated Arabian culture that prospered under the guidance of Islam, a widening distinction was made between *al-fus'ha* (the refined language taught at educational centres) and *al-ammiyyah* (the language of the common people). Pre-Islamic literature written in the vernacular – including traditional folktales – fell out of favour with the educated elite, and writers of Arabic literature turned away from composing works of imaginative prose to focus instead on poetry and non-fiction.

The appeal of stories

Yet despite the emphasis placed on the "high art" of poetry, there was a continuing public appetite for a good yarn. Although not highly regarded by Arabic scholars, the collection of tales that appeared under various titles over the next few centuries, but which are now

A Golden Age of Islamic literature

By the mid-8th century, the territory controlled by Muslims stretched from the Middle East across Persia into the Indian subcontinent, and from North Africa into Iberia. Sophisticated urban societies throughout the Islamic world became cultural as well as political centres.

This was the beginning of an Islamic Golden Age, which lasted for around 500 years. Centres of learning, such as the House of Wisdom in Baghdad, attracted polymaths – proficient in science, philosophy, and the arts – as well as scholars of the Islamic holy book, the Qur'an.

The Qur'an is the word of God, revealed to Muhammad, so it is considered not only a source of religious knowledge, but also the model for Arabic literature. Its style and language greatly influenced the classical Arabic literature that flourished from the 8th century onwards, mostly in the form of poetry, which was held in much higher regard than narrative fiction.

See also: *Mahabharata* 22–25 ▪ *The Canterbury Tales* 68–71 ▪ *The Decameron* 102 ▪ *Children's and Household Tales* 116–17 ▪ *Fairy Tales* (Andersen) 151 ▪ *Tales of the Grotesque and Arabesque* 152 ▪ *The Prophet* 223

The nights of Scheherazade

As night falls, Scheherazade enthrals her husband by continuing the previous night's story.

After concluding the tale, she starts another, often with a character telling their own story.

Having reached a cliffhanger at daybreak, her life is spared so that the ending can be heard.

known as the *One Thousand and One Nights* or the *Arabian Nights,* was perennially popular.

The collection came together in a chaotic fashion over several centuries, and no canonical version of the tales exists. Storytellers combined ancient Indian, Persian, and Arabic tales, with more stories being added over the centuries. The oldest Arabic manuscript still in existence is believed to have been put together in Syria in the late 15th century. It is written in everyday language that offers a strong contrast to the classical Arabic of poetry and the Qur'an.

Tales within tales
The structure of the *One Thousand and One Nights* takes the form of a frame narrative, where one story contains all the others within it. The framing device is the tale of Princess Scheherazade, who faces execution by her husband, Prince Shahryar. After his previous wife's adultery, the prince believes that all women are deceitful; he has vowed to marry a new bride every day, "abate her maidenhead at night and slay her next morning to make sure of his honour". The princess averts her fate by withholding the ending

of a story she tells on her wedding night, leading Shahryar to delay her execution. After 1,001 such nights, he confesses that she has changed his soul and he pardons her.

The tales told by Scheherazade intermingle fantastic tales set in legendary locations with stories involving historical figures – such as Haroun al Rashid (c.766–809), ruler of the Abbasid Caliphate during the Islamic Golden Age. The diverse nature of the tales is responsible for the wide variety of genres to be found within the

O my sister, recite to us some new story, delightsome and delectable, wherewith to while away the waking hours of our latter night.
One Thousand and One Nights

collection, from adventure, romance, and fairy tale, to horror and even science fiction.

Influence in the West
It was not until the 18th century that the stories became known in Europe, thanks to a retelling by French scholar Antoine Galland in *Les Mille et Une Nuits* (1704–17). The manuscript from which Galland translated was incomplete, falling well short of 1,001 nights worth of stories, so he added the Arabic tales of "Ali Baba", "Aladdin", and "Sinbad". These were never part of the original *One Thousand and One Nights*, but have since become some of the most well-known stories from the collection in the West.

Galland's book derived much of its popularity from its exoticism, with its tales of genies and flying carpets, and was an important influence on the folktale-collecting movement taken up by the Brothers Grimm and others in the early 19th century. A translation of the original stories by Sir Richard Burton in 1885 inspired a more serious interest in Islamic culture – but in the Arab world the tales are still regarded as entertaining fantasies rather than literature. ▪

SINCE LIFE IS BUT A DREAM, WHY TOIL TO NO AVAIL?
QUAN TANGSHI (8TH CENTURY), A COLLECTION INCLUDING POEMS BY LI BAI (LI PO), DU FU, AND WANG WEI

IN CONTEXT

FOCUS
Imperial Chinese poetry

BEFORE

c.4th century BCE A collection of lyric poems, *Songs of Chu* (*Chu Ci*), is compiled, attributed to Qu Yuan, Song Yu, and others.

2nd and 3rd centuries CE Cao Cao, later the Emperor Wu of Wei, and his sons Cao Pi and Cao Zhi, establish the *jian'an* style of poetry of the later Han dynasty.

AFTER

960–1368 During the Song and Yuan dynasties, the lyric *ci* style becomes more popular than the Tang formal *shi* style.

1368–1644 Ming dynasty poetry is dominated by Gao Qi, Li Dongyang, and Yuan Hongdao.

1644 Manchu rulers establish the Qing dynasty, opening a period of scholarship in and publication of Tang literature.

China has a tradition of poetry that can be traced back to the 11th century BCE. While some early poetry was in a lyric style – *ci* – in the shape of songs and love poems, a more formal style – *shi* – tackled reflective themes and used stricter structures. During the early Han dynasty, in the 3rd century BCE, a collection of 305 *shi* poems was compiled, the *Book of Odes* (*Shijing*). Considered one of the Five Classics of Chinese literature, it set the standard for subsequent classical Chinese poetry.

Poetic traditions

This *shi* tradition reached its apex in the Tang era (618–907 CE). In the 8th century in particular a number of brilliant poets emerged. Foremost among them were Li Bai (701–762), also known as Li Po, whose poems included nostalgic meditations on friendship; his friend Du Fu (712–770), known as the "poet-historian"; and the polymath Wang Wei (699–759), whose nature portraits seldom mentioned any human interference.

In 1705, the Kangxi emperor (reigned 1661–1722) commissioned the scholar Cao Yin to compile a definitive collection to be known as the *Quan Tangshi* ("Complete Tang Poems") with almost 50,000 poems by more than 2,000 poets. A shorter anthology was compiled in around 1763 by Sun Zhu, *Three Hundred Tang Poems* (*Tangshi sanbai shou*), which, like the *Book of Odes*, was accorded Classic status, and has remained essential reading in China to the present. ∎

We sit together, the mountain and me, until only the mountain remains.
"Alone Looking at the Mountain"
Li Bai

See also: *Book of Changes* 21 ▪ *Romance of the Three Kingdoms* 66–67 ▪ *The Narrow Road to the Interior* 92

REAL THINGS IN THE DARKNESS SEEM NO REALER THAN DREAMS
THE TALE OF GENJI (c.1000–1012), MURASAKI SHIKIBU

IN CONTEXT

FOCUS
Literature of the Heian court

BEFORE

c.920 CE The first anthology of *waka* (classical Japanese poetry) is published, known as *Kokinshū* (*A Collection of Poems Ancient and Modern*).

Late 10th century The fairytale *The Tale of the Lady Ochikubo* is written.

c.1000 Sei Shōnagon completes *The Pillow Book*, observations on life in the court of the Empress Consort Teishi.

AFTER

Early 12th century *Konjaku monogatari* (*Tales of Times Now Past*) is compiled, containing stories from India, China, and Japan.

1187 *Senzaishū* (*Collection of a Thousand Years*), the final imperial anthology of *waka* (classical poetry), is completed by Fujiwara no Shunzei.

Japanese art and culture flourished in the Heian period (794–1185), when the imperial court was located in Heian-kyō (present-day Kyoto). It was during this period that classical Japanese literature began to emerge, distinct from Chinese language and culture. And although Chinese remained the language of both officialdom and the nobility, the simpler form of the Japanese *kana* syllabic script increasingly became the national language of literature.

Imperial patronage

Poetry was highly regarded and encouraged by the Heian emperors, who commissioned eight major anthologies of poems in Japanese. At the end of the 10th century, however, works in prose also began to appear, including histories and folktales, such as *The Tale of the Bamboo Cutter*, and an original story, *The Tale of the Lady Ochikubo*, thought to have been written by a member of the Heian court.

More significantly, Murasaki Shikibu (973–1014 or 1025), a lady-in-waiting at the court, wrote what is considered to be the first Japanese novel (and what some consider the first ever novel) – *The Tale of Genji*. In its 54 chapters, it recounts the lives and loves of "Shining Genji" – the disinherited son of a Japanese emperor – and his descendants. Although presented as a sequence of events rather than a true plot, the character portrayals are compelling, giving not only an insight into the life of courtiers at the time, but also their thoughts and motivations, making this arguably a precursor of the modern psychological novel.

Murasaki probably intended *The Tale of Genji* for a readership of noblewomen, but it won a wider audience and became a classic, appearing in many editions from the 12th century onwards. Despite its status, its complex style meant it was not translated into modern Japanese until the 20th century; the text is usually annotated to explain its cultural references. ■

See also: *The Pillow Book* 56 ▪ *The Narrow Road to the Interior* 92 ▪ *The Love Suicides at Sonezaki* 93

A MAN SHOULD SUFFER GREATLY FOR HIS LORD
THE SONG OF ROLAND (c.1098)

IN CONTEXT

FOCUS
Chansons de geste

BEFORE
5th–11th century In Anglo-Saxon Britain poets known as scops entertain the courts by singing or reciting epics of mainly Scandinavian history.

880 The *Canticle of Saint Eulalia* is one of the early texts in the northern vernacular *langue d'oïl* (Old French).

AFTER
Late 11th or early 12th century Early poems of the Matter of France appear, such as the *Chanson de Guillaume* and *Gormont et Isembart*.

c.1200 *Cantar de mio Cid*, the first known Spanish epic poem, is written.

14th–15th century The great age of medieval French poetry is ended by the upheaval of the Hundred Years' War (1337–1453) and the devastation of the Black Death (c.1346–53).

A lthough some religious texts appeared in the vernacular Old French as early as the 9th century, literature in French is generally considered to have its beginnings in the epic poems known as *chansons de geste* ("songs of heroic deeds") that were recited or sung at court by minstrels or *jongleurs*. Originally, these narrative poems in verse were part of an oral tradition, but from the end of the 11th century they were increasingly written down.

Legendary exploits

The *chansons de geste* formed the basis for the Matter of France, one of three parts of a wider literary cycle of medieval works, mainly in Old French. The Matter of France featured the exploits of historical figures such as the Frankish king Charlemagne. Neither of the other two literary cycles – the Matter of Rome (the history and mythology of the classical world) and the Matter of Britain (tales of King Arthur and his knights) – was the subject of *chansons de geste*.

One of the earliest *chansons* from the Matter of France was *The Song of Roland*, a version of which was by a poet known as Turold. In some 4,000 lines of verse, it tells of the legendary Battle of Roncevaux (modern Roncesvalles) in 778, during Charlemagne's reign. In the fight for the Muslim stronghold of Saragossa in Spain, Roland is betrayed by his stepfather and ambushed. Refusing to call for help he puts up a valiant fight, but as his men are massacred he blows a call for revenge on his oliphant (an elephant-tusk horn) with such force that he dies. Charlemagne answers, arriving and defeating the Muslims.

The *chansons de geste* inspired a tradition of *cantar de gesta* poetry in Spain, including the Castilian epic *Cantar de mio Cid*, and many of the poems were retold in German and as the Old Norse *Karlamagnús saga*. Even after poets from the 12th century developed a preference for writing courtly lyric poetry, the finest *chansons de geste*, such as *The Song of Roland*, remained popular until the 15th century. ■

See also: *Beowulf* 42–43 ▪ "Under the Linden Tree" 49 ▪ *Lancelot, the Knight of the Cart* 50–51 ▪ *The Canterbury Tales* 68–71

TANDARADEI, SWEETLY SANG THE NIGHTINGALE
"UNDER THE LINDEN TREE" (LATE 12TH CENTURY), WALTHER VON DER VOGELWEIDE

IN CONTEXT

FOCUS
Troubadours and minnesingers

BEFORE
Late 11th century The troubadour tradition of courtly love poetry, written in the southern French Occitan dialect (*langue d'oc*), spreads to Spain and Italy.

12th century Poets known as *trouvères*, including Chrétien de Troyes, begin to compose lyric poems in the northern French dialect (*langue d'oïl*).

Late 12th century Der von Kürenberg and Dietmar von Aist pioneer the German *Minnesänger* tradition.

AFTER
Late 13th century Heinrich Frauenlob, one of the last of the *Minnesänger*, sets up a school for *Meistersinger*.

c.1330s Troubadour numbers wane before they vanish with the Black Death (c.1346–53).

Entertainment in the early medieval courts of Europe was provided by minstrels, who recited or sang epic poems. But in the 11th century, a number of more aristocratic poets, at first in Occitania, southern France, became travelling minstrels. In order to distinguish them from the *jongleurs*, or the common entertainers, they became known as troubadours, and their poetry moved from a focus on historical narrative to songs of courtly love – the chivalrous exploits of knights and their noble lady-loves.

Noble entertainers
Lyric poetry caught on first in northern France, and later in Italy and Spain. In the next century, the noble entertainers emerged in Germany as *Minnesänger*, or minnesingers. Foremost among these was Walther von der Vogelweide (c.1170–c.1230), who also wrote political and satirical poetry. He is best known for his charming "Under the Linden Tree", a love poem in the courtly tradition of the troubadours but distinct in key respects. With its memorable refrain of the nightingale singing "Tandaradei", he references the choruses of folk song, and more significantly, some of the poem's most beautiful words are not those of a noble lady, but a simple girl.

These features anticipated the eventual end of the age of courtly lyric poetry, which in Gemany was marked by the emergence of new, professional, poet-composers, the *Meistersinger*, or mastersingers. ∎

Still you may find there,
Lovely together,
Flowers crushed and
grass down-pressed.
"Under the Linden Tree"

See also: *The Song of Roland* 48 ▪ *Lancelot, the Knight of the Cart* 50–51 ▪ *The Canterbury Tales* 68–71

HE WHO DARES NOT FOLLOW LOVE'S COMMAND ERRS GREATLY
LANCELOT, THE KNIGHT OF THE CART (c.1175–1181), CHRÉTIEN DE TROYES

IN CONTEXT

FOCUS
Arthurian chivalric romance

BEFORE
1138 Welsh cleric and chronicler Geoffrey of Monmouth's *Historia Regum Britanniae* popularizes the legend of King Arthur.

12th century The Old French (northern vernacular *langue d'oïl*) poem *Tristan*, by Thomas of Britain, tells the legend of the knight of the Round Table Tristan and his lover Iseult.

AFTER
13th century The five-volume Lancelot-Grail cycle (also called Prose Lancelot or the Vulgate Cycle), written in Old French by anonymous clerics, gives an account of Lancelot's quest for the Holy Grail.

1485 In *Le Morte d'Arthur*, English writer Sir Thomas Malory reinterprets the traditional Arthurian legends.

The tradition of epic poetry, which had its roots in Homer and Virgil, lived on throughout the Middle Ages in the form of the *chansons de geste* ("songs of heroic deeds"), written and performed by the troubadours of southern France and their peers in other Mediterranean countries. These medieval epics conformed to the genre by telling tales of valiant acts and the battles of classical antiquity, or the wars against the Saracens and Moors. But in the 12th century, these tales of knights and their adventures assumed a different tone, as the idea of courtly love began to replace military exploits as the predominant theme, and the emphasis shifted from heroism to noble deeds.

Arthurian legend
The poet credited with introducing this change was Chrétien de Troyes, a *trouvère* (the northern French equivalent of a troubadour) who took his inspiration from the legends of King Arthur and his knights of the Round Table. In Chrétien's time there were two distinct cultures in France,

Chrétien de Troyes

Little is known about Chrétien de Troyes, a *trouvère* who, in the late 12th century, served in the court of Marie of France. His adoption of the name "de Troyes" suggests that he may have been from Troyes, in the Champagne region of France, southeast of Paris, but may instead refer to his patron, Marie, Countess of Champagne, whose court was in Troyes. His poems, which date from the period 1160–1180, suggest that he was a minor member of the clergy. Chrétien's major works were the four romances he wrote on Arthurian stories, and he is credited with introducing into the tales the new idea of courtly love, in the affair between Lancelot and Guinevere. A fifth poem, *Perceval, the Story of the Grail*, was unfinished when he died, in around 1190.

Other key works

c.1170 *Erec and Enide*
c.1176 *Cligès*
1177–81 *Yvain, the Knight of the Lion*

See also: *The Song of Roland* 48 ▪ "Under the Linden Tree" 49 ▪ *Don Quixote* 76–81 ▪
Sir Gawain and the Green Knight 102 ▪ *Le Morte d'Arthur* 102

When Lancelot is asked to ride in a cart, like a common convict, he does so very reluctantly. However, he later redeems himself for his hesitation by his chivalric deeds.

recognizable by their dialects: in the south the troubadours used the *langue d'oc*, while the language of the *trouvères* was the northern *langue d'oïl*. It is no surprise then that Chrétien should turn his attention away from the classical Mediterranean and southern French heroes, turning it instead towards the so-called "Matter of Britain", the legends of Britain and Brittany.

Love conquers all

As well as introducing the Arthurian legends to a French audience, Chrétien reinterpreted the idea of the chivalric ("knightly") romance. In the tale of *Lancelot, the Knight of the Cart*, he focused on a hitherto lesser-known character, whose quest was largely romantic in nature, and who demonstrated his nobility by defending the honour of Queen Guinevere.

Lancelot's mission is to rescue Guinevere from the evil clutches of Méléagant, and he embarks on a series of adventures. These

inevitably involve fights with Méléagant, in which he eventually emerges victorious, but they also involve his wooing of Guinevere. However, not everything goes his way: a series of misunderstandings and deceits means that Guinevere blows hot and cold along the way, and Lancelot suffers the indignity of being made to ride in a common cart normally used to transport convicts, and at one point ends up a prisoner himself. But in the end, he and his love are triumphant, and both Guinevere's honour and Lancelot's nobility survive intact.

An age of chivalry

Chrétien's innovative approach to epic poetry chimed with the mood of the time, and although the old *chansons de geste* remained popular with readers, poets across Europe adopted the new style, often on the themes of the Arthurian legends. Many chose to tell the story of lovers such as Lancelot and Guinevere, or Tristan and Iseult; others took up the story of the noble quest for the Holy Grail. During the 13th century, however, the idea of epic poetry was on the wane, and the Arthurian romances were more frequently told in prose, reaching their high point with Sir Thomas Malory's *Le Morte d'Arthur*.

The genre of Arthurian chivalric romance fell out of favour with the arrival of the Renaissance period. The portrayal of noble knights, damsels in distress, and mannered courtly love had already become a familiar cliché by the time Miguel de Cervantes wrote his *Don Quixote* in 1605, although the words "chivalry" and "romance" still retain their association with that mythical medieval world. ∎

Three distinct types of epic poetry had evolved by the medieval period in western Europe. Mainly recorded in Old French, each of these collections was distinguished by its theme or subject matter.

The Matter of Rome

The myths and legends of the classical world, including Greek and especially Roman mythology, as well as stories from history, including Alexander the Great and Julius Caesar.

The Matter of France

Legends of Charlemagne and his paladins, and the wars with the Moors and Saracens, including the stories of Roland, Guillaume d'Orange, and Doon de Mayence.

The Matter of Britain

The legends of Britain and Brittany: Arthurian legends, the quest for the Holy Grail, and the stories of Brutus of Britain, King Cole, King Lear, and Gogmagog.

LET ANOTHER'S WOUND BE MY WARNING

NJAL'S SAGA (LATE 13TH CENTURY)

Rich in heroic exploits, family feuds, love affairs, legends, and historical detail, the Nordic sagas were written between the 12th and 14th centuries. By and large their authorship is unknown. Until the 12th century, most belonged to the oral storytelling tradition, and were only written down by scribes some years later. However, unlike most medieval literature, which was recorded in Latin, the sagas were transcribed in the vernacular languages of ordinary people, in Old Norse or Old Icelandic.

The sagas divide into five main classes: sagas of the kings, mainly about the early rulers of Norway, but including Orkney and Sweden; contemporary sagas, concerning the secular matters of Icelandic chieftains (and sometimes named after the important Sturlung family); the *Fornaldsogur*, which have little historical basis and relate to legendary and mythological times; chivalric romantic sagas, such as *Alexander's Saga*, which started as translations of French *chansons de geste* ("songs of heroic deeds"); and the Icelanders' sagas.

The *Eddur*

The *Eddur* (singular *Edda*) refers to a body of ancient Icelandic literature found in two 13th-century books: the *Prose Edda* and the *Poetic Edda*. Together these two works form the most comprehensive source of Scandinavian mythology.

The *Prose Edda*, or *Younger Edda*, was written or compiled by Icelandic scholar Snorri Sturluson (1179–1241) in around 1220. It is a textbook on poetry that explains the metres of early *skalds* (court poets) and provides a guide to mythological subjects in early poetry. It consists of a prologue and three parts: Skáldskaparmál ("The Language of Poetry"); Háttatal ("A Catalog of Metres"); and Gylfaginning ("The Beguiling of Gylfi"), which tells of the visit of King Gylfi to Asgard, the citadel of the gods.

The *Poetic Edda*, or the *Elder Edda*, is a later collection that contains much older material (800–1100). It consists of heroic and mythological poems composed by unknown authors.

See also: *Iliad* 26–33 ▪ *Beowulf* 42–43 ▪ *The Song of Roland* 48 ▪ *Lancelot, the Knight of the Cart* 50–51 ▪ *Cantar de Mio Cid* 56–57 ▪ *Ivanhoe* 150 ▪ *Kalevala* 151 ▪ *The Lord of the Rings* 287

Written in the early 13th century, the Icelanders' sagas, also known as family sagas, are heroic prose narratives that focus especially on genealogical (family) history, and describe the various struggles and conflicts that took place.

The realism, starkly beautiful writing, and vivid description of character in the family sagas mark them as the highpoint of classical Icelandic saga writing. Among the better known are *Egil's Saga*, *Laxdæla Saga*, *Grettis Saga*, and *Njal's Saga*. Some scholars believe that Snorri Sturluson may have written *Egil's Saga*, but the other authors are unknown.

A tragic blood feud

Njal's Saga, or "The Story of Burnt Njal", is one of the longest of the Icelanders' sagas and is generally considered to be the finest. The saga is written in prose, with some verse embedded in the narrative, and recreates Icelandic life during its heroic period, describing events that occurred among the great families between the 10th and 11th centuries. Episodic and bleak, *Njal's Saga* is essentially the account of a 50-year blood feud that touches the lives of a wide range of complex and vividly drawn characters.

Much of the narrative focuses on the two heroes: Njal, a wise, prudent lawyer, and his friend Gunnar, a powerful but reluctant warrior. Both are peaceful men, but the demands of honour and kinship ties draw them and their families into bloodthirsty feuds with tragic consequences. In some ways – in its length, content, and psychological themes – *Njal's Saga* is similar to a modern novel. The relationships and characters are

Literature of the Northmen

Sagas of the kings		The *Konungasogur* tell of the deeds of the kings of Scandinavia and are the highest form of saga writing. Snorri Sturluson's *Heimskringla*, c.1230, about the kings of Norway, is the best known.
Contemporary sagas		The *Sturlungasogur* deal with internal struggles in Iceland in the 12th and 13th centuries. Rich in social history, they were written – unlike the family sagas – not long after the events took place.
Sagas of antiquity		The *Fornaldarsogur* deal with events before the settlement of Iceland and include the *Volsung Saga*, c.1270. As well as mythology and Germanic hero legends, there are adventures in far-off lands.
Chivalric sagas		The *Riddarasogur* contain translated Norse versions of the Romance language tales aimed at a popular readership. One of the earliest, c.1226, is the story of Tristan.
Family sagas		The *Islendingasogur* is a class of prose genealogical histories about the early generations of settler families in c.930–c.1030. Their authorship is unknown.

familiar and believable. The issue of honour and the consequences of vengeance are the key themes, but the saga also explores the role of law in settling disputes.

A powerful influence

The Icelandic sagas portray warriors, kings, strong men, and powerful matriarchs. Calling on historical events and tumultous times but containing older myths and legends, they present a realistic picture of a vanished society, as well as fantastic tales and romances.

The collection of stories represents some of the greatest writing in European medieval literature. They also had a powerful influence on later writers, notably Sir Walter Scott, the 19th-century Scottish poet and playwright, and J R R Tolkein, the 20th-century English fantasy writer. ▪

Never break the peace which good men and true make between thee and others.
Njal's Saga

FURTHER READING

EGYPTIAN BOOK OF THE DEAD
(16TH CENTURY BCE)

Illustrated and written on papyrus, the *Egyptian Book of the Dead* is a compilation of around 200 chapters of magic spells and formulas that were written by various authors for use in the afterlife. Scribes made copies, which were buried with the mummy and believed to be read by the deceased on their journey to the Underworld, as a source of protection and a guide through the hazards that lay ahead. A famous example is *The Papyrus of Ani*, now in the British Museum, London.

ODYSSEY
(c.725–675 BCE), HOMER

An epic Ancient Greek poem in 24 books (more than 12,000 lines), composed for oral performance, the *Odyssey* is traditionally attributed to Homer (see p.28). The poem is in part a sequel to Homer's other great work, the *Iliad*. Its hero is Odysseus, king of Ithaca, who is described wandering the seas, homeward-bound after the end of the 10-year Trojan War. He has vivid adventures, which include encounters with supernatural creatures and temptations of the flesh. Both his son Telemachus and wife Penelope despair for Odysseus's return – he has been absent for two decades. Penelope has to deal with a series of suitors, whose fate at the hands of the disguised Odysseus forms the dramatic denoument of the tale.

THEOGONY
(c.700 BCE), HESIOD

The 1,022-line epic poem *Theogony*, or "Birth of the Gods", was written by the ancient Greek poet Hesiod (8th–7th century BCE), and is one of the earliest mythic accounts of the origins of the cosmos and of the gods. Beginning with the formation of the Earth (*Gaia*) out of Chaos (the primordial Abyss), the poem goes on to detail the birth and overthrow of successive generations of gods, ending with the triumph of Zeus. At its centre, *Theogony* engages with some of the core themes that haunt the human imagination, including creation, the struggle between fathers and sons, and humanity's place in the universe.

DAO DE JING
(6TH–3RD CENTURY BCE), LAOZI

Traditionally attributed to the legendary Chinese sage Laozi, the *Dao De Jing* (*Classic of the Way and Virtue*), the main sacred text of Daoism, is a compilation of 81 verse chapters giving enigmatic advice on how to live harmoniously by following the Dao ("Way"). Its compelling, mysterious, poetic aphorisms – such as "Do nothing, and there is nothing that will not be done" – illustrate the practice of *wu wei*, or non-action.

ORESTEIA
(458 BCE), AESCHYLUS

Written by Aeschylus, the first of the great dramatists of classical Athens, the *Oresteia* is a trilogy (the only classical Greek example to survive) telling the tragic story of the house of Atreus. The first play portrays the return of King Agamemnon from war and the plot upon his life by his

---

Aeschylus

The seven complete tragedies that remain to us of the work of Aeschylus – who is estimated to have written between 70 and 90 plays – attest to his mastery of the genre. Thought to have been born in Eleusis near Athens in 525 or 524 BCE, he lived in the early period of the Athenian democracy, and played a part in the fight against the invading Persians – specifically at the battle of Marathon. As well as tragedies he wrote "satyr plays" in a light, burlesque style. Both genres were presented in competitions at the foremost dramatical contest in Athens, the annual festival of Dionysus, and Aeschylus was a regular winner. One exceptional year he lost to the younger tragedian, Sophocles. He died at Gela in Sicily in 456 or 455 BCE.

Key works

458 BCE *Oresteia* (see right)
472 BCE *The Persians*
467 BCE *Seven Against Thebes*
5th century BCE *Prometheus Bound*

unfaithful spouse, Clytemnestra. The second play deals with revenge by the king's daughter Electra and his son Orestes; the third concerns its consequences. The cycle of bloodshed is finally supplanted by the rule of law, under the influence of the goddess Athena.

MEDEA
(431 BCE), EURIPIDES

A tragedy by the Greek dramatist Euripides (c.484–406 BCE), *Medea* is a compelling play about injustice, jealousy, and revenge. With only two actors on stage at any time, it is based on the legendary tale of Princess Medea and her ruthless persecution of her husband Jason (hero of the Argonauts myth), after he abandons her for the daughter of the king of Corinth. Despite Medea's cruelty, and in particular her savage treatment of her own children with Jason, Euripides nevertheless elicits the audience's sympathy for her.

WASPS
(422 BCE), ARISTOPHANES

One of the world's great comedies, by Greek dramatist Aristophanes (c.450–c.388 BCE), *Wasps* satirizes

No, I know no more how to acquit than to play the lyre.
Wasps
Aristophanes

the legal system in ancient Athens by demonstrating how it could be exploited by a corrupt demogogue. The play's action centres around an ill-tempered old man who is addicted to serving on juries. The play is a classic of the Old Comedy, which is characterized by the use of a chorus, scathing inventive, ribald humour, outspoken social criticism, and elements of fantasy. The play takes its title from the chorus, a swarm of jurors.

RAMAYANA
(5TH–4TH CENTURIES BCE), VALMIKI

One of the great works of Indian literature and rivalling even the *Mahabharata*, the *Ramayana* (meaning "Rama's journey") is a Sanskrit epic of 24,000 couplets in seven books. Its moral purpose is the presentation of ideal role models – for a king, brother, wife, servant, and so on – within a narrative framework. The story describes the actions of the god Rama, with the help of the monkey-general Hanuman, against a demon-king who has abducted his wife, Sita. The Hindu sage and poet Valmiki, the reputed author, makes an appearance in the work.

SONGS OF CHU
(4TH CENTURY BCE)

A compilation of verse from the southern Chinese state of Chu, *Songs of Chu* contains many pieces attributed to exiled minister Qu Yuan (c.339–c.278 BCE), a literary innovator who introduced greater formal variety into poetry. Many of the poems here are influenced by shamanistic folk rites and by local legends. The first piece, "On Encountering Sorrow", is a long,

Valmiki

Known as the "first poet" of Sanskrit poetry thanks to his invention of the classic *sloka* ("song") verse form, Valmiki was a sage who, according to Hindu belief, lived in India at some point between the 6th and the 1st century BCE. Once a murderous highway robber named Ratnakara, he became a holy man after meditating for many years as penance after attempting to rob Narada, a divine sage. During his meditation, an ant hill grew up around him, from which he gained his name "Valmiki" (Sanskrit for "one born out of ant hills"). He reportedly composed the *Ramayana* at the command of the Hindu god Brahma.

Key works

5th–4th century BCE
Ramayana (see left)

melancholic reflection that helped to establish a tradition of romanticism in Chinese literature.

METAMORPHOSES
(c.8 CE), OVID

Roman poet Ovid (43 BCE–18 CE) brought together an array of lively mythological tales in his verse epic, *Metamorphoses*. The work marks a shift in popular taste from war to love as an appropriate subject for poetry. The stories are linked by the theme of transformation, often resulting from love or desire. Their subjects include some of the best-known legends of ancient Greece and Rome. *Metamorphoses* has had

Sei Shōnagon

Diarist-essayist Sei Shōnagon was born c.966 CE, the daughter of the scholar and *waka* poet Kiyohara Motosuke. She joined the Japanese court to serve Empress Teishi (Sadako) in the city that was later known as Kyoto. Her *The Pillow Book* is an engaging picture of court life in the Heian dynasty around 991–1000 CE. Partly due to her wit and intelligence, she was disliked by a number of her contemporaries. Her rivals included Murasaki Shikibu, who wrote *The Tale of Genji*. After her patroness died, Sei Shōnagon is reported to have left the court and married, becoming a Buddhist monk in her widowhood. She is thought to have died around 1025 CE.

Key works

c.1000 CE *The Pillow Book* (see far right)

a huge impact on both literature (including Shakespeare and Dante) and the visual arts, notably painting.

THE GOLDEN ASS
(2ND CENTURY CE), APULEIUS

Written by Apuleius (c.124–c.170 CE), a Numidian Berber who benefited from the opportunities offered by Roman rule, *The Golden Ass* is the only work of fiction in Latin to have survived in its entirety. It tells of the adventures of a young man whose fascination with magic results in his transformation into a donkey. In this new guise, he passes from owner to owner until the goddess Isis breaks the spell and frees him. The tale's principal ingredients include satire, slapstick, bawdiness, allegory, moral reflection, and, above all, humour. The idea of the transformation of humans into animals has remained a major theme in world literature.

HILDEBRANDSLIED
(c.800 CE)

An anonymous work in Old High German verse, the *Hildebrandslied* ("Song of Hildebrand") was found on the flyleaves of a theological codex, and copied by scribes between 830 and 840 CE. Only 68 lines have survived; the alliterative poem (probably intended for oral transmission) is likely to have been no more than 100 lines originally. The subject is an occasion when the warrior Hildebrand comes face to face with his son in combat and seeks to hide who he is, while ensuring the youth is not harmed.

DIGENIS AKRITAS
(c.10TH CENTURY)

The Byzantine epic hero Basil, known by his epithet Digenis Akritas (meaning "two-blood border-lord"), is the protagonist of the most famous of the so-called Akritic folk ballads, which were celebrated in vernacular Greek. *Digenis Akritas* is also the name of an anonymous, blank-verse epic that describes Basil's lineage, boyhood, and heroic later life. The son of a Saracen emir who converted to Christianity, Basil shows great strength and courage and valiantly defends the Byzantine Empire from its enemies. The epic was further developed between the 12th and 17th centuries.

THE PILLOW BOOK
(c.1000), SEI SHŌNAGON

In the Japanese tradition, a pillow book was a collection of personal musings supposedly written in the bedroom. The best-known example is that of Sei Shōnagon, a lady of the Heian-kyō court. The entries, which were arranged thematically rather than in chronological order by scribes for circulation among the Japanese court, offer observations on people and nature, ranging from caustic wit to appreciation of the finer things in life. The reader gains glimpses into the minutiae of court life, such as flutes, disobedient dogs, and ladies betting on how long it would take a mound of snow to melt.

MABINOGION
(11TH–14TH CENTURIES)

The earliest example of prose literature in Britain, *Mabinogion* is a collection of 11 anonymous Welsh prose tales, some of which reveal Celtic and French influences. Its two source manuscripts date from the late 14th century. There are elements of supernatural fantasy, probably deriving from an ancient oral storytelling tradition. Diverse in form and content, some of the tales feature the legendary king Arthur. The most sophisticated stories are the "Four Branches", which include giants, magical white horses, and incest, betrayal, and redemption.

CANTAR DE MIO CID
(c.1140)

The earliest surviving epic poem in Spanish literature, *Cantar de Mio Cid (Song/Poem of the*

Cid) tells of the exploits of the real-life Castilian hero El Cid (1043–99) in the attempt to recapture Spain from the Moors. The poem focuses on military and diplomatic prowess as well as El Cid's relationship with King Alfonso VI, using a realist tone to describe the hero's efforts to regain lost honour. The authorship of the epic, which may have been intended for public recital, has never been established – the only surviving manuscript is signed *Per Abbas*, but the identity of the writer has never been verified.

THE TALE OF IGOR'S CAMPAIGN
(LATE 12TH CENTURY)

An anonymous epic poem in the Old East Slavic language, *The Tale of Igor's Campaign* describes an unsuccessful raid by a prince of the "land of the Rus", named Igor Svyatoslavich. Igor's heroic pride leads him to face overwhelming odds, and he is taken captive by his enemies, but escapes. The tale has elements of both epic and lyric, with political overtones too. It has become a Russian national classic.

…lives are laid out on the threshing floor, souls are winnowed from bodies.
The Tale of Igor's Campaign

NIBELUNGENLIED
(c.1200)

The main characters of this work have become internationally known through Wagner's Ring cycle of operas. The *Nibelungenlied*, or "Song of the Nibelungs", is a richly imagined anonymous epic poem in Middle High German. Medieval German literature had turned to courtly refinement, but the *Nibelungenlied* looked back to older, more visceral notions of honour and vengeance. It tells of stolen treasure (Rhine gold) and magic powers (including invisibility); of the dragon-slayer Siegfried and his wooing of the princess Kriemhild; and of Kriemhild's revenge against the Nibelungen (Burgundians) after the murder of Siegfried by one of their most prominent warriors, the king's brother Hagen. Some characters – including the powerful queen Brunhild – and some of the narrative are rooted in Old Norse sagas.

ROMANCE OF THE ROSE
(c.1225–1280), GUILLAUME DE LORRIS AND JEAN DE MEUN

Frenchman Guillaume de Lorris (c.1200–c.1240) wrote 4,058 lines of the *Romance of the Rose*; Jean de Meun (c.1240–c.1305) took it to more than 21,000 lines. Based on Ovid's *Ars Amatoria* (*Art of Love*), the poem is one of the most popular French examples of the late Middle Ages. It is a dream allegory of the wooing of a young lady, symbolized by a rosebud, within courtly society, represented by the garden. De Meun gives opinions on topics of the day. The first 1,705 lines were rendered into English by Geoffrey Chaucer.

CANTIGAS DE SANTA MARÍA
(1252–1284), ALFONSO X

One of the largest collections of medieval solo songs, the *Cantigas de Santa María* ("Canticles of Holy Mary") were written in medieval Galician-Portuguese, probably (at least in part) by Alfonso X, king of Castile, León, and Galicia. Every song, or canticle, refers to the Virgin Mary, whose miracles – including local events prompted by her intercession – provide narrative content; every 10th song is a hymn in her honour. The songs – written with musical notation – have great metrical variety, with lines ranging from two to 24 syllables.

Alfonso X

Born in 1221 in Burgos, the capital of Castile (in the north of modern-day Spain), Alfonso X was a scholarly and wise king who encouraged learning and the arts. His reign began in 1252 following the death of his father Ferdinand III, who had greatly expanded Castile and fought the most successful campaigns of the *Reconquista* against the Moors. Inheriting a wealthy and stable land, Alfonso commissioned and personally oversaw a range of texts, from law and astronomy to music and history, ensuring that Castilian would be the forerunner of modern Spanish. He died in Seville in 1284.

Key works

1252–84 *Cantigas de Santa María* (see above)
c.1255–65 *Siete partidas*
1264 *Premera crónica general*

RENAISS

ENLIGHT

1300–1800

ANCE TO
ENMENT

Dante Alighieri writes *The Divine Comedy*, describing a journey through **Hell, Purgatory, and Heaven**.

Luo Guanzhong's *Romance of the Three Kingdoms* and Shi Nai'an's *The Water Margin* are written, the first two of **Chinese literature's** four great **classical novels**.

In Germany Johannes Gutenberg invents a printing process using movable type, enabling the **mass publication of printed materials** for the first time.

A **scientific, humanist revolution begins** with Nicolaus Copernicus's *On the Revolutions of the Heavenly Spheres* and Andreas Vesalius's *On the Fabric of the Human Body*.

c.1308–20　　　**14TH CENTURY**　　　**c.1439**　　　**1543**

1346–53　　　**c.1387–1400**　　　**1532–64**　　　**1604**

The Black Death causes massive **social and economic disruption**, accelerating the end of Europe's medieval era. Culturally, it brings to an end the great age of French poetry and troubadours.

In *The Canterbury Tales*, Geoffrey Chaucer recounts stories told by **a socially mixed group of pilgrims**.

A series of satirical novels by François Rabelais is published; it tells the adventures of the giants **Gargantua and Pantagruel**.

Christopher Marlowe's Elizabethan drama *Doctor Faustus* is **published after his death**, a decade after it was first performed.

From the early 14th century, the cultural movement known as the Renaissance began to spread across Europe from the Italian city of Florence. It was marked by a change from medieval attitudes – which were dominated by the dogma of the Christian Church – to a far more humanist perspective that was inspired by a rediscovery of ancient Greek and Roman philosophy and culture. But this was more than a simple rebirth of classical ideas – the period was also a time of innovation.

The epic and the everyday

In literature, although inspiration came from classical style and forms, writers chose to work in vernacular languages, as opposed to Latin or Greek, and to create their own stories rather than retell those of the past. Among the first to write in this way was the Florentine poet Dante Alighieri, whose *The Divine Comedy* was not only an epic poetic journey through the afterlife but also served as an allegory for the contemporary world.

At the same time, other writers chose to turn away from the realm of epics and legends altogether, and focus on the lives, autonomy, and ingenuity of ordinary people. In *The Decameron*, published in 1353, Giovanni Boccaccio presented a collection of 100 "novellas" in prose in the Florentine vernacular. Shortly afterwards Geoffrey Chaucer wrote a similar collection of stories, *The Canterbury Tales*. Both works contained a variety of tales of everyday life – from love stories to moral parables. With their discussions of human vices, accounts of licentiousness, and bawdy practical jokes, they soon became popular reading.

The birth of the novel

In the 15th century, the invention of Gutenberg's printing press hastened the spread of ideas, and this technology also made it easier to cater to audiences in vernacular languages. Popular demand for books had been stimulated in particular by the prose storytelling of Boccaccio and Chaucer. From these early stories emerged a form of literature as a long, prose narrative that is now ubiquitous, but was then very much "novel".

During the 16th century, prose narratives gradually replaced the epic poem as the predominant literary form in most of Europe, and readers particularly responded to

The first volume of Miguel de Cervantes' *Don Quixote* is published, marking the high point of **a golden age of Spanish literature**.

In *The Narrow Road to the Interior*, Matsuo Bashō uses **haiku** in a prose narrative to describe his **spiritual journey** through Japan.

The first volume of the *Encyclopédie*, edited by Denis Diderot and Jean le Rond d'Alembert, offers a comprehensive reference to **Enlightenment ideas and sciences**.

Friedrich Schiller's **Sturm und Drang drama** *The Robbers* portrays the violent and emotional relationship between two brothers.

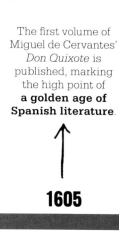

1605   **1702**   **1751**   **1781**

1623   **1719**   **1759**   **1789**

A collection of **comedies, histories, and tragedies** by William Shakespeare is published, known today as the First Folio.

Daniel Defoe's best-known book, *Robinson Crusoe*, is published in the form of a **fictional autobiography** of the eponymous hero, the lone survivor of a shipwreck.

Voltaire pokes fun at the optimism of the modern Enlightenment movement in his **satirical, philosophical, fantasy novel** *Candide*.

The fall of the Bastille in Paris, on 14 July, sparks the French Revolution, and the Enlightenment ideas of **liberty and equality** result in a secular, republican era.

---

humorous stories, such as François Rabelais' satirical adventures of Gargantua and Pantagruel. Miguel de Cervantes of Spain continued in this tradition, albeit with a gentler wit, in *Don Quixote*. However, Cervantes' satire about chivalry has a more serious undercurrent, and rather than a hero, the eponymous knight is depicted as all too human. *Don Quixote* is often considered to be the first modern novel, or at least the first European novel – China's four great classical novels and Japan's *The Tale of Genji* were all written much earlier.

Life on stage and page
In England, the prose narrative took longer to capture popular attention. Poets such as Edmund Spenser and John Milton continued to reinterpret the epic poem, but it was the theatre that most attracted the public. The plays of Christopher Marlowe and Ben Jonson built on the ideas of Greek tragedy and comedy with their dramas, but even they were eclipsed by Shakespeare's mastery of the form, which allowed him to depict very human characters in a catalogue of comedies, histories, and tragedies.

Novels began to appear in England soon after Shakespeare, and rapidly overtook the theatre in popularity. From the start, English novelists such as Daniel Defoe and Henry Fielding presented believable characters in their novels, which contain vivid descriptions of time and place that give the works a degree of realism. Defoe's *Robinson Crusoe* professes to be a "true" autobiographical account. Both Laurence Sterne's comic *Tristram Shandy* and Jonathan Swift's fantastical *Gulliver's Travels* also use the autobiographical voice, but do so in ways that test the reader's willingness to believe the narrator.

In 17th-century France, the theatre was also at the heart of literature, and was even more indebted to classical models than in England, with Jean Racine and Pierre Corneille striving to follow the "rules" of Greek drama. However, the public tended to call the tune, and it was Molière's comedies of manners that seemed more in keeping with the times. Poking fun at the contemporary mores continued to be a part of the French literary scene in the 18th century, with Enlightenment philosophers such as Voltaire wittily satirizing the conventions of the establishment. ∎

I FOUND MYSELF WITHIN A SHADOWED FOREST

THE DIVINE COMEDY (c.1308–1320), DANTE ALIGHIERI

IN CONTEXT

FOCUS
Post-classical epic

BEFORE
800 BCE Ancient Greek poet Homer writes his epic *Odyssey*, which influences much of Western literature.

29–19 BCE The *Aeneid* is written in Latin by the Roman poet Virgil. It will become a model for Latin epics of the medieval period.

AFTER
1572 Luís de Camões's Portuguese epic poem *The Lusiads (Os Lusíadas)* follows in Dante's tradition, weaving together fiction, history, and politics in a story of Portugal's voyages of discovery.

1667 The last great epic poem to be written in English, *Paradise Lost* by John Milton, reflects Britain's emerging role as a world power.

The epic was the literary form of choice for some of antiquity's greatest poets. Epics were written to celebrate the achievements of a hero – often part-divine or possessed of exceptional strength and valour – and the stories were often allegories of transitional moments in history, such as the birth of a nation or the conquest of an enemy. For example, while Homer's *Iliad* is the story of the hero Achilles, it is also, more importantly, about the defeat of Troy by the great armies of Greece. Such poems often weave together the contemporary with the mythic, and their heroes play key roles in building civilization.

See also: *Aeneid* 40–41 ▪ *Odyssey* 54 ▪ *The Faerie Queene* 103 ▪ *The Lusiads* 103 ▪ *Paradise Lost* 103 ▪ *The Red Room* 185 ▪ *The Waste Land* 213

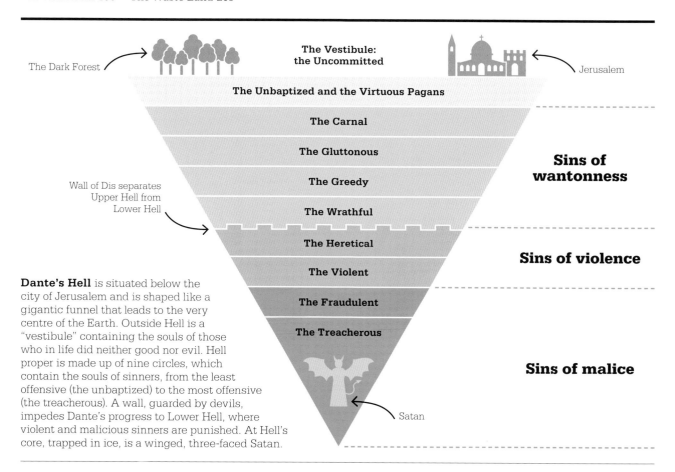

The Dark Forest

The Vestibule: the Uncommitted

Jerusalem

The Unbaptized and the Virtuous Pagans

The Carnal

The Gluttonous

The Greedy

Wall of Dis separates Upper Hell from Lower Hell

The Wrathful

The Heretical

The Violent

The Fraudulent

The Treacherous

Satan

Sins of wantonness

Sins of violence

Sins of malice

Dante's Hell is situated below the city of Jerusalem and is shaped like a gigantic funnel that leads to the very centre of the Earth. Outside Hell is a "vestibule" containing the souls of those who in life did neither good nor evil. Hell proper is made up of nine circles, which contain the souls of sinners, from the least offensive (the unbaptized) to the most offensive (the treacherous). A wall, guarded by devils, impedes Dante's progress to Lower Hell, where violent and malicious sinners are punished. At Hell's core, trapped in ice, is a winged, three-faced Satan.

Long after the fall of classical civilizations, the epic poem remained the favoured literary form through which to celebrate national power. For example, English poet Edmund Spenser's 1590 epic *The Faerie Queene* is a paean to the ascendancy of Elizabeth I and her country, while Italian Ludovico Ariosto's *Orlando Furioso*, written in 1516, applauds the increasingly influential House of Este.

A divine epic

Dante's *The Divine Comedy* fits into the post-classical epic tradition – it is long, heroic, allegorical, and often nationalistic, reflecting Dante's active role in Florentine politics.

However, it is also unusual and innovative in a variety of ways. Whereas in earlier epics the omniscient narrator remained "outside" the story, Dante sets the narrator within the text; the book audaciously uses Tuscan (Italian) vernacular language rather than traditional Latin; and Dante stretches the form of the epic by combining classical thought and mythological motifs with contemporary European philosophy and Christian symbolism.

Dante takes the reader on a journey through Hell, Purgatory, and Heaven – from sin and despair to ultimate salvation – mapping out the geography of each realm in

detail, evoking an almost physical reality. The work recalls many classical epics that describe journeys to the underworld and, like earlier epics, it is an allegory: the journey through the underworld is symbolic of Dante's search for personal meaning.

Originally, Dante called this poem simply the *Commedia*, or "Comedy", which at the time was a term used for works in which the difficulties or challenges faced by the protagonist were resolved in a broadly happy ending (in contrast to the classical tragedies, which focused on loss and suffering). It was the 14th-century poet Giovanni Boccaccio who first called the »

Purgatory is a mountain of stepped terraces where the souls of the penitent undergo a different kind of suffering on each level to purge themselves of sin and enter the Earthly Paradise.

poem "Divine", a reflection on its spiritual content as well as the extreme beauty of its style.

Politics and poetry

When Dante began *The Divine Comedy* – a work that was to take him 12 years to complete – he was already established as a poet, working in the *dolce stil novo* ("sweet new style"), a movement characterized by its introspection, and liberal use of metaphor and symbolism. Politics and personal passions were the subjects of his poetry, and late 13th-century Italy provided plenty of inspiration.

Dante himself was embroiled in the political life of his beloved Florence, which was involved, along with the rest of Italy, in struggles for power between the Church (the Pope) and the State (the Holy Roman Emperor). Key figures from these conflicts were portrayed in *The Divine Comedy,* and the inclusion of real people provided a degree of sensationalism that contributed to the poem's success.

Dante was eventually exiled from Florence for his political allegiances and, although it greatly pained him, his removal from public affairs allowed him the distance to produce his celebrated allegory of the philosophy, morals, and beliefs of his medieval world.

The Divine Comedy is structured in thirds, reflecting the significance of the number three in Christian theology (where it symbolizes the trinity of the Father, the Son, and the Holy Spirit). The journey comprises three books ("Hell", "Purgatory", and "Heaven"), each with 33 cantos, or chapters, plus one introductory chapter, to make 100 cantos in total. It is written in a verse style called

There is no greater sorrow than to recall happiness in times of misery.
The Divine Comedy

terza rima, an interlocking three-line rhyme scheme, which was developed by Dante.

Told from a first-person perspective, the work is in the form of an eschatological journey (one about death and the afterlife). The story begins in a dark forest, a symbol of sinful life on Earth. Dante attempts to climb a mountain to find his way out of the forest, but his path is blocked by wild animals (which represent sins). Hopeless, weak, and in need of spiritual guidance, he meets the Roman poet Virgil, who has been sent to guide him by Beatrice, the lost love of his past. For Dante, Virgil represents classical thinking, reason, and poetry. Virgil assures Dante he will achieve salvation – but only after he has journeyed through the afterlife. The two then begin their journey, starting with the descent into Hell.

Journey to the afterlife

The first book of *The Divine Comedy* describes the levels of Hell, and the ways in which punishments are tailored to the sins of individuals. The souls of flatterers, for example, spend eternity buried in excrement, a reminder of the excrement that they spoke on Earth. Seducers are tormented by horned devils who crack their whips over them until they become lumps of well-beaten flesh. In his visceral descriptions of the punishments and layout of Hell, Dante invites readers to reflect on their own failings, to change direction, and to live in harmony with other people and with God.

When their journey to the bottom-most reaches of Hell is complete, Dante and Virgil begin the ascent of Mount Purgatory, with its circular terraces. Purgatory is a place for sinners who lived selfishly on Earth, but showed enough remorse to offer hope for salvation. In Purgatory, they may purge themselves in preparation for entering Heaven. As they climb the mountain, passing through seven levels representing the seven deadly sins, Dante and Virgil meet individuals painfully working to overcome the flaws that led to their sins. Proud souls, for example, carry huge stones on their backs while they learn humility.

Once out of Purgatory, Beatrice takes over as Dante's guide: this is because Virgil was born before Christ and therefore could not enter the "Blessed Realms". Beatrice can be seen as the eternal feminine guide, the heart and soul of humankind. It is she who intervenes for Dante's salvation, and through her, Dante comes to understand the love of God.

Dante's legacy

Dante adapted the form of the classical epic, with its adventurer-heroes and multiple gods, to express a profound vision of Christian destiny, incorporating both personal and historical events into the story. Innumerable artists and writers have been inspired by *The Divine Comedy*, and American-born writer T S Eliot described it as "the highest point that poetry has ever reached or ever can reach". ∎

Dante Alighieri

A politician, writer, and philosopher, Durante degli Alighieri (known as Dante) was born in Florence, Italy, in 1265 to a wealthy family with a long history of involvement in Florentine politics. Dante was betrothed to be married in 1277 but he had already fallen in love with another girl, Beatrice "Bice" Portinari, who became his muse and to whom he dedicated many love poems. Tragically, she died suddenly in 1290. So grief-stricken was Dante that he immersed himself in political life, becoming a *priore* (a high official) in 1300 and acting as envoy to Pope Boniface VIII during upheavals in Florence. While he was in Rome, his enemies gained power and Dante was exiled from Florence, never to return. It is not known exactly when he began work on *The Divine Comedy*, but it may have been as early as 1304. Dante died in Ravenna, Italy, in 1321.

Other key works

1294 *La Vita Nuova* (*The New Life*)
1303 *On the Eloquence of Vernacular*
1308 *Convivio* (*The Banquet*)

Dante journeys through Heaven's nine spheres, each of which is linked with a celestial body, in line with medieval Earth-centric ideas about the structure of the universe, and with the hierarchy of angels. Beyond the spheres is God in the Empyrean – a heaven beyond time and space.

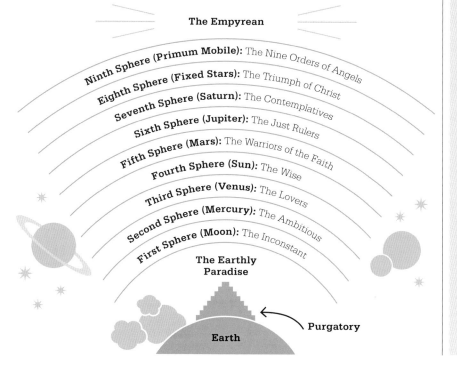

The Empyrean

Ninth Sphere (Primum Mobile): The Nine Orders of Angels
Eighth Sphere (Fixed Stars): The Triumph of Christ
Seventh Sphere (Saturn): The Contemplatives
Sixth Sphere (Jupiter): The Just Rulers
Fifth Sphere (Mars): The Warriors of the Faith
Fourth Sphere (Sun): The Wise
Third Sphere (Venus): The Lovers
Second Sphere (Mercury): The Ambitious
First Sphere (Moon): The Inconstant

The Earthly Paradise

← Purgatory

Earth

WE THREE WILL SWEAR BROTHERHOOD AND UNITY OF AIMS AND SENTIMENTS
ROMANCE OF THE THREE KINGDOMS (14TH CENTURY), LUO GUANZHONG

IN CONTEXT

FOCUS
China's four great classical novels

AFTER

14th century The second great classical novel, *The Water Margin* by Shi Nai'an, is the story of a band of outlaws who oppose a corrupt ruler.

16th century The third great classical novel, *Journey to the West,* by Wu Cheng'en, tells of a Buddhist monk's pilgrimage from China to India.

c.1618 Some scholars consider *The Plum in the Golden Vase*, its author unknown, to be the fourth Chinese classical novel. Although hugely popular, it was suppressed because of its overt sensual realism.

c.1791 The generally accepted fourth great classical novel, *Dream of the Red Chamber* by Cao Xueqin, focuses on the rise and fall of an aristocratic family.

As the first of China's four great classical novels, *Romance of the Three Kingdoms* is a hugely significant and influential work of literature. As with the other three works – *The Water Margin*, *Journey to the West*, and *Dream of the Red Chamber* – it marked a radical departure from the "high style" of Chinese poetic and philosophical literature. Aimed at an audience of common people, it employed techniques akin to oral storytelling, such as the use of vernacular language and songs, and addressed the reader directly. Despite being heavily based on historical texts, *Romance of the Three Kingdoms* (like the other three classic Chinese texts) is recognizably a novel. It is a feat of imaginative writing sustained over 800,000 words in translation, and featuring more than a thousand characters.

The first novel?

The book describes the collapse of China's Han Dynasty into three kingdoms in the 3rd century CE, and the 111 years of warfare that followed. Written over a thousand

Luo Guanzhong

Although his existence is not in question, very little else can be confirmed about the life of Luo Guanzhong (c.1330–c.1400). He is traditionally regarded as the author of the first of China's four great classical novels, *Romance of the Three Kingdoms*, and co-author or editor of the second, *The Water Margin*. He is also thought to have written story collections that deal with China's dynastic past, including the fantastical tale *The Three Sui Quash the Demon's Revolt*.

But in 14th-century China, attributing authorship to one person may in fact denote that they were the chief compiler and editor of a large number of texts by earlier storytellers.

Other key works

The Water Margin (as editor)
The Three Sui Quash the Demons' Revolt
The End of the Tang Dynasty and the Period of the Five Dynasties
Chronicle of the Sui and Tang Dynasties

See also: *The Tale of Genji* 47

History of the text

169–280 CE: the historical events – the break-up of the Han Dynasty and its eventual reunification – take place.

→

4th century CE: the story is written down by Chen Shou as *History of the Three Kingdoms*.

→

4th–14th centuries: many of the hundreds of stories become mythologized, told and retold by oral storytellers.

↓

1522: the earliest surviving text of *Romance of the Three Kingdoms* is published.

←

14th–16th centuries: the novel is copied and republished many times by anonymous hands.

←

14th century: Luo Guanzhong "authors" the huge collection of stories, both historical and fictional, editing and collating the text.

---

years after the events it describes, it takes as its historical inspiration the *History of the Three Kingdoms*, written in the 4th century CE.

Scholars believe that *Romance of the Three Kingdoms* was written nearly 250 years before *Don Quixote*, which is often regarded as the first great European novel. But, perhaps surprisingly, this early Chinese classic did not spark a profusion of prose literature – indeed, the "four great classics" were published over a period of 400 years. However, *Romance of the Three Kingdoms* has enduring appeal: it has never been out of print, and its scenes are so well known that they are familiar to Chinese speakers who have not even read the book. Its success is

partly assured by its conventional, conservative narrative: villains always get their comeuppance, and order is always restored.

One of the major themes of the book is loyalty. In perhaps the most famous scene, the Oath in the Peach Garden, future ruler Liu Bei persuades two men to join him in an oath of fraternity, thereby going against what was at the time society's strongest bond: unquestioning loyalty to family.

It is a powerful scene that has been invoked by Chinese societies and fraternities of all kinds ever since.

Despite the popularity of *Romance of the Three Kingdoms*, the other classics have not been quite so widely read. Nevertheless, all four have continued to be enjoyed and studied (*Journey to the West* has been widely acclaimed outside China), and are regarded as the pinnacles of popular Chinese literature. ∎

Many editions of *Romance of the Three Kingdoms* were richly illustrated, which helped to make the text and stories accessible to ordinary Chinese people, not just the elite.

TURN OVER THE LEEF AND CHESE ANOTHER TALE

THE CANTERBURY TALES (c.1387–1400),
GEOFFREY CHAUCER

IN CONTEXT

FOCUS
The frame narrative

BEFORE
c.8th–13th century *One Thousand and One Nights*, a collection of tales by different authors from across the Islamic world, is framed within the story of Scheherazade.

1348–53 *The Decameron*, by Italian Giovanni Boccaccio, contains 100 stories set within a tale of people fleeing the Black Death.

AFTER
1558 *The Heptameron*, by French author Marguerite de Navarre, contains 72 short stories, framed within a story of 10 stranded travellers.

2004 English writer David Mitchell's *Cloud Atlas* follows the frame-narrative tradition, including stories within stories that travel over centuries.

The use of an outer narrative that envelops within it a story (or a collection of stories, or even stories inside other stories) is a long-established literary device. "Frame narratives" provide context and structure for a tale and often include a narrator, or narrators, who can help engage the reader directly. *One Thousand and One Nights* successfully employed this technnique, as did Giovanni Boccaccio in his *Decameron*. Although most earlier works used the frame narrative to hold stories around a single theme – often religion – Geoffrey Chaucer used it to far more colourful effect in *The Canterbury Tales*, opening up

See also: *One Thousand and One Nights* 44–45 ▪ *The Decameron* 102 ▪ *Wuthering Heights* 132–37 ▪
The Hound of the Baskervilles 208 ▪ *If on a Winter's Night a Traveller* 298–99 ▪ *The Blind Assassin* 326–27

Early editions of *The Canterbury Tales* contained woodcuts to help make the text more accessible to a wide range of readers. Shown here are the pilgrims sharing a meal.

the narrative to include a range of personalities, whose stories encompassed diverse themes.

Later works of the genre include Emily Brontë's *Wuthering Heights* and Arthur Conan Doyle's Sherlock Holmes detective stories. The technique is still in use and many works of Modernist and Postmodernist fiction play with framing narratives, for example Italo Calvino's *If on a Winter's Night a Traveller*. The device is also often used in plays and films.

Literary innovation
Chaucer probably began writing *The Canterbury Tales* in about 1387, during a brief absence from his official court duties and career as a civil servant. It marked a significant change in his literary direction: his other poems – including his first major work (an elegy in the form of a dream vision) and *Troilus and Criseyde*, his retelling of the love story set during the siege of Troy – were mainly concerned with courtly themes and written primarily to he heard by court audiences. *The Canterbury*

Tales, however, was written for a far wider audience, who were probably intended to read the work rather than just listen to it.

The text is written in Middle English, as opposed to the Latin or French that was commonly used for courtly poetry of the time. Chaucer was not the first to do this, but it has been argued that he played a major role in popularizing the use of the vernacular in English literature. Significantly, too, *The Canterbury Tales* paints a remarkable picture of late medieval English society, depicting men and women of all classes, from the nobility through to the labouring classes.

Sondry folk
The Canterbury Tales opens with a General Prologue that sets the scene and creates a framework for the tales that follow. The frame story concerns a group of 29 pilgrims on their way to the shrine of St Thomas Becket in Canterbury Cathedral, in southern England. The pilgrims meet at the Tabard Inn, in Southwark, near London, where the narrator, Geoffrey Chaucer, joins »

At nyght was come into that hostelrye Wel nyne and twenty in a compaignye Of sondry folk…
The Canterbury Tales

Chaucer's characters: class and occupation

Aristocrats or nobles
• The Knight
• The Prioress
• The Monk
• The Friar

Those with commercial wealth
• The Merchant
• The Man of Law
• The Clerk
• The Franklin (landowner)

Guildsmen
• The Haberdasher
• The Dyer
• The Carpenter
• The Weaver
• The Tapestry Maker

The middle class
• The Cook
• The Shipman
• The Physician
• The Wife of Bath

The virtuous poor
• The Parson
• The Plowman

The lower class
• The Manciple
• The Miller
• The Reeve
• The Summoner
• The Pardoner

them. Pilgrimages were an everyday occurrence in medieval Europe, and Chaucer describes the pilgrims as "sondry folk", people of all social classes and occupations.

Most of the General Prologue, which consists of 858 lines of verse, describes the pilgrims, their social class, clothing, and personalities (including the narrator himself). Having introduced the pilgrims, or most of them, the Prologue ends with the innkeeper, or Host, a man called Harry Bailly, suggesting a competition. He proposes that each of the pilgrims should tell four tales, two on the outward journey and two on their return. The teller of the best tale will be rewarded with a free meal, paid for by the other pilgrims, when they return to the inn. The pilgrims draw lots and it is decided that the Knight will tell the first story.

The tales

The 24 tales within the framework include two related by the narrator, or Chaucer himself. Most are written in rhyming couplets, a few in prose. They vary enormously because Chaucer made use of a wide range of themes and literary styles. These include animal and other fables, fabliaux (ribald and satiric tales), romantic verse, pious homilies, sermons, allegories, and exempla (moral narratives). Where the Knight's Tale is a romance, which tells of a love rivalry between two brothers, the Miller's Tale is bawdy and comic, taking as its theme the cuckolding of an Oxford carpenter. The raucous and vulgar Summoner's Tale includes a description of a friar being tricked into accepting a fart as payment, while, in contrast, the Second Nun's Tale is the story of St Cecilia, a deeply spiritual woman martyred for her faith.

The tales vary considerably in length; one of the longest, and perhaps the best known, is the Wife of Bath's Tale. This begins with a prologue developing the Wife's character – domineering and pleasure-seeking – before

This world nys but a thurghfare full of wo...
The Canterbury Tales

continuing with her account of her eventful life with five husbands, the theme being women's mastery over men.

A colourful picture

Chaucer brings each story to life by ensuring that the tone and style are appropriate to each respective storyteller, reflecting his or her own status, occupation, and character. The vividness is enhanced by the use of the framing devices, which link the stories to one another through dialogue and interactions among the characters. The storytellers frequently interrupt each other with arguments, insults, or sometimes even praise. The Prioress's Tale, for example, begins after the Host has politely invited the Prioress to tell her story, while on another occasion, the Knight interrupts the Monk because he finds his tale too miserable. The wider framing story adds a further dimension to the individual tales.

The Canterbury Tales presents a colourful picture of late medieval England, its people and events. Chaucer was living and writing

The Ellesmere manuscript (c.1410) is a beautiful, exquisitely illuminated copy of *The Canterbury Tales* and is the basis for most modern versions of Chaucer's text.

during a particularly turbulent period. The Black Death of 1348–49 had killed a third of the population, the Peasant's Revolt of 1381 had demonstrated cracks in the feudal system, and the authority of the Church was being questioned, not least for its corrupt practices.

Chaucer's tales reflect many of these events, often mocking and satirizing the hypocrisy of the Church. In the Pardoner's Tale, the Pardoner is shown to be guilty of the very sins he is preaching against, while the Friar's Tale is a satirical attack on summoners – ecclesiastical officers whose role was to summon to court sinful members of the diocese. It is not surprising that the Summoner's Tale is an attack on friars.

Unfinished work
Chaucer borrowed from numerous sources when writing *The Canterbury Tales*. The Knight's Tale is based on Boccaccio's epic poem *Teseida*, and there are other references within the *Tales* to Boccaccio's work. Chaucer's other sources included Ovid, the Bible, chivalric works such as *Sir Gawain and the Green Knight*, and, possibly, works by his friend the English poet John Gower.

For though we sleep
or wake, or roam, or ride,
Ay fleeth the time;
it nyl no man abyde.
The Canterbury Tales

Scholars do not know what Chaucer's final intention was for *The Canterbury Tales*, nor even the order in which he wished the tales to appear, or whether the work was finished. The only clue is in the General Prologue, with its plan for the pilgrims to tell four stories each. However, there are only 24 tales, so not all the pilgrims tell even one tale. Nor do any of the storytellers or the Host indicate the sequence or numbering of any tale.

Enduring masterpiece
Evidence indicates that Chaucer was still working on the *Tales* when he died. There is no original manuscript in his own hand; instead there are fragments that would have been scribed by someone else. The earliest is the Hengwrt manuscript, produced shortly after Chaucer's death. The sequence most commonly used today, however, is based on the 15th-century Ellesmere manuscript, which divides the text into 10 fragments, containing varying numbers of tales. The tales are grouped according to clues or links within the text, and end with the Parson's Tale, a long prose sermon on the Seven Deadly Sins. This is followed by Chaucer's Retraction, a curious apology in which the author asks forgiveness for the vulgar, secular elements of his works. The exact significance of this apology is unclear, although some have seen it as a deathbed repentance.

Despite the uncertainties surrounding its structure and plot, *The Canterbury Tales* is recognized as a masterpiece, and one of the most important literary works in the English language. Its humour, bawdiness, pathos, and satirical observations remain unequalled today, more than 600 years after it was written. ∎

Geoffrey Chaucer

Not just a great English poet but also a courtier, civil servant, and diplomat, Chaucer was probably born in London around 1343. His father, a wine merchant, was keen to advance his son's career and secured a place for him as a page in the Countess of Ulster's household. From there, Chaucer entered the service of Edward III, first as a soldier, then as a diplomat, travelling to France and Italy, where he would have read the works of Dante and Boccaccio. From 1374 to 1386 he held a post as controller of customs.

Chaucer married in 1366, and gained a patron – John of Gaunt, the king's fourth son. Chaucer wrote his first major poem, *Book of the Duchess* (1369) as an elegy to Gaunt's first wife, Blanche. He fell on hard times during Richard II's reign; however, in 1389 was appointed clerk of the king's royal building projects. He died in 1400 and was buried in Westminster Abbey.

Other key works

1379 *The House of Fame*
c.1385 *Troilus and Criseyde*
c.1388 *The Legend of Good Women*

LAUGHTER'S THE PROPERTY OF MAN. LIVE JOYFULLY

GARGANTUA AND PANTAGRUEL (1532–1564),
FRANÇOIS RABELAIS

IN CONTEXT

FOCUS
Renaissance humanism

BEFORE
1304–74 Italian scholar and poet Petrarch translates Greek and Roman scrolls, which are the springboard for humanism and the Italian Renaissance.

1353 The 100 stories told by 10 young Florentines fleeing from the plague in Boccaccio's *The Decameron* set a standard for Renaissance literature, and influence authors from Chaucer to Shakespeare.

1460 *Ploughman of Bohemia*, a dialogue between Death and a ploughman, by Johannes von Tepl, is one of Germany's earliest humanist poems.

1522–35 Dutch humanist Erasmus publishes his own Greek and Latin translations of the New Testament; they are the basis for Martin Luther's German and William Tyndale's English translations.

I n the five-volume *Histories of Gargantua and Pantagruel*, François Rabelais builds a fantasy world around two giants and their companions. The text includes all the elements of medieval folk humour that would have been familiar to contemporary readers – bodily functions, gross sexual behaviour, birth, and death. Rich in satire, the tales are also fuelled by the energy of Renaissance humanism, which spread into northern Europe from Italy. "Humanism" at this time had a different meaning from the modern-day term, being concerned with a resurgence of interest in the wisdom of the classical world. Until this point, education had involved blindly following the Church's narrow scholastic tradition; the major humanist impetus was to build a complete programme of education that included philosophy, grammar, poetry, history, and Ancient Greek and Latin.

Scholarly and satirical
Poised at the threshold of this rapidly changing world, Rabelais finds ways to weave a humanist agenda into his giant adventures – but he first engages his reader's attention with scatological humour and absurd fantasy. At the very beginning, the text presents a midwife's-eye view of the mother in labour, as the baby Gargantua struggles up through her body to be born out of her left ear. The exploits, battles, and quests of Gargantua and his son Pantagruel rattle on, liberally embellished with descriptions of meat feasts and shovel-loads of mustard tossed into cavernous mouths; pilgrims consumed in a salad; massive codpieces; armies washed away by urination; and cannonballs that fall out of Gargantua's hair after battle.

Time, which diminishes and erodes all things, increases and augments generous deeds …
Gargantua and Pantagruel

See also: *The Decameron* 102 ▪ *The Canterbury Tales* 68–71 ▪
Don Quixote 76–81 ▪ *Tristram Shandy* 104–05

Although Rabelais wrote *Pantagruel* first, the series is usually
published in the order of the story, starting with *Gargantua*. The
first two books are characterized by satire and bawdy humour, the
third is more serious, and the fourth and fifth are darkly mocking.

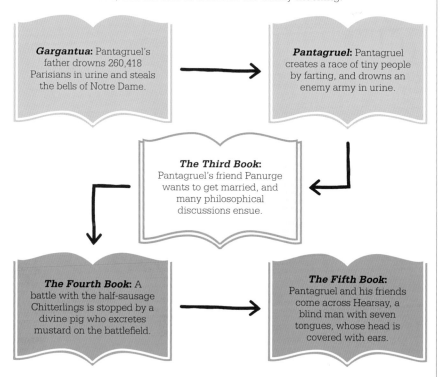

Gargantua: Pantagruel's father drowns 260,418 Parisians in urine and steals the bells of Notre Dame.

Pantagruel: Pantagruel creates a race of tiny people by farting, and drowns an enemy army in urine.

The Third Book: Pantagruel's friend Panurge wants to get married, and many philosophical discussions ensue.

The Fourth Book: A battle with the half-sausage Chitterlings is stopped by a divine pig who excretes mustard on the battlefield.

The Fifth Book: Pantagruel and his friends come across Hearsay, a blind man with seven tongues, whose head is covered with ears.

François Rabelais

Writer, medic, scholar of Greek, and priest, François Rabelais was an intellectual giant of 16th-century France. Born in the Touraine region probably around 1494, he studied law before taking holy orders with the Franciscans. He then transferred to a Benedictine order, where he studied medicine and Greek. In 1530, breaking his vows, he left the Benedictines to study medicine at Montpellier University. After graduating, he lectured on the works of ancient Greek physicians such as Hippocrates and Galen, whose work he translated, and worked as a physician in Lyon.

Using the pseudonym Alcofribas Nasier (an anagram of his name), in 1532 Rabelais published *Pantagruel*, the first of the five books that would make up *Gargantua and Pantagruel*, although Rabelais' authorship of the fifth book is doubtful. All five books were condemned by the Sorbonne and the Church, and despite being protected by powerful patrons, Rabelais was forced to live abroad from 1545 to 1547, fearing persecution. He later received a papal pardon. He died in Paris in 1553.

Yet despite such crude and extreme behaviour, Rabelais ensures that his giant creations will pass easily in the new world of Renaissance humanism by making them fully conversant in the finer points of learning, including medicine, law, and science. In a letter to his son, the old giant Gargantua contrasts his own upbringing in "dark" times with the current age, where "light and dignity have been restored".

After the arrival of the printing press in the mid-15th century, ordinary people could read the Bible in translation – for the first time they had direct access to the word of God, unmediated by the agenda of the Church. Although he was a priest, Rabelais seized his chance to satirize religious dogmatism. Gargantua's mighty warrior, Friar John, is given the sumptuous Abbey of Thélème filled with finely dressed nuns and monks who consort freely. "Do what thou wilt" is the rule of the order, as "we all engage in things forbidden, and yearn for things denied."

Witty, irreverent, and stuffed with intellectual marrow, no other novel is quite like *Gargantua and Pantagruel*. It has been celebrated by authors across the centuries, and most recently by Postmodern writers, who have found much to admire in the narrative freedom of Rabelais' great work. ▪

AS IT DID TO THIS FLOWER, THE DOOM OF AGE WILL BLIGHT YOUR BEAUTY
LES AMOURS DE CASSANDRE (1552), PIERRE DE RONSARD

IN CONTEXT

FOCUS
The Pléiade

BEFORE
1549 Joachim Du Bellay sets out the principles of the Pléiade, promoting the imitation of classical models and the revival of archaic and dialect words, as well as the invention of new words.

AFTER
1555 Taking inspiration from the Greek poet Callimachus, Ronsard's *Hymns* eloquently celebrate natural phenomena, such as the sky, as well as gods and heroes.

1576 Jean Antoine de Baïf, the most learned poet of the Pléiade and a skilled poetic experimenter, publishes a highly original work: *Mimes, Lessons, and Proverbs*.

1578 Ronsard's *Sonnets for Hélène* are full of references to the suffering of lovers, as well as to classical myth and fate.

Pierre Ronsard (1524–1585) was the leading light of a group of French humanist poets named for the bright Pleiades star cluster and also for a group of Alexandrian poets from the 3rd century BCE. The Pléiade aimed to create a French literature equal to that of Renaissance Italy. They imitated the genres and forms of the ancients, and spent much time refining and defending their controversial poetic beliefs.

A sublime art

Ronsard saw poetry as a sublime art, rather than merely a courtly pastime. He was versatile and innovative, and his poems were melodious, sensual, and pagan, despite the fact that he was a cleric in minor orders. He made important contributions to the ode (inspired by the Latin poet Horace and the Greek Pindar), the sonnet, and the elegy, and in 1558 became the official poet in the court of Charles IX, the king of France. He is best remembered today for his skilful, tender love poetry.

In the poetry collection *Les Amours de Cassandre*, Ronsard set out to rival the Italian poet Petrarch. His devotion to Cassandre is described with imagery of piercing arrows, love potions, and poisons, which Petrarch had also deployed. But in Ronsard's hands this imagery is imbued with sensuality. He often refers to a desire to be transformed – for example, into golden droplets, so that he may fall into his beloved's lap, and then into a bull so that he can carry her away on his back. ∎

I'd like to turn the deepest of yellows, / Falling, drop by drop, in a golden shower, / Into her lap...
Les Amours de Cassandre

See also: *Gargantua and Pantagruel* 72–73 ▪ *Miscellaneous Poems* (Marvell) 91 ▪ *Les Fleurs du mal* 165 ▪ *A Season in Hell* 198–203

HE THAT LOVES PLEASURE MUST FOR PLEASURE FALL
DOCTOR FAUSTUS (1604), CHRISTOPHER MARLOWE

IN CONTEXT

FOCUS
Jacobethan theatre

BEFORE
1592 Elements of Thomas Kyd's Elizabethan-period *The Spanish Tragedy* – such as its theme of revenge and the play-within-a-play – are continued in subsequent Jacobean dramas.

1598–1600 William Shakespeare's *Henry IV Parts 1 and 2* reflect ongoing Jacobethan interests in raucous comedy, history, violence, and honour.

AFTER
1610 The first performance of *The Alchemist* by Ben Jonson, indulges the Jacobean thirst for harsh satire.

1614 John Webster's five-act revenge tragedy *The Duchess of Malfi* is truly Jacobethan in its consideration of incest, torture, and madness.

The drama produced in England during the reigns of Elizabeth I (1558–1603) and James I (1603–1625) – the Elizabethan and Jacobean eras, respectively – often depicted a murky world of murder, politics, and revenge, coupled with humour and pastiche. The term "Jacobethan" is used to denote the continuity of English literature between these two periods. The Elizabethan era saw the rise of comedies and tragedies, then took on elements of psychology and the supernatural under James, whose court was a place of loose sexual morals.

A pact with the devil
Born in 1564, in the Elizabethan age, Christopher "Kit" Marlowe lived wildly and died aged 29, reportedly stabbed in a brawl. His work is a harbinger of Jacobean drama's interest in darker themes.

Based on a German story of a legendary alchemist, Marlowe's *Doctor Faustus* (originally entitled *The Tragicall History of Dr. Faustus*) recounts the tale of an academic,

The reward of sin is death? That's hard.
Doctor Faustus

highly respected as an intellect but nevertheless weary of the limits of conventional science. His thirst for knowledge is so great that he turns to magic and summons the devil Mephistopheles, who makes Faustus false promises about omnipotence and pleasure.

The two make a deadly pact: Faustus agrees to give up his soul to the devil in exchange for the devil's service for 24 years. A good man driven by pride and corrupted by power, Faustus realizes too late that he has brought great evil upon himself. ∎

See also: First Folio 82–89 ▪ *The Fairie Queene* 103

EVERY MAN IS THE CHILD OF HIS OWN DEEDS

DON QUIXOTE (1605–1615),
MIGUEL DE CERVANTES

IN CONTEXT

FOCUS
Spain's Golden Century

BEFORE
1499 The story of a procuress told in a series of dialogues, *La Celestina,* by Fernando de Rojas, marks the beginning of a literary renaissance in Spain.

1554 The anonymously published novella *The Life of Lazarillo de Tormes and of His Fortunes and Adversities* invents a new form – the picaresque novel.

AFTER
1609 Lope de Vega, Spain's most prolific playwright and a major poet, publishes his artistic manifesto *New Rules for Writing Plays at this Time* to justify his writing style.

1635 Pedro Calderón de la Barca's philosophical allegory *Life is a Dream* is one of the Golden Century's most widely translated works.

Straddling the 16th and 17th centuries, Spain's Golden Century refers to an extraordinary flourishing of the arts that began with the nation's rise to superpower status via the wealth of its colonies in America.

Under the Holy Roman Emperor Charles V (reigned 1519–56), there was a free flow of ideas across Europe, with Spain's writers responding to the excitement of the Renaissance. New techniques in storytelling, verse, and drama produced defining prose, poetry, and plays. The anonymously authored *Lazarillo de Tormes* featured a *picaro* (young rascal) narrator of mixed fortunes, giving the world a new literary genre – the picaresque novel. Experimentation with verse forms as well as metre characterized the work of poet Garcilaso de la Vega. And the dramatist Lope de Vega produced a vast and dazzling oeuvre of 1,800 plays – rich in character, plot, and history – together with sonnets, novellas, and lyric poetry.

In the same period, Miguel de Cervantes produced *Don Quixote* (originally titled *The Ingenious Gentleman Don Quixote*), the

defining literary achievement of the Golden Century. Like Lope de Vega, he was writing near the end of an era, as Spain began to decline owing to a combination of despotic rule, religious fanaticism, and dwindling fortunes after the English defeat of the Armada. Out of this climate of flux leapt Don Quixote, an eccentric hero who bestrides a romantic past and an unstable present in a chivalric adventure that continues to enchant and inspire.

Engagement with reality
Just as the plays of Cervantes' contemporary William Shakespeare are at the origin of modern drama, so *Don Quixote* is at the origin of modern fiction. Both writers delved into the motivations, actions, and emotions of their protagonists in a way that had not been attempted before, lending such characters as Hamlet, Macbeth, and Don Quixote a psychological complexity that made them seem real.

Don Quixote engages with reality on two main levels. The main character of Cervantes' novel is enthralled by the knightly heroes of earlier chivalric romances, and renames himself "Don Quixote" in

---

Miguel de Cervantes

Miguel de Cervantes was born near Madrid, Spain, in 1547. His mother was the daughter of a nobleman, his father was a medical practitioner. Little is known of Cervantes' early life, but it is likely that he lived and worked in Rome around 1569, before enlisting in the Spanish Navy. Badly wounded in the Battle of Lepanto (in which an alliance of southern European Catholic states defeated Ottoman forces), he was captured by the Turks in 1575 and spent five years in prison in Algiers; his ransom was paid by a Catholic religious order, and he

returned to Madrid. Cervantes' first major work, *La Galatea,* was published in 1585. He struggled financially but kept writing, finding success (though not wealth) with *Don Quixote.* He died in 1616, in Madrid, but his coffin was later lost. In 2015, scientists claimed to have unearthed his remains in a convent in Madrid.

Other key works

1613 *Exemplary Novels*
1617 *Persiles and Sigismunda* (unfinished)

See also: *The Canterbury Tales* 68–71 ▪ First Folio 82–89 ▪ *The Decameron* 102 ▪ *Amadis of Gaul* 102 ▪
The Tin Drum 270–71 ▪ *Hopscotch* 274–75 ▪ *If on a Winter's Night a Traveller* 298–99

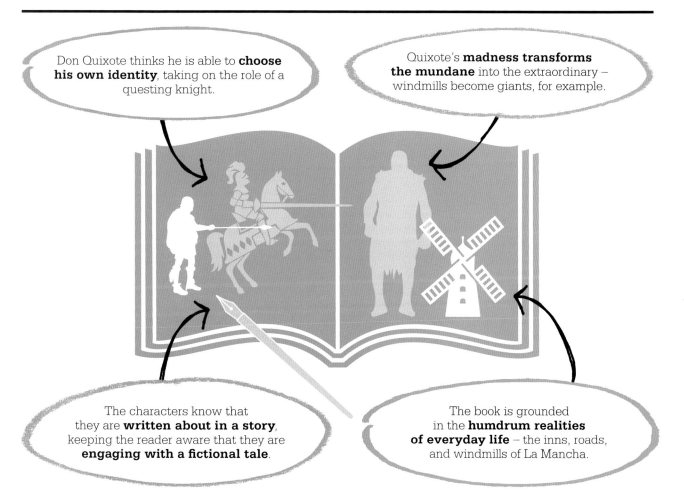

Don Quixote thinks he is able to **choose his own identity**, taking on the role of a questing knight.

Quixote's **madness transforms the mundane** into the extraordinary – windmills become giants, for example.

The characters know that they are **written about in a story**, keeping the reader aware that they are **engaging with a fictional tale**.

The book is grounded in the **humdrum realities of everyday life** – the inns, roads, and windmills of La Mancha.

imitation of them. Yet unlike these romantic heroes, the characters of *Don Quixote* worry about everyday concerns, such as food and sleep. They travel through a world of taverns and windmills, along fairly nondescript roads and paths. The characters occupy an ordinary setting that resembles our world.

On another level of engagement, the novel also operates according to the literary approach known as "realism": everything happens within the unities of time and place (the action in the book is contemporary with the time it was written, it adheres to a specifc geographical region, and is broadly chronological), without magical or mythical intervention.

Giants of the imagination

Despite this realism, illusion has its place in the novel – but only in the mind of its central character. Don Quixote's encounters with innkeepers, prostitutes, goatherds, soldiers, priests, escaped convicts, and scorned lovers are magnified by his imagination into the kind of chivalrous quests that might be undertaken by the knight Amadis of Gaul, in the romances that bear his name. Donning his rusty armour, mounting the ancient horse he renames Rocinante, and enlisting the simple labourer Sancho Panza as his "squire", Don Quixote – in the best tradition of chivalric romances – announces his love for the peasant girl he calls Dulcinea. In his realm of fantasy the everyday is transformed into the extraordinary, the lasting symbol of which are the windmills of La Mancha, elevated » by his imagination into fearsome enemies, with whom he sees fit to engage in combat.

Further complexity

The gap between reality and illusion is the source of the book's comedy (and no less its tragedy), and is a theme that has nourished fiction across the world in the subsequent four centuries. Yet, having established his theme, Cervantes deepens and complicates it in the second part of his novel, which was published 10 years after the first part.

In Cervantes' Part Two, the characters – including Don Quixote himself – have read, or at least heard of, the first part of the novel in which they appear. When strangers encounter Don Quixote and Sancho Panza in person, they already know their famous history. A duke and duchess, for example, are excited when they meet Don Quixote, having read all about his adventures. They think it amusing to deceive him for entertainment, setting in play a string of imagined adventures, which result in a series of sadistic practical jokes. Honour – Cervantes suggests – clearly has nothing to do with social position. Readers begin to laugh less.

Finally, from so little sleeping and so much reading, his brain dried up and he went completely out of his mind.
Don Quixote

In the second part of *Don Quixote*, Cervantes himself appears as a character, and other versions of Quixote are introduced. Reality is reflected by these various mirrors, deliberately confusing life and literature.

While Cervantes was writing Part Two, a spurious *Second Volume of the Ingenious Gentleman Don Quixote of La Mancha by the Licenciado Alonso Fernández de Avellaneda, of Tordesillas* appeared. Cervantes' literary creation had been stolen, inciting his comment, at the end of Part Two: "For me alone was Don Quixote born, and I for him; it was his to act, mine to write." In literary revenge, Cervantes sends his knight and squire off to Barcelona, to kidnap a character from the Avellaneda book.

Stories within stories

Literature is itself also a theme in the novel. We are told that Don Quixote's delusions result from reading too much – an interesting proposition to present to a reader of *Don Quixote*. But even when Don Quixote's books are burned by the priest, housekeeper, and barber, his improbable quest for glory continues. The role of the book's narrator is also questioned. Far from disappearing behind his characters and story, Cervantes makes frequent appearances,

ostensibly in his own voice or often in the guise of a narrator called Cide Hamete Benengeli, a Moorish storyteller. The first words of the novel – "In some village in La Mancha, whose name I do not care to recall" – exhibit the narrator's wilfulness as well as the author's control over his material.

The novel is written in episodic form, laying the groundwork for the many road novels and films that would follow. Most of the characters whom Don Quixote and Sancho Panza encounter have a story to tell, providing the novel with a format familiar to readers of Chaucer's *The Canterbury Tales* and Boccaccio's *Decameron*, and of the canon of tales from the East that entered southern Spain in the long centuries of Arab rule.

For example, one of the novel's minor characters, Ricote, a Morisco (a Muslim forcibly converted to Christianity), recounts his exile from Spain – a story within a story that introduces historical facts to the fictional narrative. The expulsion of the Moriscos in 1609 was highly topical, and whereas the earlier romances of chivalry had dwelt in a world of myth, Cervantes' novel was ready to engage with gritty, present-day issues.

Illusion and disillusion

Stories proliferate at every turn, offering further opportunities for illusion and disillusion. Quixote and Sancho hear of a young man who became a shepherd after having studied pastoral literature, but died for the love of a beautiful shepherdess, Marcella. Accused of being the cause of his death, Marcella delivers a fiery speech at the funeral defending her right to live as she wants and refusing to be the object of male fantasy. Literature is seemingly condemned for its capacity to encourage its readers to live in a dream world, while the book achieves precisely this aim.

Cervantes makes clear that as an author he will do exactly what he wants. Slowly, Don Quixote is brought back home, exhausted and disenchanted. "I was mad, now I am in my senses," he says, shortly

'Tell me, Senor Don Alvaro,' said Don Quixote, 'am I at all like that Don Quixote you talk of?'
Don Quixote

before his death. By killing him off, Cervantes clearly wished to prevent any more unauthorized sequels.

Despite Cervantes' claims of ownership, Don Quixote illustrates the way great fictional characters ultimately escape their authors, seeming to move away from the pages in which they first appear. He inspired English comic novelists such as Henry Fielding and French realists such as Gustave Flaubert, whose character Emma Bovary can

be seen as a 19th-century Quixote in her bid to escape the tedium of life by imitating fiction. In the 20th century, Cervantes' playful and metafictional side inspired Jorge Luis Borges to write "Pierre Menard, Author of the *Quixote*" (about a writer who re-creates Cervantes' novel), which Borges described, mischieviously, as "more subtle than Cervantes' [story]". Don Quixote is also immortalized as an English adjective for erratic if idealistic behaviour – quixotic.

Interpretations

Standing at the junction between medieval chivalric tales and the modern novel, *Don Quixote* bequeathed a rich cultural legacy to generations of readers, and the work has been subject to shifting interpretations over the centuries. On publication in Spain's Golden Century, it was widely perceived as a satire – with Don Quixote as the butt of the jokes; but with much of Spain's history woven into the tale, it was also seen as a critique of the country's imperial ambitions. Don Quixote's delusions of heroism can be read as a symbol of his nation's wasteful expansionism in the face of decline. For revolutionaries, Don Quixote was an inspiration – a man who was right when the system was wrong; and the Romantics transformed him into a tragic character – a man with noble intentions, defeated by the second-rate. This re-evaluation of the work over time points to the enduring power of its story and its writing, and guarantees the text a central place in literary history. ∎

La Mancha in central Spain is a dry but agriculturally important area, lacking in literary resonance and therefore an unlikely (and amusing) home for a would-be chivalric hero.

ONE MAN IN HIS TIME PLAYS MANY PARTS

**FIRST FOLIO (1623),
WILLIAM SHAKESPEARE**

When William Shakespeare died, his friend and rival playwright Ben Jonson wrote that his works would prove "not of an age, but for all time". The prediction proved true: Shakespeare's name is known across the globe, and he continues to be regarded as one of the most iconic writers of all time. His works have been translated into more than 80 languages; his dramas have been transformed into movies, animations, and musicals; and his words have inspired politicians, artists, and advertisers around the world.

Enduring appeal

In 1999 Shakespeare was voted "Man of the Millennium" in the UK, and speeches from *The Tempest* were used in the opening ceremony for the 2012 Olympic Games. He is one of the UK's greatest cultural exports, and each year around 800,000 visitors make the trip to Stratford-upon-Avon to visit the houses where his life story began.

Why should Shakespeare, a man who died in 1616, continue to be so relevant for readers and theatre-goers today? Much of his appeal

Some are born great, some achieve greatness, and some have greatness thrust upon 'em.
Twelfth Night

lies in his ability to capture in words what it feels like to be human. His mastery of language allowed him to convey complex emotions with great impact and economy. The fact that Shakespeare's audiences represented a cross-section of society, from cobblers to courtiers, encouraged the playwright to develop a poetic voice that spoke across social rank, education, and age. His plays had to appeal to those who had paid one penny to stand in the yard, while also on occasion satisfying the tastes of the monarch and the court. It is

William Shakespeare

William Shakespeare was born in Stratford-upon-Avon in April 1564. Aged 18 he married Anne Hathaway, already pregnant with the first of their three children. Records reveal that Shakespeare was in London in the early 1590s, working as an actor. The first reference to him as a playwright in 1592 is somewhat unflattering: fellow dramatist Robert Greene labelled him an "Upstart crow, beautified in our feathers".

Shakespeare's History plays about King Henry VI had proved very popular by the late 1590s, and his reputation was such that

in 1598 Francis Meres described the "mellifluous and honey-tongued Shakespeare".

The pre-eminent writer for the King's Men acting troupe and a shareholder in the Globe theatre on Bankside, he was able to buy a house in Stratford-upon-Avon, to which he returned in his later years. He died on St George's Day, 23 April, 1616.

Other key works

1593 *Venus and Adonis*
1594 *The Rape of Lucrece*
1609 *Shakespeare's Sonnets*

See also: *Oedipus the King* 34–39 ▪ *Metamorphoses* 55 ▪ *The Canterbury Tales* 68–71 ▪ *Doctor Faustus* 75 ▪
Moby-Dick 138–45 ▪ *Ulysses* 214–21

Shakespeare was born in the market town of Stratford-upon-Avon. He lived in this house on Henley Street into adulthood, including the first five years of marriage to Anne Hathaway.

little wonder then that the works of Shakespeare remain accessible to a broad audience; Shakespeare's imaginative tales have the capacity to delight schoolchildren as well as veteran playgoers.

A writer for all worlds

Shakespeare's genius lies in his talent for holding a mirror up to nature and reflecting his audience in it; people recognize themselves and others in his works. His most effective technique for engaging his audience was through use of soliloquy. It is in these moments when a character is left alone on stage, and begins to reveal the core of their being, that a strong connection is built between the world of the play and that of the onlookers. Soliloquy allows characters to share their innermost fears, disappointments, dreams, and ambitions. In moments of privacy, Shakespeare's characters can appear fragile and vulnerable;

All the world's a stage,
And all the men and
women merely players.
As You Like It

they can also be revealed to be duplicitous and villainous. By allowing them to speak in private to the audience, Shakespeare created the illusion that the spectators were privy to every thought. His characters moved beyond being mere vehicles for plot development, and appeared to be individuals living in the moment, making decisions from scene to scene.

Shakespeare's plays were designed to be enjoyed in the theatre, but readers could also experience some of them in print after they had appeared on stage: *Hamlet*, *Romeo and Juliet*, *A Midsummer Night's Dream*, and *Henry V* were printed as individual works (known as quartos) during Shakespeare's lifetime. However, other plays such as *Julius Caesar*, *Macbeth*, *As You Like It*, and *Twelfth Night* do not seem to have been printed before the dramatist died, and would have disappeared

completely had it not been for the publication in 1623 of *Mr. William Shakespeares Comedies, Histories, & Tragedies*, otherwise known as the First Folio.

The First Folio

There are only some 240 copies of the First Folio still in existence and it has become one of the world's most valuable books, with a price of around US $6 million at auction. Were it not for this book, many of Shakespeare's masterpieces would have been lost forever.

In the Elizabethan and Jacobean periods there was no guarantee that a play would be published simply because it had been performed. Publishers tended to think that dramas had a "fashionable" rather than "enduring" appeal, and they preferred to put their energies (and finances) into publishing Bibles, sermons, and chronicles of English history. Ben Jonson was the first dramatist to have his works »

Plays included in the First Folio

Comedies	Histories	Tragedies
The Tempest	King John	Troilus and Cressida
The Two Gentlemen of Verona	Richard II	Coriolanus
The Merry Wives of Windsor	Henry IV Part 1	Titus Andronicus
Measure for Measure	Henry IV Part 2	Romeo and Juliet
The Comedy of Errors	Henry V	Timon of Athens
Much Ado About Nothing	Henry VI Part 1	Julius Caesar
Love's Labour's Lost	Henry VI Part 2	Macbeth
A Midsummer Night's Dream	Henry VI Part 3	Hamlet
The Merchant of Venice	Richard III	King Lear
As You Like It	Henry VIII	Othello
The Taming of the Shrew		Antony and Cleopatra
All's Well That Ends Well		Cymbeline
Twelfth Night		
The Winter's Tale		

collected together and published as a whole. His *Works* appeared in 1616, the year of Shakespeare's death, and its popularity inspired others to consider similar volumes.

Two of Shakespeare's fellow actors and close friends, John Heminges and Henry Condell, oversaw the mammoth task that went into producing the First Folio. This would have been a difficult job and their first priority was to locate the play texts. The playwright's original manuscript was either used, or transcribed, by the company, and then served as the text from which "cue scripts" were created: each actor would have their own lines transcribed with just a line or more to listen out for as their cue. Over time manuscripts disappear, or are altered, revised, and covered in ink. Today there are no Shakespearian manuscripts in existence, although there are 147 lines in a play called *Sir Thomas More* that are thought to be in Shakespeare's own hand. The First Folio serves as a monument then to Shakespeare's memory; it proved so popular that it had to be reprinted (with revisions) just nine years later, and it has continued to be republished in differing formats ever since. It is little wonder that the First Folio is regarded as such an important book today, given the vision and determination that went into ensuring its publication.

A threefold division
The First Folio divides the plays of Shakespeare into Comedies, Histories, and Tragedies. The division into three genres is somewhat arbitrary, and is more reflective of the publisher's desire than it is suggestive of the way

The Globe theatre, co-owned by Shakespeare, opened in 1599 on the south bank of the Thames, but by 1644 it had been demolished. A re-created Globe opened at the site in the 1990s.

in which Shakespeare viewed his plays. *Julius Caesar*, for example, is listed as a tragedy when it could just as readily be a history play; similarly, *Richard III* is listed under the Histories when it could also be under the Tragedies.

Shakespeare did not necessarily think in terms of writing for one particular genre. As an innovative writer he would frequently blend characteristics associated with different genres to create variety in his own work. At moments of great sorrow, for example, he occasionally injects an element of black humour, which serves to alter the pervading mood: the gravedigger sings as he digs a grave in *Hamlet*; the Porter jokes with the audience as Macbeth and his wife leave the stage to wash their hands of blood; and Cleopatra is moved to mirth as she contemplates her own suicide in *Antony and Cleopatra*.

The Egyptian queen Cleopatra, here played by Harriet Walter, clasps the "worme" and succumbs to its bite, like a "lover's pinch", during the passionate, deadly climax to *Antony and Cleopatra*.

Similarly, Shakespeare's comedies, which one might expect to be light and frivolous in tone, can sometimes prove dark and dangerous: Isabella is sexually harassed by Angelo in *Measure for Measure*; Oberon enchants Titania's eyes with a potion that will lead her to fall in love with the first thing she sees in *A Midsummer Night's Dream*; and Malvolio's puritanical streak in *Twelfth Night* leads to a very public humiliation.

Relationships tested

While Shakespeare's comedies share many similarities, they also differ markedly from one another. They almost all end with the prospect of marriage, which helps to unite individuals and communities simultaneously; it also brings a celebratory, festive quality to the play's close and distances the memory of any misunderstandings that have thwarted the merriment beforehand. *Love's Labour's Lost* is unusual among the comedies, because the play ends not with

Our revels now are ended. These our actors … Are melted into air. ***The Tempest***

a marriage, but an agreement between the couples to meet again after a year spent apart.

While the comedies ordinarily end in harmony and reunion, the tragedies are altogether more destructive in their dramatic trajectory. Relationships are tested, put under stress, and eventually broken, often resulting in a tableau of death to close the play. The same trajectory can be followed in some of the history plays as well. Tales of kingship, government, and rule are often driven by conflict, feud, and **»**

Recurring motifs in Shakespeare's plays

Women disguised as men		*The Two Gentlemen of Verona, The Merchant of Venice, As You Like It, Twelfth Night, Cymbeline*
The fool		*King Lear, Twelfth Night, As You Like It*
Play within a play		*A Midsummer Night's Dream, Hamlet, Love's Labour's Lost*
The supernatural		*Macbeth, Hamlet, A Midsummer Night's Dream, The Tempest, Julius Caesar, Richard III, Cymbeline*
Overhearing		*Twelfth Night, Love's Labour's Lost, Hamlet, Othello*
Mistaken identity (as a comic motif)		*The Comedy of Errors, Much Ado About Nothing, Measure for Measure, All's Well That Ends Well*
Storm and shipwreck		*Macbeth, King Lear, The Tempest, Pericles, The Comedy of Errors*

alone. King Lear is another of the tragic creations that speaks directly to Shakespeare's understanding of the human condition. In old age Lear's understanding of himself and the world around him is at odds with the views of a younger generation. His pride leads him to make rash judgements, which serve to ostracize him from friends and family, leaving him to reflect upon his actions and his relationships with other people. Lear, like so many of Shakespeare's other tragic figures, is tormented by his own thoughts, and it takes the duration of a play for him to reassess his situation and "see better".

Questions of identity

A Midsummer Night's Dream is one of Shakespeare's most popular comedies, and Bottom one of his most memorable creations. When rehearsing in the woods, Bottom's head is magically transformed into that of an ass by the knavish sprite Puck. Visual effects have a much stronger impact on the stage than on the page. The hilarity of seeing an actor alter their whole being to

rivalry. Despite the differences, Shakespeare's plays are connected through the dramatist's desire to give voice to a socially diverse cast of characters: pimps, bawds, and prostitutes rub shoulders with the future king of England in *Henry IV Part 1* and *Part 2*; Bottom the weaver encounters the fairy world in *A Midsummer Night's Dream*; and the monarch listens to the thoughts of a fool and a beggar in *King Lear*.

The torment of the tragic

Of the plays included in the First Folio there are certain works that have acquired the status of Shakespearian masterpieces. People do not always need to have read or seen *Hamlet* in performance to be familiar with the words, "To be, or not to be; that is the question". Hamlet's association with melancholy and deep thought is now famous the world over. In him, Shakespeare created one of the most poetic voices of all time, and the literary illusion of a troubled conscience. Shakespeare walks listeners through the twists and turns of Hamlet's imagined mind as he struggles with issues of morality and mortality. Hamlet is troubled with the idea of "what dreams may come / When we have shuffled off this mortal coil"; as countless poems, novels, and dramas suggest, Hamlet is not

Prince Hamlet of Denmark, here portrayed by Laurence Olivier in the 1948 film version he also directed, is a pychologically complex character who feigns madness to exact revenge.

The enchanted Bottom the weaver, of *A Midsummer Night's Dream*, whose head has beed replaced with that of an ass, becomes desirable to Titania, who is under the spell of a love potion.

convey this metamorphosis can only really ever be fully appreciated in performance, but readers will appreciate that Bottom's experience of life has been overturned, and for a brief moment he gets to feel life as someone other than himself. This technique is repeated in some of Shakespeare's other comedies where disguise allows characters to alter their identity: Rosalind in *As You Like It* and Viola in *Twelfth Night* both cross-dress as young men; and in *The Comedy of Errors* two sets of twins are mistaken for one another to great comic effect.

Perils of power

Shakespeare's history plays are filled with duplicitous characters. In *Richard III*, Richard of Gloucester disguises his intentions to murder his way to the throne and becomes arguably Shakespeare's greatest villain. Set apart by his misshapen body, the hunchback Richard is forcefully charismatic from his first soliloquy, which opens the play. He informs the audience that he is "determined to prove a villain", and proclaims that he is "subtle, false, and treacherous". The soliloquies, and the symbolism of his deformity, cast Richard as the vice figure of the drama: audiences love to hate him. And yet, as is the case in all of Shakespeare's history plays from *Richard II* to *Henry VI*, power is shown to be fragile. Shakespeare notes in *Henry IV Part 2*, "Uneasy lies the head that wears a crown": those in power are never free from danger. This is a lesson that Richard III learns to his surprise. Having murdered his way to the throne he has to continue killing until he feels that all threats to his crown have been wiped out.

Works for the ages

The First Folio stretches to over 900 pages, contains 36 plays, and features the best-known portrait of Shakespeare on its title page, but it does not include *Pericles* or *The Two Noble Kinsmen*, which can be found in most copies of Shakespeare's complete works today. *The Tempest*, *Cymbeline*, and *The Winter's Tale* are often referred to as romances in modern editions, while *Coriolanus*, *Julius Caesar*, and *Antony and Cleopatra* are sometimes spoken of today as his "Roman plays".

Shakespeare's works have burst beyond the generic confines in which they were first published, but it is thanks to the First Folio that Shakespeare's works have survived at all. ∎

The authorship debate

Various conspiracy theories have circulated since the late 18th century claiming that William Shakespeare of Stratford-upon-Avon was not the author behind the works published in the First Folio.

There is a long catalogue of alternative candidates, and it continues to grow. The list includes figures such as Sir Francis Bacon, Christopher Marlowe, Edward de Vere, and even Queen Elizabeth I, all of whom died a decade before Shakespeare's last plays were staged or published. How could the Elizabethan playwright Christopher Marlowe have written the plays when he was murdered in 1593? One story goes that Christopher Marlowe did not really die in a tavern brawl in 1593, but went into hiding and continued to supply the public theatres with plays under the pseudonym "William Shakespeare". The arguments for the other contenders are equally improbable.

TO ESTEEM EVERYTHING IS TO ESTEEM NOTHING
THE MISANTHROPE (1666), MOLIÈRE

IN CONTEXT

FOCUS
French neoclassicism

BEFORE
1637 Pierre Corneille's "tragicomedy" *Le Cid* is performed in Paris to popular acclaim, but criticized by the Académie française for not observing the classical unities.

1653 Earliest performance of *The Rivals*, the first of Philippe Quinault's prolific output of comedies, tragicomedies, and lesser known tragedies.

AFTER
1668 Jean de la Fontaine adapts his collection of *Fables* from classical sources, including Aesop and Phaedrus, stretching the metrical verse of the time.

1671 Molière, Corneille, and Quinault collaborate on *Psyché*, a tragicomic ballet.

1677 *Phèdre* continues Jean Racine's series of tragedies on Greek mythological themes.

A fascination with all things classical overtook Europe during the Enlightenment period (1650–1800). The ancient Greek ideals of form, clarity, and elegance inspired a neoclassical movement in all the arts, with France leading the way in the field of literature. The classical influence was most apparent in French drama, which during the 17th century adopted a reinterpretation of the conventions of Greek theatre, as described in Aristotle's *Poetics.*

This stylized drama in verse frequently took the form of tragedies, which often reflected Greek mythological themes (a notable source of inspiration for Jean Racine), but there was a growing public demand for comedy, which was met by the witty plays of Molière (1622–1673).

A comedy of manners
Molière's major contribution was the "comedy of manners", satirizing the mores of the time with larger-than-life characters such as Alceste, the protagonist of *The Misanthrope,* whose cantankerous rejection of *politesse* (superficial, insincere politeness) is challenged when he falls for a society girl, Célimène. Fooled by her flirting, he begins to act in exactly the manner he despises in others, but reverts to his usual character when criticizing the sentimental poem of a nobleman. This gets him into legal trouble, and loses him friends, so he seeks solace (in vain) with the flighty Célimène. While poking fun at Alceste's misanthropy, Molière also exposes the hypocrisy of 17th-century courtly manners, in the spirit of the comedies of the Greek dramatist Aristophanes.

The success of Molière's comedies, including *The School for Wives*, *Tartuffe*, and *The Miser*, marked the beginning of an era of elegant, witty theatre that continued through the 18th century. The genre caught on in England, inspiring a line of work that can be traced from Restoration comedy, through Oliver Goldsmith and Richard Brinsley Sheridan (and novelists such as Jane Austen), to Oscar Wilde. ∎

See also: *Oedipus the King* 34–39 ▪ *Candide* 96–97 ▪ *Le Cid* 103 ▪ *Phèdre* 103–04 ▪ *Pride and Prejudice* 118–19 ▪ *The Picture of Dorian Gray* 194

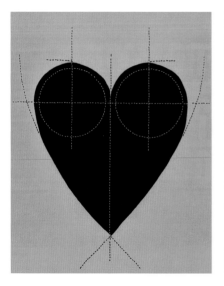

BUT AT MY BACK I ALWAYS HEAR TIME'S WINGED CHARIOT HURRYING NEAR
MISCELLANEOUS POEMS (1681), ANDREW MARVELL

IN CONTEXT

FOCUS
The Metaphysical Poets

BEFORE
1627 John Donne deploys Metaphysical exaggeration in his melancholic love elegy "A Nocturnal Upon St Lucy's Day" – "Oft a flood / Have we two wept, and so / Drowned the whole world, us two…"

1633 "The Agony", by George Herbert, applies Metaphysical wit to matters of belief – "Love is that liquore sweet and most divine, / Which my God feels as blood; but I, as wine."

1648 Robert Herrick's book *Hesperides* includes the famous *carpe diem* ("seize the day") poem, "To the Virgins, to Make Much of Time", with its famous line, "Gather ye rosebuds while ye may".

1650 Henry Vaughan, inspired by George Herbert, publishes "The World", a poem of mystical devotion.

The term "Metaphysical Poets" was coined by the essayist and literary critic Samuel Johnson to describe a group of 17th-century English writers that included John Donne, George Herbert, and Andrew Marvell (1621–1678). Their style was marked by wit, sophisticated logic, and occult metaphor, and often focused on themes of love, sexuality, and faith.

Sensual pleasures
Better known as a politician than a poet during his lifetime, Marvell produced a body of work, published posthumously as *Miscellaneous Poems*, that contains the famous love poem "To His Coy Mistress". In the poem, the speaker tries to persuade the object of his desire to seize the day and sleep with him. His argument to break down her resistance contains typically Metaphysical conceits – fanciful ideas pursued to an imaginative conclusion: "The grave's a fine and private place, / But none I think do there embrace."

History, theology, and astronomy are all brought into play by Marvell, who challenges the puritanical Christianity of the 17th century as a barrier to sensual pleasures.

He also brings vivid imagery and intellectual vitality to the pastoral, in poems such as "The Mower to the Glow Worms" and "The Garden", where he achieves a beautiful balance between abstraction and the senses, as he eulogizes the pleasure of withdrawing "To a green thought in a green shade". ∎

Stumbling on melons, as I pass, / Ensnared with flowers, I fall on grass.
"The Garden"

See also: *Metamorphoses* 55–56 ▪ *Les Amours de Cassandre* 74 ▪ *Paradise Lost* 103 ▪ *The Waste Land* 213

92

SADLY, I PART FROM YOU; LIKE A CLAM TORN FROM ITS SHELL, I GO, AND AUTUMN TOO

THE NARROW ROAD TO THE INTERIOR (1702), MATSUO BASHŌ

IN CONTEXT

FOCUS
Haiku and haibun

BEFORE
1686 Matsuo Bashō composes one of his most famous haiku, about a frog plopping with a splash into an ancient pond. It inspires a competition on the same theme among other haiku writers in Edo.

AFTER
1744 The great haiku poet Yosa Buson publishes his travel notes after following in the footsteps of Bashō.

1819 Kobayashi Issa proves a worthy successor to Bashō with *The Spring of My Life*, combining prose and haiku in a haibun. Issa was prolific, writing around 20,000 haiku, including 230 on the firefly.

1885 Masaoka Shika starts to write haiku on portraits he draws – he advocates writing from life, in the field, as an artist would paint a landscape.

Matsuo Bashō (c.1644–1694) of Edo (modern Tokyo) was the master of the haiku, a short Japanese verse form. Rendered in English in three or (more rarely) four lines, the haiku captures a fleeting moment, often with poignancy as well as sharp observation. But Bashō's greatest work is in a composite genre – the haibun – in which haiku is embedded in a prose narrative.

A noble journey

Bashō's aim in *The Narrow Road to the Interior* was to record a spiritual pilgrimage to the far north of the country, undertaken in the spirit of Zen Buddhism and to honour poets who had travelled before him. On this journey, direct encounters with nature, enriched by cultural associations, and visits to Shinto shrines, confirm Bashō's liberation from selfish attachments. The poetry and the prose are in perfect equilibrium, illuminating each other like a pair of mirrors facing inwards. Journeying mostly on foot, for hundreds of miles,

Bashō searches for wisdom, relating his discoveries in prose that is vivid and frequently tinged with elegiac melancholy – even a reference to "pines shaped by salty winds, trained by them into bonsai" appears solemn and resigned. His haiku achieve the sought-after quality of *kenshō*, or glimpse of enlightenment – a brief awakening into truth. ∎

Those who float away their lives on boats or who grow old leading horses are forever travelling, and their homes are wherever those travels take them.
The Narrow Road to the Interior

See also: *The Tale of Genji* 47 ▪ *On the Road* 264–65

NONE WILL HINDER AND NONE BE HINDERED ON THE JOURNEY TO THE MOUNTAIN OF DEATH
THE LOVE SUICIDES AT SONEZAKI (1703), CHIKAMATSU MONZAEMON

IN CONTEXT

FOCUS
Kabuki and Bunraku

BEFORE
c.1603 Kabuki drama – an unruly theatrical form that blends song, dance, action, and mime – originates with a female dancer called Okuni, an attendant at the Shinto shrine of Izumo.

c.1680 Bunraku develops as a form of musical puppet theatre in which half-lifesize puppets act out a chanted romantic narrative called *jōruri*.

AFTER
1748 *Chūshingura*, or *The Tale of the 47 Ronin*, by Takedo Imuzo, Namiki Sosuke, and Miyoshi Shoraku, is performed. Composed as Bunraku and adapted into a Kabuki, it is the nearest rival to Chikamatsu's work for popularity.

1963 Osaka's Bunraku Association rescues the *jōruri* theatrical form from decline.

Kabuki and Bunraku are both forms of traditional Japanese theatre that originated in the 17th century. Kabuki dealt with ribald material and was performed by wandering troupes of women who were often available as prostitutes. Bunraku is a form of puppet theatre, in which each puppet has a lead puppeteer who moves the right hand, another the left, and a third the legs and feet. The three men remain in full view of the audience, although they are often dressed in black. There is usually a single chanter, who portrays different characters by changing his pitch.

Japan's national bard
The greatest dramatist in either of these forms remains Chikamatsu Monzaemon (1653–1725). He was born into the samurai class but chose instead to write drama, and in time became Japan's most famous playwright. His work often features individuals caught in a conflict between ethical and personal demands.

Produced as Bunraku and adapted for Kabuki, Chikamatsu's play *The Love Suicides at Sonezaki* is his masterpiece; it was written within two weeks of the real event it was based on – that of a young couple who took their lives in a forest.

In his play, Chikamatsu created two characters who, like William Shakespeare's star-crossed couple Romeo and Juliet, have become synonymous with the theme of ill-fated lovers. Tokubei is a young man whose family has received a dowry, but he refuses to marry the chosen bride because he loves Ohatsu, a prostitute. A rival for her favours threatens to frame him as a thief. Unable to do his duty to his family, Tokubei can neither redeem his honour, nor have a future with Ohatsu, and so the two decide to make a death pact. The play and similar ones provoked a spate of copycat lovers' suicides, leading to a ban on the genre for a period after 1723. However, the play's language is considered to be some of the most beautiful in Japanese literature. ∎

See also: First Folio 82–89 ▪ *The Well Cradle* 102 ▪ *The Temple of the Golden Pavilion* 263

I WAS BORN IN THE YEAR 1632, IN THE CITY OF YORK, OF A GOOD FAMILY
ROBINSON CRUSOE (1719), DANIEL DEFOE

IN CONTEXT

FOCUS
Fictional autobiography

AFTER
1726 *Gulliver's Travels*, by Anglo-Irish author Jonathan Swift, is published as a traveller's tale and fictional autobiography and becomes an immediate success.

1740 English author Samuel Richardson publishes *Pamela*, a fictional autobiography that chronicles the life of its lead character, a maidservant, through a series of letters.

1749 The comic novel autobiography *Tom Jones*, by English writer Henry Fielding, is published and follows the adventures of a high-spirited foundling boy.

1849–50 *David Copperfield*, by English author Charles Dickens, is published; although a fictional work, the life of the main protagonist has close parallels to Dickens' own.

Constructing the narrative of a literary text around a fictional autobiography is a device that not only enables a writer to tell the tale of the life of an individual as if that person were the author but also gives the impression that the words spoken are a direct transcription of actual events. Daniel Defoe's *Robinson Crusoe* (originally entitled *The Life and Strange Surprizing Adventures of Robinson Crusoe*) was the progenitor of this fictional autobiographical voice. A number of other notable 18th- and 19th-century characters followed Crusoe, including Jonathan Swift's Gulliver, Henry Fielding's Tom Jones, and Charles Dickens' David Copperfield.

The title page of the first edition of *Robinson Crusoe* did not cite Defoe as the author: instead, the words "Written by Himself" appeared beneath the title – and so readers may well have imagined the story to be true. The book's opening sentence, which begins "I was born in the year 1632", suggests that this is a real tale recounted by the individual who experienced these adventures.

Daniel Defoe

Daniel Foe is thought to have been born in London in 1660 (he later added the prefix "De" to his name). In 1684 he married Mary Tuffley, then spent many years as a businessman and merchant, but went bankrupt in 1692. In 1697, he became a confidant of King William III and travelled Britain as a secret agent. In 1702, his pamphlet *The Shortest-Way with the Dissenters* led to his imprisonment, due to its political content, and to a second bankruptcy. Released thanks to politician Robert Harley, Defoe acted as Harley's spy, travelling around Britain and reporting back on public opinion. Defoe did not turn to novel writing until his late 50s, and became a key figure in the construction of the form, finding great success with *Robinson Crusoe*. Defoe died in 1731.

Other key works

1722 *Moll Flanders*
1722 *A Journal of the Plague Year*
1724 *Roxana*

See also: *Gulliver's Travels* 104 ▪ *Tom Jones* 104 ▪ *David Copperfield* 153 ▪ *The Catcher in the Rye* 256–57

> Makes use of an autobiographical voice to endorse the text as a true narrative.

> Promotes individualism: solitary, self-sufficient man mastering nature through reason.

> Crusoe becomes "King and Lord" of his isle.

Robinson Crusoe and *Gulliver's Travels* both use an autobiographical voice to present their tales of travel as factual accounts of real-life experiences; they nevertheless differ in several crucial respects.

Robinson Crusoe

Gulliver's Travels

> Makes use of an autobiographical voice to parody claims of truth in contemporary fiction.

> Satirizes the concept of individualism and the use of reason.

> Gulliver becomes a prisoner on the island of Lilliput.

The details of the "author's" birth lend authenticity to the work as an autobiographical text – and therefore also as a true narrative. Such verisimilitude is enhanced by the fact that parts of the novel take the form of a journal.

Island castaways

Robinson Crusoe is widely credited as a foundational text of realism, and, for many, it also ranks as the first English novel. It is believed that Defoe's work was inspired by the account of a real-life castaway, Alexander Selkirk, who, in the early 18th century, was marooned on an island in the Pacific. An instant success on publication, Defoe's story mentions expeditions in exotic regions of Africa and Brazil, and a slaving mission that leads to shipwreck on a Caribbean island.

Crusoe tells of his attempts to rescue provisions from the ship and of his solitary existence on the island. He builds a shelter and makes tools with which to hunt,

farm, and forage. He keeps track of the days by cutting notches in a wooden cross; he reads the Bible and thanks God. He domesticates a parrot. For years this is his life.

Then – in one of the most iconic moments in literature – Crusoe discovers a footprint in the sand, leading to an obsessive fear that he will be attacked by "savages". After two years spent barricading himself in a fortress, he encounters a native from a nearby island who is fleeing from cannibals. Crusoe "rescues" him, puts him to work, and names him Friday, after the day on which they met. The relationship between the two has been critiqued as one of master and slave (a European explorer/exploiter and an indigenous local); Crusoe, as a bearer of "civilization", is a symbol of burgeoning British imperialism. Just as European nations claim land for colonies, so Crusoe assumes dominion over the island, and sees himself as an owner and "absolute Lord".

Crusoe's "autobiographical" island memoir proved remarkably resilient, inspiring endless re-imaginings and giving rise to an entire subgenre, the Robinsonade. A pivotal text in English literature, it has had a significant influence – perhaps unrivalled by any other individual work – and its motifs have become part of the general culture. ▪

[H]e kneeled down again, kissed the ground, and … set my foot upon his head; this it seems was in token of swearing to be my slave forever.
Robinson Crusoe

IF THIS IS THE BEST OF ALL POSSIBLE WORLDS, WHAT ARE THE OTHERS?

CANDIDE (1759), VOLTAIRE

A diverse group of writers and intellectuals who lived in France in the 18th century came to be known as the *philosophes* ("philosophers"); their work nevertheless extended beyond philosophy into social, cultural, ethical, and political realms. The *philosophes* – who included Voltaire, Jean-Jacques Rousseau, Denis Diderot, and Montesquieu – were part of the widespread intellectual shift in Europe that was known as the Enlightenment: the assault on superstition, intolerance, and injustice in the name of reason and intellectual freedom that

Man was born to live either in the convulsions of misery, or in the lethargy of boredom.
Candide

lasted from the late 17th century to the French Revolution of 1789. Indeed, the Revolution was inspired by the ideas of philosophers and scientists, together with the prevailing spirit of rationalism and political liberalism.

Supreme optimism
Candide (originally titled *Candide, ou l'Optimisme*, and translated into English as *Candide: or, All for the Best*) is a *conte philosophique*, a philosophical fable in which Voltaire gave narrative expression to Enlightenment values. He turned his ferocious satirical scrutiny in particular on the ideas expressed by the German Gottfried Wilhelm von Leibniz in his philosophy of optimism, which held that because God is a benevolent deity, this world must be the best possible (optimal) world.

Leibniz's ideas are echoed in the novel by the philosopher Dr Pangloss, who utters his mantra "All is for the best in the best of all possible worlds" even in the face of repeated disaster. In a way that challenges this rosy metaphysics, the young hero, Candide, suffers a series of ordeals, including expulsion from a baronial home,

See also: *Gulliver's Travels* 104 ▪ *Jacques the Fatalist* 105

Gullible and naive, Candide is incapable of forming his own opinions on life: his vision of the world – his ideas on determinism, optimism, and free will, for example – is constructed by the views of the people around him.

Dr Pangloss (Candide's old tutor): Everything that happens reflects God's supreme and harmonious purpose for humankind.

The old woman (daughter of Pope Urban X and the Princess of Palestrina): Everybody's life is a tale of misfortune and suffering.

Martin (scholar and former publishing hack): The world is senseless and detestable. It was created by the forces of evil to drive us to complete madness.

Count Pococurante (a Venetian nobleman): No product of the arts can give untainted pleasure. Artistic endeavour is always overpraised.

The Turkish farmer: Politics brings misery: it is better to cultivate your farm, since work banishes boredom, vice, and poverty.

numerous violent misadventures, and an eventual reunion with his lost love, Cunégonde, only to find that he no longer desires her. Yet the misfortunes come so thick and fast and are related in so matter-of-fact a tone that the overall effect is comic. Women are violated by men; armies destroy each other; people are robbed and enslaved. Reversals of all kinds make life, health, and happiness precarious. In a world of greed, lust, and brutality (often in the name of religion), good deeds are scarce. Measured against the heartlessness of reality, Panglossian optimism is patently naive.

Personal influences

Although vibrant with melodramatic incident, *Candide* is a tale of ideas, albeit with autobiographical roots. Voltaire had known personal misfortune, including abuse by Jesuit teachers, loss of favour in the French court, and expulsion from Prussia. In addition, two public

catastrophes worked on his imagination and profoundly affected his views on God and free will: the earthquake that destroyed Lisbon, Portugal, in 1755, and the start of the Seven Years' War (1756–63), which unleashed destruction in Europe. Both events feature in *Candide* in fictionalized form.

Within the book, a narrative of intertwining personal stories becomes a thread that connects depictions of contrasting social systems. The first community we encounter is the feudal castle from which the hero gets expelled. There is a utopian interlude in Eldorado, an egalitarian nation of natural plenty. Finally, Candide, now living on a farm in Turkey, visits a family farm dedicated to cooperative work, where the people are happy. The ending, with Candide saying "We must go and cultivate our garden", indicates that it is possible to be happy – by means of hard work, and an absence of philosophy. ∎

Voltaire

Son of a notary, François-Marie Arouet was born in Paris, France, in 1694. A dramatist and poet, he adopted "Voltaire" as a *nom de plume*. His satirical verse earned him a spell in the Bastille prison, Paris, in 1717–18. After two years in England (a country that he found more tolerant and rational than France), his *Letters Concerning the English Nation* (1733) was suppressed in his homeland; it was seen as a critique of the government.

A study of Louis XIV restored him to favour at Versailles, where he became royal historiographer in 1745. Later, in Berlin, he become close friends with the Prussian king, Frederick the Great. He wrote his philosophical tales at his estate at Ferney, France, when in his 60s – including *Candide*. He also worked for agricultural reform as well as for greater justice for wronged individuals. He died in Paris in 1778, aged 84.

Other key works

1718 *Oedipus*
1733 *Philosophic Letters*
1747 *Zadig*
1752 *Micromégas* (short story)

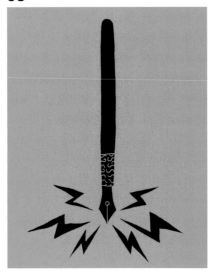

I HAVE COURAGE ENOUGH TO WALK THROUGH HELL BAREFOOT
THE ROBBERS (1781), FRIEDRICH SCHILLER

IN CONTEXT

FOCUS
Sturm und Drang

BEFORE
1750 Swiss-born philosopher Jean-Jacques Rousseau writes *Discourse on the Arts and Sciences*, an essay in which he condemns the Enlightenment drive towards pure rationalism.

1774 *The Sorrows of Young Werther*, a novel by German writer Johann Wolfgang von Goethe, is an immediate success and contains the elements that will characterize Sturm und Drang, such as high-flown expressions of intense emotion and the futile struggle of a young hero.

1777 Friedrich Maximilian von Klinger's play *Sturm und Drang* is first performed, giving the movement its name.

AFTER
1808 Goethe moves away from Sturm und Drang with his dramatic masterpiece *Faust*.

The Sturm und Drang movement (often translated as "storm and stress" but "storm and urge" is more accurate) was a sudden and brief explosion of German literature that lasted around 10 years. Sturm und Drang consisted of plays and novels characterized by great energy, physical and emotional violence, fierce and anguished lyricism, and the breaking of taboos (both social and artistic) in order to express the essential drama of the human heart.

The movement was a reaction to the Enlightenment (and particularly the French Enlightenment) values of pure reason and rationalism. Some early Enlightenment thinkers

Never has law formed a good man: 'tis liberty that breeds giants and heroes.
The Robbers

felt that genius could be attained through hard work and practice, and that good literature must adhere to classical forms. But to the Sturmer und Dranger (as the writers of the movement are known) these ideas were stifling – and were discarded with abandon.

Sturm und Drang plays ignored the established formal structures: they might not have five acts, or dialogue might not be written in perfectly formed sentences. And aside from being expressive, the language could be shocking, too: both Friedrich Schiller's play *The Robbers* and Johann Wolfgang von Goethe's novel *The Sorrows of Young Werther* exist in several editions, because the original language had to be toned down.

Youthful exuberance
Schiller's *The Robbers*, first performed in 1782, was the final flowering of a fading movement. The plot concerns two aristocratic brothers with opposing outlooks: Karl, an honourable idealist; and Franz, who is cold, materialistic and manipulative. Karl takes to the Bohemian woods to lead a band of robbers after Franz has turned their father against him, and stolen his

See also: *Candide* 96–97 ▪ *The Sorrows of Young Werther* 105 ▪ *Nachstücke* 111 ▪ *Faust* 112–15 ▪ *Jane Eyre* 128–31 ▪ *Wuthering Heights* 132–37 ▪ *The Brothers Karamazov* 200–01

inheritance. *The Robbers* broke taboos. The plot involved violence, robbery, and murder, and it is the hero, Karl, who leads the gang that commits the illegal and violent acts. In the depths of his passion he even kills his innocent cousin Amalia, to whom he is betrothed. The language of the play is as wild and stormy as the emotions it expresses, but it is also lyrical too, and *The Robbers* is regarded as one of the finest examples of dramatic writing in German literature. It is still considered a masterpiece today, and many critics also see in it the beginnings of European melodrama.

The Sturm und Drang movement was made up of energetic young men – most were in their 20s, the oldest only in their 30s. Perhaps as the authors grew older, they lost their taste for youthful rebellion, which might account for the movement's brevity. Many chose more reflective modes of expression thereafter, as the storm-and-urge era settled into a long and fruitful period of Weimar Classicism and German Romanticism. ▪

Freedom
In *Götz von Berlichingen* (1773) by Johann Wolfgang von Goethe, an honourable noble who prizes his freedom is unable to adapt to a world in which cynical forces pursue power politics.

Manipulation
The Soldiers (1776), by Jakob Michael Reinhold Lenz, tells the story of the beautiful Marie, who becomes the plaything of chauvinist young noble officers, resulting in murder and suicide.

Sturm und Drang
The subjects of Sturm und Drang works were typically sensational, reflecting the passions of their writers.

Desire and envy
A melancholic, violent twin murders his gentler brother over a woman he desires for himself in *Die Zwillinge* ("The Twins"; 1776) by Friedrich Maximilian von Klinger.

Oppression
In Friedrich Schiller's play *Don Carlos* (1787), the main protagonist tries to free the oppressed people of Flanders. The work aimed to expose the horrors of the Inquisition.

Friedrich Schiller

Johann Christoph Friedrich von Schiller (1759–1805) was born in Württemburg, Germany. A poet, playwright, philosopher, and historian, he wrote *The Robbers* while still at school. The play made him an overnight sensation, but it did not provide financial independence. Schiller later became a professor of History and Philosophy in Jena, whose university is now named after him. His friendship with Goethe led, in the late 18th century, to their setting up the Weimar Theatre, which would become the leading theatre in Germany.

Schiller was ill throughout his life, and he died of tuberculosis aged 45 in 1805, after making a fruitful return to playwriting in his last few years. He is still considered by many to be Germany's greatest classical playwright.

Other key works

1784 *Intrigue and Love*
1786 "Ode to Joy"
1787 *Don Carlos*
1794 *On the Aesthetic Education of Man*
1800 *Wallenstein*

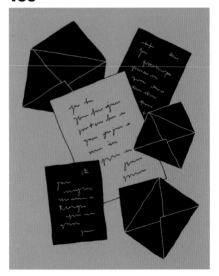

THERE IS NOTHING MORE DIFFICULT IN LOVE THAN EXPRESSING IN WRITING WHAT ONE DOES NOT FEEL

LES LIAISONS DANGEREUSES (1782), PIERRE CHODERLOS DE LACLOS

IN CONTEXT

FOCUS
The epistolary novel

BEFORE
1669 One of the earliest epistolary novels is published, *Letters of a Portuguese Nun*. It is attributed to French author Gabriel-Joseph de La Vergne, comte de Guilleragues.

1740 The hugely popular novel *Pamela*, by English author Samuel Richardson, details the corruption of an innocent maidservant.

1747–48 Richardson's tragic tale *Clarissa* is one of the longest novels in the English language and considered to be his masterpiece.

1761 Swiss-born philosopher Jean-Jacques Rousseau writes *Julie, or the New Heloise*, in which he uses the epistolary form to explore philosophical questions of rationality, morality, and autonomy.

L etters, diaries, and notes were the primary written means by which people communicated with one another in both daily life and literature during the 18th century. *Les Liaisons dangereuses* is an example of a literary style known as the epistolary novel (after the Greek for "letter"), which tells a story in the form of letters and, sometimes, other documents. Although it largely died out after the 1800s, in its heyday the epistolary novel was a popular and fashionable genre, reflecting the social world of a great age of correspondence.

When one woman stabs another to the heart … she rarely misses the vital spot and the wound can never be healed.
Les Liaisons dangereuses

Laclos did not simply imitate this genre, he radically extended it. The most famous epistolary novels of the period, such as Samuel Richardson's *Clarissa* and Jean-Jacques Rousseau's *Julie, or the New Heloise*, were often tedious in their meticulous and lengthy descriptions, and moralistic tone. Unlike his contemporaries, Laclos used the epistolary form to provide an exciting pace of action, and his characters often speak in the witty and urbane manner of the time.

The ruin of innocents
In France, the epistolary novel was linked with narratives of passion and the calculated seduction of women. Key to the success of these novels was the philosophy of "libertinage", in which eroticism, sexual depravity, and a lifestyle of excess and vice were intermingled with sophisticated wordplay.

In *Les Liaisons dangereuses* letters between multiple characters expose the moral decline of the French aristocracy just before the Revolution. Laclos' key "actors" in this form of seduction as sport are the libertine Vicomte de Valmont, and the Marquise de Merteuil – with her public façade of a virtuous

See also: *Robinson Crusoe* 94–95 ▪ *Clarissa* 104 ▪ *The Sorrows of Young Werther* 105 ▪ *Dracula* 195 ▪ *The Moonstone* 198–99

lady. Former lovers, they try to outdo each other in their cruelty and manipulative degradation of others through sexual exploitation. Their own and others' letters show how they plot the pursuit of their entertainment like a military campaign, the narrative tracing a calculated process of ruination involving rape, sexual corruption, and humiliation.

Moral ambiguity

Unlike his contemporaries, who often addressed the reader directly in their epistolary novels, Laclos removed his authorial presence from the narrative, leaving his characters to speak for themselves. Because of his absent narrational voice and the lack of any authorial condemnation of his characters'

actions, contemporary reviewers wondered if Laclos too was as wicked as Merteuil and Valmont.

The cleverness of *Les Liaisons dangeureses* lies in its moral ambiguity and the extent to which Laclos implicates the reader in society's treatment of women as pawns in games of ownership and sexual domination. In her own words to Valmont, Merteuil views her actions as part of a wider battle of the sexes in which she is "born to avenge my sex and subjugate yours" – although in doing this, she brings destruction as much to other women as to men. In the letters through which he presents this battle, Laclos seduces his reader via the "pleasure" to be found in a voyeuristic literary exploration of artful temptation. ■

Pierre Choderlos de Laclos

Pierre Choderlos de Laclos was born in 1741 in Amiens, to a family that had only recently become part of the French nobility. The family's relative unimportance in the social hierarchy meant that as a young man Laclos looked to the military for a viable career. While captain of an artillery regiment at Besançon in 1778, he began writing his only novel, influenced by the work of Jean-Jacques Rousseau.

Although *Les Liaisons dangereuses* was scandalous because of its libertine characters and themes of sexual vice, Laclos himself was not a faithless seducer. He married his lover, Marie-Soulange Duperré, when she fell pregnant; they went on to have two children and live a happy life. He escaped the guillotine in 1794 and devoted himself to his family until his death in 1803 from fever.

Other key works

1777 *Ernestine*
1783 *Des Femmes et de leur éducation*
1790–91 *Journal des amis de la Constitution*

The letters that form Laclos' text are also objects in the plot, used to manipulate. Merteuil and Valmont, the orchestrating villains, are adept at writing letters in ways that exploit how others will read meaning into them.

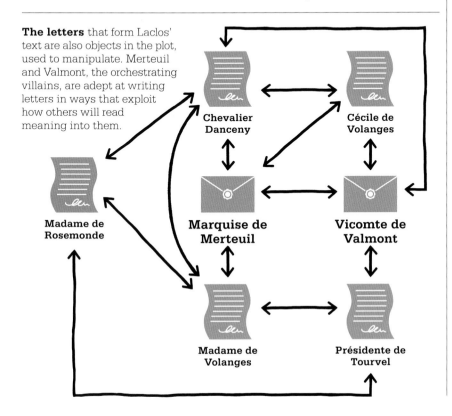

Chevalier Danceny

Cécile de Volanges

Madame de Rosemonde

Marquise de Merteuil

Vicomte de Valmont

Madame de Volanges

Présidente de Tourvel

FURTHER READING

THE DECAMERON
(1353), GIOVANNI BOCCACCIO

Structured as a frame narrative, *The Decameron* by Italian writer, poet, and scholar Giovanni Boccaccio (1313–75) is a collection of 100 tales. The frame story uniting them is that of 10 young adults – seven women and three men – who flee plague-ridden Florence to an attractive villa in nearby Fiesole. The group decides that every day, each of them should tell a story, resulting in 100 stories over 10 days. Whoever is nominated leader for the day chooses the subject and stipulates rules for the stories to be told. Each day ends with one person singing a *canzone* or song, while the others dance. The result is a dazzling collection of exquisitely written tales – ranging from stories of tragic love and bawdiness through to the power of human will and tricks that women play on men – that inspired writers of the Renaissance and beyond.

A kissed mouth does not lose its freshness, for like the moon it always renews itself.
The Decameron
Giovanni Boccaccio

SIR GAWAIN AND THE GREEN KNIGHT
(c.1375)

Consisting of some 2,500 lines, *Sir Gawain and the Green Knight* is one of the best-known examples of Middle English alliterative verse. Of unknown authorship, the poem is a chivalric romance set in the early days of the legendary King Arthur's court. A beautifully written tale of enchantment that is full of psychological insight, the poem describes a series of challenges and temptations faced by the hero, Sir Gawain, following an encounter with the mysterious Green Knight.

THE WELL CRADLE
(c.1430), ZEAMI MOTOKIYO

The Well Cradle (*Izutsu*) is a classical Noh play by Zeami Motokiyo (1363–1443), the greatest dramatist and theorist of the Japanese Noh theatre. The play, which takes its name from the protective railing around a well, is framed within an encounter between a Buddhist monk and a village woman, who tells the monk a story. Highly stylized, the play is based on a visionary Noh story of a boy and girl who meet at a well, fall in love, and marry.

LE MORTE D'ARTHUR
(1485), SIR THOMAS MALORY

Printed by William Caxton in 1485, although an earlier manuscript version from around 1470 exists,

Therein stuck a fair sword naked by the point ... Whoso pulleth out this sword of this stone and anvil, is rightwise king born of all England.
Le Morte d'Arthur
Sir Thomas Malory

Le Morte d'Arthur is a compilation of stories about the legendary King Arthur and the knights of the Round Table. Deriving from older French romances, the stories were translated into English prose and compiled by English knight, soldier, writer, and Member of Parliament Sir Thomas Malory (d.1471). Malory arranged the stories in chronological order, starting with the birth of Arthur, and chose to focus on the brotherhood of the knights rather than the theme of courtly love so popular with the French.

AMADIS OF GAUL
(1508), GARCI RODRÍGUEZ DE MONTALVO

A chivalric prose romance written in Spanish by Montalvo (c.1450–1504), *Amadis of Gaul* probably had its origins in the early 14th century, but its original date and authorship is uncertain. Written in four volumes, Montalvo's version recounts the story of Amadis – a handsome, valiant, yet gentle knight – and his love for Princess Oriana, in whose service he undertakes chivalric adventures and bold feats against giants and monsters. Its high ideals, gallantry, and romance set the standard for chivalric works that followed.

THE *BARCAS* TRILOGY
(1516, 1518, 1519), GIL VICENTE

A devotional work, the *Barcas* ("Ships") trilogy by Portuguese playwright Gil Vicente (c.1465–1573) – often described as the "father of Portuguese drama" – consists of three one-act plays: *The Ship of Hell*; *The Ship of Purgatory*; and *The Ship of Heaven*. Satirical and allegorical, these three plays – which together are considered Vicente's most masterful work – portray the passengers, who reflect all classes of Lisbon society, and their mainly unsuccessful attempts to enter Heaven.

THE LUSIADS
(1572), LUÍS DE CAMÕES

Often regarded as Portugal's national epic, *The Lusiads* is a 10-canto epic poem by the great Portuguese poet de Camões (1524–80) recounting Vasco da Gama's sea route to India. After the introduction, an invocation to river gods, and a dedication to King Sebastian, the poem includes orations by a series of narrators, including a history of Portugal, recounted by da Gama, as well as descriptions of adventures, storms, and interventions by Greco-Roman gods. Overall it is a homage to the Portuguese and their achievements.

THE FAERIE QUEENE
(1590, 1596), EDMUND SPENSER

The defining work of English poet Spenser (c.1552–99), and one of the great long poems of the English language, *The Faerie Queene* is a religious, moral, and political allegory. Set in a mythical Arthurian world, symbolizing Tudor England, the poem consists of six books, each of which describes the exploits of a knight who represents a moral virtue, such as Chastity. The knights serve Gloriana, the Faerie Queene, who represents Queen Elizabeth I. Spenser had planned 12 books, but died in London at the age of 46 before completing his great work.

LE CID
(1637), PIERRE CORNEILLE

A verse tragedy in five acts, *Le Cid* by French tragedian Pierre Corneille (1606–84) is seen as the defining example of French neoclassical tragedy. Inspired by the story of Spain's national hero, El Cid, the play relates Le Cid's coming of age

John Milton

English poet John Milton is best known for *Paradise Lost*, considered the greatest epic poem in the English language. Born in Cheapside, London, in 1608, he began writing while still a student. But with the outbreak of the English Civil War in 1642, he devoted himself to revolutionary politics, producing pamphlets defending religious and civil liberties. Following the execution of Charles I in 1649 and the overthrow of the English monarchy, he became

and an incident when he is asked by his father to challenge his future father-in-law to a duel. In so doing, he is forced to choose between the woman he loves and family honour.

PARADISE LOST
(1667), JOHN MILTON

Milton's masterwork, and a supreme triumph of rhythm and sound, the epic poem *Paradise Lost* relates the biblical story of the fall from grace of Adam and Eve, and hence of all humanity. Organized into 12 books for the final 1674 edition (the first edition contained 10 books), the poem interweaves two themes: the rebellion of Satan against God and Heaven; and the temptation of Adam and Eve and their expulsion from the Garden of Eden.

PHÈDRE
(1677), JEAN RACINE

The dramatic tragedy *Phèdre* by French playwright Jean Racine (1639–99) is a supreme example of French neoclassicism. It consists

secretary to the council of state. Completely blind by 1654, he was able to continue working by dictating his verse and prose to an assistant. Following the Restoration in 1660, he devoted himself to producing his greatest literary works. He died in 1674 in London at the age of 65.

Key works

1644 *Areopagitica, A Speech for the Liberty of Unlicensed Printing*
1667 *Paradise Lost* (see above)
1671 *Paradise Regained*
1671 *Samson Agonistes*

Samuel Richardson

A true man of letters, English novelist Samuel Richardson was born in Derbyshire in 1689 and is best remembered for developing the innovatory epistolary novel, in which the story is told through letters. Moving to London, where he had only a meagre education – something that would always trouble him – he became a master printer. Richardson's domestic life was tragic: his first wife died, as did his six children, and he married again. He was 50 when he wrote his first novel, becoming a popular and respected author. He died in 1761 of a stroke in London.

Key works

1740 *Pamela: Or, Virtue Rewarded*
1747–48 *Clarissa* (see right)
1753 *The History of Sir Charles Grandison*

of five acts written in verse, and takes its subject matter from Greek mythology that had already been explored by the classical dramatists Euripides and Seneca. Racine's play portrays the incestuous love of Phèdre (Phaedra), married to the king of Athens, for her stepson Hippolyte (Hippolytus) who, shocked and in love with another woman, rejects her advances.

THE PRINCESS OF CLEVES
(1678), MADAME DE LA FAYETTE

The Princess of Cleves by French author Madame de La Fayette (1634–93) appeared at a time when women could not openly declare authorship, and was published anonymously. Seen as the first novel to explore the psychology of character, events take place at the royal court of Henry II of France, which La Fayette reproduces with historical accuracy. Her heroine, the Princess of Cleves, suppresses her love for a young nobleman, but misunderstandings and court intrigues damage her marriage.

GULLIVER'S TRAVELS
(1726), JONATHAN SWIFT

An influential satirical novel by Anglo-Irish writer Jonathan Swift (1667–1745), *Gulliver's Travels* is narrated by ship's surgeon Lemuel Gulliver, who visits various fantasy regions: Lilliput, where inhabitants are six inches tall; Brobdingnag, a land of practical giants; Laputa, a flying island; Glubdubdrib, the Island of Sorcerers; and the land of the Houyhnhnms. Humorous and fantastical, Swift's novel lampoons travel books and pokes fun at much of contemporary society, satirizing political parties, religious dissenters, scientists, and philosophers, as well as mocking small-minded attitudes.

CLARISSA
(1747–1748), SAMUEL RICHARDSON

Clarissa, also entitled *The History of a Young Lady*, is an epistolary novel by Samuel Richardson and, at over a million words, is one of the longest novels in the English language. It traces the tragic history of the virtuous heroine, Clarissa Harlowe, who is rejected by her family and abused by the unscrupulous Lovelace. Events are recounted mainly through a four-way correspondence of letters between Clarissa and her friend Miss Howe, and Lovelace to his friend John Belford.

TOM JONES
(1749), HENRY FIELDING

A comic novel by English writer Henry Fielding (1707–54), *Tom Jones* (originally titled *The History of Tom Jones, a Foundling*) is one of the earliest works to be defined as a novel. It follows the adventures of the eponymous hero, a foundling who is brought up by the wealthy Squire Allworthy, and his pursuit of the virtuous Sophia Western. Rich in coincidences and misadventures, the novel makes a moral point in highlighting differences between the lusty but essentially well-meaning Tom Jones, and his hypocritical half-brother, Blifil.

TRISTRAM SHANDY
(1759–1767), LAURENCE STERNE

A bawdily humorous novel, *The Life and Opinions of Tristram Shandy, Gentleman*, by Irish clergyman and

I wish either my father or my mother, or indeed both of them, as they were in duty both equally bound to it, had minded what they were about when they begot me.
Tristram Shandy
Laurence Sterne

writer Laurence Sterne (1713–68), was published in nine volumes over eight years, and is a fictionalized biography of its hero and a parody of the novels of its day. Narrated in an endless series of digressions and speculations by Shandy, the novel begins with his botched conception (though he is not born until Volume II) and then ambles through his life, introducing unfinished anecdotes, shifts in time, and various colourful characters – Shandy's parents, his Uncle Toby and his servant Trim, the parson Yorick, and household servant Obadiah. Its experimental approach – as well as the erratic narrative, Sterne left some pages blank and littered others with asterisks – has led some to describe it as a forerunner of 20th-century stream-of-consciousness writing.

THE SORROWS OF YOUNG WERTHER
(1774), JOHANN WOLFGANG VON GOETHE

A significant novel in the Sturm und Drang (literally, "Storm and Stress") movement, *The Sorrows of Young Werther* established its 26-year-old German author, Goethe

It is certain that nothing on earth but love makes a person necessary.
The Sorrows of Young Werther
Johann Wolfgang von Goethe

(1749–1832), as an internationally acclaimed writer. Completed in just six frenetic weeks, Goethe's debut novel is epistolary in form and loosely autobiographical. It consists of a series of letters written by the hero, Werther, a young artist in the Romantic tradition, to his friend William. The letters describe his tormented passion for a young woman, Lotte, who is promised to another. The novel's popularity was such that "Werther Fever" spread across Europe, with young men adopting the dress and habits of its eponymous, tragic hero.

SONGS OF INNOCENCE AND OF EXPERIENCE
(1794), WILLIAM BLAKE

Blake's *Songs of Innocence and of Experience* – masterpieces of English lyric poetry, rich in rhythmic subtlety – explore what the poet defined as "Two Contrasting States of the Human Soul". *Songs of Innocence*, first published in 1789, portrays the innocence of childhood through the eyes of the child or as observed by adults. The edition of 1794 was expanded to include the contrasting "Songs of Experience", including "The Tyger" and "The Fly". These explore experiences of fear, aggression, conflict, and oppression, which come with the loss of innocence and childhood.

JACQUES THE FATALIST
(1796), DENIS DIDEROT

Published posthumously, *Jacques the Fatalist and his Master* by French Enlightenment philosopher and writer Diderot (1713–84) explores issues of moral responsibility, free will, and determinism. Much of the

William Blake

Born in Soho, London, in 1757, Blake left school at the age of 10. Profoundly influenced by the Bible from an early age, he experienced visions on angelic and heavenly themes throughout his life; religious and spiritual motifs figured heavily in both his poetry and his engravings. After being apprenticed to a distinguished London printmaker, Blake developed his own method of relief etching in 1789, which he used in his finest illustrated works. Now considered the earliest and most original of the Romantic poets, at the time of his death in 1827 many contemporaries dismissed his work and regarded him as mad.

Key works

1794 *Songs of Innocence and of Experience* (see left)
1804–20 *Jerusalem*

novel consists of dialogue between Jacques and his unnamed master who are riding through France; on his master's prompting they begin to talk about their loves. A picture emerges not just of 18th-century France, but also of a world in which events occur at random and, as personified by Jacques, where history determines an individual's fate. Diderot's novel is complex and multi-layered – the haphazard progress of Jacques' journey is frequently interrupted by long, often-comedic digressions, other characters, other narratives, and chance events. This playful and modern narrative style has led to Diderot's book being hailed as a precursor of the 20th-century novel.

ROMANTI

AND THE

OF THE N

1800–1855

CISM
RISE
OVEL

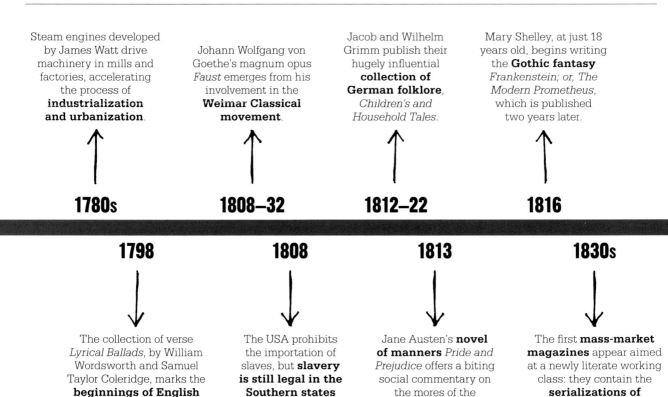

Steam engines developed by James Watt drive machinery in mills and factories, accelerating the process of **industrialization and urbanization**.

Johann Wolfgang von Goethe's magnum opus *Faust* emerges from his involvement in the **Weimar Classical movement**.

Jacob and Wilhelm Grimm publish their hugely influential **collection of German folklore**, *Children's and Household Tales*.

Mary Shelley, at just 18 years old, begins writing the **Gothic fantasy** *Frankenstein; or, The Modern Prometheus*, which is published two years later.

1780s   **1808–32**   **1812–22**   **1816**

1798   **1808**   **1813**   **1830s**

The collection of verse *Lyrical Ballads*, by William Wordsworth and Samuel Taylor Coleridge, marks the **beginnings of English Romantic literature**.

The USA prohibits the importation of slaves, but **slavery is still legal in the Southern states** of the union.

Jane Austen's **novel of manners** *Pride and Prejudice* offers a biting social commentary on the mores of the English landed gentry.

The first **mass-market magazines** appear aimed at a newly literate working class: they contain the **serializations of popular novels**.

The late 18th century was a period of revolutionary change across Europe. The Enlightenment, or Age of Reason, had fostered the scientific advances that brought about the Industrial Revolution, as well as the various philosophical ideas that had led to the political revolutions in North America and France. The effects of growing industrialization and urbanization on society had a significant impact on the way that many people lived and worked.

During the Renaissance and the Enlightenment periods, humankind and reason were the twin focuses of cultural interest. But in the early 19th century, the individual came to the fore. Partly as a reaction to the cool rationality of the Enlightenment, a movement in the arts arose, which placed emphasis on subjective feelings and faculties such as intuition, imagination, and emotion. This movement became known as Romanticism.

Romantic literature

Romanticism had its roots in the German Sturm und Drang movement, from which the writers Johann Wolfgang von Goethe and Friedrich Schiller emerged. In this transition from the classical style of the Enlightenment to 19th-century Romanticism, they introduced the idea of an unconventional protagonist whose actions are less important than his thoughts and feelings. This "Romantic hero" later became more of an anti-establishment figure, epitomizing the rebellious spirit of the period, and a recurrent character in the growing number of novels that appeared at the time. By the mid-19th century, Romanticism had spread across Europe to Russia, and writers such as Alexander Pushkin, Mikhail Lermontov, and Ivan Turgenev developed the idea into that of the "superfluous man", whose unorthodox ideas isolate him completely from society.

Another characteristic of Romantic literature was an affinity with the natural world. English poets such as William Wordsworth and Samuel Taylor Coleridge offered an antidote to the industrial age by portraying the beauty and power of nature, and celebrating the innocence and impulsiveness of childhood. A similar reaction to urbanization was evident in the work of American transcendentalist writers Ralph Waldo Emerson, Henry David Thoreau, and Walt

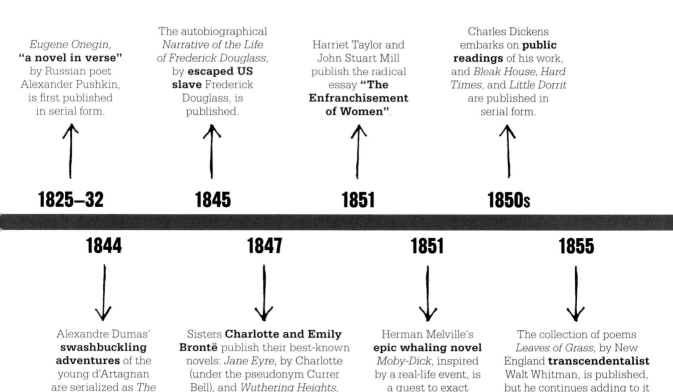

Eugene Onegin, **"a novel in verse"** by Russian poet Alexander Pushkin, is first published in serial form.

The autobiographical *Narrative of the Life of Frederick Douglass*, by **escaped US slave** Frederick Douglass, is published.

Harriet Taylor and John Stuart Mill publish the radical essay **"The Enfranchisement of Women"**.

Charles Dickens embarks on **public readings** of his work, and *Bleak House*, *Hard Times*, and *Little Dorrit* are published in serial form.

1825–32 **1845** **1851** **1850s**

1844 **1847** **1851** **1855**

Alexandre Dumas' **swashbuckling adventures** of the young d'Artagnan are serialized as *The Three Musketeers*.

Sisters **Charlotte and Emily Brontë** publish their best-known novels: *Jane Eyre*, by Charlotte (under the pseudonym Currer Bell), and *Wuthering Heights*, by Emily (writing as Ellis Bell).

Herman Melville's **epic whaling novel** *Moby-Dick*, inspired by a real-life event, is a quest to exact revenge on nature.

The collection of poems *Leaves of Grass*, by New England **transcendentalist** Walt Whitman, is published, but he continues adding to it until his death in 1892.

Whitman who evoked the spirit of humanitarian liberty, culminating in their call to go "back to nature".

Gothic novels
However, many Romantic writers recognized that nature (and human nature) also has a dark side, and can arouse feelings of terror as well as pleasure. This fascination with the destructive power of nature, and even the supernatural, inspired the genre that came to be known as Gothic literature. The tone was set in Germany by Goethe's play *Faust*, and the short stories by E T A Hoffmann, but the genre was most eagerly adopted by English novelists, such as Mary Shelley, who wrote *Frankenstein*. Elements of the Gothic run through many Victorian novels, often stressing the untameable nature of a Romantic

hero in a wild landscape, as in Emily Brontë's *Wuthering Heights*, or the grotesque characters in grim urban surroundings that feature in the works of Charles Dickens. The genre also became popular in the USA, as exemplified by Edgar Allan Poe's tales of the macabre; it also influenced the style adopted by Herman Melville in his haunting short stories and *Moby-Dick*.

History and identity
As society industrialized, levels of literacy increased, and literature was no longer solely for an educated elite. Novels in particular reached a mass readership in 19th-century Europe and the USA, and many were made available in serial form. Especially popular were historical novels by the likes of Walter Scott, Alexandre Dumas, and James

Fenimore Cooper, which catered for an urban public's desire for romance and adventure, but included graver fare such as Leo Tolstoy's *War and Peace*. There was also an appetite for folk stories and fairy tales which, like historical novels, were often specific to a culture. This focus on regional traditions chimed with the era's growing nationalism.

As well as a broader readership, increased literacy spawned a greater variety of authors, most noticeably a generation of women writers such as the Brontë sisters and George Eliot of England, who (albeit under pseudonyms) pioneered a female perspective in literature, and the first freed slaves, such as Frederick Douglass, Harriet Jacobs, and Solomon Northup, who gave a voice to the USA's oppressed black people. ∎

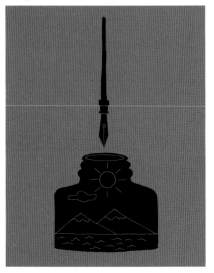

POETRY IS THE BREATH AND THE FINER SPIRIT OF ALL KNOWLEDGE

LYRICAL BALLADS (1798–1800), WILLIAM WORDSWORTH AND SAMUEL TAYLOR COLERIDGE

IN CONTEXT

FOCUS
The English Romantic poets

BEFORE
1794 William Blake's *Songs of Innocence and of Experience* marks the early phase of Romanticism, anticipating the esteem placed by Wordsworth on the purity of childhood and giving a voice to society's marginalized figures.

AFTER
1818 Percy Bysshe Shelley's sonnet about the statue of Ozymandias points to a Romantic interest in the insignificance of man.

1819 Romantic poetry's link with intoxicants, death, and the imagination is expressed in John Keats's poem "Ode to a Nightingale".

1818–1823 Lord Byron's *Don Juan* – cynical, subversive, and witty – undermines his earlier Romanticism.

William Wordsworth (1770–1850) and Samuel Taylor Coleridge (1772–1834) were two of the "Lake Poets", so called because they lived and wrote in the inspirational setting of England's Lake District. The friends collaborated on the *Lyrical Ballads*, a collection of Romantic verse with the ambition (stated in the preface of the book's second edition of 1800) to "follow the fluxes and refluxes of the mind when agitated by the great and simple affections of our nature". In part a reaction to the acute rationalism of the industrial age, English Romanticism (c.1790s–1830s) took human experience, imagination, nature, and individualistic freedom as its inspiration.

Democratizing poetry

Lyrical Ballads starts with "The Rime of the Ancient Mariner", Coleridge's seven-part ballad with otherworldly overtones: it was agreed that supernatural poetry with a "semblance of truth" would be this writer's remit. Wordsworth's brief was to give "the charm of novelty" to everyday life and awaken the reader to the loveliness of the familiar. Both writers believed that poetry should be written in transparent, unadorned language for the general populace, with simple metre and rhyme, and chose subject matter consistent with this democratizing impulse: the lives of uneducated rustic folk, whose emotions were pure and universal. Poems dealing with royalty or lofty allegory were replaced with themes of poverty, crime, and madness.

Purity and reflection

Some of Wordsworth's poems focus on children, whom he thought lived closer to nature and form a bond with it – childhood being a time of innocence, impulse, and play. Most of the poems are deeply felt rather than deeply thought, but two have a more reflective manner: Coleridge's "The Nightingale", a conversational poem, and Wordsworth's "Lines written a few miles above Tintern Abbey". ∎

See also: *Songs of Innocence and of Experience* 105

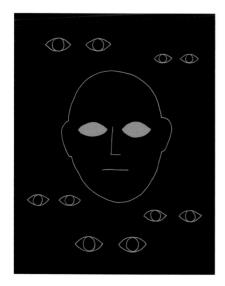

NOTHING IS MORE WONDERFUL, NOTHING MORE FANTASTIC THAN REAL LIFE
NACHTSTÜCKE (1817), E T A HOFFMANN

IN CONTEXT

FOCUS
German Romanticism

BEFORE
1797–99 Best known as a poet, Friedrich Hölderlin writes the lyrical and tragic two-part novel *Hyperion*. The book reflects the typically German Romantic fascination with ancient Greek culture.

AFTER
1821 Heinrich von Kleist's *The Prince of Homburg* is staged for the first time – 10 years after the author's death by suicide. The patriotic play, in which the prince fails to follow orders and faints in a dream scene, has been edited so as not to offend the Prussian elite.

1827 *The Book of Songs* by Heinrich Heine is published. A five-section collection of Romantic poetry that wins Heine fame, many of the poems were later set to music by Franz Schubert and Robert Schumann.

German Romanticism came after, and was a reaction to, Weimar Classicism; its proponents rejected calm restraint and cared only about the artist's perceptions. Romantic literature in Germany looked to the medieval past as a period of intellectual simplicity that could be re-created. It also explored the supernatural, the uncanny, and the fantastical as realms of the imagination – the Romantics wanted the world to become dream-like, and for dreams to be so realistic they resembled the world. German Romanticism tended to be less serious than British Romanticism, and often made use of playful wit.

Dark revelations

Nachtstücke by E T A Hoffmann (1776–1822), from Königsberg in Prussia, is a collection of eight short stories that combine a spirit of light-heartedness with darker themes of human irrationality. The stories are written in a simple and populist tone, accessible to all, and not self-consciously intellectual.

Hoffman was a musician, rather than a writer; *Nachtstücke* ("Night Pieces") is a musical title, and one of many German Romantic texts that were adapted into songs or operas.

The most famous of the stories is "The Sandman", in which this traditionally sympathetic figure, who blesses children with their dreams, is revealed as a monster who instead plucks out their eyes. The Gothic and fantastical tales offer a disturbing insight into the human psyche and the individual's struggle to feel at ease in society. ∎

He puts their eyes in a bag and carries them to the crescent moon to feed his own children...
"The Sandman"

See also: *The Robbers* 98–99 ▪ *The Sorrows of Young Werther* 105 ▪ *Lyrical Ballads* 110 ▪ *Faust* 112–15 ▪ *Frankenstein* 120–21

MAN ERRS, TILL HE HAS CEASED TO STRIVE

FAUST (1808, 1832), JOHANN WOLFGANG VON GOETHE

IN CONTEXT

FOCUS
Weimar Classicism

BEFORE
1776 Under the auspices of the young Goethe, German philosopher Johann Gottfried Herder comes to Weimar and begins to write works on literary aesthetics that hark back to the values of the Greek classics. His ideas provide the philosophical underpinning for the movement known as Weimar Classicism.

1794 Friedrich von Schiller writes to Goethe. Their friendship, after they meet in Weimar, forms the backbone of Weimar Classicism.

1799 Schiller completes his *Wallenstein* drama trilogy, often said to be the greatest historical drama in the German language and a key work of Weimar Classicism.

It was not until shortly before his death in 1832 that Johann Wolfgang von Goethe finally completed the work for which he is best remembered – *Faust*, a tragic play in two parts, the first of which was completed in 1808. *Faust* is also the most notable achievement of the movement known as Weimar Classicism, a period of prolific cultural and literary activity centred on the German city of Weimar, which began in the 1780s and lasted for nearly 30 years.

The two writers most closely associated with Weimar Classicism are Goethe and his friend and collaborator, the playwright Friedrich von Schiller (1759–1805).

See also: *Doctor Faustus* 75 ▪ *The Robbers* 98–99 ▪ *Les Liaisons dangereuses* 100–01 ▪ *The Sorrows of Young Werther* 105 ▪ *The Magic Mountain* 224–27 ▪ *The Catcher in the Rye* 256–57

Age is no second childhood
– age makes plain,
Children we were, true
children we remain.
Faust

As young men, both had been involved with the late 18th-century movement known as Sturm und Drang ("storm and stress"), which featured novels and plays that broke with the literary traditions of the Enlightenment and promoted passionate emotional expression. However, in the 1780s, as the fire of their youth subsided, Goethe and Schiller began to look back at the Enlightenment values that they had previously rejected, reconciling them with the energy of Sturm und Drang, and revisiting the Greek classics with a view to creating new and finer aesthetic standards.

Collaborative classicism

Weimar Classicism is often regarded as Goethe and Schiller's joint achievement, although it included other writers – notably the philosopher Johann Gottfried Herder (1744–1803) and Christoph Martin Wieland (1733–1813), a poet and novelist.

In formulating their ideas about good literature, Goethe and Schiller agreed that aesthetic perfection was an impossible goal. Instead, they emphasized the importance of balance and harmony, arguing that a literary work could be considered great if it existed in perfect balance with its own imperfect elements. In this way, a work could achieve the unity and wholeness that the authors of the Greek classics had sought.

This balance, according to Goethe and Schiller, was achieved by a combination of the three elements essential to a work of art. The first, *gehalt*, the author's primary inspiration or vision, combined with the second, *gestalt*, the aesthetic form of the work, which might be based on close study of classical models. The third element, the *inhalt*, is the bulk of the author's invention – the "content" or, in effect, the words in a work of literature. The *inhalt* is therefore the element that must

Here deeds have understood
Words they were darkened by;
The Eternal Feminine,
Draws us on high.
Faust

be managed carefully because it can create an imbalance that could distract from the *gehalt* and the *gestalt*.

Goethe and Schiller collaborated on each other's productions and encouraged one another – it was »

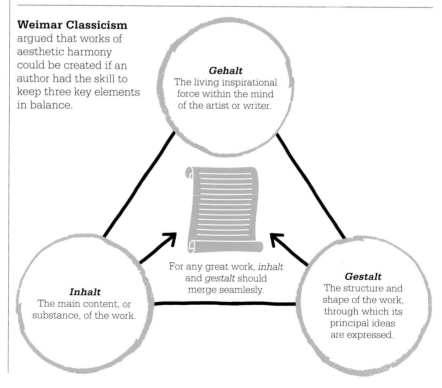

Weimar Classicism argued that works of aesthetic harmony could be created if an author had the skill to keep three key elements in balance.

Gehalt
The living inspirational force within the mind of the artist or writer.

Inhalt
The main content, or substance, of the work.

For any great work, *inhalt* and *gestalt* should merge seamlessly.

Gestalt
The structure and shape of the work, through which its principal ideas are expressed.

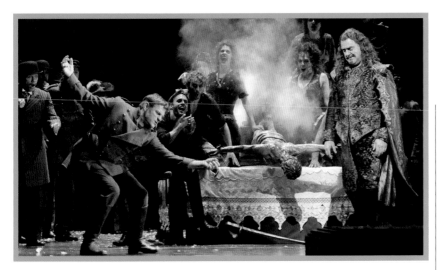

A man who sells his soul for worldly gain is an idea that has long captivated writers. Part One of Goethe's play inspired Charles Gonoud's opera. Here, Bryn Terfel (right) plays Mephistopheles.

Faust: Part One begins in heaven where Mephistopheles (the devil) muses on mankind and wagers with God that he can turn one of God's favourite subjects, Faust, to sinful ways and win his soul. God accepts the bet but asserts his belief that Faust will stay faithful, pointing out that while a man may make mistakes in his life, he is basically good.

A deadly deal

Moving the action to Earth with its contemporary German setting, Goethe introduces Faust, a learned professor, doctor, and theologian. Faust is sitting in his study in despair, feeling that he has reached the limit of his learning and that he is merely "a wretched fool, no wiser than I was before"; he even contemplates suicide. The devil appears and an agreement is made between the two: Mephistopheles agrees to fulfil Faust's wishes on Earth; in return Faust will serve the devil in hell. As part of the deal, Faust declares that if the devil can provide him with a moment that is so absolutely rewarding that he wishes to remain in it forever, then he will die at that precise moment. The pact is signed in blood.

Faust meets and is attracted to a young woman called Gretchen. With the devil's help, he seduces her, but what Faust hoped would bring happiness quickly turns to death and tragedy, and in this first part, Faust is denied fulfilment.

Faust: Part Two is the more complex part of the tragedy. It consists of five acts, each different from the others, which leap around

Schiller who insisted that Goethe should return to his work on *Faust*, a work he had begun in his 20s and later put to one side. The two men corresponded daily until Schiller's death in 1805, a date many critics take to be the end of Weimar Classicism.

A universe on stage

The story of Faust is based on many popular legends about pacts with the devil that circulated throughout Europe from the early 16th century onwards, and which had inspired Christopher Marlowe's 1604 play, *Doctor Faustus*, among others.

While earlier versions presented the Faust legend as a relatively simple contest between God and the devil, or between good and evil, Goethe's *Faust* is a more profound tale that moves beyond simple morality. Goethe argues that through living, doing, and striving humans may make mistakes, but that learning from these mistakes will lead them to righteousness.

Goethe starts his play (after a verse dedication) with a prologue. Here a director, a poet, and a clown discuss what characteristics are needed to make a good play. Each has his own agenda: the

director wishes to make a play that will draw in the crowds and be well received by its German audience; the poet is an idealist, trying to portray eternal values and make a work of integrity and inspiration – a masterpiece that will endure; and the clown wishes to entertain the audience through comedy and action. The three finally reach a compromise – the poet can create a play with profound meaning as long as it includes action, comedy, and tragedy. The discussion ends with a promise to the audience – that the whole universe, from heaven,via the world, to hell – will be presented on the stage.

Whoever strives,
in his endeavour,
We can rescue
from the devil.
Faust

between settings: real, magical, historical, and mythical. In effect Goethe, having explored Faust's personal small world in Part One, now places events in the wider world. Part Two introduces many fantastical, and often confusing, plot strands, such as the marriage of Faust to Helen of Troy (in Greek mythology, the most beautiful woman in the world).

A literary landmark

Faust typifies Weimar Classicism in its richness of classical allusion: the play's characters include gods, goddesses, and heroes from Greek mythology and settings from classical antiquity. It is written in a staggering array of literary styles, referencing Greek tragedies as well as mystery plays about biblical subjects, which were popular in the

Weimar's Courtyard of the Muses, painted by Theobald von Oer in 1860, depicts Goethe (right, hand on hip) opposite Schiller (reading, left), with Herder and Wieland seated behind.

Middle Ages. It takes inspiration from Renaissance masque and *commedia dell'arte* (a form of theatre from 17th-century Italy, in which actors improvised around stock characters), and makes use of a variety of poetic forms.

Faust is without question the greatest accomplishment of Weimar Classicism, yet it took such an astonishingly long time to complete, that by the time Part Two was published, a few months before Goethe's own death in 1832, the movement had long finished.

Faust did not exert a strong influence on the "next generation" of writers, since many had already published numerous works by the time of the play's appearance. Instead, German Romanticism (which ignored classical "balance") held sway across much of Europe. Despite its lack of contemporary influence, *Faust* went on to become one of the most famous and studied works of German literature, and is now considered one of the greatest plays ever written. ∎

Johann Wolfgang von Goethe

Born on 28 August 1749 in Frankfurt to a wealthy middle-class family, Goethe was not only a great writer and literary figure but also knowledgeable in many fields from law and philosophy through to botany, zoology, science, and medicine.

Goethe was home-tutored until 1765 when he was sent to Leipzig to study law. There he began to write lyric poetry and his first full-length plays. After graduation, he continued writing, establishing his reputation as an innovatory and outstanding writer.

In 1775 he was invited to take a position at the Weimar court, where he held public offices for 10 years. In 1786 he left for a two-year tour of Italy. From around 1794 he began a collaboration with Friedrich von Schiller that resulted in some sublime and influential literary and cultural work. He died on 22 March 1832.

Other key works

1773 *Götz von Berlichingen*
1774 *The Sorrows of Young Werther*
1795–96 *Wilhelm Meister's Apprenticeship*

ONCE UPON A TIME…

CHILDREN'S AND HOUSEHOLD TALES (1812–1822), BROTHERS GRIMM

IN CONTEXT

FOCUS
Folklore collections

BEFORE
c.1350–1410 Welsh stories based on oral tales are collected in the *Mabinogion*, the earliest prose literature of Britain.

1697 French author Charles Perrault writes *Tales of Mother Goose*, a collection of rewritten and original tales.

1782–87 German author Johann Karl August Musäus publishes a popular collection of satirical folk stories.

AFTER
1835–49 Finnish folklore is celebrated in the epic poem the *Kalevala* by Elias Lönnrot.

1841 *Norwegian Folktales*, by Peter Christen Asbjørnsen and Jørgen Moe, is published.

1979 *The Bloody Chamber*, by English novelist Angela Carter, challenges traditional folktale portrayals of women.

olklore collections that synthesize into a single written text cultural traditions such as fairy tales, oral history, and popular beliefs (as told in homes and at social gatherings) have been compiled since the Middle Ages. The term "fairy tale" was coined by French writer Madame d'Aulnoy in the late 17th century, but it is her contemporary Charles Perrault's retellings of old fairy tales that are better known. English antiquarian William Thoms first defined "folklore" in a letter to *The Athenaeum* magazine in 1846.

Some tales, such as the 14th-century Welsh *Mabinogion*, have a religious or spiritual function –

In olden days, when wishing still worked…
Children's and Household Tales

but folk stories do not usually contain references to religion. Real places, people, or events are not cited. Instead, these stories are ahistorical, existing "once upon a time…", and readers and audiences expect stock characters, random magic, reward and revenge, and a "happily ever after" ending. Poetic or literary references and realism are rarely used; fairy tales are written in a plain style, using mainly straightforward imagery, and plot is key: these stories power along with astonishing swiftness.

Enriching Western culture
The Brothers Grimm, like many folklorists since, embarked on a scholarly project to identify and preserve the spirit of the people by recording the fairy tales being told across their culture.

This was an epic romantic venture: interest in folklore was inspired by a rise in nationalism and cultural pride, and the purpose of the Grimms' collection was no different. Nor were they the only European scholars to undertake such an enterprise, and their peer group at university shared their enthusiasm for folk traditions. But the Grimms' work, as reflected in

See also: *One Thousand and One Nights* 44–45 ▪ *Fairy Tales* 151 ▪ *Kalevala* 151 ▪ *The Bloody Chamber* 332

their *Children's and Household Tales*, represents the greatest body of stories collected in Europe and is the most widely translated and read. W H Auden declared Grimms' tales "among the few common-property books upon which Western culture can be founded".

The methodology for gathering stories did not include sorties into the woods, as is often picturesquely believed. The Grimms' sources generally came to them, and some stories were already written down, such as "The Juniper Tree", sent to them by painter Philip Otto Runge.

In their first edition, the Grimms wrote for a mainly adult audience. It was only after Edgar Taylor's English translation of their work in 1823 was successful with children that they made revisions to sanitize the German stories. For example, their first version of "Rapunzel" openly referred to her pregnancy (outside marriage), but in the revised version she simply fattens. Yet violence was not necessarily minimized. The French Cinderella, Cendrillon, in Charles Perrault's tale, forgives her stepsisters and finds good husbands for them. But in the Grimms' punitive version, Cinderella's helper-birds blind the sisters by pecking out their eyes.

Violence notwithstanding, the popularity of the Grimms' collected tales has endured, and they have sustained multiple interpretations and rewrites in various media over the years. The romantic depiction of "Once upon a time" continues to manifest inextinguishable truths, which, along with the allure of a happy and harmonious ending, appeal across the generations. ∎

Jacob Grimm and Wilhelm Grimm

Known as the Brothers Grimm, Jacob (1785–1863) and Wilhelm (1786–1859) were celebrated German academics, cultural researchers, linguists, and lexicographers.

The oldest surviving sons of a family of six children, they were raised in Hanau, Hesse. Despite poverty following the death of their lawyer father, they were educated at the University of Marburg, thanks to a well-connected aunt.

The Grimms are credited with developing an early methodology for collecting folk stories that is now the basis of folklore studies. They were also notable philologists (studying the language in written historical sources). Both brothers also worked on a monumental (32-volume) German dictionary, which was unfinished in their lifetimes.

Other key works

1813–16 *Old German Forests*
1815 *Poor Heinrich by Hartmann von der Aue*
1815 *Songs from the Elder Edda*
1816–18 *German Sagas*
1852–1960 *German Dictionary*

Archetypal characters in folklore

The magical helper		In the Grimms' version, Cinderella weeps by her mother's grave, marked by a hazel tree that then gives her an outfit to go to the ball (Perrault has a fairy godmother instead of the tree).
The wicked stepmother		These characters were mothers in the Grimms' early versions: the sanctity of motherhood was preserved by changing the texts to "stepmother".
The witch or sorceress		This archetype creates opportunities for shifts in plot and for the triggering of magical but often terrible events.
The trickster		This archetype creates menace and obstacles in a story to challenge the natural order.
The transformed animal		Grimms' tales are littered with characters that have been transformed into birds and other animals and that might become human again under the right circumstances.

FOR WHAT DO WE LIVE, BUT TO MAKE SPORT FOR OUR NEIGHBOURS, AND LAUGH AT THEM IN OUR TURN?
PRIDE AND PREJUDICE (1813), JANE AUSTEN

IN CONTEXT

FOCUS
The novel of manners

BEFORE
1740 English author Samuel Richardson's *Pamela* is a story about a servant girl climbing the social ranks; it is considered to be an early novel of manners.

AFTER
1847 *Jane Eyre*, by Charlotte Brontë, critiques Victorian class divisions and prejudice, as well as the constricting expectations faced by women.

1847–48 The duplicity and dishonesty of society life are satirized via the exploits of Becky Sharp in *Vanity Fair*, by English novelist William Makepeace Thackeray.

1905 An American novel of manners, Edith Wharton's *The House of Mirth* reflects the social, economic, and moral constraints that are placed on women.

The early to mid-18th century saw the rise of the novel and, a little later, the development of Romanticism in literature. By the close of the 18th century, however, a new genre had emerged in England – the novel of manners, which moved away from the excesses of emotion and flights of fancy common to Romanticism. Instead, it placed emphasis on the beliefs, manners, and social structures of particular groups of people. These novels were often dominated by women – both as authors and as protagonists – and for this reason were sometimes wrongly dismissed as trivial.

A lady's imagination is very rapid; it jumps from admiration to love, from love to matrimony in a moment.
Pride and Prejudice

Jane Austen's novels are the prime examples of such literature, gently satirizing the social mores of the English country gentry, as well as poking fun at the overindulgent drama of Gothic Romanticism. Austen highlights the vulgarities and follies of the English upper classes: the importance of rank, the stigma of social inferiority, and the system of patronage are played out via balls, visits, and society gossip.

Social ups and downs
In *Pride and Prejudice*, the reader follows the Bennet sisters in their quest for an eligible bachelor. For women, a good marriage was key to maintaining or improving one's social status. The novel is told mainly through the eyes of its principal character, Elizabeth Bennet (Austen's own favourite among her heroines), a good and well-intentioned young woman. She is one of the five daughters of the intelligent but put-upon Mr Bennet, a country gentleman, and his pushy, vulgar wife; their own marriage being a perfect example of how not to do it.

Elizabeth meets the aristocratic Fitzwilliam Darcy, who is drawn to her despite himself; however, she

See also: *Jane Eyre 128–31* ▪ *Vanity Fair 153* ▪ *North and South 153* ▪ *Middlemarch 182–83*

Fanny Price (*Mansfield Park*) is undervalued by the family she lives with.

Emma Woodhouse (*Emma*) is a matchmaker who is oblivious to people's feelings.

Elinor Dashwood (*Sense and Sensibility*) is unable to display her emotions.

The lives of Austen's heroines are influenced and often circumscribed by their social class and the customs of their time. Austen draws each individual character in a nuanced way.

Catherine Morland (*Northanger Abbey*) believes herself to be a Gothic heroine.

Marianne Dashwood (*Sense and Sensibility*) displays her emotions too freely.

Anne Elliot (*Persuasion*) is thrown into confusion when her old love reappears.

finds his haughty pride and his supercilious behaviour offensive. He is contrasted with his equally wealthy but unaffected friend, Bingley, who takes a liking to Elizabeth's older sister, Jane. Yet when the flighty younger sister, Lydia, scandalously elopes with the dashing officer George Wickham, threatening to disgrace the entire family, it is Darcy who unexpectedly steps in to help. Elizabeth's pride, prejudice, and inexperience lead her to make errors of judgement (concerning both Wickham and Darcy) that she must pay for, but

through these trials, she grows into a mature adult. Darcy, similarly, has to grow out of his own pride to prove he is a worthy match for her, in spite of his higher social class.

Indeed, through the use of subtle wit and irony, Austen makes clear that good breeding does not necessarily equate with good manners (although good manners may well be indicative of good morals). While the landscape of *Pride and Prejudice* might appear to be narrow, it nevertheless keenly probes the manners and morals of its day. ∎

Jane Austen

The daughter of a relatively prosperous country parson, Jane Austen was born in Steventon rectory, Hampshire, England, in 1775, the seventh of eight children. As a child she read voraciously, having access to her father's library, which was uncommon for girls at the time. She started writing in her early teens, producing an embryonic version of *Pride and Prejudice*, entitled *First Impressions*, between 1796 and 1797. In 1800 her father decided to retire and the family moved to Bath; Jane was unhappy there. In 1809 she moved to Chawton, Hampshire, with her mother and sister, where she wrote daily. It was her observations of genteel life in Hampshire that furnished her novels. Despite writing a great deal about marriage, she never married herself, although she did receive a proposal. She died in 1817, at the age of 41.

Other key works

1811 *Sense and Sensibility*
1814 *Mansfield Park*
1815 *Emma*
1818 *Northanger Abbey*
1818 *Persuasion*

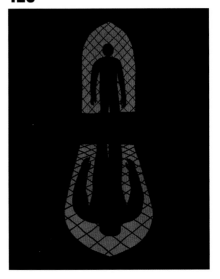

WHO SHALL CONCEIVE THE HORRORS OF MY SECRET TOIL

FRANKENSTEIN (1818), MARY SHELLEY

Gothic fiction established its main themes in the late 18th century, years before the publication of Mary Shelley's *Frankenstein*. Works such as Horace Walpole's *The Castle of Otranto*, Ann Radcliffe's *The Mysteries of Udolpho*, and E T A Hoffmann's *Nachtstücke*, set out the key elements of the genre. In these books, exiles roam sublime foreign landscapes, or are trapped in ruined castles in nightmarish tales of abuse, tyranny, and murder.

At the heart of early Gothic fiction was a combination of Romantic preoccupations with the power of the mind, the limits of the imagination, and contemporary social questions, coupled with Gothic tropes of evil aristocratic villains, gory deaths, and gloomy medieval settings. This mixture was frequently embodied in beings such as vampires, ghosts, monsters, and terrifying and mysterious female figures.

In *Frankenstein*, Mary Shelley expanded on these elements, linking them to wider philosophical debates, and forever changing the Gothic genre in the process. The inspiration for the novel came from conversations she had with, among others, the English Romantic poets Percy Bysshe Shelley and Lord Byron. One evening, the group told stories around the fire, as a storm raged outside. Byron suggested they devise ghost stories, and Mary Shelley's imagination was stirred.

An unsettling age
Although the stormy origins of *Frankenstein* are perhaps fitting, the novel is much more than a simple tale of terror. One of Shelley's most significant contributions to the Gothic genre is her ability to expand on the stock themes of persecution, threat, and monstrous hauntings into a more

A flash of lightning illuminated the object ... it was the wretch, the filthy daemon, to whom I had given life.
Frankenstein

See also: *Doctor Faustus* 75 ▪ *Nachtstücke* 111 ▪ *Faust* 112–15 ▪ *Wuthering Heights* 132–37 ▪ *The Picture of Dorian Gray* 194 ▪ *Dracula* 195

Elements of Gothic

Gloomy settings		Crumbling castles, dark forests, mysterious towers, wild and remote places, graveyards, and tombs.
Stock characters		The villainous tyrant, the maiden in distress, madwomen and maniacs, the femme fatale, and the evil monk or nun.
Foreboding signs		Omens, portents, visions, dreams, storms, and full moons.
The supernatural		Ghosts, monsters, inexplicable events, vampires, or werewolves.
Overwrought emotions		Terror, madness, mental anguish, fury, passion, curiosity, or screaming.

sophisticated exploration of one of the key Romantic preoccupations of the period: the alienated individual in the modern world.

A fable for the times

The title name of Frankenstein refers not to the infamous monster, but to Victor Frankenstein, the novel's protagonist – the scientist, artist, and creator of the unnamed creature whom he describes as "the demoniacal corpse to which I had so miserably given life". Frankenstein is a solitary creative genius, whose "secret" horror stems from within, as he overreaches the ethical laws of humankind in typical Romantic fashion. Through him, Shelley reworks the Gothic theme of monstrosity in the form of the idealized persona of the exiled or wandering outsider. As scholar David Punter suggests, the book focuses on "rejection of the strange, at both social and psychological levels". *Frankenstein*'s monster is a product of the moment of his creation in the new and unsettling age of industrialization and of the author's negotiation of the political and social upheaval of the time.

The horror of *Frankenstein* lies not with its monster but rather – in its melding of key Gothic tropes of haunting, exile, and isolation – with the anxieties of the period that so preoccupied the Romantics, such as questions about religion versus science; philosophies of justice; debates about the origins of life; and the role of education, culture, and nurture in shaping identity.

Frankenstein's downfall through his own monstrous creation is the ultimate modern fable, cleverly wrapping moral and social issues in the guise of Gothic terror. ▪

Mary Shelley

The birth of novelist Mary Wollstonecraft Shelley on 30 August 1797 in London, England, was closely followed by the death of her mother, the feminist author Mary Wollstonecraft, 11 days later. Her father was the radical philosopher William Godwin.

At the age of 14, Shelley was sent to live in Scotland. In 1814 she returned to her (remarried) father's London home and met the young poet Percy Bysshe Shelley. He was already married, but the pair eloped to Europe and wed in 1816. It was a loving but tragic union: only one of their four children survived, and in 1822 Percy drowned. Mary wrote until her death in 1851. She is best remembered for her novel *Frankenstein*, which she began drafting in 1816, during happier times with her husband and their circle of close friends.

Other key works

1817 *History of a Six Weeks' Tour*
1819 *Mathilda*
1826 *The Last Man*
1830 *The Fortunes of Perkin Warbeck*
1835 *Lodore*

ALL FOR ONE, ONE FOR ALL

THE THREE MUSKETEERS (1844), ALEXANDRE DUMAS

IN CONTEXT

FOCUS
The historical novel

BEFORE
1800 Anglo-Irish writer Maria Edgeworth's *Castle Rackrent* is in the vanguard of a fashion for historical fiction.

1814 *Waverley*, by Scottish writer Walter Scott, is the first in a series of historical novels that includes *Rob Roy* (1817) and *Ivanhoe* (1820).

1823–41 US author James Fenimore Cooper writes his "Leatherstocking Tales", historical fictions that include *The Pioneers* (1823) and *The Last of the Mohicans* (1826).

AFTER
1829 Honoré de Balzac's *The Chouans* tells of the 1799 royalist uprising in France.

1989 Gabriel García Márquez's *The General in His Labyrinth* is a postmodern historical novel about Simon Bolivar, "Liberator of South America".

Although the idea of setting a novel in a previous period of history was not a new one – fictional tales of the past are as old as literature itself – the historical novel as a distinct genre achieved unprecedented popularity in the 19th century. Demand came first in Britain, and was stimulated by the novels of the Scottish writer Sir Walter Scott, which appeared between 1814 and 1832. These had a huge readership, in Britain and abroad, and their success inspired a wave of similarly themed novels.

By the 1820s, the influence of Scott's novels in particular had spread as far as the USA, where James Fenimore Cooper wrote the popular "Leatherstocking Tales".

Never fear quarrels, but seek hazardous adventures.
The Three Musketeers

Translations of British historical fiction were also creating a market for the genre across Europe, notably in France, where it was taken up by writers such as Victor Hugo and Honoré de Balzac. The most popular of the French historical authors, however, was Alexandre Dumas.

A thirst for adventure

The first of Dumas' novels, *The Three Musketeers*, appeared in serial form in 1844, and almost immediately made him a household name. The novel contained all the ingredients of the popular fiction of the time: dashing, romantic heroes and wily villains; plots involving derring-do and camaraderie; and the backdrop of a period that was well known to its readers for political intrigue.

At the time of the book's publication, France had undergone a turbulent period post-Revolution: tensions between monarchists and republicans were unresolved, and the romantic depiction of a fictionalized past appealed to those yearning for a more settled time.

At the heart of Dumas' story is d'Artagnan, a young nobleman who leaves his home in Gascony to join the Musketeers of the Guard in

See also: *Ivanhoe* 150 ▪ *The Last of the Mohicans* 150 ▪ *Les Misérables* 166–67 ▪ *War and Peace* 178–81 ▪ *A Tale of Two Cities* 198

Alexandre Dumas

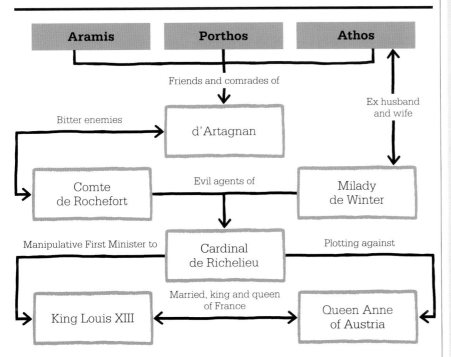

The Musketeers of the Guard, a brotherhood of bodyguards, are the focal point of a story that combines international politics, courtly intrigue, friendship, enmity, and romantic entanglements: a historical tale with timeless themes that guarantee its enduring popularity.

Paris, in 1623. Through a series of misadventures, his ambition is thwarted, but he ends up first duelling with, and then befriending, the three musketeers of the title, Athos, Porthos, and Aramis. Together they embark on a series of missions to save the honour of the queen, and to ensure that the king is not hoodwinked by the machinations of First Minister Cardinal de Richelieu into a war with the English. Along the way, there is much carousing, and inevitable romantic liaisons.

Beneath the swashbuckling, however, Dumas makes some serious points, and is critical in his portrayal of the period. His musketeer heroes are brave and attractive, but show a blind allegiance to the monarchy, and are not always gentlemanly in their treatment of others. And the object of their loyalty, King Louis XIII, is portrayed as gullible and weak: he is ruthlessly manipulated by the cardinal and his agents, the Comte de Rochefort and Milady de Winter.

The instalments of the story were eagerly awaited by the French public in the summer of 1844, and were translated widely. Building on this success, Dumas serialized two further "d'Artagnan Romances", *Twenty Years After* and *The Vicomte of Bragelonne*, and the similarly styled *The Count of Monte Cristo*, all of which have remained popular, both in their original novel form and as adaptations for television and the cinema. ▪

Alexandre Dumas was born Alexandre Davy de la Pailleterie in Picardy, France, in 1802. His father was the son of the governor of Saint-Domingue (now Haiti) and an Afro-Caribbean slave woman, Marie-Cessette Dumas.

Like his father, Alexandre later adopted the surname of his grandmother, but it was his aristocratic ancestry that helped to launch his career as a writer. He found work with the Duke of Orléans (who later became the "Citizen King" Louis-Philippe), and after initial success with historical drama, turned to writing novels. These included the adventures of d'Artagnan, for which he became famous. When Louis-Philippe was deposed, Dumas fled France in 1851 and did not return until 1864.

Dumas had many affairs, and is said to have fathered at least four children, including a son Alexandre, who also became a writer and is often known as *fils* (son).

Other key works

1845 *Twenty Years After*
1847–50 *The Vicomte of Bragelonne*

BUT HAPPINESS I NEVER AIMED FOR, IT IS A STRANGER TO MY SOUL

EUGENE ONEGIN (1833), ALEXANDER PUSHKIN

IN CONTEXT

FOCUS
The superfluous man

BEFORE
1812–24 English poet Lord Byron's characters Childe Harold and Don Juan are the precursors of the superfluous man in Russian literature.

AFTER
1840 Mikhail Lermontov's only novel, *A Hero of Our Time*, builds on the superfluous man theme with its hero Grigory Pechorin, a Byronic figure desperate for activity that will stave off his world-weariness.

1850 In the figure of the Hamlet-like Tchulkaturin, Ivan Turgenev's novella *The Diary of a Superfluous Man* further develops the idea of the idealistic, inactive man.

1859 Idle dreamer Oblamov, in Ivan Goncharov's novel of the same name, epitomizes the laziness and inertia of the superfluous man's character.

Like the main protagonist in *Eugene Onegin*, Alexander Pushkin (1799–1837) was killed in a duel. In spite of this early end to his career, he is considered to be Russia's greatest poet. His work was extremely influential, particularly his masterpiece *Eugene Onegin*, whose eponymous hero established the concept and character of "the superfluous man".

A disillusioned individual, often born into wealth and privilege, the superfluous man regards the society around him with boredom, cynicism, and lack of interest, at the same time feeling himself to be morally and intellectually superior.

A life unfulfilled

Set in imperial Russia during the 1820s, *Eugene Onegin* is written in the form of "a novel in verse", as Pushkin called it. It follows the life and destiny of Eugene Onegin, a bored landowning man about town; his friend Vladimir Lensky, a young, romantic dreamer; and the beautiful and intelligent Tatyana Larina and her vain and flirtatious sister, Olga. Tatyana falls in love with Onegin, but is rejected by him because he does not want "life restricted to living in domestic bliss". Unable or unwilling to prevent tragedy, he fights a duel with Lensky, leaves his estate for some years, and returns to find that Tatyana has married someone else.

Lonely destiny

Writing in a lively and often ironic tone, Pushkin not only describes the lives of his main characters, but also introduces a large cast of other individuals. He realistically depicts scenes from Russian life and there are numerous wide-ranging literary references and philosophical observations, some satirizing the society of the time.

At the end, Eugene Onegin, who has spent most of his life distancing himself from those around him, is left regretting his lonely destiny. Pushkin's superfluous man was adopted by other writers and embedded as a recurring motif in much Russian literature of the 1840s and 1850s. ∎

See also: *Tristram Shandy* 104–05 ∎ *A Hero of Our Time* 151

LET YOUR SOUL STAND COOL AND COMPOSED BEFORE A MILLION UNIVERSES
LEAVES OF GRASS (1855), WALT WHITMAN

IN CONTEXT

FOCUS
Transcendentalism

BEFORE
1840 Author and literary critic Margaret Fuller and essayist and poet Ralph Waldo Emerson become founding editors of the Transcendentalist journal *The Dial*, publishing on literature, philosophy, and religion.

1850 Emerson, spokesman of Transcendentalism, proposes a "general mind" that expresses itself through the lives of geniuses such as Plato and Shakespeare.

1854 The rewards of a simple life in nature are described in *Walden; or a Life in the Woods* by Henry David Thoreau.

AFTER
1861–65 The great US poet Emily Dickinson enjoys her most prolific period. Her poems have Transcendentalist overtones mixed with a fear of cosmic immensities.

The Transcendentalist movement thrived in the USA in the mid-19th century, inspired by German philosopher Immanuel Kant's idea that knowledge is concerned "not with objects, but our mode of knowing objects". This fusion of the intellectual and metaphysical – combined with a celebration of physicality, sexuality, and nature – characterized the work of the US poet Walt Whitman (1819–92) and other Transcendentalist writers.

In praise of body and spirit
Whitman's collection *Leaves of Grass* contains poems such as "I Sing the Body Electric", where, at the same time as revering the soul, he displays a desire to liberate Americans from shame about the body, to foster egalitarian instincts, and to promote human connection. "Song of Myself" is a eulogy to all of humanity, in which the poet imagines himself returned to the cycles of nature. With the hypnotic rhythm of his verse, Whitman revels in the senses: "I will go to the bank by the wood and become undisguised and naked, / I am mad for it to be in contact with me."

Whitman delighted in nature and its cycles, in which, for him, God was self-evidently present. He shared a conviction with the poet Emerson that humankind was innately good, and this became a hallmark of Transcendentalism. Later poems in the book, such as "A Noiseless Patient Spider", also show a mystic fascination with the "measureless oceans of space". ■

This is the grass that grows wherever the land is and the water is, / This the common air that bathes the globe.
"Song of Myself"

See also: *Lyrical Ballads* 110

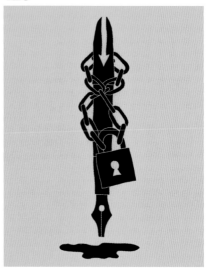

YOU HAVE SEEN HOW A MAN WAS MADE A SLAVE; YOU SHALL SEE HOW A SLAVE WAS MADE A MAN

NARRATIVE OF THE LIFE OF FREDERICK DOUGLASS (1845), FREDERICK DOUGLASS

IN CONTEXT

FOCUS
Slave narratives

BEFORE
1789 *The Interesting Narrative of the Life of Olaudah Equiano, or Gustavus Vassa, the African* is published in England; it is narrated by an enslaved boy from Benin (now Nigeria).

AFTER
1853 Solomon Northup's autobiographical *Twelve Years a Slave* contrasts the lives of free blacks in the North and enslaved blacks in the South of the USA.

1861 In *Incidents in the Life of a Slave Girl*, ex-slave Harriet Jacobs focuses on the experiences of slave women.

1979 In Octavia E Butler's novel *Kindred*, a neo-slave narrative, the main character time-travels between present-day California and pre-Civil War Maryland, USA.

n the decades leading up to the US Civil War (1861–65), around four million slaves were held in the Southern states of the USA, while abolitionists in the North campaigned to bring an end to the inhuman practice of slavery. In 1841 Frederick Douglass – a mixed-race slave who had escaped north – was invited to address an Anti-Slavery Society meeting in Massachusetts, and was found to be a powerful orator for the cause. He went on to chronicle his life in a book that sold 5,000 copies within four months of its publication in

It was new, dirty, and hard work for me; but I went at it with a glad heart and a willing hand. I was now my own master.
Narrative of the Life of Frederick Douglass

1845 and created the template for the slave narrative genre in American literature.

Douglass asked in the book, "How is a man made a slave?". He told how he was removed from his slave mother within a year of his birth. Always hungry and cold, he saw overseers whipping male workers for the smallest excuse. He witnessed slaves murdered for disobedience; the young Frederick became aware that "killing a slave or a colored person … is not treated as a crime, either by the courts or the community".

Literature as liberation
Published by the Anti-Slavery Office, and prefaced by two leading abolitionists, *Narrative of the Life of Frederick Douglass, an American Slave* was crafted in part to suit the needs of the abolitionist cause. In eloquent, compelling text laced with biblical imagery, the fugitive slave debunked myths peddled by the South, such as the ineducable character of blacks and the benign nature of slave-holding. Christianity in the South, he concluded, was "a mere covering for the most horrid crimes, a justifier of the most appalling barbarity…".

See also: *Uncle Tom's Cabin* 153 ▪ *The Adventures of Huckleberry Finn* 188–89 ▪ *Invisible Man* 259 ▪ *Beloved* 306–09

As his story gradually unfolds, Douglass asks "How is a slave made into a man?". He answers this question by writing himself into existence in a picaresque coming-of-age tale. As a boy, Frederick was taught to read and write by a mistress and quickly grasped the power of literacy to both expose injustice and unlock a future self. Although he was denied further teaching, he enlisted poor white boys and fellow workers as teachers. A turning-point came when, aged 16, he won a fight with a brutal overseer: there is a strong sense of self-discovery in the rest of the story of his growing into a man.

Lasting influence

After the US Civil War, interest in slave narratives declined. However, the language and sentiment of the writing resurfaced in the rhetoric of activists such as Martin Luther King during the Civil Rights campaigns of the mid-20th century. Stories told by slaves then became central to black studies, and to the canon of American literature. ▪

The writing of narratives by slaves had a dual effect: as well as furthering the cause of the abolitionists, the texts marked the beginning of a uniquely African-American literature.

Writing the truth
Fugitive slaves escaping to the North have poignant stories to tell that reveal the injustice and brutality of their lives.

Propaganda
These widely read narratives are powerful propaganda for the abolitionist and anti-slavery societies.

Finding a voice
The stories give an empowering voice and history to people silenced by slavery.

Frederick Douglass

The son of Harriet Bailey and an unnamed white man, Frederick Augustus Washington Bailey was born into slavery in Maryland in February 1818. At the age of 20 he escaped to New York and married Anna Murray, a free black woman. They had five children.

Moving to Massachusetts, Frederick adopted the name Douglass to avoid capture, and spoke regularly at abolitionist meetings. He lectured in Great Britain, where friends raised funds for his release from slavery in Baltimore in 1846. Douglass settled in New York, where he published newspapers, assisted fugitive slaves, and recruited black troops for the Union cause. After the death of his wife, he married Helen Pitts, a white editor and feminist. Douglass became US Marshall for the District of Columbia and Consul General for Haiti. He died in Washington, DC, in 1895.

Other key works

1855 *My Bondage and My Freedom*
1881 *Life and Times of Frederick Douglass* (revised 1892)

I AM NO BIRD; AND NO NET ENSNARES ME

JANE EYRE (1847), CHARLOTTE BRONTË

IN CONTEXT

FOCUS
Victorian feminism

AFTER
1847 Emily Brontë publishes *Wuthering Heights*, exploring feminist issues of gender, domesticity, and women's status in Victorian society.

1853 Charlotte Brontë's *Villette* is published. It is considered a more mature reworking of her earlier themes of women's self-determination, identity, and independence.

1860 George Eliot's *The Mill on the Floss* contrasts themes of female intellectual growth with notions of family duty.

1892 Charlotte Perkins Gilman publishes her short story "The Yellow Wallpaper", an early example of US feminist literature that shows women's mental health in relation to patriarchal oppression.

When *Jane Eyre* was first published in 1847, it was credited to Currer Bell, a pseudonym used by Charlotte Brontë to conceal her gender (the work of women writers was often considered by critics to be second-rate). The book was also subtitled *An Autobiography*, signalling that it had borrowed from the 19th-century German Bildungsroman genre (the "novel of formation"). In these coming-of-age stories, readers typically followed protagonists through their lives from childhood to adulthood as they overcame obstacles to reach maturity. Significantly, the development of selfhood and

See also: *Wuthering Heights* 132–37 ▪ *Middlemarch* 182–83 ▪ *The Magic Mountain* 224–27 ▪ *Wide Sargasso Sea* 290

Haddon Hall, a picturesque medieval manor house in Derbyshire, England, has been used as the fictional setting of Thornfield Hall for two film adaptations of *Jane Eyre*.

identity was often explored through male characters because at that time women were not generally thought to possess the same depth. What makes *Jane Eyre* radical for its time is that it assumes that women have a complex interior the equal of men's, rather than merely being superficial exteriors defined by their beauty alone.

Character development

Brontë's plain, passionate, and intelligent heroine enlists her readers to follow her emotional development and her relationships, and through these to sympathize and empathize with the plight of women of her class and the inequalities in the lives of young girls and women. Unlike many contemporary male authors who presented female characters as general figures of aesthetic beauty or morality, there is no distanced contemplation of Jane as a "type" in the novel.

The book tells the story of Jane Eyre, from her childhood as an orphan in the care of her aunt and her education at a charity boarding school, Lowood Institution, to her employment as a governess at a country house, Thornfield Hall. Brontë presents Jane as a complex, three-dimensional human being, and her readers are emotionally invested in her, from her childhood abuse to the later injustices of her lack of freedom and independence. These are expressed in numerous memorable passages that link Jane's wish for liberty and her restlessness with the language of revolt and rebellion.

At Thornfield Hall, Jane meets (and falls in love with) the owner, the mysterious Mr Rochester. She becomes embroiled in his complex affairs – in particular, with his insane first wife, Bertha Mason, who is imprisoned in the attic of the house. Unable to marry Rochester, Jane leaves Thornfield. »

Charlotte Brontë

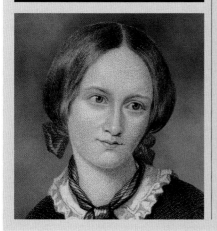

Born on 21 April 1816 in Yorkshire, England, Charlotte Brontë was the third daughter of the Reverend Patrick Brontë and his wife Maria Branwell. In 1824, she and her elder sisters, Maria and Elizabeth, were sent to a boarding school, where poor conditions resulted in a typhoid outbreak. Charlotte blamed this for the early death of Maria and Elizabeth and used her experiences at the school as the basis for Lowood in *Jane Eyre*.

Charlotte worked as a governess and teacher. Her first novel, *The Professor*, was rejected and only published posthumously. The immediate success of *Jane Eyre* in 1847 was soon followed by tragedy, when first her brother Patrick and then her two remaining sisters, Emily and Anne, died. Of the six Brontë children, Charlotte was the lone survivor. She married Reverend A B Nicholls in 1854, and died during childbirth in March the following year.

Other key works

1849 *Shirley*
1853 *Villette*
1857 *The Professor*

Some feminists view Bertha Mason – the deranged, imprisoned wife of Edward Rochester,
Jane Eyre's employer – as a metaphorical reflection of Jane and her own status in society.
Bertha Mason is Jane's antagonist, but can be considered her psychological Gothic double,
a feminist version of Robert Louis Stevenson's Jekyll and Hyde.

Jane hears voices.

Jane has been taught to repress expressions of her emotions as a child and young woman.

Jane reacts "like a mad cat" on being locked in a room as a child by her aunt.

Jane is imprisoned within the domestic household.

Bertha is considered to be mad.

Bertha enacts her rage, turbulent emotions, and passions.

Bertha growls "like some strange wild animal".

Bertha is literally imprisoned.

Jane Eyre   Bertha Mason

At first she is penniless, but fate restores her fortunes, and draws her back to Rochester.

Domestic slavery

Jane Eyre's compelling story is far more than an English Bildungsroman. Brontë infused the work with the anti-slavery and revolutionary rhetoric that she and her sisters had read in many 19th-century political tracts. In *Jane Eyre*, this political language is not used in reference to humanity in general, but with specific regard to middle-class women in Victorian society and the domestic constraints placed upon their lives. In one of the most passionate passages of the novel, Jane tells her readers that women "suffer from too rigid a restraint, too absolute a stagnation, precisely as men would suffer; and it is narrow-minded in their more privileged fellow-creatures to say that they ought to confine themselves to making puddings and knitting stockings, to playing on the piano and embroidering bags." This plea for equality among the sexes runs throughout the novel as Jane Eyre progressively builds a case for women's need for liberty, independence, and action.

These feminist aspects of the novel did not go unnoticed by Brontë's contemporaries. While many early reviews praised the novel, some criticized its radical content and "unfeminine" view of womanhood. Jane Eyre, however, quickly became one of the most influential literary heroines of her time. After the publication of the novel a new type of female protagonist was apparent in Victorian literature – a plain, rebellious, and intelligent one. She offered a counterpart to the passive, sweet, pretty, and domestic heroines who were usually championed by male authors such as Charles Dickens and William Makepeace Thackeray.

Female spaces

Jane Eyre opened the door for other female writers of the period to explore the limitations of women's lives and their desire for equality. It was a theme that was apparent in many of the great Victorian stories. George Eliot's *Middlemarch*, for example, criticizes patriarchy and its moral weaknesses, and brings the frustration of women's ambitions into focus. The reality of domestic responsibility dictating women's lives, which Brontë introduced into the Victorian novel through her own evocative use of domestic spaces in *Jane Eyre*, continued to haunt women writers throughout the 19th century.

Many feminist readings of *Jane Eyre* focus on key spaces such as specific rooms, windows, and the infamous attic at Thornfield Hall in which Jane's love interest, Edward Rochester, locks up his first "mad" wife. The domestic sphere is intimately linked with the female body and the female self, and for this reason, much women's fiction of the time is riddled with details of domesticity. Feminist critics have argued that these are the natural fictional manifestations of women reacting to the strict boundaries and gender ideologies of the time.

Madness and savagery

Jane is a woman who wants more than the predefined life of a Victorian woman, and reacts against her domestic confines as a prison from which she must escape. At a turbulent moment in their relationship, Rochester calls Jane a "resolute wild free thing", noting that "Whatever I do with its cage, I cannot get at it – the savage beautiful creature!". His description of Jane as a "savage" creature in a cage could also be a description of his first wife, Bertha, who is literally caged in the attic of his home. Bertha's madness is a manifestation of the limitations that were placed on women's lives and it mirrors Jane's sense of imprisonment throughout her life. Bertha is the most extreme and literal depiction of what happens to 19th-century women when they

Women are supposed to be very calm generally: but women feel just as men feel; they need exercise for their faculties and a field for their efforts as much as their brothers do.
Jane Eyre

marry and lose their identity; she is not just a metaphor or mirror for Jane's constraint and rage but also represents the "madness" of being restricted in life.

Later authors produced more explicitly feminist interpretations of Bertha's predicament. When the US writer Charlotte Perkins Gilman published her feminist short story "The Yellow Wallpaper" in 1892, she developed Brontë's representation of Bertha's insanity by calling into question the medical and cultural

oppression of women within a patriarchal society. In her widely acclaimed 1966 novel *Wide Sargasso Sea*, Dominica-born British author Jean Rhys would go on to tell Bertha's story from another perspective: Bertha (originally named Antoinette), a Creole woman in colonial Jamaica, marries an Englishman and is taken by him to England, where she is trapped in an oppressive patriarchal society, losing her identity and becoming mad.

Not mad but trapped

From a feminist perspective, Jane's double is not "mad" but is forbidden her freedom – like all other women. In this context, Jane's passionate comment to Rochester that "I am no bird; and no net ensnares me: I am a free human being with an independent will" becomes a poignant reminder of the social nets that trapped women in the 19th century, inducing a psychological madness within them. When Brontë wrote *Jane Eyre* she, perhaps unwittingly, created not one but two feminist icons: Jane herself, and the "Madwoman in the Attic". ∎

The Madwoman in the Attic

The most famous feminist interpretation of *Jane Eyre* is *The Madwoman in the Attic* by US scholars Sandra M Gilbert and Susan Gubar. Published in 1979, this influential book borrows its title from *Jane Eyre* and examines Brontë's novel alongside the works of other female writers of the era, including Jane Austen, Mary Shelley, Emily Brontë, George Eliot, Elizabeth Barrett Browning, Christina Rossetti, and Emily Dickinson.

A major theme in their analysis is that of the concept of "madness" in relation to the emotional, psychological, and physical confinement of women in the 19th century.

The authors argue that 19th-century women were represented by male writers as either angels or monsters; women writers expressed their anxieties about these stereotypes by depicting their own female characters as either submissive or entirely mad.

I CANNOT LIVE WITHOUT MY LIFE! I CANNOT LIVE WITHOUT MY SOUL!

WUTHERING HEIGHTS (1847),
EMILY BRONTË

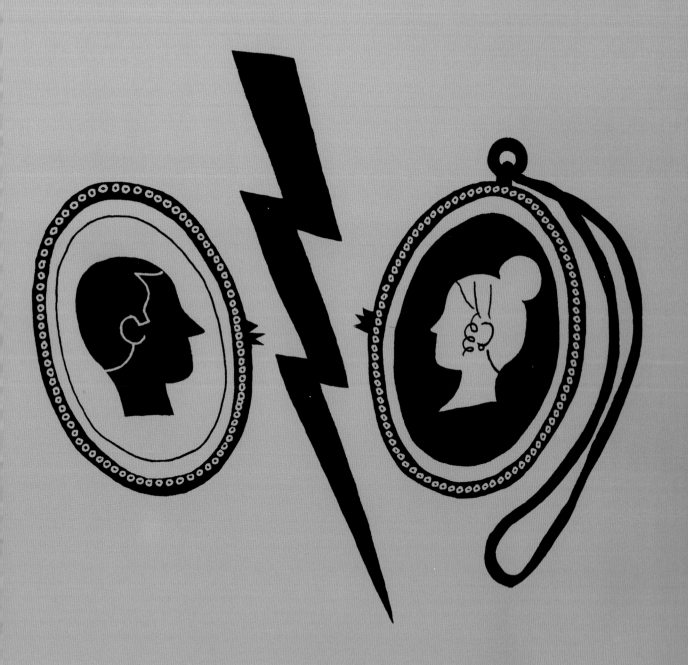

IN CONTEXT

FOCUS
Victorian Gothic

BEFORE
1837–39 Charles Dickens'
Oliver Twist shifts the gloomy
atmosphere of early Gothic
fiction to the streets of London.

1840 Edgar Allan Poe writes
stories of intense relationships
mixed with Gothic themes of
unsettling, crumbling houses;
ghosts; and corpses coming
back to life.

1847 Charlotte Brontë's *Jane
Eyre* is published: its themes
of Gothic domestic abuse and
confinement are mirrored in
Wuthering Heights.

AFTER
1852–53 Charles Dickens
writes *Bleak House* and
reworks the ruined Gothic
castle of earlier fiction as the
slum tenements of London in
the development of the
Victorian urban Gothic.

E mily Brontë's *Wuthering
Heights* is considered
one of the most famous
love stories in Western culture.
This is, however, a questionable
assessment: while the intense
but doomed affair between its two
main characters, Catherine and
Heathcliff, is certainly captivating,
readers soon discover that – rather
than romance – the novel presents
a tale of violence, haunting, and
abuse. In this book, Emily Brontë
expands and reworks Gothic
themes in a way that exposes
Victorian concerns about gender,
class, poverty, and domesticity.

Myth on the moors

The story told in the novel is one
of revenge, dependence, and
passionate longing, centred on the
manor called Wuthering Heights,
set in the harsh landscape of the
Yorkshire moors. It follows the life
of the antihero, Heathcliff, an
orphan adopted from the streets of
Liverpool by the Earnshaw family.
Heathcliff is brought up alongside
the family's daughter, Catherine,
and son, Hindley, and the book tells
of their complex relationships and
power struggles over the following

Oh I am burning! I wish I were
out of doors – I wish I were a
girl again, half savage and
hardy, and free.
Wuthering Heights

years, Heathcliff's loss of his
soulmate, Catherine, to Edgar
Linton, and the revenge he takes.

Structurally, the novel uses
a framing device – a separate
story within which the main
narrative is presented. This frame
consists in the tale of the visit of
a gentleman named Lockwood to
Wuthering Heights. An unsettling
encounter with what he believes to
be Catherine's ghost traumatizes
him deeply, and he quizzes Nelly
Dean, a former servant of Catherine,
about the history of the house. The
story recounted by Nelly unfolds for
the reader as it does for Lockwood.

Emily Brontë

Born on 30 July 1818, Emily Brontë
was the fifth daughter of the
Reverend Patrick Brontë. The
family lived in the village of
Haworth, on the edge of the moors
in Yorkshire, a location that had
a profound influence on Emily's
writing, and that of her literary
sisters, Charlotte and Anne.

Her mother died in 1821, and
in 1824 Emily was sent with her
sisters to the Clergy Daughters'
School in Lancashire. After the
death of her eldest sisters,
Elizabeth and Maria, from
typhoid, the remaining three
siblings returned home. Later, at

Haworth, they decided to start
publishing their work under
male pseudonyms, Emily's being
"Ellis Bell". Her only published
novel was *Wuthering Heights*
(1847), although she and her
sisters had brought out a volume
of their poems the previous year.
Tragically, Emily never lived to
witness the success of her novel
as she died from tuberculosis
just a year after its publication.

Other key works

1846 *Poems by Currer, Ellis, and
Acton Bell*

See also: *Jane Eyre* 128–31 ▪ *Bleak House* 146–49 ▪ *Oliver Twist* 151 ▪ *Tales of the Grotesque and Arabesque* 152 ▪ *Great Expectations* 198

Wuthering Heights did not enjoy immediate success when it was published in 1847, perhaps because Victorian sensibilities could not cope with its unbridled passion and cruelty. But the tide of public opinion turned when later critics championed the novel. An essay on the work by English writer Virginia Woolf in 1916 marked a shift in how the text was interpreted. Woolf describes the book as being like a fairy tale or myth that is timeless in nature. This perspective on the novel became popular and is current today; however, it tends to ignore or diminish the significance of Brontë's use of Gothic literary conventions in her narrative, and her work's own relationship with the literature and issues of its time.

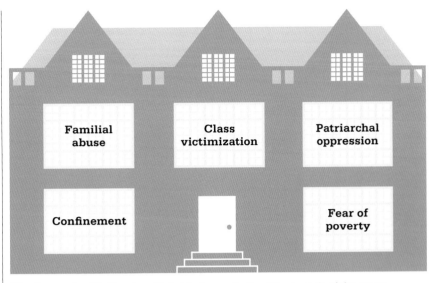

The house in *Wuthering Heights* is symbolic of the tumult of the story, and of the emotional turmoil of its protagonists. Rather than functioning as a place of refuge from the outside, the home is transformed into a Gothic site of abuse, fear, claustrophobia, exploitation, and oppression.

(house labels: Familial abuse · Class victimization · Patriarchal oppression · Confinement · Fear of poverty)

Gothic themes

What is particularly striking about *Wuthering Heights* is the way that it adapts Victorian Gothic themes. Other contemporary writers, such as Charles Dickens, used Gothic elements within realist novels,

Terror made me cruel; and finding it useless to attempt shaking the creature off, I pulled its wrist on to the broken pane, and rubbed it to and fro until the blood ran down and soaked the bed-clothes.
Wuthering Heights

thus deepening the themes, style, and meanings associated with earlier Gothic literature. Instead of the crumbling medieval castle, for example, Dickens portrayed teetering urban landscapes, rife with poverty and exploitation. In place of the terrifying manor house, with its victimized inhabitants within, Dickens presented the horrifying abuse that occurred in the gloomy London streets outside the home.

Brontë took things further than Dickens, expanding on Gothic literary traditions through the character of Heathcliff, who is brought to the house of Wuthering Heights as a boy. When he arrives in the household, and indeed throughout the story, he is referred to as a "gypsy". For the Victorians, the word "gypsy" had several connotations: it indicated someone of a different race, and it was also used as an insult for someone who was homeless, a wanderer, and therefore to be feared.

Brontë's more complex take on the Gothic is also evident in her portrayal of the conflicts within her characters' minds. Catherine, for example, when forced to choose between Heathcliff and Linton, does not sleep for three days and is unable to distinguish between imagination and reality.

Victorian respectability

Racial difference and working-class poverty were significant concerns for the Victorians. They fashioned their ideas of respectability and of English national identity through the idealized domestic space of the middle-class home. For example, Dickens himself often depicted clichéd domestic scenes where the respectability of the bourgeois »

The wild moorland setting symbolizes the barbaric threat presented by nature. The desolate landscape, in which it is easy to get lost, is one of the book's characters.

space was contrasted with the literal and moral poverty of the streets outside. Brontë, however, brought the raw realities of the outside into the home, recalling earlier Gothic narratives where households were not sites of refuge or comfort, but spaces of familial abuse. In doing so, she reveals to her contemporary reader that the "slavery" and "homelessness" associated with Heathcliff are also evident within the idealized domestic sphere: in effect, the home is no safer than the crime-ridden Gothic streets.

As an abandoned waif found in Liverpool, Heathcliff has been associated not only with gypsies but also with the slave trade of the period. As a character, he may be seen as a Gothic manifestation of the outside, bringing the terror of the unfamiliar into the domestic environment. Through his strong attachment to Catherine, who, like him, experiences only neglect and abuse within the house of Wuthering Heights, his presence

reveals that crime and exploitation were not simply the domain of the urban working-class poor.

Lovers or vampires?
Catherine and Heathcliff's relationship is more vampiric than romantic. They draw the life force from each other in pursuit of their needs and revenge, and often mirror each other's desires and frustrations with society. Heathcliff's plea to Catherine that "I cannot live without my life! I cannot live without my soul!" is an indicator of how theirs is not a flowery love union, but an existential meeting of souls.

My great miseries in this world have been Heathcliff's miseries, and I watched and felt each from the beginning.
Wuthering Heights

Catherine utters a similar line: "Whatever our souls are made of, his and mine are the same." For her, Heathcliff is not a source of girlish infatuation and she even warns her sister-in-law not to idealize him as the hero of a romance book. Instead, she sees him for what he is: selfish and predatory. She is also a wilfully stubborn and selfish character and her actions mirror Heathcliff's unbending will.

Bred on poverty and abused at Wuthering Heights for his lower class, Heathcliff desires social power through class elevation, money, and the ownership of property, represented by Catherine. Like other middle-class women of the period, Catherine is herself regarded as a piece of property, a feature of the household in which she is confined. For her, Heathcliff represents a weapon against the respectable middle-class world she is expected to conform to as she enters womanhood.

Gender and the domestic
The relationship between Victorian Gothic and gender is an important aspect of *Wuthering Heights* that is strongly evident in one of the most violent and famous passages in the novel. When the hapless Lockwood

first comes to Wuthering Heights, he expects to find a typical Victorian country house – the kind of domestic home Dickens was famous for writing about, with its comforting hearthside scenes of familial bliss and harmony. Instead, he seems to stumble into the pages of a Gothic novel, where strange dogs attack him, a surly owner banishes him, and a mysterious housekeeper sends him to sleep in a haunted room.

Lockwood's encounter with Catherine's child-ghost in her old bedroom culminates in a startling and gory image of him deliberately rubbing the ghost's bare wrist on the jagged glass of a broken window. This violent, disturbing image could be interpreted as simple Gothic melodrama were it not for the fact that Catherine's relationship with her home is a complex one. Throughout her life, she experiences households as sites of confinement. She seeks escape from them and yet, ironically, haunts the edges of Wuthering Heights, seeking entry into it after her death. Like Heathcliff, she is a "homeless" character who does not belong

anywhere. For her, the real Gothic terror is the house's inability to accommodate her and her desires. Instead, like Lockwood's fracturing of her skin in death, her identity is broken in life. Through her, Brontë reveals the limits of the Victorian domestic ideology that was often used to define women in the period.

Imprisoned by the home

During the 19th century, women were intimately linked with the site of the home to the extent that eminent Victorian critics such as John Ruskin described women's bodies themselves as private spaces of domesticity. This claustrophobic limiting of women's lives is an issue that is echoed in Charlotte Brontë's *Jane Eyre* through the literal imprisonment of a woman within the household. In *Wuthering Heights*, this Gothic theme of female imprisonment, expressed through Catherine, suggests that the only way out for women is through a violent self-destruction that results in a permanent homelessness.

For Catherine, Victorian domestic ideology is not only a prison, it is also an existential

The Brontë sisters (Anne, Emily, and Charlotte), shown here in a painting by their brother Bramwell, collaborated on literary works and explored similar themes in their writing.

dilemma that makes her question where she belongs and drains her of her life and vitality, leaving only a spectral "shadow" of her former self, first metaphorically, then literally. This is the power of *Wuthering Heights* and its use of Victorian Gothic elements; it reveals that the fundamental tragedy of the tale lies not in the doomed relationship between Catherine and Heathcliff, but rather in the lack of a true space of belonging for either of them. ∎

The destinies of two families are intertwined in *Wuthering Heights*. Brontë tends to repeat names, often causing confusion in the minds of readers.

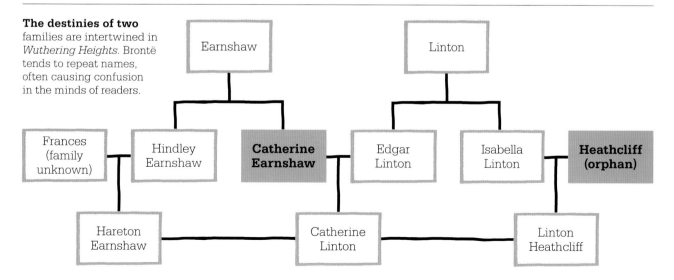

THERE IS NO FOLLY OF THE BEAST

OF THE EARTH WHICH IS NOT INFINITELY OUTDONE BY THE

MADNESS OF MEN

MOBY-DICK (1851), HERMAN MELVILLE

IN CONTEXT

FOCUS
Dark Romanticism

BEFORE
1845 In "The Raven", a poem by Edgar Allan Poe, the bird repeats the word "Nevermore" to accelerate a grief-stricken lover's descent into madness.

1850 In Nathaniel Hawthorne's *The Scarlet Letter*, Hester Prynne has a daughter out of wedlock. The scarlet letter is "A" for "Adulteress", which she must wear on her dress.

1851 *The House of the Seven Gables*, also by Hawthorne, explores guilt, retribution, and atonement, with hints of the supernatural and witchcraft.

AFTER
1853 In a foreshadowing of existential literature, a legal copyist in Melville's story *Bartleby, the Scrivener* politely refuses to accept his tasks, dwindling to mere existence.

Early to mid-19th-century America witnessed the development of two strands of Romanticism. One, practised notably by Ralph Waldo Emerson and Henry David Thoreau, was Transcendentalism, an idealistic movement centred on a belief in the soul or "inner light", and the inherent goodness of humans and the natural world. The other was Dark Romanticism, which took a less optimistic view of human nature; writers such as Edgar Allan Poe, Nathaniel Hawthorne, and Herman Melville explored ideas of the individual susceptible to sin and self-destruction, in a reaction against Trancendentalist idealism.

The dark side

Both schools recognized a spiritual energy in nature, but whereas the Transcendentalists saw nature as a mediating channel between God and humanity, the Dark Romantics were less sanguine about human perfectibility. They saw nature as embodying dark, mysterious truths that humans confront at their peril. In the same spirit of pessimism, they regarded attempts at social reform as dubiously utopian.

> … all that cracks the sinews and cakes the brain; all the subtle demonisms of life and thought; all evil, to crazy Ahab, were visibly personified, and made practically assailable in Moby Dick.
> **Moby-Dick**

In their poetry and prose from about 1836 through the 1840s, exponents of Dark Romanticism often depicted individuals failing in their attempts to bring about positive change. Drawn to horror, the supernatural, and the macabre, as well as to suffering and tragedy, they were fascinated by the human propensity for evil and by the psychological consequences of sin, guilt, revenge, and insanity. Such elements were also found in Gothic literature, and paved

---

Herman Melville

The son of an importer and merchant, Melville was born in 1819 in New York. Starting his working life at his late father's business, he then taught at local schools, worked on his uncle's farm, and clerked in a bank. At age 20, he enrolled as cabin boy on a merchant ship sailing to Liverpool. In 1841 he got a job aboard the *Acushnet*, a whaling ship. An interlude of living in the Marquesas Islands in the South Pacific inspired his first novel, *Typee*. Later he served on further whalers and on a US Navy frigate. Seafaring provided material for

Moby-Dick, and Melville hoped to capitalize on popular interest in marine adventure. But by the time the book was published, public interest had shifted to the American West, and *Moby-Dick* was not seen as a masterpiece in Melville's lifetime. He died of a heart attack in 1891.

Other key works

1846 *Typee*
1853 *Bartleby, the Scrivener*
1857 *The Confidence-Man*
1888–91 *Billy Budd* (published posthumously in 1924)

See also: First Folio 82–89 ▪ *Frankenstein* 120–21 ▪ *Leaves of Grass* 125 ▪ *Wuthering Heights* 132–37 ▪ *Tales of the Grotesque and Arabesque* 152 ▪ *The Scarlet Letter* 153 ▪ *Dracula* 195 ▪ *Gravity's Rainbow* 296–97

Transcendentalism and Dark Romanticism were two opposing sides of the American Renaissance of the mid-19th century. The Transcendentalists saw both nature and people as inherently good; conversely, for the Dark Romantics, nature was a potentially sinister force and humans infinitely fallible.

Nature is a divine spiritual force that mediates between man and God.

Humankind possesses a divine spark, making humans innately good.

Individuals are at their best when self-reliant and independent.

Nature is a sinister spiritual force that reveals terrifying truths.

Humankind is imperfect, and inclined towards sin and self-destruction.

Individuals fail when trying to change things for the better.

Transcendentalism   **Dark Romanticism**

the way for the modern horror story. As the truths the Dark Romantics sought to reveal were primitive and irrational, they favoured the use of symbolism – a mode of communication that bypassed the faculty of reason. Edgar Allan Poe wrote stories and poems featuring sombre, dreamlike details such as people being buried alive, decaying mansions, and a raven that inflicts psychological torment. Nathaniel Hawthorne, who found his own nightmares in the hypocrisy of Puritanism in the real world, wrote about shame and secret sin.

On 5 August 1850 two of the great writers of Dark Romanticism, Hawthorne, aged 46, and Herman Melville, aged 31, met on a hike up a mountain in Massachusetts. Melville, in the throes of writing his great whaling novel *Moby-Dick*,

was greatly inspired by the older writer's intense Romantic inwardness and his rejection of conformity. Later he moved with his wife and family to live near Hawthorne, and he included a dedication to him in the opening pages of *Moby-Dick*, which read "in token of my admiration for your genius".

The revenge quest
Rich in language, incident, character, and symbolism, and displaying an extraordinary depth and breadth of knowledge within its maritime subject area, *Moby-Dick; or, The Whale* is the first great American fictional epic. It is a book driven by an intense literary ambition; from its famous opening line, "Call me Ishmael", it sweeps the reader along, following the

narrator's quest to discover meaning "in the damp, drizzly November of [his] soul".

In fact, Ishmael's own quest is paired with an obsessive and ultimately tragic adventure »

For all men tragically great are made so through a certain morbidness ... all mortal greatness is but disease.
Moby-Dick

The persona of Ahab as a hate-filled, obsessive sea captain is at first built through second-hand information and hearsay; Ahab only physically appears more than 100 pages into the novel.

conducted by Ahab, the captain of the whaling ship *Pequod*, as he searches the seas for the gigantic albino sperm whale known as Moby Dick that has bitten off one of his legs below the knee. Ahab, "a grand, ungodly, god-like man", who stomps around the deck on his prosthesis made from whale bone, sends out a satanic charisma. At a profound pyschological level he is

engaged in a battle with God, the ineffable presence behind Moby Dick's "unreasoning mask" – Ahab's vision of the world being one in which all objects represent something unknown, inscrutable, and malign. By striking at the whale, he strikes at God, or that unknown agent. The story of his obsession, as the novel relates it, is also an enquiry into the meaning of life and death, with insights on subjects from religion to madness.

Ahab's violent craving for revenge is tempered only by his tender feelings, towards the end, for the young black deckhand named Pip, and by a short interlude of nostalgia, when he drops a single tear into the sea. Speaking to the *Pequod*'s chief mate, Starbuck, of his 40 years of oceanic solitude, he thinks of his wife ("I widowed that poor girl when I married her, Starbuck") and of his little boy. These regrets are overwhelmed by his hate-filled lust (two deadly sins in one) for vengeance.

A nation afloat

The *Pequod*'s voyage, and even the name of the ship itself, has allegorical overtones: the Pequod (or Pequot) was a Native American tribe that was almost exterminated by the British Puritan settlers during the 17th century. The story therefore hints at the doom of a civilization brought about by unquenchable thirst for material progress, imperial expansion, white supremacy, and the exploitation of nature. The ship may be seen as a microcosm of the world, and of the USA in particular; and since Ahab's obsession infects the whole ship, a whole society is implicated.

The crew are a mixture of races and creeds, reflecting the universality of Melville's vision. Working together, the shipmates are mutually dependent. Freedom of movement and communication takes place across the hierarchical boundaries of status and command.

And of all these things the Albino whale was the symbol.
Moby-Dick

The giant albino whale that gives its name to Melville's novel is a vivid symbol of Ahab's quest for vengeance. However, the animal is interpreted by other characters in various ways, depending on their education, class, and faith – or lack thereof.

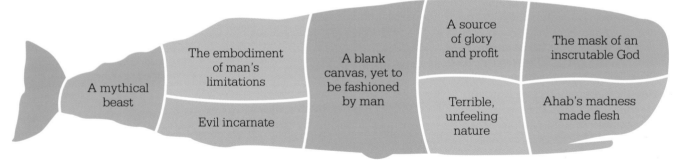

A mythical beast

The embodiment of man's limitations

Evil incarnate

A blank canvas, yet to be fashioned by man

A source of glory and profit

Terrible, unfeeling nature

The mask of an inscrutable God

Ahab's madness made flesh

> Moby Dick seeks thee not. It is thou, thou, that madly seekest him!
> **Moby-Dick**

However, this diverse floating society is far from democratic: social and racial distinctions make for inequality and all on board bend to the iron rule of Ahab. The diversity of thoughts and feelings experienced by the crew of the whaler forms a dramatic counterpoint to the monomania of the captain and the monolithic energy of the whale that he is determined to track down and kill.

The ship is a floating factory, as well as a vessel of pursuit, and Melville was fully conscious of the parallels that readers would see between the ship and US capitalism, the machine age, and the market economy.

The Bible and prophecy

Moby-Dick is an epic tale of blasphemous aspiration ("Talk not to me of blasphemy, man;" says Ahab, "I'd strike the sun if it insulted me"), and it uses biblical references to add meaning to its structure. Its two main characters, Ishmael and Ahab, are named after figures in the Bible. In Genesis

Whaling ships were a regular sight in New Bedford, Massachusetts, where Melville worked and where the early parts of *Moby-Dick* are set. The last whaler left the harbour in 1925.

16–25, Ishmael, the illegitimate son of the patriarch Abraham, was cast out in favour of the legitimate son, Isaac. By giving his narrator this name, Melville underlines the fact that Ishmael is a wanderer and an outsider: his inexperience at whaling prevents his unqualified acceptance by the crew. Ahab, in Kings 1.21, is a ruler who covets a vineyard and obtains it by means of deceit, but is destined to come to an inglorious end. His namesake follows a loosely analogous pattern in *Moby-Dick*, finding success in a way that seals his own doom.

Melville, concerned with the machinations of chance and fate, uses prophecy to create a sense of ominous foreboding. Before

Ishmael signs up on the *Pequod*, a character named Elijah (in another biblical equivalence) predicts a vague doom for the vessel. Later, a prophecy by Fedallah, a harpooner, foreshadows the final stages of the narrative's trajectory. He says that the captain will die only after seeing two hearses, one "not made by mortal hands" and one made of wood grown in the USA – which Ahab interprets as a sign of his surviving the voyage.

Hellfire and retribution

Ishmael comments tartly, after making the acquaintance of the harpooner Queequeg: "Better sleep with a sober cannibal than a drunken Christian." Such »

The Nantucket whaling ship _Essex_ encountered a large sperm whale in the Pacific Ocean in 1820 and sank. It was one of several events that inspired Melville to write _Moby-Dick_.

undermining of Christian orthodoxy, and of other religions too, is a strand running through the novel. Assembling the crew on deck, Ahab makes the three "pagan" harpooners drink from the hollow heads of their steel harpoons, in a scene that resembles a sacrilegious mass. He calls them his cardinals and their drinking vessels chalices, urging them to swear death to Moby Dick. To the harpoon point, anointed with blood, that he will use to skewer the whale, he later says mockingly in Latin: "I baptize you, not in the name of the Father but in the name of the Devil" – a sentence that Melville described to Hawthorne as the book's "secret motto". He wrote to Hawthorne that he had written "a wicked book", and, in an earlier letter, that his novel was "broiled in hell-fire".

The ship itself, painted black and festooned with the enormous teeth and bones of sperm whales, is reminiscent of the funeral ship of some dark, tribal religion – Melville describes it as a "cannibal of a craft, tricking herself forth in the chased bones of her enemies". At night, the fires used to melt the whale blubber turn it into a "red hell". In this way, even the setting of the novel picks up the note of subverted faith that is so often sounded in the action and dialogue.

Drama and poetry

The book uses devices that are more often associated with drama than with novels, including soliloquies (speeches sharing a character's thoughts directly with the audience), stage directions, and even, in Chapter 40 ("Midnight, Forecastle"), a short dramatization. In depicting self-destructive ambition, Melville was inspired by the Elizabethan tragic hero: Ahab has echoes of Shakespeare's tragic hero-villain Macbeth, of King Lear in his heartless unreason, and of Hamlet in his impulse to avenge. In an essay of 1850, Melville wrote of admiring the "deep far-away things" in Shakespeare and the vital truths that are spoken by his "dark characters". Melville used explicitly Shakespearean means to express his vision, from the soliloquies already mentioned (used with great power by Shakespeare) to intense, elevated language to prose that actually has the cadence of blank verse (the unrhymed, rhythmic poetic line).

Melville also drew inspiration for the language of the book from John Milton's epic blank-verse poem _Paradise Lost_. There are parallels too with Samuel Taylor Coleridge's poem _The Rime of the Ancient Mariner_ – the albatross brought down by the mariner is equivalent to Melville's whale.

Encylopedic elements

The use of various elements from drama and poetry, with the bold originality that helps to make _Moby-Dick_ such a major landmark

I see in him outrageous strength, with an inscrutable malice sinewing it.
Moby-Dick

Queequeg, the tattooed Polynesian harpooner, is part of the international crew of the *Pequod*. Although said to be a pagan and a cannibal, he is calm, generous, honest, and loyal.

in fiction, is offset by borrowings from another literary genre: the encyclopedia. As the suspense of the story is ratcheted up through a series of increasingly dramatic whale hunts, the momentum is deliberately frozen, at strategic intervals, by chapters that present a wealth of anthropological, zoological, and other factual information on whales and the activity of whaling – for example,

an account of the extraction of whale oil, or a discussion about the portrayal of whales in art. The prodigious volume and density of knowledge on display seem appropriate to Melville's experience as a self-taught man: "I have swam through libraries," declares Ishmael, and Melville did the same, absorbing mountains of knowledge through his own reading, often while at sea himself. The content and tone of the encyclopedic chapters provide the novel with a vastly detailed infilling of factual realism. This helps to relate Melville's Dark Romantic world view to the civilization inhabited by the book's readers, and taught to them through science and history.

A compelling mix

The strands of Shakespearean drama and factual content give the novel two of its characteristic prose styles, and offset against both is a third: conversational casualness. This mode announces itself in Ishmael's second sentence ("Some years ago – never mind how long precisely – having little or no money …") and surfaces frequently in the midst of writing of elaborate

How can'st thou endure without being mad? Do the heavens yet hate thee, that thou can'st not go mad?
Moby-Dick

impressiveness and theatrical exclamation. Genres and styles are mixed to powerful effect.

Moby-Dick has an encyclopedic depth and wide-ranging literary styles; since the oceans occupy two-thirds of the Earth's surface, it could perhaps be described as a psychological drama conceived on the largest imaginable scale. With its consideration of good and evil in an indifferent cosmos, and its realization of a detailed social world, this monumental epic of fanaticism infused with a tragic vision set a new benchmark for fictional ambition. ∎

The Great American Novel

Writing the "Great American Novel", as an expression of nationalist pride and a challenge to the European fictional canon, became an explicit ambition in the 19th century.

The phrase "Great American Novel" was devised by the novelist John De Forest in 1868. An essential qualification was that the book should capture a distinctively American ethos. A family saga addressing race and other social tensions, such as *Uncle Tom's Cabin* (Harriet

Beecher Stowe, 1852) and, later, *Beloved* (Toni Morrison, 1987), was deemed appropriate. Some candidates for the label focused on self-creation, which in the 20th century became the cornerstone of the American Dream; these themes were scrutinized in *The Great Gatsby* (F Scott Fitzgerald, 1925) and *Invisible Man* (Ralph Ellison, 1952). Another suitable type was the so-called "mega-novel", with multiple characters and plot lines presenting a microcosm of contrasting social

and philosophical ideas. *Moby-Dick*, the first Great American Novel, belongs to both the second and the third of these categories; the next major contender, *The Adventures of Huckleberry Finn* (Mark Twain, 1884), largely to the second.

In the 21st century, the Great American Novel remains an ideal for writers and readers, although the notion has lost its swagger, and the idea of a unifying "American" voice is rejected by many critics.

ALL PARTINGS FORESHADOW THE GREAT FINAL ONE

BLEAK HOUSE (1852–1853), CHARLES DICKENS

IN CONTEXT

FOCUS
Serial fiction

BEFORE
1836–37 Charles Dickens' *The Pickwick Papers* is published in 20 monthly instalments. It establishes the popularity and financial viability of serializing narrative fiction.

1844–45 *The Count of Monte Cristo,* a thrilling adventure of a man's false imprisonment and his subsequent revenge, by Alexandre Dumas, is published in instalments.

AFTER
1856 Gustave Flaubert's debut novel *Madame Bovary* appears in serial form in the literary magazine *Revue de Paris*.

1868 Wilkie Collins' *The Moonstone* proves so popular that it is extended from 26 to 32 serialized episodes.

Readers on both sides of the Atlantic Ocean could barely contain themselves as they awaited the final instalment of Charles Dickens' serialized *The Old Curiosity Shop* – so much so, that when the ship carrying it finally docked in New York, USA, in 1841, excited readers waiting at the port rushed forwards across the wharf, desperate to find out whether Little Nell, the novel's protagonist, had died.

Such enthusiasm showed just how popular the work of Charles Dickens had become. But it also highlighted the popularity of serialization – a process by which a novel was published in episodes

See also: *Oliver Twist* 151 ▪ *The Count of Monte Cristo* 152–53 ▪ *Vanity Fair* 153 ▪ *David Copperfield* 153 ▪ *Madame Bovary* 158–63 ▪ *The Moonstone* 198–99

The one great principle of the English law is, to make business for itself.
Bleak House

before being offered in book form. Improved printing technology, cheaper paper, the growth of the railways, and a rise in literacy all contributed to the emergence of serial fiction. Price, too, played a part: readers were more willing or able to pay per episode than to buy an expensive book outright. In this way serial fiction enabled the growth of a mass reading public.

Serial pioneer

When Charles Dickens embarked on his novel-writing career, he had intended to produce a three-volume novel, in the conventional tradition of the time. However, his publishers suggested that he write a series of articles to accompany some sporting prints. According to Dickens, "My friends told me it was a low, cheap form of publication, by which I would ruin all my hopes", but he accepted and began work on the first episode of *The Pickwick Papers*. It was a huge success, and from then on Dickens published all of his novels in serial form.

Despite the stress involved in meeting a weekly or monthly deadline, the serial format perfectly suited Dickens' energetic and

dramatic storytelling style. It also helped to create an intimacy between him and his readers – he sometimes even altered the plot of later instalments in response to his readers' reactions.

Mature complexity

Bleak House was published in monthly instalments between March 1852 and September 1853. It was Dickens' ninth novel and is thought by many to be one of his most mature. English writer and critic G K Chesterton considered it to be his best novel, a view shared by many readers, then and now.

An immense and complex novel, *Bleak House* is set mainly in London but also in Lincolnshire in the east of England. Its main theme is the iniquities of the English legal system at that time, which through delays, obfuscation, and lack of humanity, destroyed the lives of innocent individuals. Central to the story, and woven through it, is the fictional case of Jarndyce and Jarndyce, a legal »

Each instalment of *Bleak House* was accompanied by two illustrations by Hablot Knight Browne, enhancing the mood of the text – this illustration shows the stately home Chesney Wold.

Charles Dickens

Born in Portsmouth, England, on 7 February 1812, Charles Dickens was the second of eight children. When he was 12, his father was imprisoned for debt. Charles left school and worked in a shoeblacking factory, a grim experience that he would describe in *David Copperfield*. Later he worked as a legal clerk and started writing as a journalist.

In 1836 Dickens married Catherine Hogarth and began work on *The Pickwick Papers*, establishing his reputation as a novelist. Over the next 30 years, he published 12 major novels; he also edited periodicals and wrote numerous articles, short stories, and plays. He separated from Catherine in 1858, having fathered 10 children. Dickens died in 1870 and was buried in Poets' Corner, Westminster Abbey.

Other key works

1836–37 *The Pickwick Papers*
1837–39 *Oliver Twist*
1843 *A Christmas Carol*
1849–50 *David Copperfield*
1855–57 *Little Dorrit*
1859 *A Tale of Two Cities*
1860–61 *Great Expectations*
1864–65 *Our Mutual Friend*

Pea-soupers, heavy fogs containing soot and other pollutants, were a feature of 19th-century London. In *Bleak House*, fog serves as a symbol of confusion and oppression.

dispute over an inheritance that has already lasted several decades by the time the novel begins, and which has become "… so complicated that no man alive knows what it is".

Multiple layers

However, *Bleak House* is not just an attack on the English legal system: it is also a murder mystery, a whodunnit, and a searing exploration of the poverty, disease, and neglect that were part of 19th-century England. The novel includes plots and subplots that touch on themes of secrets, guilt, greed, self-interest, love, and kindness. Like all of Dickens' novels, it includes a huge and memorable cast of characters, who interlink with each other in ways that are both obvious and extremely subtle (introducing surprise into the serial form), most of them drawn into each other's lives through the complex web of Jarndyce and Jarndyce. Such features grew out of the serial nature of the work, its episodic creation allowing for many subplots involving numerous characters.

Dickens starts to lay the basis for his story in the very first episode, introducing the reader to places, events, and several of the main characters. He also provides clues to mysteries that will eventually unfold.

The book's memorable opening describes London in November, fog on the river seeping into the bones of the characters, symbolizing the confusion and corruption that emanate from the fog's densest point – the High Court of Chancery. Moving outwards to Lincolnshire, it reappears as mist around Chesney Wold, the estate of the aristocratic Lord and Lady Dedlock.

We are introduced to three main characters: Esther Summerson, Ada Clare, and Richard Carstone. All are orphans, their lives already affected by the long-running Jarndyce and Jarndyce case.

Fog everywhere. Fog up the river, where it flows among green aits and meadows; fog down the river…
Bleak House

They go to live in the eponymous Bleak House with their guardian, John Jarndyce, a kindly man and benefactor who has resolutely distanced himself from the infamous lawsuit and warns his young wards to do the same. But each is touched by the case, and Carstone becomes dangerously sucked into it.

Brought up as a child by a harsh aunt, and with a shameful mystery surrounding her birth, Esther plays a central role in the novel. She is a modest, shy, self-effacing young woman, who says of herself, "I know I am not very clever".

Esther is also one of the two narrators that Dickens uses. Her first-person narrative weaves in and out of the story, describing people and events from a personal and retrospective view. She provides insight into and criticism of the other characters. The other narrator is an anonymous third-person voice that describes events in the present tense, creating dramatic tension and highlighting social injustice – the voice of conscience.

Remarkable characters

Each member of *Bleak House*'s large cast is carefully named and presented to make social points; characters are often larger than life, but are never oversimplified. The complexity of Dickens' characters made them compelling to readers, who followed their fortunes in instalments in much the same way that today's television viewers tune in to weekly soap operas.

Lord and Lady Dedlock epitomize the deadness, sterility, and aloofness of the aristocracy, although the haughty coldness of Lady Dedlock hides a dark secret. Miss Flite, who befriends the young wards, is a half-crazed old woman, driven mad by the Jarndyce and Jarndyce case. Carrying a bag of documents, she haunts Chancery, expecting a day of judgement when she will release the birds she keeps in cages, whose names chillingly include Ashes, Waste, Ruin, and Despair. Krook, a scrap merchant fond of rum and obsessed by the court case, plays a critical role until one day, in a startling end to the tenth instalment, he spontaneously combusts. And Tulkinghorn, Dedlock's lawyer, haunts the pages, stalking the mystery that links the Dedlocks and Esther Summerson.

Neglect vs kindness

Selfishness, greed, hypocrisy, and neglect are common themes of the book: Mrs Jellyby neglects her own children for her philanthropic interests; self-centred "model of Deportment" Mr Turveydrop shows little interest in his hard-working, impoverished son; the grotesque Smallwood family are obsessed by "compound interest"; and all of society neglects Jo, a poor young crossing sweeper, who is constantly told to "move on". Hypocrisy is caricatured in the persons of Chadband, a greasy Evangelical churchman, and Harold Skimpole, who presents himself as untouched by the monetary realities around him, yet cadges money from all his friends. By contrast, kindness is shown to all by Esther, Ada, and their benefactor John Jarndyce.

Serial success

Bleak House is also arguably one of the earliest detective novels in English literature. The detective is Mr Bucket, a genial, terrier-like man, who, after a ghastly murder,

Dickens treats the locations in *Bleak House* almost as characters in their own right. Vividly portrayed, they serve as a shorthand for class and provide a credible backdrop for people of very different social status to meet and interact.

Lincoln's Inn
Much of the action – especially the legal machinations of Jarndyce and Jarndyce – occurs in and around Lincoln's Inn, one of four Inns of Court in London. This was the home of Tulkinghorn and also of Dickens' lawyer in real life.

Tom-All-Alone's
The poverty and ruinous living and working conditions in Dickensian London are encapsulated in the tumbling slum called Tom-All-Alone's. Although this area is fictional, it may have been based on an area called Devil's Acre in London's Westminster.

St Albans
Dickens locates John Jarndyce's middle-class home, Bleak House, in St Albans, Hertfordshire, but it is believed to have been modelled on the house in Broadstairs, Kent, where he stayed with his family every summer for several years.

Lincolnshire Wolds
Dickens placed Chesney Wold – the grand home of Sir Leicester and Lady Honoria Dedlock – in Lincolnshire. Its description is based on Rockingham Castle in Leicestershire, which was owned by his friends Richard and Lavinia Watson.

tracks down the culprit. Dickens creates false clues in this subplot; these appeared tantalizingly as cliffhangers at the end of two instalments, keeping readers in suspense and eager to read more.

Some early reviews were critical of *Bleak House*, feeling that it was too gloomy and lacking in humour. Dickens' friend and biographer John Forster described it as "too real", but readers clearly disagreed: sales were between 34,000 and 43,000 copies a month. Following the success of Dickens, other writers also gained readers via

serialization. Wilkie Collins' detective novel *The Moonstone* first appeared in instalments, and episodes of Sir Arthur Conan Doyle's Sherlock Holmes tales were published in *The Strand Magazine*. Outside Britain, Leo Tolstoy's *Anna Karenina* was published serially, as was Fyodor Dostoyevsky's *The Brothers Karamazov*. Radio and television eventually took over from magazine serials, but in 1984 US writer Tom Wolfe returned to serialization with *The Bonfire of the Vanities*, which was first published in *Rolling Stone* magazine. ∎

FURTHER READING

RENÉ
(1802), FRANCOIS-RENÉ CHATEAUBRIAND

The melancholic figure of René, wandering the lands from France to the Americas, finding only *ennui* both in the city and the countryside, offered a perfect protagonist for early Romanticism. *René* by French writer, diplomat, and politician Chateaubriand (1768–1848) shocked readers with its plot revelation that René's sister Amélie joined a convent to conquer her feelings of incestuous love. The novella was an instant success.

THE SKETCH BOOK OF GEOFFREY CRAYON, GENT.
(1819–1820), WASHINGTON IRVING

Penned by US writer Washington Irving (1783–1859), *The Sketch Book* is a collection of short stories and essays. It includes tales such as "Rip van Winkle", in which the main character sleeps through the War of Independence, and "The Legend of Sleepy Hollow", with its account of Ichabod Crane's pursuit by the Headless Horseman. Irving's book was one of the first American literary works to be successfully received in Britain and Europe, and raised the reputation of American literature in the early 19th century.

IVANHOE
(1820), SIR WALTER SCOTT

Set in 12th-century England, *Ivanhoe* was based on the tensions between the brutal Norman rulers and the dispossessed Saxon population. Scott's romance tells the love story of two high-born Saxons, Rowena and Ivanhoe; they live alongside many noble and ignoble knights who duel and joust. Legendary figure Robin Hood makes an appearance as an outlaw with exemplary archery skills and a compelling sense of justice. Scott's characterization in *Ivanhoe* helped rejuvenate Robin Hood's reputation for a Victorian readership.

THE LAST OF THE MOHICANS
(1826), JAMES FENIMORE COOPER

Set in the 1750s at the height of the Seven Years' War (1754–63), known in the USA as the French and Indian War, *The Last of the Mohicans* tells of Chingachgook and his son Uncas, the eponymous last pure-blooded member of the Mohican tribe. US writer Cooper (1789–1851) details their brave efforts, with their white trapper friend Natty Bumppo, to save innocent lives. By far the most popular of the five-part series the "Leatherstocking Tales", Cooper's novel helped to create several enduring stereotypes of the Western genre, such as the romantic notion of the brave, fearless frontiersman and the wise, stoic indigenous tribesman.

THE RED AND THE BLACK
(1830), STENDHAL

Told over two volumes, *The Red and the Black* describes the formative years of Julien Sorel, a provincial young man who attempts to scale the social order in 19th-century France. Through detailed personal, historical, and psychological accounts of Julien's early life, from his beginnings as

Sir Walter Scott

Scott (1771–1832) was born in Edinburgh, and Scotland is central to much of his work. Considered by some to be the inventor and greatest exponent of the historical novel, Scott's childhood love of nature, the Scottish landscape, and traditional folktales helped to foster his strong sense of national identity. In poetry and prose, Walter Scott's meshing of romance and historical fiction set against the passionate depiction of his homeland – especially in the Waverley novels (1814–32), which he wrote anonymously – delighted huge audiences and changed the way Scotland was viewed culturally. Scott suffered ill health for much of his life, finally sailing to Italy for respite, before dying at Abbotsford, the estate he had built over many years in Scotland, in 1832.

Key works

1810 *The Lady of the Lake*
1814 *Waverley*
1820 *Ivanhoe* (see above)

Honoré de Balzac

One of France's leading writers of the 19th century, Balzac is known for his development of realism in the novel form, especially in *Old Goriot*. Born in Tours in 1799, he moved to Paris as a child, attended the Sorbonne from 1816, and was heading towards law as a profession when he turned to writing. By 1832, he had plans for *La Comédie humaine* – a collection of nearly 150 of his works, including essays, novels, and a range of analytical and philosophical texts. Balzac intended this vast compendium to capture the nature of the human condition, but he died in 1850, his life's work unfinished.

Key works

1829 *The Chouans*
1834–35 *Old Goriot* (see below)
1841–42 *The Black Sheep* (see p.152)

the sensitive child of a carpenter, to his rise into upper-class echelons via affairs with aristocratic women, the book leads up to Sorel's eventual fall into disgrace. French writer Stendhal (1783–1842) set his novel in early 19th-century France, both parodying and satirizing the excesses of the Bourbon regime prior to the July Revolution of 1830.

OLD GORIOT
(1834–1835), HONORÉ DE BALZAC

Set in Paris in 1819, *Old Goriot* by Balzac tells of life during the Bourbon Restoration. The 1789 revolution seems far away, though class divisions are tense once more.

Balzac employed realist depiction in recounting his brutal vision of early 19th-century Paris society, and in particular the social climbers willing to tread on others to achieve their ends. Considered by many to be his finest novel, it was the first of Balzac's stories to feature characters from his other books, a practise that became a trademark of his fiction.

FAIRY TALES
(1835–1837), HANS CHRISTIAN ANDERSEN

Danish writer Hans Christian Andersen (1805–75) created some of his fairy tales by retelling tales he heard as a child and others by inventing his own bold, original stories. Published in three volumes, *Fairy Tales* consists of nine tales, including classics such as "The Princess and the Pea", "The Little Mermaid", and "The Emperor's New Clothes". Andersen's works prefigured the explosion of children's literature in the 19th century and continue to hold enormous cultural significance today.

KALEVALA
(1835–1849), ELIAS LÖNNROT

Taken from folklore tales of the Karelian and Finnish indigenous peoples, the *Kalevala* – meaning "the land of Kaleval" – is a collection of epic poetry that is considered one of the most significant works of Finnish literature. Brought together by the ethnographic research of Finnish doctor and philologist Elias Lönnrot (1802–84), who travelled across the expanses of Finland and Karelia recording oral folksongs, the *Kalevala* is written in a distinctive metre, with each line featuring four

pairs of stressed and unstressed syllables. It retold mythological tales, building a literary and cultural heritage that awakened Finnish nationalism in the 19th century.

OLIVER TWIST
(1837–1839), CHARLES DICKENS

In his second novel, English writer Dickens (see p.147) paints a bold depiction of the social underclass of Victorian Britain, and of the poor fending for themselves in a hostile world. Seen as an early example of the social protest novel, *Oliver Twist* tells the story of Oliver as he flees the workhouse for London and joins a criminal child-gang. Like many of Dickens' novels, it was published serially, with cliff-hangers to keep readers hungry for each installment.

A HERO OF OUR TIME
(1840), MIKHAIL LERMONTOV

In *A Hero of Our Time*, Russian writer, poet, and painter Lermontov (1814–41) introduces the protagonist Grigory Pechorin, an idle, nihilistic, "superfluous man" figure. Pechorin acts as an antihero through a series of adventures and love affairs set

I was ready to love the whole world – no one understood me: I learned to hate.
A Hero of Our Time
Mikhail Lermontov

against the landscape of the Caucasus region of Russia. The author arranged his novel in five parts, portraying the complex nature of a sensitive, emotional, yet brutally cynical antihero who despairs at the pointlessness of life.

TALES OF THE GROTESQUE AND ARABESQUE
(1840), EDGAR ALLAN POE

Originally published in two volumes, *Tales of the Grotesque and Arabesque* consists of 25 short stories or "tales". Many of them are written with elements of Gothic form, and some delve into the darker psychological aspects of the protagonists' minds. US writer Poe (1809–49) is regarded as the creator of "dark Romanticism" – a specifically American form of Romanticism. "The Fall of the House of Usher", best known of the tales, sees Roderick Usher's home cracking and breaking and finally collapsing in sympathetic parallel with his own psychological breakdown.

There was an iciness, a sinking, a sickening of the heart – an unredeemed dreariness of thought which no goading of the imagination could torture into aught of the sublime.
"The Fall of the House of Usher"
Edgar Allan Poe

Much analysis of Poe's collection has centred on the meaning of the terms "Grotesque" and "Arabesque": whatever Poe's exact intention, the tales are significant for their treatment of terror and horror.

THE BLACK SHEEP
(1841–1842), HONORÉ DE BALZAC

Long overlooked but now considered to be one of the masterpieces of French novelist and playwright Balzac (see p.151), *The Black Sheep* tells the story of the competing plots, manipulations, and schemes of the members of a bourgeois family to secure a substantial inheritance. Titled *La Rebouilleuse* – someone who stirs waters in order to trap fish – in French, in reference to a controlling mistress of the story, it is a compelling exploration of the nature of deceit. Money, status, and legitimacy, and the lengths to which human beings will go in order to secure financial reward are among the themes explored by Balzac.

DEAD SOULS
(1842), NIKOLAI GOGOL

Dead Souls is often seen as the first great novel of the Russian Golden Age. Inspired by his friend, the poet Pushkin, Ukraine-born writer Gogol intended to write a three-part epic, but only produced the first two parts, and burned the manuscript of the second volume when close to his death. The remaining novel satirizes the practices of serfdom in Russia. Since tax must be paid by landowners on all their serfs – even those who have died since the last census – lead character Chichikov colludes illegally with estate owners to buy their dead serfs. He plans to

Nikolai Gogol

Born in 1809 in Sorochintsy in the Russian Empire (now part of Ukraine), Gogol was the progenitor of the great 19th-century tradition of Russian realism. Raised in the Cossack heartlands and shaped by the folklore of his native people, Gogol's early works displayed a lively and often colloquial style, winning instant acclaim from the Russian literary public. His short stories, novels, and plays spanned Romanticism, Surrealism, comedy, and satire, but his creative capacity waned in the years before his death in 1852.

Key works

1831–32 *Evenings on a Farm near Dikanka*
1836 *The Government Inspector*
1842 *Dead Souls* (see left)

borrow money against the value of his "dead souls" to start his own estate. Chichikov's travels across Russia are a comic tale reminiscent of Cervantes' *Don Quixote*.

THE COUNT OF MONTE CRISTO
(1844–1845), ALEXANDRE DUMAS

The most popular book throughout Europe at the time of its serialization, *The Count of Monte Cristo*, by French playwright and novelist Dumas (see p.123), was set during the Bourbon Restoration. It tells the story of the revenge inflicted by Edmond Dantès on his enemies, following his imprisonment on false charges of treason. In prison he meets Abbé Faria, who tells him of hidden treasure on the island of Monte Cristo. After escaping and finding the treasure, Dantès rises again as the Count of Monte Cristo.

VANITY FAIR
(1847–1848), WILLIAM MAKEPEACE THACKERAY

Vanity Fair follows the fortunes of two women – Amelia Smedley, from a decent family, and the orphan Becky Sharp – as they head out into a swirling social world seeking wealth and standing. They are polar opposites: Amelia is innocent and gentle, while Becky is ferocious in her ambition to climb the social strata. English author Thackeray (1811–63) paints a vivid parody of society and creates an essentially amoral heroine in the impish Becky.

Vanity Fair is a very vain, wicked, foolish place …
Vanity Fair
William Makepeace Thackeray

DAVID COPPERFIELD
(1849–1850), CHARLES DICKENS

Describing the coming of age of the title character, *David Copperfield* was first published in serial form, and of all the novels of Dickens (see p.147), it is the one closest to an autobiographical work. The details of Copperfield's life show parallels

with the author's own, although places and settings were altered. Characters such as great aunt Betsy Trottwood, the obsequious Uriah Heep, and penniless Mr Macawber are among Dickens' best-known and best-loved creations.

THE SCARLET LETTER
(1850), NATHANIEL HAWTHORNE

Set amid the Puritan world of mid-17th-century Massachusetts, Hawthorne's historical romance tells the tale of Hester Prynne, a young woman found guilty of adultery and forced to wear a scarlet letter "A" to signify her crime. Her husband has long disappeared, and is presumed dead. She defiantly refuses to name the father of her daughter, Pearl – against the demands of her public trial and her church minister – so is sent to prison. Hester's alienation from the strict religious creeds of Puritan society allows US writer Hawthorne (1804–64) to explore wider spiritual and moral issues, such as attitudes to the notion of sin. *The Scarlet Letter* was an immediate success, becoming one of the first mass-produced books in American history.

UNCLE TOM'S CABIN
(1852), HARRIET BEECHER STOWE

The hugely successful anti-slavery tale by US writer Stowe (1811–96) helped to persuade readers that Christian beliefs and slavery were incompatible. *Uncle Tom's Cabin* tells of noble slave Tom, who is sold and forced to leave his wife and family, yet never loses his moral values. In its first year of publication Stowe's story sold some 300,000 copies in the USA,

highlighting the country's race issue and North–South division. It was even seen by some as a spark for the US Civil War (1861–65).

NORTH AND SOUTH
(1854–1855), ELIZABETH GASKELL

English novelist Gaskell despised social inequality and poverty. Her tale of heroine Margaret Hale's journey from prosperous southern England to the north allowed readers to see the dire state of the lowest classes in Britain's industrial northern cities. The work graphically depicts the division between the north and south of England and the lives of those who provided the labour for the Industrial Revolution. It was published serially just after *Hard Times* by Dickens, at whose request Gaskell wrote her novel.

Elizabeth Gaskell

Born in London in 1810, Gaskell was the daughter of a Unitarian minister. Married to a church minister in industrial Manchester, she began writing in her 30s after beginning a diary to record the day-to-day life of her family. Her first books drew on her early life in rural Cheshire, but it was her later novels, set amid the poverty and strife of the working class, that made her name. She died in 1865, her finest work – *Wives and Daughters* – unfinished.

Key works

1848 *Mary Barton*
1853 *Cranford*
1854–55 *North and South* (see above)

DEPICTI
REAL LI
1855–1900

NG
FE

In *The Condition of the Working Class in England in 1844*, German political theorist Friedrich Engels exposes the **squalor of ordinary people's lives** caused by industrialization.

Charles Darwin's *On the Origin of Species by Means of Natural Selection* provokes debate, and whets the **public appetite for scientific knowledge**.

Lewis Carroll's first **fantasy novel for children**, *Alice's Adventures in Wonderland*, is published.

Leo Tolstoy finishes his historical epic *War and Peace*, which is set during the Napoleonic era and the 1812 **French invasion of Russia**.

1845   **1859**   **1865**   **1869**

1856   **1862**   **1866**   **1871–72**

Gustave Flaubert's *Madame Bovary* contrasts **ordinary life in provincial France** with the heroine's romanticized view of the world.

In *Les Misérables*, Victor Hugo **highlights social injustice** by recounting the events leading up to the anti-monarchist uprising in Paris in 1832.

Fyodor Dostoyevsky's novel *Crime and Punishment* describes **the thoughts and motivations of a murderer**, Raskolnikov.

Under the pen name George Eliot, Mary Ann Evans portrays **the complexity of ordinary life** in *Middlemarch*.

By the mid-19th century, the novel was firmly established as the predominant form of literature, with an unprecedented number of readers creating demand for new fiction across the world. No longer restricted to a cultural elite, reading had become a popular pastime, and readers increasingly sought books that were relevant to their own experiences and the world they lived in.

Realism gains momentum

The portrayal of believable characters and stories had been pioneered by the earliest novelists, such as Daniel Defoe and Henry Fielding, and in the 19th century the trend towards ever greater authenticity continued, resulting in contemporary fiction about ordinary people and their everyday lives.

This literary approach, known as "realism", began in earnest in France, where a generation of writers – uncomfortable with the tendency of Romanticism towards idealization and dramatization – sought to depict familiar scenes and characters as accurately as possible. One of the first to embrace the style was Honoré Balzac, whose monumental series of stories *La Comédie Humaine* was intended to provide an encyclopedic portrait of society, revealing the principles governing individual lives and their effects. This grand vision inspired not only French realist novelists such as Gustave Flaubert, but also a literary genre that spread across the Western world. By the latter half of the 19th century, elements of realism – and in particular the depiction of human preoccupations

and fallibilities – could be found in novels from as far apart as Russia, Britain, and the USA.

Authors enhanced the realism of their novels by various means. Some used the *roman à clef*, presenting historical events as fiction; others wrote from an omniscient narrator's perspective, enabling them to describe the thoughts and feelings, as well as the actions, of the characters. This emphasis on internal characterization developed into psychological realism, a subgenre that Russian authors in particular adopted, including Leo Tolstoy and Fyodor Dostoyevsky.

Social protest

In their striving for authenticity, many writers turned their attention to the lives of working people rather than the middle classes. In contrast

In the "Scramble for Africa" **European powers compete to establish colonies** and extend control over a still largely unexplored continent.

Mark Twain's *The Adventures of Huckleberry Finn*, written in a regional vernacular, **subverts the racist attitudes of the USA's South**.

A killer dubbed "Jack the Ripper" brutally murders several women in squalid East London, providing **dark and disturbing material for urban Gothic fiction**.

Oscar Wilde's *The Picture of Dorian Gray*, is published – a novel that explores sensual pleasure and **the superficial nature of beauty**.

1880s   **1884**   **1888**   **1891**

1881   **1885**   **1891**   **1899**

Henry James's *The Portrait of a Lady* contrasts **the Old and New World cultures** of Europe and North America.

The hope of a better future for humanity is at the heart of Emile Zola's *Germinal*, set in a mining community in northern France in the late 1800s.

In his novel *Tess of the D'Urbervilles*, Thomas Hardy explores **the destructive effects of modern life** on traditional English values.

Joseph Conrad's masterpiece, *Heart of Darkness*, juxtaposes **colonial ideals with human despair** in a primeval setting.

---

to the depiction of the humdrum existence of a character like Madame Bovary, Victor Hugo and Charles Dickens showed in graphic detail the grim conditions of the peasantry and industrial working class, not only for literary effect, but also as a form of social and political commentary. Others, including Emile Zola, emphasized the role that social conditions play in shaping character.

From Gothic to fantasy

The focus on the harsh, squalid realities of working-class life contributed to a gradual shift in perspective towards the dark side of city life. One result was the development of the Gothic tradition that became known as urban Gothic, epitomized by Bram Stoker's *Dracula* and Robert Louis

Stevenson's *Dr Jekyll and Mr Hyde*. The hope that this distressing era of dirt, disease, and death might be transformed for the better by advances in science enthralled the public and inspired authors such as Jules Verne and Arthur Conan Doyle to write "scientific romances". These precursors of science fiction had plots that featured invented discoveries and technologies, presented as if they were real.

A taste for the fantastical was also a prominent feature in the growing number of children's books that appeared at this time, notably in the "nonsense" fantasy of Lewis Carroll's surreal *Alice* novels. This strange, adventurous material began a "golden age" of children's literature, which included perennial favourites, such as Rudyard Kipling's collection of fables *The Jungle Book*

and the more down-to-earth yarn of *The Adventures of Huckleberry Finn* by Mark Twain.

Symbolist expression

Some writers argued that art should represent beauty and depict sensual pleasure rather than suffering. Writers of this Aesthetic movement used an indirect style influenced by the symbolism of French poets such as Charles Baudelaire and Stéphane Mallarmé. The symbolists had reacted against what they saw as the prosaic description of realist novels, instead emphasizing the importance of metaphor, imagery, and suggestion. Symbolist poets also explored new means of expression, experimenting with poetic techniques, which were later to inspire the coming generation of Modernist writers. ∎

BOREDOM, QUIET AS THE SPIDER, WAS SPINNING ITS WEB IN THE SHADOWY PLACES OF HER HEART

MADAME BOVARY (1856), GUSTAVE FLAUBERT

IN CONTEXT

FOCUS
French realism

BEFORE
1830 With its detailed analysis of French society and psychological depth, Stendhal's *The Red and the Black* marks a definitive shift from Romanticism to Realism.

1830–56 The interlocking novels and stories of Honoré de Balzac's monumental *La Comédie humaine* provide a panoramic view of French society from 1815 to 1848.

AFTER
1869 Flaubert's *A Sentimental Education* adds to the body of French realism with its vast presentation of France under Louis-Philippe.

1885 Guy de Maupassant portrays the rise to power of a ruthless social climber in *Bel Ami*, a Realist novel set in fin-de-siècle Paris.

Romanticism, with its focus on emotion, nature, and the heroic, dominated French literature from the end of the 18th century, but by the 1830s a new literary genre was gathering force: realism. Although the genre went on to spread throughout Europe and beyond, its beginnings and its development are particularly associated with France.

Emerging partly as a reaction to Romanticism, and reflecting the evolution of science and the social sciences, this new genre sought to depict contemporary life and society with detail and precision, in an unadorned and unromantic way. Realist writers put familiar situations and events under the literary microscope, representing them realistically rather than idealistically, even if some of the subject-matter might have been considered banal when compared with the Romantics.

Realism gathers force

One of the first French novelists of the period to take this approach was Stendhal, who incorporated both Romanticism and realism in his novels *The Red and the Black*

Her heart was just like that: contact with the rich had left it smeared with something that would never fade away.
Madame Bovary

and *The Charterhouse of Parma* (1839). Honoré de Balzac was a key pioneer of French realism, creating a keenly observed and realistic portrayal of ordinary life in his masterpiece, *La Comédie humaine*, which incorporated a vast series of more than 100 novels and stories. However, Gustave Flaubert's *Madame Bovary* moved much further along the path of realistic depiction, and it is considered to be the finest and most influential example of French realism.

On the surface, *Madame Bovary* has a fairly simple plot. A young woman, Emma Bovary, is unhappily

Gustave Flaubert

Gustave Flaubert was born in Rouen, France, on 12 December 1821. His father was chief surgeon at the main hospital in Rouen. Flaubert began writing while still at school, but in 1841 he went to Paris to study law. At age 22 he developed a nervous disorder, and he left the law to devote himself to writing. In 1846 his father and his sister Caroline died; with his mother and niece, Flaubert moved to Croisset, near Rouen, where he lived for the rest of his life. He never married, but between 1846 and 1855 he carried on an affair with poet Louise Colet.

Flaubert began to work on his novel *Madame Bovary* in 1851, completing it five years later. In 1857 he travelled to Tunisia, collecting material for his next novel, *Salammbô* (1862), which was set in ancient Carthage. Other works would follow, but none ever achieved the acclaim of his first novel. Flaubert died on 8 May 1880 and was buried in Rouen cemetery.

Other key works

1869 *Sentimental Education*
1877 *Three Tales*

See also: *The Red and the Black* 150–51 ▪ *Old Goriot* 151 ▪ *Germinal* 190–91 ▪ *A Sentimental Education* 199 ▪ *Lolita* 260–61

married to a rather dull doctor in provincial Normandy, in northern France. Influenced by the romantic reading of her youth, she dreams of a more exciting and fulfilling life, but her attempts to force reality to live up to her fantasies have devastating results.

Life in the provinces

The novel is more complex than the outline of its plot would suggest. From its beginning, when the reader is introduced to the young Charles Bovary, to its tragic ending, which supposedly had Flaubert himself in tears, *Madame Bovary* is deeply rooted in mid-19th-century provincial France. Events in the wider world were moving fast, and for the newly emerging middle classes, the centre of sophistication was Paris. But Flaubert chose to focus on the petit bourgeois in the provinces, whose lives he portrayed with an acute – and not always kindly – psychological perception.

Flaubert had begun his literary career as a Romantic, working on an exotic and mystical novel,

> There was no fire in the fireplace, the clock was still ticking, and Emma felt vaguely amazed that all those things should be so calm when there was such turmoil inside her.
> ***Madame Bovary***

The Temptation of Saint Anthony. However, some of his close friends, particularly his mentor, author Louis Bouilhet, reacted critically to an early draft of this work and urged him to attempt something more realistic. Drawing on a real-life event (the death of a doctor whose wife had caused a scandal), Flaubert began work on his new book. His aim was to write about the lives of ordinary people.

Creativity in detail

The project took Flaubert five years and involved meticulous research. He set his novel in the region around Rouen, where he spent most of his life and which he knew in intimate detail; he modelled places in his novel – the villages of Tostes and Yonville – on real country towns. He walked around the region and even made maps to ensure the greatest

Rouen, the capital of Normandy, is the provincial setting of Flaubert's text – a perfect backdrop for his skilful rendering of the lives and preoccupations of the middle class.

accuracy; he drew up biographies of his fictional characters, and set out to create a prose style that was totally stripped of all Romanticism, labouring over every sentence. Sitting in his room by the river Seine at Croisset, near Rouen, he constantly corrected and rewrote every page of his manuscript, a time-consuming process. His aim was to write in an entirely new and objective fashion, without "a *single* subjective reaction, nor a *single* reflection by the author". The result, as Flaubert had hoped, was a "tour de force".

Divided into three sections, *Madame Bovary* contrasts the hopelessness of sentimental »

Fantasy, reality, and realism

Emma yearns for:
thrilling adventures
in far-flung places;
love, passion, and
"intoxication"; wealth
and a "luxurious life".

**Emma's life is
characterized by:**
the tedium and mediocrity
of a provincial town;
boredom and dissatisfaction
with marriage;
insurmountable debt.

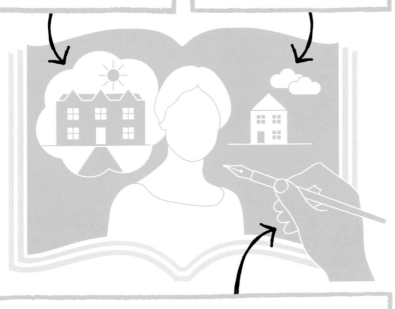

Flaubert achieves penetrating realism by means of:
his insistence on finding *"le mot juste"* – exactly the
right word; unrelenting attention to detail;
rigorous objectivity.

Flaubert dissects Madame Bovary
in this 1869 caricature. The novel is
a dissection of Emma's inner mind,
exploring her private thoughts with
an intense psychological realism.

romanticism with the monotonous reality of everyday life. In particular, Flaubert criticizes the foolishness and dullness of the middle classes, whom he held in contempt, even though he was himself middle class. Emma Bovary, around whom the novel rotates, symbolizes unrealistic romanticism. She is the convent-educated daughter of a wealthy farmer. Fed by the romances of Walter Scott and the "meanderings of Lamartine", a

Romantic poet scorned by Flaubert, she dreams of living "in some old manor-house, … looking out far across the fields for the white-plumed rider galloping towards her on his black horse".

Passion and reality

Seeking a "marvellous passion", Emma marries Charles Bovary, a kindly but boring doctor in the small rural village of Tostes. Almost immediately she is disappointed,

not just by Charles's dullness and lack of ambition, but also sexually. The disparity between her dreams and the unstimulating reality of her marriage, so perceptively described by Flaubert, lies at the heart of the novel.

Emma and Charles move to Yonville, a provincial town that Flaubert portrays in painstaking and often ironic detail, describing it as a "bastard region where the language is without accentuation, as the landscape is without character". Flaubert's ability to capture the mundane and commonplace contributed to establishing the novel as a key work in French realism. No detail is too small to be included: he describes roof-thatches like fur caps, sickly pear trees, ancient farmhouses and barns, and small graveyards typical of the region. His description of the country fair where local dignitaries make pompous speeches, aping the urban middle classes, is masterly. Dramatically, he counterpoises the tedious speeches against the passionate conversations and actions of Emma Bovary, behind a window overlooking the fair.

Unattainable dreams

Flaubert introduces other characters who live in Yonville, among them the town pharmacist, Monsieur Homais, an atheist and self-opinionated individual who practises medicine without a licence and uses every opportunity to display his apparent knowledge in the most pompous manner; and Monsieur Lhereaux, a merchant, who callously encourages Emma to run up debts, as she seeks to overcome marital boredom with what would today be described as retail therapy. Flaubert knew such characters very well and portrays them in intimate and realistic detail; throughout the novel he brilliantly captures their dullness and their small-minded attitudes, while never allowing his writing to become dull. Just as Flaubert gently mocks Emma's completely unachievable dreams and romanticism (and describes the tragic consequences that

Never touch your idols: the gilding will stick to your fingers.
Madame Bovary

She wanted equally to die and to live in Paris.
Madame Bovary

they have), so he also mocks the unsympathetic and pretentious aspirations of the merchant class.

Set among the realistic details of everyday routine, Flaubert's descriptions of Emma's romantic hopes and her frustrations within her provincial marriage are even more powerful, and appear surprisingly modern. Almost inevitably, Emma seeks romance and grand passion outside her marriage, embarking on two doomed affairs, first with the wealthy landowner and womanizer Rodolphe Boulanger, and then with Léon Dupois, a young law student, who shares her yearnings for glorious landscapes, music, and Romantic literature. Although initially excited and apparently fulfilled, Emma ultimately becomes disillusioned. As Flaubert writes: "Adultery, Emma was discovering, could be as banal as marriage." Abandoned by one lover and rejected by the other, she spirals into a self-destructive path of increasing debt and alienation.

Realism on trial

Madame Bovary first appeared in serial form in the *Revue de Paris*. Almost immediately, Flaubert, the printer, and the manager of the *Revue* were brought to trial on charges of obscenity, and

there was an attempt to ban the novel on the grounds of "outrage against public and religious morality". It was not only its content but also the realism of the style itself that was considered vulgar and shocking. But Flaubert and his colleagues were acquitted, and although the novel initially received a mixed reception, it went on to become a bestseller.

Madame Bovary and Flaubert's subsequent novel, *Sentimental Education*, with their objective, detailed, and stark portrayal of everyday life, marked the coming of age of French realism and at the same time its highest point. Within France, Flaubert's work influenced other major writers, including Guy de Maupassant, whose economical style and approach reflected the realism of his mentor; and Émile Zola, who, in novels such as *Germinal* (1885), focused on the harsh realities of day-to-day life, and who, like Flaubert, often spent months researching his subject-matter. ∎

Rodolphe Boulanger, Emma's first lover, recognizes her boredom, her frustrated passion, and her willingness to be seduced, and manipulates her expertly into an affair.

I TOO AM A CHILD OF THIS LAND; I TOO GREW UP AMID THIS SCENERY

THE GUARANI (1857), JOSÉ DE ALENCAR

IN CONTEXT

FOCUS
Indianism/Indianismo

BEFORE
1609 Garcilaso Inca de la Vega, son of a Spanish conquistador and an Incan princess, writes *Comentarios Reales de los Incas*, a prose work about Incan traditions and customs, and Spain's conquest of Peru.

1851 Brazilian poet Gonçalves Dias publishes one of the most famous poems of the Indianism movement, *I-Juca-Pirama*, about a Tupi warrior. The title is in Tupi and means, "He who must die that is worthy to be killed."

1856 *A Confederação dos Tamoios* is published. An epic poem about the Tupi people by Brazilian poet and playwright Gonçalves de Magalhães, it was commissioned by Brazilian Emperor Pedro II.

Indianism was a literary and artistic movement in mid-19th-century Brazil, in which writers and artists cast the country's indigenous people, the Indians, in a heroic light.

Two main factors contributed to Indianism. First, Brazil had only recently gained independence from Portugal (in 1821–24), so authors were expressing the idea that their new nation was one in which tribes and Europeans were united and equal. The second factor was the arrival in Brazil of Romanticism from Europe, which cherished the indigenous people for their perceived innocence and spiritual purity (views that derived from the 18th-century sentimental vision of the "noble savage").

Romantic idealism

José de Alencar (1829–77) is regarded as the father of the Brazilian novel, and *The Guarani* first brought him to the attention of the public. Set in 1604, it tells the story of an early settler whose daughter, Cecilia, has a suitor but instead falls for Peri, the Guarani Indian of the book's title. Peri is an idealized creation, exotic yet noble, who abandons his tribe and approves of Christian teachings.

Alencar's inclusion of native vocabulary, such as terms for flora and fauna, was seen as scandalous by the Portuguese literary establishment, but it freed Brazil's literature to develop in its own way. Highly romantic and lyrical, *The Guarani* is still taught in Brazilian schools today. ∎

They were brave, fearless men, uniting with the resources of civilized man, the cunning and agility of the Indian.
The Guarani

See also: *The Last of the Mohicans* 150 ▪ *The Gaucho Martín Fierro* 199

THE POET IS A KINSMAN IN THE CLOUDS
LES FLEURS DU MAL (1857), CHARLES BAUDELAIRE

IN CONTEXT

FOCUS
The French Symbolists

BEFORE
1852 *Enamels and Cameos*, a collection of poems by Théophile Gautier, departs from Romanticism, focusing on form rather than emotion.

AFTER
1865–66 Stéphane Mallarmé, in "The Afternoon of a Faun", gives a dreamlike account of a faun conversing with two nymphs – one representing the material, one the intellectual.

1873 Arthur Rimbaud, in *A Season in Hell*, presents two sides to himself – the poet intoxicated by light and childhood and the down-to-earth peasant.

1874 Paul Verlaine brings out *Songs without Words*, which is inspired by his relationship with Arthur Rimbaud.

The work of the French Symbolist poets of the 19th century focused on sensation and suggestion rather than plain description and rhetorical effects, and made use of symbols, metaphors, and imagery to evoke subjective moods. The leading Symbolists included Paul Verlaine, Arthur Rimbaud, and Stéphane Mallarmé, but the pioneer was Charles Baudelaire (1821–67).

Art from decay

In *Les Fleurs du mal* (*The Flowers of Evil*) – the title suggests the flowering of moral decay into art – Baudelaire turns his back on Romantic outpourings in favour of suggestive symbolism and frank expression. Using the traditional alexandrine metre – in which lines of 12 syllables are divided into two parts by a pause, or caesura – he addresses non-traditional new subjects that were shocking at the time, such as prostitution, interracial sex, drink, and drugs. Baudelaire paints a pessimistic portrait of modern man, inflected with his personal concerns – including his ambitions as a poet. At the book's heart is *ennui*, the deadening of the soul, as well as an existential dread and fear of death.

A search for meaning

In the opening section, a series of poems explores the role of the artist as visionary, martyr, performer, outcast, and fool. The poet tries to find meaning through sex, but initial excitement is followed by disenchantment – to which art offers some consolation. In the second section, "Parisian Tableaux", which was added for a new edition of 1861, the poet roams the city as a *flâneur* (an idle observer), finding only reminders of his own misery. The old Paris is gone, the new street scene alienating.

The following sections describe the poet's resulting flight to drink, sex, and even satanism. The last poem, "The Voyage", is a miniature odyssey tracing the travels of the soul to its final adventure, where at last there might be something new to experience. ∎

See also: *The Picture of Dorian Gray* 194 ▪ *A Season in Hell* 199 ▪ *The Waste Land* 213 ▪ *The Outsider* 245

NOT BEING HEARD IS NO REASON FOR SILENCE

LES MISÉRABLES (1862), VICTOR HUGO

IN CONTEXT

FOCUS
Social protest novel

BEFORE
1794 English radical writer William Godwin deplores an unjust social system in *The Adventures of Caleb Williams*.

1845 English politician Benjamin Disraeli writes *Sybil, or The Two Nations*, which shows that England has two worlds: the rich and the poor.

1852–65 English novelist Charles Dickens criticizes the poverty and greed of Victorian society in *Bleak House*, *Little Dorrit*, and *Our Mutual Friend*.

AFTER
1870s–80s French writer Émile Zola attacks urban poverty and the social system in novels such as *L'Assommoir* (1877) and *Germinal* (1885).

1906 *The Jungle*, a novel by US journalist Upton Sinclair about Chicago's meatpacking industry, shocks readers.

An immense novel, *Les Misérables* is comprised of five volumes, each of which is subdivided into books of several chapters. Victor Hugo's motivation was also vast – namely, to write a novel that protested the social conditions existing in France at that time. For him, as long as there was "social condemnation, which … creates hells on earth, … books like this cannot be useless".

Hugo was not the only writer to highlight injustice in an attempt to bring about social change. In England, his contemporary Charles Dickens was doing the same, while Elizabeth Gaskell's portrait of the poor in the industrialized north

Social prosperity means man happy, the citizen free, the nation great.
Les Misérables

of the country, *Mary Barton* (1848), contributed to England's mood of social reform. Meanwhile, in the USA, Harriet Beecher Stowe's *Uncle Tom's Cabin* (1852) helped mobilize public opinion against slavery.

Hugo's book features a huge cast of characters and a vast historical sweep, spanning as it does the era from 1815 to the June 1832 uprising in Paris. It is a panoramic novel that embraces themes of hardship, poverty, greed, bitterness, politics, compassion, love, and redemption.

Hell in need of humanity
The main story in *Les Misérables* focuses on Jean Valjean, released after spending 19 years in prison for the theft of some bread. Now a social outcast, he steals from a bishop, who covers for him and whose kindness sets him on a path towards redemption. Under a false name, Valjean starts a business, becomes wealthy, and adopts a young girl, Cosette, whose mother, Fantine – forced into prostitution by poverty – has died. Despite his efforts, Valjean is haunted by his criminal past, and he is relentlessly pursued by an implacable police inspector, Javert.

See also: *Bleak House* 146–49 ▪ *Oliver Twist* 151 ▪ *Uncle Tom's Cabin* 153 ▪ *War and Peace* 178–81 ▪ *Germinal* 190–91

Les Misérables has a large cast of intertwining characters. Although a mix of social classes is depicted, those whose wretched lives are swallowed up in the labyrinth of Paris's underworld are the focus. At the heart of the book is the fate of Cosette, the orphaned child of a prostitute.

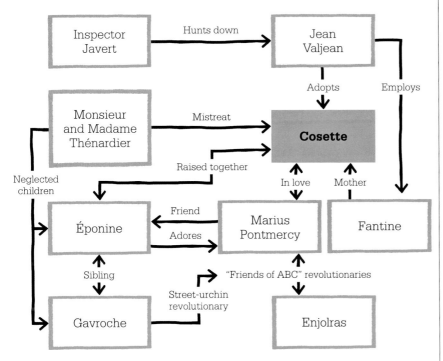

Victor Hugo

Victor Hugo, one of France's leading writers, was born in 1802 in Besançon, eastern France, the son of an officer in Napoleon's army. Raised in Paris and well educated, by the age of 20 he had published his first volume of verse.

Hugo was a prodigious writer, producing some 20 volumes of poetry, 10 plays, nine novels, as well as many essays. A liberal republican and supporter of universal suffrage, he was also active politically. Following the revolutions of 1848 that shook Europe, he was elected to the National Assembly. He was, however, highly critical of the Second Empire of Louis Napoleon and went into exile in 1851 with his wife, Adèle, and his long-standing mistress, Juliette Drouet.

Returning to Paris as a national hero in 1870, Hugo became a senator in the Third Republic. He died in 1885 and was buried in the Pantheon.

Other key works

1827 *Cromwell*
1831 *The Hunchback of Notre-Dame*
1859–83 *The Legend of the Ages*

Many other characters weave in and out of his story: Marius, an idealistic law student, who falls in love with Cosette; the Thénardiers, unscrupulous innkeepers, who mistreat Cosette; their neglected children, Gavroche and Éponine, who live on the streets; and many revolutionary students. All are caught up in a hellish society that Hugo vividly describes.

From time to time Hugo digresses to write about related topics, or to present his opinions. He writes in detail about such subjects as the Battle of Waterloo (1815), street urchins, Parisian architecture, the construction of the Paris sewers, and religious orders. Towards the end of the novel, Hugo moves away from the action at the barricades to reflect on the role of revolution in creating a better society, before returning to the story and its conclusion.

Les Misérables was widely advertised before publication and caused a considerable stir: several reviewers were critical, accusing Hugo of being either dangerously revolutionary or overly sentimental. However, the book was an instant success, not just in France but also in Britain and beyond. Although it did not directly bring about change, its historical sweep and powerful description of social injustice meant that, like all great protest novels, it provoked thought and helped to raise social consciousness. ■

CURIOUSER AND CURIOUSER!

ALICE'S ADVENTURES IN WONDERLAND (1865), LEWIS CARROLL

The concept of "childhood" was really only invented in the 18th century, when the middle classes began to see the value of a child's innocence and play. For most of literary history, children were rarely mentioned, occasionally appearing in such works as Jean-Jacques Rousseau's *Émile* and William Wordsworth's *The Prelude*. In the 19th century, Charles Dickens sometimes placed children in the foreground of his stories, but only in books for adults.

Most tales written for, as opposed to about, children were adaptations of adult stories, or morally didactic. In the early 19th century, the Brothers Grimm's

See also: *Robinson Crusoe* 94–95 ▪ *Gulliver's Travels* 104 ▪ *Children's and Household Tales* 116–17 ▪ *Fairy Tales* 151 ▪ *Little Women* 199 ▪ *Treasure Island* 201

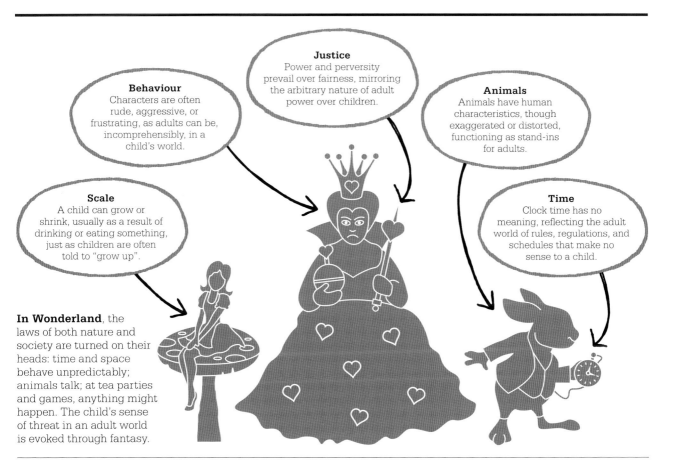

Justice
Power and perversity prevail over fairness, mirroring the arbitrary nature of adult power over children.

Behaviour
Characters are often rude, aggressive, or frustrating, as adults can be, incomprehensibly, in a child's world.

Animals
Animals have human characteristics, though exaggerated or distorted, functioning as stand-ins for adults.

Scale
A child can grow or shrink, usually as a result of drinking or eating something, just as children are often told to "grow up".

Time
Clock time has no meaning, reflecting the adult world of rules, regulations, and schedules that make no sense to a child.

In Wonderland, the laws of both nature and society are turned on their heads: time and space behave unpredictably; animals talk; at tea parties and games, anything might happen. The child's sense of threat in an adult world is evoked through fantasy.

illustrated folktales, originally collected for adults, were criticized as being unsuitable for young people because of their sexual and violent content – later editions were adapted to be more child-friendly. Hans Christian Andersen, who wrote his *Fairy Tales* (1835–37) specifically for children, caused an outcry by failing to include a moral.

A golden age
In the late 19th and early 20th centuries, writing for children enjoyed a golden age, founded on increasing literacy, the growth of commercial publishing, and recognition of the imaginative potential of a child's world. *Tom*

Brown's School Days (1857), by English author Thomas Hughes, started the tradition of the school story; another new genre was the coming-of-age tale, such as Louisa May Alcott's *Little Women* (1868–69) in the USA. Other classics include Johanna Spyri's *Heidi* (1880–81), from Switzerland, and Scotsman J M Barrie's *Peter Pan* (1911).

Alice's Adventures in Wonderland is one of the most influential books of this flowering. Regarded as the first masterpiece for children in English, its fantastical story is a marked departure from the prevailing realism of literature at the time. On a July day in 1862, Charles

Dodgson, a young mathematics don, went rowing with a male friend and three young sisters on the Thames near Oxford, and told a story about a girl named Alice – which was also the name of one of his passengers, Alice Liddell, aged ten. So *Alice's Adventures in Wonderland* took shape, appearing as a handwritten book, and then as a publication under the pseudonym Lewis Carroll.

A surreal world
In the story, seven-year-old Alice falls down a rabbit hole and finds herself in a surreal universe. She negotiates alone a world of strange creatures, strange attitudes, »

The brusque, hookah-smoking Caterpillar intensifies Alice's insecurity: she is so confused by Wonderland that she cannot even answer his question "Who are you?"

strange happenings, and strange linguistic logic. This is the focus of the book and its principal theme.

Part of the book's coherence comes from the fact that Alice herself entertains unorthodox logic. As she falls down the rabbit hole she wonders if she is going to land in the "Antipathies" (Antipodes), and imagines herself appearing ignorant when she has to ask whether she is in Australia or New Zealand. Her next observation

shows Carroll brilliantly inhabiting a child's ingenuousness: "No, it'll never do to ask: perhaps I shall see it written up somewhere."

Alice constantly wonders: about who she is, what are the rules of this peculiar world, and how she is to regain normality; common issues of childhood. Her bewilderment at first focuses on her being the wrong size, either too big or too small to do as she wants. After she meets the Caterpillar a new anxiety arises: the challenge of being repeatedly, often rudely, contradicted. Towards the end, with the Queen's repeated plea for a beheading, the possibility of violence adds to the tension.

Escape from rules

The characters that Alice meets are mostly animals. Apart from Alice and her sister, who features before and after the adventure, the only human characters are the Mad Hatter and the Duchess, since the King and Queen of Hearts are playing cards. Parents do not make an appearance, nor is there any reference to them.

Yet the inversions of everyday life that imprison Alice might also, at the same time, be seen as

'Well! I've often seen a cat without a grin,' thought Alice; 'but a grin without a cat! It's the most curious thing I ever saw in all my life!'
Alice's Adventures in Wonderland

liberating by Victorian adults accustomed to convention. One of the attractions of nonsense is that it offers a playground for the imagination, and arguably for the satisfaction of subliminal needs, including occasional escape from social rules.

Alice makes no reference at the end to having learned any lessons from her adventures. However, she does, in the course of the book, become more forthright, and by the time of the trial scene near the end she is capable of saying to the

The Harry Potter phenomenon

For Harry Potter, mortality lurks in the shadows: he is a hero fighting the forces of darkness, and learning life lessons in the process.

J K Rowling's Harry Potter novels (1997–2007), featuring the adventures of a young wizard, show how powerful children's writing can be. Rowling owes the phenomenal success of the books partly to her skilful mixing of genres, combining fantasy, coming of age, and school story, together with elements of the thriller and romance. Rowling has stated that death is a major theme in the books, but this does not prevent them from containing a strong vein of humour.

The publication schedule of the series allowed Harry to grow up in real time, so that the first generation of young Harry Potter readers literally grew up along with him, making their experience of reading the books particularly powerful.

Immensely popular with children and also garnering a substantial adult readership, the books have generated great wealth for their author. More than 450 million of the seven books had been sold by 2013.

Queen that her perverse sense of justice is "Stuff and nonsense!" Her final act, by which time she is child-sized again, is to insist that the playing cards are just that – inanimate things – whereupon they fly into the air. By force of character she has punctured the illusion.

The coda, featuring Alice's older sister, is beautifully judged. It starts with her dreaming "after a fashion", since a fully-fledged dream would be less subtle than this elusive mind-state. First, she affectionately imagines Alice herself; then the weird characters Alice has been describing pass in front of her. Finally, she imagines Alice turning into a "grown woman", but keeping the "simple and loving heart" of her childhood, and passing on the story of Wonderland to a new generation.

The meaning of nonsense

Fantasy conveyed with as much vividness, wit, and sensitivity as Carroll's has immediate impact but will raise questions about hidden meanings. Food in the book often triggers unease – did Carroll suffer from an eating disorder? Since the brand of mathematics he taught at Oxford was conservative, at a time when more abstract ideas were taking root, some of the weird logic may be a satirical side-sweep at the new maths. And as the book was a gift for the real Alice, it may contain private references for her.

Carroll's sources of inspiration will never be comprehensively recovered, yet any in-jokes in no way diminish the universality of Alice's adventures, grounded as it is in the vulnerability of children, a theme as relevant today as it was in Carroll's time.

Carroll brought out a second and similar book about Alice in 1871: *Through the Looking-Glass, and What Alice Found There*. Here too

are memorable characters (such as the Walrus and the Carpenter, and Tweedledum and Tweedledee), nonsensical songs, and witty aphorisms that flirt with alternative logic. As in Wonderland, meaning is slippery: a word, claims Humpty Dumpty, "means just what I choose it to mean". However, the sequel is more menacing than the first Alice story, perhaps reflecting Carroll's grief over the loss of his father.

The lure of fantasy

A line of influence stretches from the magical transformations of Wonderland through J R R Tolkien's *The Hobbit* and C S Lewis's Narnia series, the whimsical rhyming world of Dr Seuss, Roald Dahl's beloved *Charlie and the Chocolate Factory*, and J K Rowling's wizard stronghold Hogwarts. Although in the 21st century a new realism has entered writing for children, with stories of abandonment, homelessness, and alienation, fantasy remains perennially compelling to young minds. ∎

Humpty Dumpty, in common with characters in Wonderland, has conversations with Alice that are characterized by riddles, wordplay, and perverse logic posed as rationality.

Lewis Carroll

Born in 1832 in Cheshire, England, Charles Dodgson (best known later by his pen name, Lewis Carroll) was the son of a clergyman. He took a first-class degree in mathematics from Christ Church, Oxford, and from 1855 he held a lectureship there until his death. He was also ordained as a deacon. His first published work, in 1856, was a poem on solitude. Dodgson was well connected, his friends including the critic and writer John Ruskin, and the painter and poet Dante Gabriel Rossetti. He was a notable photographer, taking portraits of the poet Alfred Tennyson, the actress Ellen Terry, and many children. He died in 1898, aged 65, as a result of pneumonia after a severe dose of influenza. By this time *Alice's Adventures in Wonderland* was the most popular children's book in Britain. Queen Victoria was one of its admirers.

Other key works

1871 *Through the Looking-Glass, and What Alice Found There*
1876 *The Hunting of the Snark*

PAIN AND SUFFERING ARE ALWAYS INEVITABLE FOR A LARGE INTELLIGENCE AND A DEEP HEART

CRIME AND PUNISHMENT (1866), FYODOR DOSTOYEVSKY

IN CONTEXT

FOCUS
Psychological realism

BEFORE
c.1000–12 Murasaki Shikibu's *The Tale of Genji* offers psychological insights into the lives of its characters.

1740 English writer Samuel Richardson's sentimental novel *Pamela* explores the inner nature of the novel's heroine.

1830 *The Red and the Black*, by French author Stendhal, is published and is seen by many as the first psychological realist novel.

AFTER
1871–72 George Eliot's *Middlemarch* traces the psychological landscape of a provincial English town.

1881 *The Portrait of a Lady*, by US author Henry James, delves into the consciousness of the character Isabel Archer.

P sychological realism is the depiction in literature of the personality traits and innermost feelings of a character, casting a spotlight on their conscious thoughts and unconscious motivations. The plot itself often takes a secondary role in works that focus on psychological realism, and is there to set out the relationships, conflicts, and physical settings within which these mental dramas are played out.

Delving into the psyche of a character in this way marked a radical departure from Romantic fiction, in which plotlines typically saw wrongdoing punished and virtue rewarded. Literary works had, however, long explored the workings of the human mind, though uninformed by the emerging science of psychology. For example, mental machinations are central in the 11th-century Japanese story *The Tale of Genji*; in William Shakespeare's *Hamlet* (1603), it is the inner conflicts of the hero that drive the drama; and the 18th century saw the heyday of the genre known as the epistolary novel, in which personal letters and journal

All is in a man's hands and he lets it all slip from cowardice.
Crime and Punishment

entries were used to give the reader an insight into a character's intimate thoughts and feelings.

Exposing minds
In his masterpiece *Crime and Punishment*, Fyodor Dostoyevsky introduces the reader to his antihero, the student Rodion Romanovich Raskolnikov, also called Rodya or Rodka by the few people who love him. The author dissects – by means of a third-person narrative – Raskolnikov's psychological motivations in a way that presages the work of Sigmund Freud and other psychoanalysts.

Fyodor Dostoyevsky

Fyodor Dostoyevsky was born in Moscow, Russia, in 1821 to parents of Lithuanian descent. He trained and worked as an engineer before writing his first novel, *Poor Folk* (1846), which depicts the mental as well as the material condition of poverty.

In 1849, Dostoyevsky was arrested for being a member of the Petrashevsky Circle, a socialist intellectual group. After the torment of a mock execution by firing squad, he endured several years of hard labour in Siberia, where he began to suffer from epilepsy. After his release, issues with creditors prompted his voluntary exile in western Europe. After the death of his first wife, in 1867 he wed Anna Grigoryevna Snitkina, who gave birth to their four children, acted as his secretary, and managed the family's finances. Haunted by infirmity, he died in 1881.

Other key works

1864 *Notes from the Underground*
1866 *The Gambler*
1869 *The Idiot*
1880 *The Brothers Karamazov*

See also: *The Tale of Genji* 47 ▪ *The Princess of Cleves* 104 ▪ *Madame Bovary* 158–63 ▪ *Middlemarch* 182–83 ▪ *The Portrait of a Lady* 186–87

Summertime in St Petersburg is the setting for *Crime and Punishment*. The crowded, stifling conditions in the city mirror the troubled student Raskolnikov's feverish inner drama.

It is precisely this opening up of the protagonist's mind to the reader that secured the book's status as one of the most important and influential literary works to emerge in the 19th century.

Crime and Punishment opens on a "hot evening early in July" in St Petersburg, Russia. Raskolnikov, a shabbily dressed young man, steps from his tiny, garret flat, skips past his landlady, and slips away into the heat and the stench of the city. He is ill and also suffering from some form of mental dislocation. He mutters to himself. He is hungry. He walks the streets, disturbed by the presence of others. The reader is drawn ever closer to his innermost thoughts, fears, and anxieties.

Raskolnikov is poor, and this motif of poverty is pervasive in the text. The reader wanders with him, seeing with his eyes a city that is striving to survive – a place in which many struggle against hunger and mental torment.

Inner conflicts

Dostoyevsky inserts a variety of colourful and brilliantly observed characters into the narrative, as seen through Raskolnikov's eyes. He ventures to the house of Alyona Ivanovna, a local pawnbroker, "a diminutive, withered up old woman of sixty, with sharp malignant eyes and a sharp little nose". Raskolnikov has come to pawn his father's watch and, poverty-stricken, he is forced to accept a pitiful sum for it. As he leaves the apartment block, a

thought enters his mind. He stops on the stairs, shocked at himself, and once back on the crowded streets, he walks as though in a dream, "regardless of the passers-by, and jostling against them", until he finds himself by a flight of steps leading down into a tavern. Although he has never been into a tavern before, he enters and orders a beer, and immediately "he felt easier; and his thoughts became clear". But Dostoyevsky informs the reader that Raskolnikov is far from well, because "even at that moment he had a dim foreboding that this happier frame of mind was also not normal".

He has a conversation with a drunken man, Marmeladov, who tells a pitiful story of poverty and his daughter's prostitution, both

brought about by his alcoholism. Marmeladov acknowledges his vice and reveals that he is confessing this to Raskolnikov, a chance encounter, rather than the regular patrons, because in his face he can read "some trouble of mind". »

Only to live, to live and live! Life, whatever it may be!
Crime and Punishment

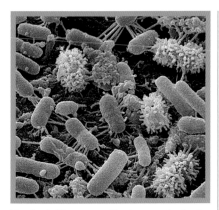

Raskolnikov recalls dreams he had while delirious in hospital. In one a plague of microbes had infected people and driven them mad, all convinced that they "alone had the truth".

Raskolnikov finally returns to his own hovel where he broods all the following day. Dostoyevsky paints a desperate picture of destitution and Raskolnikov's isolation from society.

The author's mastery of psychological realism fully exposes Raskolnikov's inner deliberations and machinations over how to act on his thought, which is to commit a crime (by killing the pawnbroker, Alyona Ivanovna), and he draws the reader tangibly and empathetically close to Raskolnikov's mind – the mind of a murderer. We feel his terror, and we experience the dirty

The really great men must, I think, have great sadness on earth.
Crime and Punishment

streets and depraved citizens of St Petersburg through his eyes. We become witnesses as scenes are played out in his mind, and we lie beside him in his squalid home. We, too, start to feel the awful sense of the inevitability of the act, from its imagined conception through to its grim and bloody reality.

Just as Freud would later argue that dreams enable understanding of waking experience, Dostoyevsky offers insights into his antihero's mind through his dreams. In one dream, Raskolnikov witnesses drunken peasants beating a horse to death. Heavy with symbolism, the dream foreshadows the crime he is about to commit, but it is also a reference to his desensitization to atrocity, and to the loss of his free will to act. Much later, he dreams that microscopic bugs cause insanity, dissent, and a propensity to violence in humans – an allusion to Raskolnikov's state of mind.

The shock of violence
The murder of Alyona Ivanovna is portrayed with a powerfully visceral actuality. Raskolnikov clubs the old woman with an axe until her skull is "broken and even battered in on one side". Over the floor lies "a perfect pool of blood". The moments hang in chillingly real tension as Raskolnikov unlocks a wooden chest under the bed and retrieves the riches of "bracelets, chains, ear-rings, pins". And the scene is not complete. There are further footsteps in the room where Alyona Ivanovna lies. "Suddenly, he jumped up, seized the axe and ran out of the bedroom". So ends the first part of the novel.

Dostoyevsky presents several potential motives for this crime, the most prominent of which is Raskolnikov's perception of himself as a "superman" – someone superior

to others, above the law, who feels a disgust for society and the mindless behaviour of the herds of "ordinary" people. At one point, Raskolnikov remarks that all great men have been criminals, transgressing ancient laws and shedding blood if it were "of use to their cause".

Dostoyevsky's exposition of this motive is thought to reflect his anguish at the changes he observed in Russian society – the rise of materialism, the decline of the old order, and the popularity of selfish and nihilistic philosophies. Raskolnikov's crime, and his later unravelling, serve as a caution to those of Dostoyevsky's compatriots inclined to revolutionary change.

Guilt and redemption
In the unfolding consequences of the murder, we follow Raskolnikov around the streets of St Petersburg in his desperation and fevered delirium. He stumbles upon the drunk, dying Marmeladov who has been run over by a carriage and horses, and is drawn closer to Marmeladov's daughter, Sonya, who is left to support the family alone. Raskolnikov meets Porfiry

Tsar Alexander II abolished serfdom in Russia in 1861. The prostitutes found in St Petersburg's seedy Haymarket area, a haunt of Raskolnikov, were predominantly desperate peasant girls.

Raskolnikov's motives for killing Alyona Ivanovna are a central theme of *Crime and Punishment*. Dostoyevsky shows that his antihero's actions are prompted by a complex interplay of motives, internal dialogues, and unconscious drives that combine social, individual, philosophical, and religious imperatives.

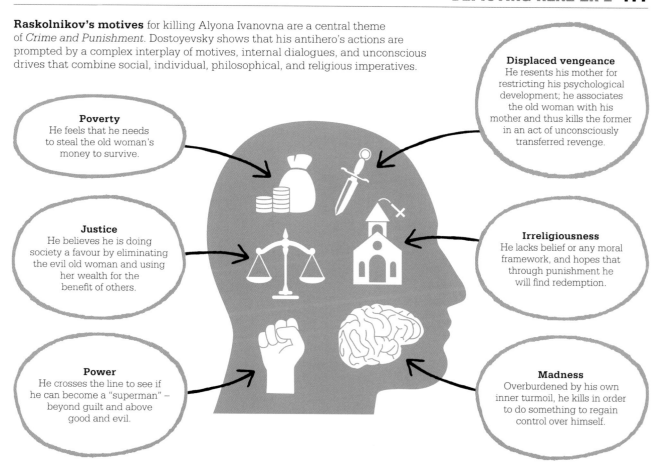

Poverty
He feels that he needs to steal the old woman's money to survive.

Displaced vengeance
He resents his mother for restricting his psychological development; he associates the old woman with his mother and thus kills the former in an act of unconsciously transferred revenge.

Justice
He believes he is doing society a favour by eliminating the evil old woman and using her wealth for the benefit of others.

Irreligiousness
He lacks belief or any moral framework, and hopes that through punishment he will find redemption.

Power
He crosses the line to see if he can become a "superman" – beyond guilt and above good and evil.

Madness
Overburdened by his own inner turmoil, he kills in order to do something to regain control over himself.

Petrovitch, a detective who becomes increasingly convinced that Raskolnikov is guilty of the crime, but lacks the evidence to prove it. Raskolnikov's nerves are in shreds. Would confessing and taking the punishment of the law be preferable to the torture of his own conscience? Does his sense of remorse suggest that he is ordinary rather than extraordinary?

Representing reality

In *Crime and Punishment*, Dostoyevsky masterfully explores and dissects the immensely complex nature of the mind of his protagonist. The novel's powerful exploration of the meaning of life and the existence in the world of horror, evil, suffering, and brutality is matched by its examination of guilt, conscience, love, compassion, relations with our fellow humans, and the possibilities of redemption.

Dostoyevsky's concern for representing the reality of the psychological processes in Raskolnikov's mind ensured that *Crime and Punishment* became a significant touchstone for future novelists. This approach to writing coincided with – and was arguably influenced by – the rise of the science and practice of psychology. One of the late 19th century's most psychologically attuned writers, novelist Henry James, was brother of the pioneering psychologist William. The existential writers of the mid-20th century, including Jean-Paul Sartre and Albert Camus, also owe much to the ground-breaking narrative form created by Dostoyevsky. ∎

A hundred suspicions don't make a proof.
Crime and Punishment

TO DESCRIBE DIRECTLY THE LIFE OF HUMANITY OR EVEN OF A SINGLE NATION, APPEARS IMPOSSIBLE

WAR AND PEACE (1869), LEO TOLSTOY

Russia in the 19th century
was the seat of enormous
creativity in prose, poetry,
and drama. Critics have dubbed
the period the country's "Golden
Age", not for any unity of intent
among the authors, but for the
sheer number of literary works of
international significance that
emerged there over a short time.

The literature of the Golden
Age was heavily influenced by
the modernization of Russia in the
18th century. The country, which
had been insulated by culture and
geography from the Renaissance
that affected the rest of Europe
from the 14th to the 17th centuries,
was rapidly Westernized under

See also: *Eugene Onegin* 124 ▪ *A Hero of Our Time* 151–52 ▪ *Dead Souls* 152 ▪ *Crime and Punishment* 172–77 ▪ *The Idiot* 199 ▪ *Anna Karenina* 200 ▪ *The Brothers Karamazov* 200–01 ▪ *Uncle Vanya* 203

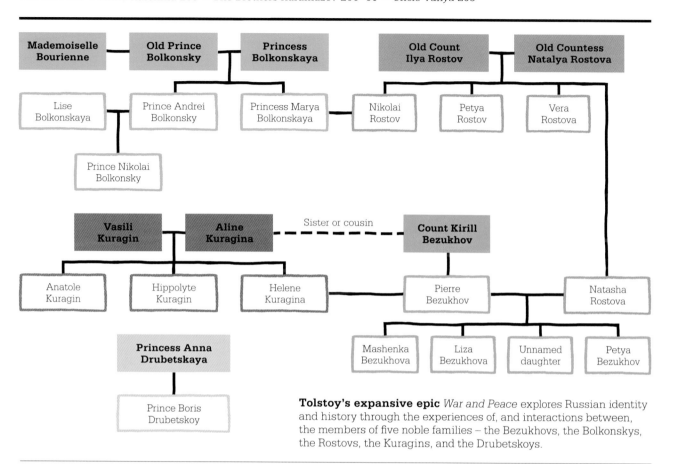

Tolstoy's expansive epic *War and Peace* explores Russian identity and history through the experiences of, and interactions between, the members of five noble families – the Bezukhovs, the Bolkonskys, the Rostovs, the Kuragins, and the Drubetskoys.

Peter the Great, tsar from 1682 to 1725. Peter oversaw the adoption of Western customs, learning, and even language, to the extent that – by the early 19th century – the primary tongue spoken by the Russian aristocracy was French.

The traditional literature of "old Russia", notably the folk epic, was displaced by writing that focused on more modern themes, and the Russian language itself developed new literary forms that carried through to the 19th century. However, Russian writers did much more than ape the conventions of Western literature. They reacted to and defied its assumptions, and carved out their own uniquely

Russian forms of expression, which often looked back to the themes of earlier folktales, and sometimes even challenged the very concept of writing as art. In the West, the writers of Russia's Golden Age were regarded with curiosity – they were certainly brilliant, but they were also considered savage and unschooled.

The first flowering of the Golden Age early in the 19th century included works from writers such as Alexander Pushkin, Nikolai Gogol, and Ivan Turgenev. A second blossoming in the 1860s and 1870s produced the greatest works of the period, including Fyodor Dostoyevsky's *Crime and*

Punishment (1866) – a visceral exercise in psychological realism – and Tolstoy's *War and Peace* (1869) and *Anna Karenina* (1875–77). »

If no one fought except on his own conviction, there would be no wars.
War and Peace

High-society balls of the early 19th century, where attendees dressed in military finery and expensive gowns, characterize Tolstoy's depiction of the shallow liberalism of St Petersburg.

Within a single lifespan, Russian literature had made a series of incredible leaps from a folkloric tradition to far more complex and extensive literary styles.

History writing

A typically Russian ambivalence about Western literary tropes led Tolstoy to write that "There is not a single work of Russian artistic prose... that quite fits the form of a novel, a poem, or a story." He was reluctant to categorize his masterful *War and Peace*: "[it is] not a novel, even less is it a poem, and still less a historical chronicle", he stated in 1868. Tolstoy's concern was that all historical records had their pitfalls and that the "truth" of history was hard to grasp without an omniscient view. He attempted to achieve such a wide perspective in *War and Peace* by exploring the experiences of a vast cast of characters – more than 500 in all – from across society. Some of the characters were inspired by people Tolstoy knew in real life: Natasha Rostova, for example, was based on Tolstoy's wife's sister. Many of the aristocratic characters were given authentic, but slightly bastardized names: the name of reckless and wilful Bezukhov, for example, translates as "earless".

War and Peace spans a period of eight years from July 1805, narrating the events of Napoleon's invasion of Russia up to the eventual burning of Moscow in September 1812. The main narrative follows the rise and fall in the fortunes of five fictional, aristocratic Russian families set against the backdrop of the Napoleonic Wars of the 19th century, linking their personal lives to the history of Russia. Alongside these fictional characters, Tolstoy casts a series of actual historical figures, such as Tsar Alexander and Napoleon, as key players in his epic.

Introductions

The book begins in the most Westernized of Russian cities – St Petersburg – at a high-society soirée. While Napoleon's army marches through Italy and heads east, the city's aristocrats meet to gossip (in French), gamble, drink, and flirt. Significantly, the opening lines of the book, spoken by the hostess of the soirée, Anna Pavlovna Scherer, establish the book's focus on history, war, and the state of European affairs: "Well, Prince, so Genoa and Lucca are now just family estates of the Buonapartes."

Tolstoy uses this gathering to introduce readers to some of his leading characters, including Prince Andrei Nikolaevich Bolkonsky, a handsome, intelligent and wealthy figure who will emerge as one of the heroes of the book, and Andrei's friend Pierre Bezukhov, the ungainly and bulky son of a Russian count, through whom Tolstoy relays his own thoughts and concerns on the best way to live a moral life in an immoral world.

Tolstoy's narrative then moves to Moscow, where both the city and its people have more traditionally Russian qualities. Here, the reader is introduced to further characters, including Countess Rostova and her four children, one of whom is Natalia Ilyinichna (Natasha) – "black-eyed, wide-mouthed" and "full of life" – whose vibrant energy flits through the pages of the book.

Russia at war

Soon, Russia is at war. Napoleon's forces march towards Moscow and are met by the Russians some 100km (70 miles) west of the city at the Battle of Borodino on 7 September 1812. Tolstoy paints a vivid image of the bloodbath in

There's nothing stronger than those two old soldiers – Time and Patience.
War and Peace

which more than 25,000 men were killed in a single day. He presents the thoughts and actions of real-life characters, such as Napoleon and his Russian counterpart Kutusov, alongside those of imagined characters like Andrei and Pierre, allowing readers to see the chaos and brutal truth of war from every perspective. The battle – which was an indecisive victory for the French – marks the turning point of the war.

While life for St Petersburg's aristocrats continues almost unaffected, Moscow is sacked and burned by Napoleon's Grand Armée before it retreats. Napoleon's forces suffer enormous hardships as they withdraw: facing freezing conditions and starvation, they are slaughtered in their thousands by the Russians.

In the book's two-part epilogue, Tolstoy tells of life in 1813 and beyond, after Napoleon's army

The Battle of Borodino is a key moment in Tolstoy's *War and Peace*. In his account, it is the chaos of battle, rather than the orders of leaders, which decide the conflict's outcome.

has fled and the war is over, with peace finally restored to Russia and her people.

The small actions of many

After finishing the stories of his fictional characters, Tolstoy reappraises the historical roles played by Napoleon and Tsar Alexander. He concludes that history is not driven by the actions of great leaders, but by many, small and ordinary events: "History is the life of nations and of humanity." In *War and Peace* that vast scale is finely observed, and Tolstoy's penetrating vision into everyday truths makes the book the vast, grand work that it is.

War and Peace captured the essence of an era. In 1875, it was described by the Russian novelist Ivan Turgenev as "the vast picture of the whole nation's life". A century on from its publication, Ernest Hemingway declared that it was from Tolstoy that he had learned to write about war, for no one wrote "about war better than Tolstoy did". Nor indeed, have many written better on peace. ∎

Leo Tolstoy

Leo Tolstoy was born near Moscow in 1828 to a noble Russian family. After leaving Kazan University early, Tolstoy led a dissolute life in Moscow and St Petersburg, running up significant gambling debts. He toured Europe in 1860–61, meeting the novelist Victor Hugo and the political thinker Pierre-Joseph Proudhon. Both inspired Tolstoy to return to Russia to write and educate the impoverished serfs. In 1862, Tolstoy married Sophia Andreevna Behrs with whom he had 13 children. Sophia looked after their financial matters, although their marriage became increasingly unhappy. After completing *War and Peace* and *Anna Karenina*, Tolstoy sought spiritual and moral truth through his Christianity and by espousing pacifism, influencing figures such as Gandhi and Martin Luther King. He died of pneumonia in 1910, aged 82.

Other key works

1875–77 *Anna Karenina*
1879 *A Confession*
1886 *The Death of Ivan Ilyich*
1893 *The Kingdom of God Is Within You*

IT IS A NARROW MIND WHICH CANNOT LOOK AT A SUBJECT FROM VARIOUS POINTS OF VIEW
MIDDLEMARCH (1871–1872), GEORGE ELIOT

IN CONTEXT

FOCUS
The omniscient narrator

BEFORE
1749 Henry Fielding's omniscient narrator in *Tom Jones* exposes the process of constructing a narrative.

1862 The omniscient voice in Victor Hugo's *Les Misérables* comments on politics, society, and the characters in the text.

1869 *War and Peace* by Leo Tolstoy includes an omniscient voice to enable "philosophical discussion".

AFTER
1925 The omniscient narrator in *Mrs Dalloway* lets Virginia Woolf create characters with great "inner space" and depth.

2001 Third-person omniscient narration by Jonathan Franzen, in *The Corrections*, suggests that cultural commentary and authority is a revived function of literary fiction.

The omniscient (all-knowing) narrator writes from a perspective outside the story but knows everything about the characters and events in the story. This authorial voice was widely used by 19th-century novelists in the context of social realism. Many of the best-known writers of the period – Charles Dickens, Victor Hugo, and Leo Tolstoy, for example – often wrote in the third-person omniscient, and the narrative device was ideal for George Eliot in *Middlemarch*, as it helped her to draw her readers into "watching keenly the stealthy convergence of human lots".

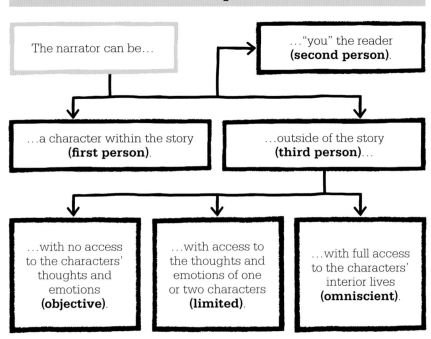

The narrator's point of view

The narrator can be…

…"you" the reader **(second person)**.

…a character within the story **(first person)**.

…outside of the story **(third person)**…

…with no access to the characters' thoughts and emotions **(objective)**.

…with access to the thoughts and emotions of one or two characters **(limited)**.

…with full access to the characters' interior lives **(omniscient)**.

See also: *Pride and Prejudice* 118–19 ▪ *The Three Musketeers* 122–23 ▪ *Vanity Fair* 153 ▪ *Les Misérables* 166–67 ▪
Crime and Punishment 172–77 ▪ *War and Peace* 178–81 ▪ *Tess of the D'Urbervilles* 192–93

Through the intertwining storylines of a large cast of characters – who live in the provincial English town of the title – *Middlemarch* explores tensions between marriage and vocation. In particular, it focuses on the dreams of two idealistic individuals, the intelligent and philanthropic heiress Dorothea Brooke, and the talented but naive doctor Tertius Lydgate.

A world of hard choices

Eliot steers clear of conformist happy endings – a fantasy that she considered the territory of "silly" lady novelists. Her ambition was to create a portrait of the complexity of ordinary human life: minor flaws and failings, small tragedies, quiet triumphs, and moments of dignity. It is the omniscient voice that regularly turns our focus back to this ambition.

Eliot admired the German writer Johann Wolfgang van Goethe, and also shared his philosophy that the efforts of each single individual are essential to the overall progress of humankind. In *Middlemarch* she refines and fictionalizes this tenet, proposing that women play a unique and significant role in the trajectory of progress and change. In particular, Eliot (as omniscient narrator) poses the question of how to do this as a woman in the real and changing world.

An invitation to think

There are many discussions about the role of women, between the novel's characters, as well as in the authorial asides. Male characters describe a range of qualities that are expected of women, from Dorothea's husband Mr Casaubon's ideal of "self-sacrificing affection" to Lydgate's daydream of beautiful companionship, "reclining in a paradise with sweet laughs for bird-notes". Yet there is a reluctance to promote a single, conclusive opinion regarding women's lot in society. Instead, the authorial voice invites us to reach our own conclusions by posing questions such as, "Was [Dorothea's] point of view the only possible one with regard to this marriage?"

What do we live for, if not to make life less difficult to each other?
Middlemarch

Although Eliot has been accused by critics of authorial bullying – Henry James read the novel as "too clever by half" – she succeeds in sustaining a discursive tone, particularly in interjections by the omniscient narrator.

George Eliot remains faithful to her own conviction that we must concern ourselves with real-life issues by inviting readers to perceive their own interconnected web of complex and often opposing tendencies in all people, whether those people are fictional or real. ▪

George Eliot

George Eliot was born Mary Ann Evans in 1819 in Warwickshire, England. Unusually for a girl, she was educated at private schools until the age of 16; after her mother died in 1836, she became housekeeper for her father. After his death, in 1849, Eliot travelled to Geneva, then London, where she settled and in 1851 became editor of John Bray's journal, *The Westminster Review*.

She formed a number of unreciprocated attachments, including to philosopher Herbert Spencer, but found true love with fellow intellectual George Henry Lewes, who was separated but could not divorce. In 1854, they chose to live together openly, and Evans began writing her novels, using a male pseudonym to lend authority to her work. Her writing ended after Lewes died in 1878. In 1880 she married John Walter Cross, but died just seven months later.

Other key works

1859 *Adam Bede*
1860 *The Mill on the Floss*
1861 *Silas Marner*
1876 *Daniel Deronda*

WE MAY BRAVE HUMAN LAWS, BUT WE CANNOT RESIST NATURAL ONES
TWENTY THOUSAND LEAGUES UNDER THE SEA (1870), JULES VERNE

IN CONTEXT

FOCUS
Scientific romance

BEFORE
1818 *Frankenstein*, by the English author Mary Shelley, is published; it is often seen as the first fictional work with a scientific focus.

1845 The term "scientific romance" is used for the first time, in a review of the anonymously authored 1844 work *Vestiges of the Natural History of Creation*, to describe its unorthodox scientific ideas as literary fiction.

AFTER
1895 *The Time Machine*, H G Wells's first science fiction novel, popularizes the concept of time travel and offers a dystopian view of the future.

1912 Sir Arthur Conan Doyle's *The Lost World* extends the genre of scientific romance by envisioning dinosaurs in contemporary South America.

The term "scientific romance" originated in the 19th century to describe speculative writings about natural history or to condemn scientific ideas as fanciful. But over time, as scientific knowledge meant that ideas about the future grew more plausible, the label came to be applied to fictional works that incorporated aspects of scientific wonder in the plotline.

This was an era in which Europeans – now obsessed with technology, social progress, travel, and adventure – dominated the world, and it was hoped that science could help to transform an era of grime and squalor into one of comfort and wealth.

Science and exploration
Frenchman Jules Verne (1828–1905) is the best remembered of the 19th-century scientific romance writers, demonstrating in his works a prescient and imaginative taste for futuristic travel. Verne's travelogue *Five Weeks in a Balloon* (1863) established his style of action-packed adventure, playing with the possibilities of exploration. From journeying into the air, Verne turned terrestrial with *Journey to the Centre of the Earth* (1864), but it was in the oceans that he achieved his greatest success in the genre.

In the 1850s Verne began to develop the idea of an underwater boat, which became *Nautilus*, the ship of Captain Nemo in *Twenty Thousand Leagues Under the Sea*. Verne's narrative relates the fabulous tale of Nemo and his crew; of their spectacular submarine adventures finding kelp forests and giant squid in the watery regions of the world. The wonderfully creative Verne gave his travellers diving suits and "air-guns" to use under water – an amazing vision of the potential power of scientific development to enable exploration of the furthest reaches of the world.

In the early 20th century, "scientific romance" was largely superseded by the term "science fiction", and the focus shifted to outer space and the future rather than "terra incognita". ∎

See also: *Frankenstein* 120–21

IN SWEDEN ALL WE DO IS TO CELEBRATE JUBILEES
THE RED ROOM (1879), AUGUST STRINDBERG

IN CONTEXT

FOCUS
Roman à clef

BEFORE
1642–69 Readers would have recognized depictions of important society figures in the *roman à clef* novels of French writer Madeleine de Scudéry, such as *Clelia*.

1816 The characters in the scandalous novel *Glenarvon*, by the English aristocrat Lady Caroline Lamb, are thinly disguised versions of her ex-lover Lord Byron and others in her own privileged London social circle.

AFTER
1957 *On the Road*, by Jack Kerouac, continues the tradition of the *roman à clef*, detailing his time travelling in North America.

1963 US writer Sylvia Plath's semi-autobiographical *The Bell Jar* depicts a young woman's descent into mental illness.

The *roman à clef*, or "novel with a key", is literature that depicts real people or events thinly disguised as fiction, the "key" being the relationship between the real and the fictitious. Such works often use satire and humour to comment on politics, scandals, and controversial figures.

Deceit and corruption

The Red Room, a novel by Swedish author August Strindberg (1849–1912), who was also a much admired playwright, is a satire of Stockholm society, akin to the work of English writer Charles Dickens in its biting critique. Considered to be the first modern Swedish novel in its style and content, the book introduces Arvid Falk, Strindberg's alter ego and a naive idealist.

Falk is a young civil servant when we meet him, so frustrated by the bureaucracy and drudgery of his job that he gives it up to become a journalist and author. He encounters characters from theatre, politics, and business, drawn from real personalities in the Stockholm

elite – and, disheartened, he soon realizes that Swedish society is riddled with deceit and corruption.

The title of the novel refers to a room in a Stockholm restaurant where bohemians gathered. Here, Falk seeks solace with artists and writers to contemplate the vicissitudes of life. The comic descriptions of the characters he encounters provide a sense of the tensions between bohemian and bourgeois life in Stockholm. ■

Train yourself to regard the world from a bird's-eye view, and you will discover how petty and insignificant everything is.
The Red Room

See also: *Bleak House* 146–49 ▪ *On the Road* 264–65 ▪ *The Bell Jar* 290 ▪ *Fear and Loathing in Las Vegas* 332

SHE IS WRITTEN IN A FOREIGN TONGUE

THE PORTRAIT OF A LADY (1881), HENRY JAMES

IN CONTEXT

FOCUS
Transatlantic fiction

BEFORE
1844 In *Martin Chuzzlewit*, Charles Dickens offers an early piece of transatlantic fiction, set in England and the USA.

1875 *The Way We Live Now*, a satirical novel by English writer Anthony Trollope, follows corrupt European financier Augustus Melmotte and his American investments.

AFTER
1907 US author Edith Wharton's *Madame de Treymes* revolves around Americans living in France.

1926 In *The Sun Also Rises*, US author Ernest Hemingway presents a group of young American and British expatriates in Paris and Spain.

1955 In Vladimir Nabokov's *Lolita*, European Humbert Humbert pursues the young Lolita across the USA.

Much has been made of the supposed psychological and cultural differences between Europeans (notably the British) and Americans – whether in language, humour, or social etiquette. In Europe, the debate often centres on Americanisms that are seen to be creeping into European cultures.

Similar preoccupations have been reflected in literature, with early transatlantic fiction often exploring cultural differences, but with a particular focus on the impact of the Old World (Europe) on US sensibilities. Although the

If we're not good Americans we're certainly poor Europeans; we've no natural place here.
The Portrait of a Lady

18th century had seen a political and economic breach in Anglo–American relations that led to US independence in 1776, there remained a strong, though at times antagonistic, bond between the two. As a nation, the USA gained in confidence, and saw a growth in the affluent classes and an increase in tourism and transatlantic travel.

Innocents abroad
One prominent example of an American with a taste for travel and an eye for cultural difference was the expatriate Henry James. He viewed his fellow Americans with detachment, and his novels examined in depth what it meant to be an American.

Like so many of his works, *The Portrait of a Lady* depicts a cast of mainly American characters in a European setting. The self-made Caspar Goodwood is a symbol of his nation – enterprising and forthright. He is contrasted with Gilbert Osmond, who has adopted European manners and values, a morally corrupt man who poses as an aesthete, a man of taste.

It is through the novel's central character, Isabel Archer, that the tensions between Old and New

See also: *The Turn of the Screw* 203 ▪ *Lolita* 260–61

USA

A young, independent outlook based on belief in "Life, Liberty, and the pursuit of Happiness".

Culturally barren, coarse, vulgar, and unrefined.

Meritocratic values rooted in optimism, dynamism, and individual ambition.

Early transatlantic literature typically contrasted US vulgarity and enthusiasm with European sophistication and cynicism. Europe remained hugely compelling and attractive to Americans, in both real life and fiction.

Europe

Older, complex societies, rigid with tradition, and tainted by despotism and decadence.

Culturally rich, refined, elegant, and sophisticated.

Restrictive values, world-weariness and cynicism, fear of loss of privilege.

World values are most starkly played out. Isabel is an intelligent, imaginative woman, who reflects the optimism and individualism of the USA. Travelling to England and then to Europe, Isabel, despite her independent spirit, also desires to conform to the social proprieties she encounters abroad. Her charm and sincerity make her attractive to suitors, but she believes marriage will curtail her freedom. To secure her independence, her cousin Ralph Touchett persuades his father to bequeath a large inheritance to Isabel, so that she will never have to marry for money. Ironically, her fortune renders her vulnerable to the seductions of sinister Gilbert Osmond, as Old World cunning ensnares New World innocence.

James continued these themes in his later works, including *The Ambassadors* and *The Wings of a Dove*, and inspired several authors, such as Edith Wharton, to focus on similar concerns. ▪

Henry James

New York-born Henry James (1843–1916), the son of wealthy intellectual Henry James Sr, spent his childhood travelling across Europe. After returning to the USA to attend Harvard University, he decided he wanted to be a writer, and published his short stories and reviews in periodicals.

From 1875 James settled in Europe, eventually moving to London. His nomadic childhood and life abroad as an adult allowed him to critique both American and European society. He was a prolific writer, producing short stories, plays, essays, travel sketches, and reviews as well as novels, and was nicknamed "The Master" by his friend Edith Wharton. In his writing, he remained very much an American, with his greatest characters being from his birth-nation. In 1915 he became a British citizen.

Other key works

1879 *Daisy Miller*
1886 *The Bostonians*
1902 *The Wings of a Dove*
1903 *The Ambassadors*
1904 *The Golden Bowl*

HUMAN BEINGS CAN BE AWFUL CRUEL TO ONE ANOTHER
THE ADVENTURES OF HUCKLEBERRY FINN (1884), MARK TWAIN

IN CONTEXT

FOCUS
American voices

BEFORE
1823 *The Pioneers*, the first of James Fenimore Cooper's saga the "Leatherstocking Tales", offers conflicting views of life on the frontier in one of the first original US novels.

1852 Harriet Beecher Stowe creates multiple vernacular voices in *Uncle Tom's Cabin*, a sentimental story that inflames the anti-slavery debate.

AFTER
1896 In *The Country of the Pointed Firs*, Sarah Orne Jewett paints a vivid picture of life in an isolated fishing village on the coast of Maine.

1939 John Steinbeck's Pulitzer Prize-winning novel *The Grapes of Wrath* mixes local colour with social injustice in an epic story of a family's journey west in the midst of the Great Depression.

With little history to speak of and few literary traditions to anchor them, US writers in the 19th century were engaged in holding up a mirror to the varied, complex populations of their rapidly evolving nation. One author blazed a trail, siting his story specifically in the Mississippi Valley in the Midwest with a poor white boy narrator like no other. Mark Twain's Huck Finn relates his adventures in regional dialect, salted with philosophical musings and homespun wisdom, and along the way becomes one of the first authentic voices in American literature.

What is it about *The Adventures of Huckleberry Finn* that led Ernest Hemingway to declare it to be the starting point for all American

The Country of the Pointed Firs (Jewett, 1896, Maine)
"'Tain't worthwhile to wear a day all out before it comes."

The Grapes of Wrath (Steinbeck, 1939, Oklahoma)
"There ain't no sin and there ain't no virtue. There's just stuff people do."

Uncle Tom's Cabin (Stowe, 1852, Kentucky)
"It don't look well, now, for a feller to be praisin' himself."

The Sound and the Fury (Faulkner, 1929, Mississippi)
"Hush, now. We be gone in a minute. Hush, now."

Huckleberry Finn (Twain, 1884, Mississippi Valley)
"Say, who is you? Whar is you? Dog my cats ef I didn' hear sumf'n."

The use of regional dialect in notable examples of 19th- and early 20th-century American literature gave a voice – and thereby a form of representation – to races, regions, cultures, and classes that had previously been denied one.

See also: *Uncle Tom's Cabin* 153 ▪ *The Sound and the Fury* 242–43 ▪ *Of Mice and Men* 244 ▪ *The Grapes of Wrath* 244 ▪ *To Kill a Mockingbird* 272–73

literature? For a start, it empowered generations of American writers to shift literature from its centre in the New England colonies and site their works on home soil with local colour and vernacular speech. But what is also remarkable is the radical heart of this free-flowing "boy's own" story. Twain's novel was published after the American Civil War (1861–65), but is set 40 to 50 years earlier, when slaveholding persisted in the South and settlers were scrabbling for land in the West. Huck's ingenuous thoughts reflect the numerous contradictions at the heart of American society.

Adventures down the river

Early on in the narrative, Huck introduces himself to the reader as an established character from a previous novel by Twain, *The Adventures of Tom Sawyer*, which gives his account the credibility of social history. He feigns death to escape the civilizing folk of Missouri and the brutality of his father, and begins his journey down the Mississippi on a raft, in the company of Jim, a runaway slave. As they drift south, the barbarous reality of backwoods society encroaches whenever they make contact with the shore. In these one-horse towns, lynch mobs and gangs administer justice; tricksters play to the weakness of the crowd; loud-mouthed drunks are summarily shot; and a young gentleman who befriends Huck is murdered in a family feud.

In a text that is peppered with the offensive word "nigger", subversion is played out through the talks between Huck and Jim. Newly escaped from being sold down the river by his mistress, Jim concludes:

"Yes – en I's rich now … I owns myself, en I's worth eight hund'd dollars. I wished I had de money."

Living on the raft in idyllic self-sufficiency, Huck and Jim are cast adrift from their social order, and a friendship develops. Later, as Huck wrestles with a Southern ideology that demands he should turn Jim in, he can remember the man only as a friend: "we a floating along, talking, and singing, and laughing … somehow I couldn't seem to strike no places to harden me against him…" By the time Tom Sawyer, the eponymous hero of Twain's earlier novel, steps on to the page, Huck's emotional development is almost complete.

Although it was condemned as "coarse" when it was first published in 1884, *Huckleberry Finn* injected American writing with a new energy, style, and colour. Its focus on the speech of real Americans stretched on through the voices of John Steinbeck's dispossessed farmers in *The Grapes of Wrath* (1939) to recent first-person narratives such as *Drown* (1996), Junot Díaz's stories of Dominican-Americans in New Jersey. ▪

You feel mighty free and easy and comfortable on a raft.
The Adventures of Huckleberry Finn

Mark Twain

Born on 30 November 1835, Samuel Langhorne Clemens grew up in Hannibal, Missouri, which served as the model for "St Petersburg" in *Huckleberry Finn*.

After the death of his father, Clemens left school at the age of 12; he worked as a typesetter and occasional writer, and in 1857 became a steamboat pilot on the Mississippi. During the Civil War he prospected for silver in Nevada, then started writing for newspapers, adopting the pen name Mark Twain.

In 1870 Clemens married Olivia Langdon; they settled in Connecticut and had four children. Despite the success of his novels, a series of poor investments bankrupted him, but from 1891 he lectured widely, enjoyed international celebrity, and restored his finances. As Mark Twain, he wrote 28 books, and many short stories, letters, and sketches. He died in 1910.

Other key works

1876 *The Adventures of Tom Sawyer*
1881 *The Prince and the Pauper*
1883 *Life on the Mississippi*

HE SIMPLY WANTED TO GO DOWN THE MINE AGAIN, TO SUFFER AND TO STRUGGLE
GERMINAL (1885), ÉMILE ZOLA

Naturalism was a literary movement that evolved in mid-19th-century France, in reaction to the sentimental imagination of Romanticism. Rather than depicting an idealized world, Naturalism focused on the harsh lives of those in the lowest social strata. It had much in common with realism, which aimed to present an accurate evocation of ordinary life, as exemplified in Gustave Flaubert's *Madame Bovary*. Naturalism had similar literary ambitions and used detailed realism, but was rooted in the theory that humans are unable to transcend the impact of their environment. Therefore, Naturalist authors applied quasi-scientific principles of objectivity and observation to examine how characters react when placed in adverse conditions. In effect, all Naturalist fiction is also realist, but the reverse is not always true.

Documentary realism
The leading figure of the Naturalist movement was the French writer Émile Zola. *Germinal* is Zola's 13th novel in the 20-volume Rougon-Macquart series, subtitled "The natural and social history of a family under the Second Empire", in which he studies the deterministic effects of heredity and environment on different characters within a single extended family. In the new French revolutionary calendar, "Germinal" was the name of the spring month, when plants begin to sprout: the title thus refers, optimistically, to the possibility of a better future.

Zola depicts the life of a mining community in northern France, portraying the struggle between capital and labour as well as the inexorable workings of the environment and heredity on his frequently ill-fated characters. He researched the background to his story minutely, inspired in part by miners strikes in 1869 and 1884.

Blow the candle out.
I don't need to see what colour my thoughts are.
Germinal

See also: *Tess of the D'Urbervilles* 192–93 ▪ *Far from the Madding Crowd* 200 ▪
A Doll's House 200 ▪ *The Red Badge of Courage* 202 ▪ *Sister Carrie* 203

Claude Lantier
The Masterpiece (1886)

Jacques Lantier
La Bête humaine
(1890)

Jean Macquart
The Earth (1887),
The Debacle (1892)

Étienne Lantier
Germinal (1885)

Gervaise Macquart
L'Assommoir (1877)

Anna Coupeau
Nana (1880)

Antoine
Macquart
*The Fortune of the
Rougons* (1871)

Lisa Macquart
*The Belly of
Paris* (1873)

Pauline Quenu
The Joy of Life
(1884)

Adelaïde
Fouque
*The Fortune of the
Rougons* (1871)

In Zola's Rougon-Macquart series, the main
characters are all descended from a single matriarch,
Adelaïde Fouque. Through them, Zola explores his
theories of heredity – the way in which inherited traits,
such as alcoholism or madness, play themselves out
differently but inexorably in generation after generation.

Émile Zola

Émile Zola was born in Paris
in 1840; his father died in 1847,
leaving the family to struggle
financially. In 1862 Zola got
a job at the publishing firm
Hachette and supplemented
his income by writing critical
articles for periodicals. Three
years later, his reputation
established, he made the
decision to support himself
by literary work alone, and
in 1865 published his first
novel, *Claude's Confession*.

In 1898 Zola famously
intervened in the Dreyfus
Affair, in which a Jewish
army officer was wrongfully
convicted of treason: Zola
wrote an open letter critical of
the general staff that became
known as *"J'Accuse"*. This act
led to his being found guilty
of libel and he fled to England.
He was allowed to return to
France in 1899. Zola died in
1902, from carbon monoxide
poisoning due to a blocked
flue. Some believe that his
death may not have been an
accident, but instead the
work of anti-Dreyfusards.

Other key works

1867 *Thérèse Raquin*
1877 *L'Assommoir*
1890 *La Bête humaine*

Zola deploys a forensic realism to
evoke the mine, which becomes
almost a character in itself. The use
of imagery and metaphors give it a
heightened reality – it is an ogre, a
voracious monster, sucking in and
devouring the insect-like workers.

Hope for the future
The novel's main protagonist is
the educated but volatile Étienne
Lantier, the son of an alcoholic, who
loses his job after assaulting his
boss. Étienne arrives in Montsou,
where he finds work in the mine.
Wary of an inherited propensity for
violence, he tries to avoid alcohol.
His position as an outsider allows
him to evaluate the suffering and
injustice he sees, and to pity the

plight of the people. As the novel
progresses, poverty and working
conditions worsen, to such an
extent that the workers go on
strike, with the idealistic Étienne
as their leader; when riots and
violent repression ensue, the miners
blame him. Despite the brutality
and desolation, Étienne retains his
belief in the potential germination
of a better society.

Dominated by Zola, literary
Naturalism was a relatively short-
lived movement in Europe, but it
went on to flourish in the USA,
where authors such as Stephen
Crane, Jack London, Theodore
Dreiser, and Upton Sinclair explored
in diverse ways the effects of
environment on their characters. ▪

THE EVENING SUN WAS NOW UGLY TO HER, LIKE A GREAT INFLAMED WOUND IN THE SKY
TESS OF THE D'URBERVILLES (1891), THOMAS HARDY

IN CONTEXT

FOCUS
Pathetic fallacy

BEFORE
1807 William Wordsworth employs pathetic fallacy in his poem "I wandered lonely as a cloud / That floats on high o'er vales and hills."

1818 "It was on a dreary night in November…". Mary Shelley opens Chapter 5 of *Frankenstein* with foreboding elemental forces.

1847 *Wuthering Heights* by Emily Brontë uses the weather on the moors to represent human emotion.

AFTER
1913 In *Sons and Lovers* by English novelist D H Lawrence, the moods of characters are reflected by evoking the environment around them.

1922 The opening of T S Eliot's Modernist poem *The Waste Land* portrays the season of spring as "cruel".

A strong connection with the landscape and nature runs through the works of the English writer Thomas Hardy. This relationship was a reflection of the author's tremendous love of Dorset, the county where he was born, and where he set all of his major novels. In *Tess of the d'Urbervilles*, nature represents the authenticity and spontaneity of traditional, rural life: if nature suffers, then Hardy is pointing to powerful "modern" forces, which are depicted not only as destructive but also more broadly as indicative of human suffering.

Through Hardy's use of pathetic fallacy, Tess Durbeyfield is shown as being in harmony with nature, which reflects her character and moods. The term "pathetic fallacy" was coined by art critic John Ruskin in 1856, and refers to the attribution of human behaviour and emotions to nature; this device was often used in 19th-century novels.

Pathetic fallacy is used by Hardy and other writers to link human emotions to aspects of nature – for example, using references to the weather to indicate mood: sunshine suggests happiness, rain misery, and a storm inner turmoil.

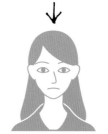

See also: *Frankenstein* 120–21 ▪ *Wuthering Heights* 132–37 ▪ *Bleak House* 146–49 ▪ *Far From the Madding Crowd* 200 ▪ *The Waste Land* 213

Tess is first shown as an innocent. She is dancing – a "maiden" in white – as part of a May Day celebration, and captures the attention of Angel Clare, whom she too notices. Although the author asserts in his subtitle (*A Pure Woman*) that Tess is "pure", evoking a Christian sentiment, she appears at first to be the embodiment and celebration of the pagan, feminine, and natural.

The series of misfortunes that shapes Tess's story is precipitated by the suggestion that she is descended from an aristocratic Norman family, the d'Urbervilles. This revelation distances Tess from her natural self – Angel's "new-sprung child of nature" – and eventually leads to consequences.

As events unfold, and Tess's life becomes entangled with Alec d'Urberville, she is depicted in more disturbing settings, such as beneath an "inflamed" sun or in bewildering, mist-shrouded forests. In an intense example of pathetic fallacy, she wakes in a wood to find herself surrounded by dying pheasants, hunted and abandoned, and she is forced to show mercy by ending their agony. Reflecting on her own misery, she is humbled by the suffering of the birds.

Virtuous victim

But Tess's love for Angel is pure and Hardy shows that they can overcome adverse circumstances. They marry, but their happiness is disrupted; a cock crowing in the afternoon after their marriage ceremony is a bad omen.

Angel is compelled by his background and upbringing to turn against Tess after she confesses to a turbulent past, despite agreeing

that she was "more sinned against than sinning". Hardy no longer represents her in nature, working in the fields or with animals – he places her in the new and lonely environment of a town, Sandbourne, living as a kept mistress.

The inevitability of fate

When Angel finally accepts that he wants to be with Tess, the lovers are reunited and experience a short-lived pastoral bliss before darkness sets in again. They retreat to the New Forest, where, like nymphs, "they promenaded over the dry bed of fir-needles, thrown into a vague intoxicating atmosphere at the consciousness of being together at last…". Here Hardy again suggests Tess's oneness with nature. The forest atmosphere evokes a joyful, pure love, which triumphs even over the prospect of death. The stone circle at the end of the novel represents both paganism and nature; and Tess's sleep on the altar-stone symbolizes her final, willing surrender to her fate. ▪

The atmosphere turned pale, the birds shook themselves in the hedges, arose and twittered; the lane showed all its white features and Tess showed hers, still whiter.
Tess of the d'Urbervilles

Thomas Hardy

Thomas Hardy was born in Dorset in 1840, the son of a stonemason and builder, and at the age of 16 became an architect's apprentice.

When he was 22 he moved to London, but after five years, concerned for his health and yearning to write, he returned to Dorset. Hardy set all his major novels in the southwest of England, and named his fictional landscape "Wessex" after the medieval Anglo-Saxon kingdom. Although many of the novels' locations are real, he always gave them fictional names.

Hardy was disposed to write about suffering and tragedy. The death of his estranged first wife, Emma, in 1912 led him to write some of his finest love poetry. After his death in 1928, his ashes were interred in Poets' Corner at Westminster Abbey while his heart was buried with Emma.

Other key works

1874 *Far from the Madding Crowd*
1878 *The Return of the Native*
1886 *The Mayor of Casterbridge*
1887 *The Woodlanders*
1895 *Jude the Obscure*

THE ONLY WAY TO GET RID OF A TEMPTATION IS TO YIELD TO IT

THE PICTURE OF DORIAN GRAY (1891), OSCAR WILDE

IN CONTEXT

FOCUS
Aestheticism

BEFORE
1884 In French writer Joris-Karl Huysmans' *Against Nature*, the eccentric aesthete antihero, Jean des Esseintes, loathes middle-class morality.

AFTER
1901 German novelist Thomas Mann's *Buddenbrooks* details the decline of bourgeois culture in the 19th century.

1912 Thomas Mann's novella *Death in Venice* charts the succumbing to temptation of Gustav von Aschenbach, an artist who goes down a self-destructive path of erotic infatuation and excess.

1926 The novella *Dream Story*, by Austrian writer Arthur Schnitzler, is published; it is considered a key piece in the turn-of-the-century Viennese decadence movement that is associated with Aestheticism.

When the dandy Lord Henry first seduces the title character of Oscar Wilde's *The Picture of Dorian Gray* into a life of debauchery, his advice to yield to temptation summarizes the basic tenets of Aestheticism. The Aesthetic movement developed in late 19th-century Europe and Britain, emphasizing the primacy of "art for art's sake" rather than for its social, political, or moral "value".

In pursuit of pleasure

In Wilde's novel, the beautiful Dorian lives the life of the ideal aesthete, embracing all forms of hedonism in pursuit of new sensations. As he enters further into a life of dissipation and corruption, behind closed doors his magical portrait conceals the horrors of his sins, his painted image becoming older and uglier while he remains young and unblemished in the flesh.

While the story is considered a prime example of the creed of appreciating art and life for sensual pleasure alone, Dorian's path of excess is a destructive one and he leaves many victims in his wake. His is not a straightforward tale of aesthetic pleasure, but, like the Aesthetic movement, it questions the bourgeois morality of the 19th century, which required art to serve a higher purpose. Wilde's portrayal of Aestheticism attacks this by suggesting that art should be removed from morality. Wilde saw his celebration of amoral sensuality and destruction as a critique of the middle-class ideology that, he felt, was stifling art with its didacticism.

Beauty and decay

Just as Dorian superficially thrives while his painting decays, the façade of Aestheticism disguised the loss of a middle-class social order in the waning of the British Empire. The beautiful decay that so "fascinates" Lord Henry represents the society from which it stems, where temptation is overly indulged as a symbol of a world in decline. Beauty might reign, but at a terrible cost – for Dorian, the ultimate price is his soul. ∎

See also: *Death in Venice* 240

THERE ARE THINGS OLD AND NEW WHICH MUST NOT BE CONTEMPLATED BY MEN'S EYES
DRACULA (1897), BRAM STOKER

IN CONTEXT

FOCUS
Urban Gothic

BEFORE
1852–53 In Charles Dickens' *Bleak House,* urban fog is used to signify claustrophobia and confusion; it becomes a key symbol of mystery and terror in Urban Gothic fiction.

1886 *The Strange Case of Dr Jekyll and Mr Hyde*, by Scottish writer Robert Louis Stevenson, puts a horrific spin on the tedium of middle-class decency.

1890 With its fixation on social degeneration and mortality, *The Picture of Dorian Gray* by Irish author Oscar Wilde is a classic Urban Gothic novel.

AFTER
1909 French writer Gaston Leroux's *The Phantom of the Opera* takes the Gothic novel to the heart of Paris. Stage and film adaptations later bring the story to a huge audience.

Stories of the supernatural and the macabre, set within ruins and wild landscapes, characterized the Gothic novel of the late 18th to early 19th centuries. The later Urban Gothic novel turns city settings into places of horror, playing on the anxieties of the time, such as moral degeneration.

Dracula, by the Irish novelist Abraham (Bram) Stoker (1847–1912), takes the reader into the heart of Victorian London, where a vampiric foreign Count threatens middle-class society. Living for the most part undetected, he is free to choose his victims – the novel reveals the horror that comes with urban anonymity.

Horror from the east
Dracula is about east versus west: the Count comes from the east (Transylvania), lands on England's east coast, and resides in Purfleet, to the east of London. This, for the Victorian reader, would associate him with foreigners, violence, and crime (the horrors of Whitechapel, East London, where Jack the Ripper murdered several women in 1888, would still have been fresh in readers' minds).

All that is modern – gas lights, science, technology, the police – is no help in the face of this ancient invader from lands of myth and folklore. Count Dracula is depicted as a foreign, dark, animalistic force. Contagion, sexuality, and degeneration, associated with the squalor of urban living, feature too, as the Count threatens to spread his curse of the undead. ■

What manner of man is this, or what manner of creature is it in the semblance of a man?
Dracula

See also: *Bleak House* 146–49 ■ *The Picture of Dorian Gray* 194 ■ *The Strange Case of Dr Jekyll and Mr Hyde* 201–02 ■ *The Turn of the Screw* 203

ONE OF THE DARK PLACES OF THE EARTH

HEART OF DARKNESS (1899), JOSEPH CONRAD

IN CONTEXT

FOCUS
Colonial literature

BEFORE
1610–11 Prospero enslaves Caliban in Shakespeare's *The Tempest*, one of the earliest fictional works to depict colonial attitudes.

1719 In *Robinson Crusoe,* Daniel Defoe's hero teaches the native Friday the "superior" ways of the Western world.

AFTER
1924 E M Forster's *A Passage to India* questions whether there can ever be a true understanding between the colonizer and the colonized.

1930s The Négritude literary movement, led by Aimé Césaire and L-S Senghor, rejects French colonial racism for a common black identity.

1990s The study of colonial representation in literature – Postcolonialism – becomes popular in literary theory.

During the 19th century, imperialism reigned supreme, and many European countries wielded immense power over their distant colonies. Western writers often held fiercely colonial attitudes, and the sense of superiority felt by the colonizing nation can be seen in novels of the period.

But at the turn of the 20th century, colonialism, and its brutal effects on subjugated peoples, was starting to be questioned. Authors moved away from imperialist perspectives to explore the complexities of colonialism, and the rights and wrongs of empire.

Going up that river was like travelling back to the earliest beginnings of the world.
Heart of Darkness

For example, Rudyard Kipling's work subtly challenges the image of the benevolent British Empire. But nowhere are the themes of colonial exploitation and intolerance seen more clearly in the literature of this era than in the works of Joseph Conrad, in particular in his short novel *Heart of Darkness*.

The darkness within
Africa, the setting of the novel, was for Victorian Britain "the dark continent". Conrad uses this image of darkness throughout the book – he refers, for example, to the River Thames leading out towards "the heart of an immense darkness". Yet London was also "one of the dark places of the earth". The novel suggests that this darkness can exist within as well as without – a white man operating beyond the confines of the European social system, such as the book's enigmatic ivory-trader Kurtz, might begin to glimpse the darkness in his own soul.

At the beginning of the novel, a group of friends sit in a boat moored in the Thames. One of them, Marlow, tells the story of his time in the Belgian Congo, prefacing it with thoughts about

See also: *Robinson Crusoe* 94–95 ▪ *The Story of an African Farm* 201 ▪ *Nostromo* 240 ▪ *A Passage to India* 241–42 ▪ *Things Fall Apart* 266–69

what he calls "the conquest of the earth", which is "Not a pretty thing when you look into it too much". Conquest relies on dispossession, on taking "from those who have a different complexion or slightly flatter noses than ourselves".

Marlow's journey up the Congo reads like a voyage into hell: black Africans dying of overwork and malnutrition; white Europeans going slowly mad; his boat under attack from those who live in the jungle. He is obsessed with stories about Kurtz, who has amassed huge amounts of ivory but has embraced the darkness around him – or within him. The report that Kurtz has written about how

to suppress "savage customs" ends, Marlow discovers, with a scrawled sentence: "Exterminate all the brutes!" Conrad here suggests that under the surface of the supposed mission to "civilize" Africa lies an urge to exterminate those of a different complexion.

But just as Marlow realizes his kinship with his cannibal crew ("good fellows", he calls them), so he understands his kinship with Kurtz. Conrad, a contemporary of psychoanalyst Sigmund Freud, offers the suggestion that the "heart of darkness" may lie inside, that Marlow's voyage deep into the African continent can be read as a voyage into the human psyche. ∎

Joseph Conrad

Joseph Conrad was born Jozef Teodor Konrad Korzeniowski on 3 December 1857, in the Polish Ukraine. After his mother's early death and his father's political exile to Siberia, Conrad was brought up by his mother's brother in Kraków. At the age of 17, he moved to France and made many bohemian friends; he took work at sea as a pilot, and his observations during this time laid the groundwork for much of the detail in his novels. Conrad later settled in England, with the intention of becoming a naval officer. He spent 20 years as a sailor, slowly learning English and beginning to write. He became a British subject in 1886 and began his first novel, *Almayer's Folly*, in 1889. The time he spent in command of a steamship named *Le roi des Belges* in the Belgian Congo in 1890 provided the outline for *Heart of Darkness*. Conrad died in 1924 at the age of 67.

Other key works

1900 *Lord Jim*
1904 *Nostromo*
1907 *The Secret Agent*
1911 *Under Western Eyes*

Marlow's journey up the Congo

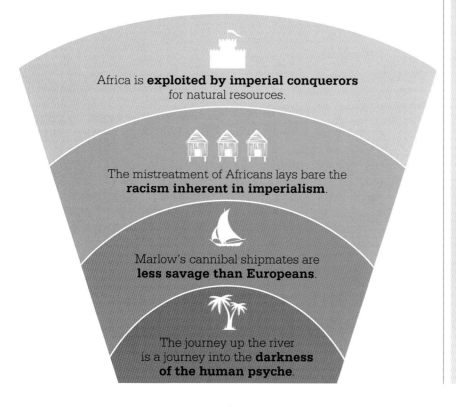

Africa is **exploited by imperial conquerors** for natural resources.

The mistreatment of Africans lays bare the **racism inherent in imperialism**.

Marlow's cannibal shipmates are **less savage than Europeans**.

The journey up the river is a journey into the **darkness of the human psyche**.

FURTHER READING

A TALE OF TWO CITIES
(1859), CHARLES DICKENS

One of only two historical novels written by the prolific English writer Charles Dickens (see p.147), *A Tale of Two Cities* is set in London and Paris before and during the 1789 French Revolution. Notable for its lack of humour, it tells the story of Dr Manette; his granddaughter Lucie; her husband, *émigré* Charles Darnay; and Darnay's lookalike, Sydney Carton. Describing the plight of the peasantry, the storming of the Bastille, and the horrors of the guillotine, Dickens creates suspense when a long-buried secret is revealed, putting Darnay's life at risk.

GREAT EXPECTATIONS
(1860–1861), CHARLES DICKENS

One of Dickens' greatest critical and popular successes, *Great Expectations* opens on the misty Kent marshes where Pip, an orphan

We need never be ashamed of shedding tears … they are rain on the blinding dust of earth …
Great Expectations
Charles Dickens

raised by a harsh sister and her kindly husband, blacksmith Joe Gargery, encounters an escaped convict. Time passes and Pip's life changes dramatically with news of "great expectations" from an anonymous benefactor, who enables him to become a gentleman. Written with perhaps the finest examples of Dickens' much-loved humour, the plot features many unforgettable characters: faded and embittered Miss Havisham; cold and haughty Estella, her adopted daughter; and convict Abel Magwitch. Ultimately the discovery of his benefactor's identity turns Pip's life upside down.

THÉRÈSE RAQUIN
(1867), EMILE ZOLA

Initially serialized, *Thérèse Raquin* by French writer Zola (see p.191) tells the tragic story of the heroine, Thérèse. Unhappily married to her sickly cousin Camille, she embarks on a torrid love affair with Laurent, a friend of her husband's. The two lovers murder Camille, an act that haunts them for the rest of their lives, turning their passion to hatred. Remarkable for Zola's scientific study of "temperament", the novel, which was criticized by some for being "putrid", helped to establish him as a great writer.

THE MOONSTONE
(1868), WILKIE COLLINS

Described by T S Eliot as "the first, the longest and the best of the modern English detective

Wilkie Collins

Born in London in 1824, the son of the landscape painter William Collins, Wilkie Collins discovered a gift for devising tales as a teenager while at boarding school, thanks to a bully who demanded a story before allowing him to sleep each night. He was introduced to Dickens in 1851 and became protégé to the literary colossus, with whom he collaborated and formed a close friendship that grew over the next two decades. In the 1860s Collins wrote his most celebrated and enduring works, becoming established as the pioneer of mystery stories and suspense fiction, a genre that later gave rise to the detective novel. He died in 1889 of a stroke.

Key works

1859–60 *The Woman in White*
1868 *The Moonstone*
(see below)

novel", *The Moonstone* by Wilkie Collins concerns the mysterious theft of a priceless Indian diamond from an English country house. It utilizes the same method of multiple narrators that Collins had deployed to great effect in his earlier work *The Woman in White*. First published in serial form, the book established what would later become the classic detective novel elements: suspense, misleading clues and happenings, a bungling local policeman, a brilliant but idiosyncratic detective (Sergeant Cuff), false suspects, a locked room, and a dramatic denouement.

LITTLE WOMEN
(1868–1869), LOUISA MAY ALCOTT

Originally published in two volumes, *Little Women* by US author Alcott (1832–88) is set in New England during the US Civil War of 1861–65. It traces the various activities and aspirations of four sisters – Meg, Jo, Beth, and Amy – as they develop into young women. The book was an enormous success on both sides of the Atlantic, establishing a genre that approached young womanhood in a new and modern way, rejecting traditional feminine roles. Alcott's characters, although sometimes seen as sentimental, are strong-minded women, particularly Jo, a tomboy who challenges conformity.

THE IDIOT
(1868–1869), FYODOR DOSTOYEVSKY

Writing *The Idiot* – considered to be one of the most brilliant works of Russia's literary "Golden Age" – writer and philosopher Dostoyevsky

They had both failed in their objects – the one who dreamed only of love, and the other of power.
A Sentimental Education
Gustave Flaubert

(see p.174) intended "to depict a completely beautiful human being". The result was Prince Myshkin, the protagonist and "idiot" of the novel, a nobleman with almost Christ-like compassion, but who is ultimately naive. Returning from a Swiss sanatorium, Myshkin finds himself torn between romantic love for Aglaya Yapanchin and compassionate love for Nastassya Filippovna, a kept and oppressed woman. His goodness is tested but ultimately there is no place for Myshkin's compassion and integrity in an increasingly corrupt society.

A SENTIMENTAL EDUCATION
(1869), GUSTAVE FLAUBERT

Set during the period of the 1848 Revolution and the ensuing Second French Empire of Napoleon III, *A Sentimental Education* by French novelist and playwright Flaubert (see p.160) recounts the activities of a young and somewhat rootless lawyer, Frédérick Moreau, and his infatuation with an older married woman, Madame Arnoux. Calling on events from his own life, Flaubert writes in a sparse, objective, and occasionally ironic style to create a realistic picture of bourgeois society that existed in France at the time, which he criticizes for its posturing and lack of refinement.

SEVEN BROTHERS
(1870), ALEKSIS KIVI

Ten years in the writing, *Seven Brothers* by Finnish writer Kivi (1834–72) describes the boisterous and often disastrous adventures of seven brothers who, rejecting social conventions, escape into the forest

to live as hunters. Combining Romanticism, realism, and a great deal of humour, the novel was harshly received by critics, which may have contributed to Kivi's early death. Today it is regarded as a masterpiece and the first significant novel to be written in the Finnish language, breaking the dominance of Swedish literature in Finland.

THE GAUCHO MARTÍN FIERRO
(1872), JOSÉ HERNANDEZ

Largely social protest, *The Gaucho Martín Fierro* by Argentinian poet Hernandez (1834–86) is an epic poem that describes the way of life of the *gauchos*, cattle ranchers whose traditional life on the grassy plains of the *pampas* is threatened by industrialization and political manipulation. Through the poem, Martín Fierro, a *payador* (*gaucho* minstrel), sings of his oppressed life and the starkness of the *pampas*. Hernandez championed the cause of the *gauchos* and his poem, with its nostalgic view of a vanished life, was a literary and popular success.

A SEASON IN HELL
(1873), ARTHUR RIMBAUD

Written by French prodigy Rimbaud (1854–91) at the age of just 19, *A Season in Hell* is a complex work of prose and verse that reflects the poet's tumultuous life. Arranged in nine sections, the poem consists of scenes in which the narrator examines the hells through which he has travelled, mirroring Rimbaud's moral crisis and reflective state of mind following the breakdown of his relationship with his lover, the artist Paul Verlaine. The book was

Henrik Ibsen

Considered to be the "father of realism" and seen as one of the trailblazers of Modernism in theatre, Ibsen was born in Skien, southern Norway, in 1828. He began writing plays when he was 15, and was determined to make this his career. His play *Brand* (1865) gained him recognition, while the plays that followed, with their biting social realism, established him internationally. Most of his dramas are set in Norway, although he spent his most productive years, from 1868 onwards, working in Italy and Germany, returning to Norway in 1891 as a national hero. Following a series of strokes he died in 1906.

Key works

1879 *A Doll's House* (see right)
1881 *Ghosts*
1884 *The Wild Duck*
1890 *Hedda Gabler*
1892 *The Master Builder*

to prove an inspiration to the Symbolist movement, and to future generations of poets and writers.

FAR FROM THE MADDING CROWD
(1874), THOMAS HARDY

The English author's first popular success, and the first to be set in Wessex, *Far from the Madding Crowd* by Thomas Hardy (see p.193) centres on Bathsheba Everdene, an independent and bold woman who attracts three contrasting suitors: devoted shepherd Gabriel Oak, neighbouring farmer Boldwood, and the dashing Sergeant Troy. Creating evocative descriptions of rural life, Hardy explores the themes of rejection, poverty, faithful love, and unprincipled passion.

ANNA KARENINA
(1875–1877), LEO TOLSTOY

A novel described by Dostoyevsky as "flawless", *Anna Karenina* by Russian author Leo Tolstoy (see p.181) traces the adulterous liaison between Anna, the beautiful and intelligent wife of Aleksy Karenin, and Count Vronsky, a young bachelor. Karenin discovers his wife's affair but, desirous of maintaining his public position, he refuses to divorce his wife. The lovers move to Italy, have a child, and live troubled lives. Having broken the social codes of the day, Anna is shunned by society. Running parallel to Anna's story is that of country landowner Levin – a character that Tolstoy based on himself – and Kitty, who is related to Anna by marriage and who was originally infatuated with Vronsky. Following a difficult courtship, Levin and Kitty ultimately have a happy and fulfilling marriage, reflecting Tolstoy's belief in the simple, pastoral life.

DANIEL DERONDA
(1876), GEORGE ELIOT

Daniel Deronda is the last work that English novelist Eliot (see p.183) completed. Notable for its exposure of anti-Semitism in Victorian Britain and its sympathetic treatment of Jewish ideals, the novel incorporates two strands. The first concerns Gwendolen Harleth, stifled and frustrated in an unhappy marriage; the second describes Daniel Deronda, a wealthy and compassionate man who, by rescuing a young Jewess – Mirah Lapidoth – discovers his own Jewish roots. After Deronda and Gwendolen meet by chance, their lives begin to intertwine. Deronda's decision to support the Jewish cause enables Gwendolen to seek her own freedom.

A DOLL'S HOUSE
(1879), HENRIK IBSEN

A three-act play by Norwegian playwright, poet, and theatre director Henrik Ibsen, *A Doll's House* sparked outrage and controversy when it was first performed. The play portrays an ordinary family – Torwald Helmer, a bank lawyer, his wife Nora, and their three children. However, the play also expresses Ibsen's critical opinion of conventional marriage when, after a serious disagreement with her husband, Nora leaves both him and their children to seek independence and self-fulfilment.

THE BROTHERS KARAMAZOV
(1880), FYODOR DOSTOYEVSKY

Some two years in the writing, *The Brothers Karamazov* by Russian writer Dostoyevsky (see p.174) was the author's final novel, and is often considered to be his masterpiece. Recounted by an unnamed first-person narrator, the novel tells the story of irresponsible wastrel Fyodor Karamazov and his sons from two marriages – Dimitri, a hedonist; Ivan, a rationalist and atheist; Alyosha, a man of deep faith – and an illegitimate son, Smerdyakov, who is morose and epileptic. Describing family struggles over an inheritance, a love rivalry between Dimitri and Fyodor, and introducing the theme of patricide, Dostoyevsky creates a complex novel in which he explores profound questions of faith and doubt, the problem of free will, and the issue of moral responsibility. Dostoyevsky died within four months of the novel's completion.

TREASURE ISLAND
(1881–1882), ROBERT LOUIS STEVENSON

First serialized in a children's magazine, *Treasure Island* by Robert Louis Stevenson is a masterpiece of children's literature, featuring pirates, buried treasure, and a swamp-ridden tropical island. Creating a gripping read that has entertained children around the world, Stevenson also interweaves a coming-of-age novel, as teenager Jim Hawkins gains sensitivity and maturity. The author also explores moral issues with his descriptions of the ever-changing character of one-legged pirate Long John Silver.

THE STORY OF AN AFRICAN FARM
(1883), OLIVE SCHREINER

Feminist South African writer Olive Schreiner (1855–1920) set *The Story of an African Farm* in the South African *veld* – the grassy scrubland on which the region's Dutch settlers reared cattle – where she grew up. Reflecting her strongly held views, the novel features a young woman, Lyndall, who challenges the Bible-led restrictions of Boer society, and her suitor Waldo, who also rebels against convention. Schreiner's

Nothing is despicable – all is meaningful; nothing is small – all is part of a whole.
The Story of an African Farm
Olive Schreiner

portrayal of Lyndall won her both feminist acclaim and notoriety, while her use of a fictionalized South African landscape was regarded as pioneering.

LA REGENTA
(1884–1885), LEOPOLDA ALAS

Published initially in two volumes, *La Regenta* by Spanish novelist Alas (1852–1901) tells the story of a magistrate's wife (*la Regenta* of the title – a pun in Spanish meaning

Robert Louis Stevenson

When living in Samoa, Robert Louis Stevenson took the nickname *Tusitala*, or "Teller of Tales", a perfect description for the man who wrote some of the world's most famous adventure stories. Born in Edinburgh in 1850, Stevenson decided early in life to make a career in writing, although he agreed to study law to please his father. Dogged by ill-health, he was nevertheless a keen adventurer and traveller, visiting the USA and spending time in France where, although

"the woman in command") who, living in a provincial town, seeks fulfilment through religion and adultery. Rich in characters, such as the cathedral's priest and the local casanova, Alvaro Mesia, the novel presents a remarkable picture of provincial life as well as exploring the psychology of the characters by allowing them to narrate events.

THE STRANGE CASE OF DR JEKYLL AND MR HYDE
(1886), ROBERT LOUIS STEVENSON

The defining novel that cemented its author's reputation and ensured his celebrity, *The Strange Case of Dr Jekyll and Mr Hyde* by Robert Louis Stevenson is best known for its remarkable portrayal of what is sometimes described as a "split personality". The book initially relates the mystery of two men – respectable and sociable Dr Henry Jekyll and the vice-ridden, brutal murderer Edward Hyde – who appear to be connected in some way. As the story progresses the reader learns that Jekyll has created a potion to suppress hedonistic

bedridden, he wrote some of his best-known work, much of it for children. After leaving Europe for the USA in 1887, in search of more favourable climes to suit his poor health, Stevenson set out with his family in 1888 on a voyage to the South Seas. He settled in Samoa in 1890, where he died four years later.

Key works

1881–82 *Treasure Island* (see left)
1886 *Kidnapped*
1886 *The Strange Case of Dr Jekyll and Mr Hyde* (see above)

aspects of his personality, only to create Hyde, seemingly an evil manifestation of the darkest attributes of his character.

THE MAIAS
(1888), EÇA DE QUEIRÓS

Regarded as the masterwork of one of the greatest European realist novelists, Eça de Queirós, *The Maias* is set in fin-de-siecle Lisbon. Notable for its satire and realism, its central character, Carlos Maia, is a wealthy and talented doctor who is keen to do good work, but lives a dissolute life. Maia embarks on an affair with a beautiful but mysterious woman, but a shocking discovery brings the relationship to an end.

Eça de Queirós

Considered Portugal's greatest novelist, Eça de Queirós was also a political activist. Born in northern Portugal in 1845, he studied law but his real interest was literature, and his short stories and essays soon began appearing in the press. By 1871 he was part of the "Generation of 70", a group of rebellious intellectuals who were committed to social and artistic reform; he denounced Portuguese literature as unoriginal. He served as consul in Cuba, England – where he wrote the satirical novels for which he is best known – and Paris, where he died in 1900.

Key works

1876 *The Crime of Father Amaro*
1878 *Cousin Bazilio*
1888 *The Maias* (see above)

HUNGER
(1890), KNUT HAMSUN

Norwegian writer Knut Hamsun (1859–1952) was 30 when his first successful novel, *Hunger*, was published. He had previously spent many impoverished years travelling and working in various jobs, and his novel reflects those experiences. Set in Kristiania (Oslo), it describes the poverty and psychological despair of a young man so bent on success as a writer that he becomes almost demented. The novel's portrayal of obsession and alienation established it as a literary landmark.

THE JUNGLE BOOK
(1894–1895), RUDYARD KIPLING

A collection of stories, linked by poems, *The Jungle Book* by English writer Kipling (1865–1936) is most famous for its tales of Mowgli, an Indian boy raised by wolves and taught the laws of the jungle by Baloo, the brown bear; Bagheera, the panther; and the wolves of the pack. Kipling, who lived in India for many years, used the animals in the tales – which are effectively fables – to present moral lessons about good behaviour by contrasting irresponsible humans with animals that follow a strict jungle code.

EFFI BRIEST
(1894–1895), THEODORE FONTANE

Considered to be a landmark of Prussian realism, *Effi Briest* by German writer Fontane (1819–98) tells the story of its 17-year-old protagonist, who is married to Geert von Innstetten, an ambitious nobleman twice her age. Effi has a secret affair with a local womanizer. Six years later, the affair – long-since ended – comes to light and, with the characters bound by a strict Prussian social code so well depicted by Fontane, the story moves towards its tragic end.

JUDE THE OBSCURE
(1895), THOMAS HARDY

In his fatalistic *Jude the Obscure*, English writer Hardy (see p.193) tells the story of Jude Fawley, a villager with scholarly ambitions that are never achieved. Married reluctantly and under false pretence, Jude falls in love with his cousin, Sue Bridehead, who then marries a local schoolmaster. Repelled by sex within her marriage, Sue turns to Jude. They live together but poverty and society's disapproval take a dreadful toll. Critics and readers were so shocked by the novel's sexual frankness and pessimism that Hardy wrote no further novels, turning from fiction to poetry.

THE RED BADGE OF COURAGE
(1895), STEPHEN CRANE

One of the great war novels and noted for its realism, terse style, and modern approach, *The Red Badge of Courage* by US author Crane (1871–1900) is set during the US Civil War (1861–65). The protagonist is Henry Fleming, a young private in the Union Army. He dreams of glory but, when faced with the stark and terrifying reality of fighting on the battlefield, flees from the advancing Confederate forces. Overwhelmed by his shame, he seeks redemption and meaning in a heroic act.

UNCLE VANYA
(1897), ANTON CHEKHOV

A masterly study of aimlessness and hopelessness, *Uncle Vanya* is thought by many to be Chekhov's finest work. Set on a country estate in turn-of-the-century Russia, the play focuses on estate manager Voynitsky (Uncle Vanya), estate owner Professor Serebryakov and his second wife Yelena and daughter Sonya, and Sonya's unrequited love for local physician Astrov. Vanya, frustrated by his wasted life and failure to seduce the beautiful Yelena, attempts to shoot Serebryakov but fails. The play ends with nothing having changed.

THE TURN OF THE SCREW
(1898), HENRY JAMES

A novella by US writer Henry James (see p.187), *The Turn of the Screw* is one of the best-known ghost stories ever written. Narrated mainly through the diary of a governess, the story describes her struggle to save her young charges, Flora and Miles, from the demonic clutches of two deceased former servants. Ambiguous in approach – some critics suggested that the governess was hysterical rather than haunted – the story has been influential, paving the way for subsequent tales of innocent children possessed by evil spirits.

Whatever I had seen, Miles and Flora saw *more* – things terrible and unguessable …
The Turn of the Screw
Henry James

THE AWAKENING
(1899), KATE CHOPIN

Set in New Orleans, *The Awakening* by US writer Kate Chopin (1851–1904) tells the story of Edna Pontellier and her struggle to break free from the restrictions imposed upon her by both marriage and motherhood. Pontellier seeks her "awakening" through two sexual affairs, but more importantly through independent thinking, art, music, and swimming. With its explicit portrayal of marital infidelity and female independence, the novel shocked readers and critics, and was censored on its first publication. Today it is regarded as a landmark feminist novel and an early example of Southern literature.

LORD JIM
(1900), JOSEPH CONRAD

Lord Jim, by Poland-born English novelist Joseph Conrad (see p.197), describes the efforts of Jim, a young British seaman, to overcome an act of unwitting cowardice that leaves his name tarnished. Helped by a sea captain, Marlow, who narrates much of the story, Jim becomes "Tuan" (lord) of Patusan – a fictional South Sea country – and ultimately overcomes his guilt through self-sacrifice. The novel is notable not just for its exploration of idealism and heroism, but also for its sophisticated use of a frame narrative structure.

Anton Chekhov

Celebrated as one of the greatest Russian playwrights, Anton Chekhov was born in 1860. He qualified as a doctor and, despite writing prolifically, continued practising medicine, once describing the latter as "his lawful wife" and literature as his "mistress". Initially it was short stories that brought him fame – in 1888 he won the Pushkin Prize for his short story *The Steppe*. From the 1890s he produced the plays for which he is remembered, which were performed at the Moscow Art Theatre. He married actress Olga Knipper in 1901 but died of tuberculosis in 1904.

Key works

1897 *The Seagull*
1897 *Uncle Vanya* (see left)
1904 *The Cherry Orchard*

SISTER CARRIE
(1900), THEODORE DREISER

The first novel by US novelist, journalist, and socialist Theodore Dreiser (1871–1945), *Sister Carrie* concerns the young woman of the title, Carrie, who leaves her home in Wisconsin for Chicago. She gains work in a shoe factory, but after two affairs – one with a married man – finally achieves success and wealth in a stage career. Dreiser's publisher, Doubleday, accepted the book but considered the subject matter so shocking in the moralistic climate of fin-de-siecle USA that they delayed publication, altering the text and agreeing to only a limited print run. An uncut version did not appear until 1981.

BREAKIN
WITH TR
1900–1945

G

ADITION

Austrian neurologist Sigmund Freud develops his **theories of the unconscious** and invents the clinical treatment known as psychoanalysis.

The Qing (Manchu) dynasty in China is overthrown, and a constitutional **republic declared**, ending around 4,000 years of dynastic rule in China.

Franz Kafka's existential novella *Metamorphosis*, **a nightmarish tale of alienation**, is published in Germany.

"Dulce et Decorum Est" and other **war poems** by British soldier Wilfred Owen are published posthumously.

1890s   1912   1915   1920

1901   1914–18   1917   1922

The Hound of the Baskervilles, by Arthur Conan Doyle, is serialized in *The Strand Magazine*.

The Great War, later known as World War I, rages in Europe, with an **unprecedented loss of life** among a generation of young men.

In March the Russian Revolution topples the tsar, and by November a **radical Bolshevik government** has seized power under Lenin.

James Joyce's *Ulysses* uses a **stream of consciousness** technique to describe a day in the life of Leopold Bloom..

The dawn of the 20th century was characterized by an almost worldwide feeling of optimism that this was a cultural turning point – a stately progress from the pessimism that typified the end of the 19th century toward a more vibrant, modern era. Industrialization and empire-building had brought prosperity – to the Western world at least – and with it the hope of creating a better, fairer society. At the same time, new scientific ideas, such as Sigmund Freud's concept of the unconscious and Albert Einstein's theory of relativity, influenced the way that people thought about themselves and the world.

However, the new century turned out to be a turbulent one, as hopes for the future were first shattered by the catastrophic carnage of World War I, and then, after a brief period of hedonistic confidence, dashed by a global economic depression and the rise of Nazism and fascism, which resulted in World War II.

Modernism

In the world of literature, the new century was characterized by a move away from gritty realism to distinctly modern forms and genres. Taking their cue from the French symbolists, poets such as Ezra Pound developed a new style that stretched the conventions of verse. In 1922 *The Waste Land*, by Anglo-American poet T S Eliot, captured the disillusionment of the age.

Novelists also found a variety of new means of expression. Influenced by existentialist philosophy and the new theories emerging in the field of psychology, Franz Kafka created a fantastic and often nightmarish world of the alienated individual in modern society, while in Japan Natsume Sōseki pioneered a similar genre of first-person "I-novel".

Another form that was adopted by modernist novelists was the "stream of consciousness" novel. Although this approach was not a new idea, it was given a particular boost by psychological theories, and it provided Irishman James Joyce with the framework on which he built his modernist style, first in *Ulysses* and then more experimentally in *Finnegans Wake*.

Modernism also featured in more conventional prose narratives. German author Thomas Mann, for example, took the Bildungsroman, or formative, rite-of-passage story,

Left-wing nationalist writer Lu Xun produces a collection of stories in the **Chinese vernacular**, *Call to Arms*.

F Scott Fitzgerald's social commentary on **life in the USA during the Jazz Age**, *The Great Gatsby*, is published.

The Wall Street Crash marks the starting point of **the Great Depression**, ending the boom years of the "Jazz Age" and Roaring Twenties.

Raymond Chandler's first novel, *The Big Sleep*, introduces **hard-boiled private detective** Philip Marlowe in a dark, complex plot.

Exiled in the USA during World War II, Antoine de Saint-Exupéry writes the novella ***The Little Prince***.

1922   **1925**   **1929**   **1939**   **1943**

1924   **1929**   **1937**   **1939–45**

Thomas Mann completes his complex epic **Bildungsroman** *The Magic Mountain*.

Alfred Döblin uses a variety of **experimental techniques** in his Weimar-era novel *Berlin Alexanderplatz*.

Their Eyes Were Watching God, by Zora Neale Hurston, presents a realistic picture of the life of a **young black woman** in 20th-century USA.

Allied forces fight against **Nazism** in Europe and imperial Japanese **militarism** in the Pacific region during World War II.

---

and reshaped it into a modern form, first in the novella *Death in Venice*, and later in his masterpiece *The Magic Mountain*.

A warring world

It was not only ideas that shaped the literature of the 20th century, but also events. The Great War of 1914–18 inevitably had a profound effect, which is most obviously seen in the work of poets, such as Wilfred Owen, who served in the forces. However, there was also the "lost generation" of US writers who had come of age during the war, which included T S Eliot, Ernest Hemingway, and F Scott Fitzgerald. Although writing ostensibly about the heady days of the 1920s, Fitzgerald portrays the world beneath the superficial and ephemeral Roaring

Twenties in *The Great Gatsby*, evoking a mood that anticipates the Great Depression of the coming decade. The 1920s also saw the rise of a generation of African-American writers, whose authentic depictions of their lives contrasted with the popular portrayal of the black entertainers of the Jazz Age.

In Germany and Austria too, there was a brief period of post-war optimism that was captured vividly by novelists such as Alfred Döblin, but this was as short-lived as elsewhere in Europe and the USA. Hitler's rise to power forced many writers and artists to flee into exile until the end of World War II. The repressive Nazi regime was hostile to "degenerate" modern art, and so too was the newly formed Soviet Union under Stalin, drawing to a close a century of great Russian

writing. In China the end of four millennia of dynastic rule inspired a generation of nationalist writers.

The detectives

Popular fiction flourished in the first half of the 20th century and the detective genre in particular appealed to a mass readership. Pioneered by Victorian writers such as Wilkie Collins in the UK and Edgar Allan Poe in the USA, detective fiction really came into its own with Scotsman Arthur Conan Doyle's creation of Sherlock Holmes. This marked the beginning of a long line of fictional sleuths, as diverse as British writer Agatha Christie's genteel Miss Marple and Hercules Poirot, and the hard-boiled Philip Marlowe, hero of US author Raymond Chandler's dark and tangled noir novels of the 1940s. ∎

THE WORLD IS FULL OF OBVIOUS THINGS WHICH NOBODY BY ANY CHANCE EVER OBSERVES

THE HOUND OF THE BASKERVILLES (1901), ARTHUR CONAN DOYLE

IN CONTEXT

FOCUS
Detective fiction comes of age

BEFORE
1841 US writer Edgar Allan Poe's hero detective in *The Murders in the Rue Morgue* applies observation, deduction, and intuition to solve a murder.

1852–53 Inspector Bucket investigates a murder in *Bleak House*, by the English writer Charles Dickens, sifting through a variety of suspects.

1868 English author Wilkie Collins' *The Moonstone* is published, arguably the first full-length detective novel in English.

AFTER
1920 English writer Agatha Christie publishes her first detective novel, *The Mysterious Affair at Styles*, marking the start of what is often called the "Golden Age" of detective fiction.

The sleuth, who uses acute powers of observation and deduction to solve near-impossible puzzles and catch wrongdoers, appears in earlier texts from several cultures. However, detective fiction as a distinct genre emerged only in the 19th century, with the stories of US author Edgar Allan Poe featuring C Auguste Dupin, and reached its zenith in inter-war Britain. At its heart was the detective: cerebral, often at the expense of social skills; usually accompanied by an assistant (who is often also the narrator); and possessed of an ability to identify and decipher clues that baffle the police. Sherlock Holmes – created by Scottish writer Arthur Conan Doyle (1859–1930) – epitomized this modern detective.

Conan Doyle trained as a doctor in Scotland and pursued his medical career even after writing had brought him acclaim. His true interest was writing historical fiction, but he found far more success with his detective stories, many of which were serialized in *The Strand Magazine*. *The Hound of the Baskervilles* was the third full-length novel to feature Holmes.

Foul play
The story centres on a strange crime on Dartmoor: Sir Charles Baskerville has apparently been terrified to death on his own estate by a ghostly hound. Foul play is suspected, and Holmes investigates. The main story, and a subplot involving an escaped criminal on the moor – are told by Dr Watson, Holmes's friend and ally and the book's narrator.

Like most other works of early detective fiction, *The Hound of the Baskervilles* features a dastardly crime (a murder), a closed group of suspects, an inspired sleuth who arrives to carry out an investigation, and a solution that readers may arrive at themselves through logical deduction. The appeal of the novel lies as much in its plot – the triumph of reason over evil and superstition – as in its eerie, Gothic atmosphere. ■

See also: *Bleak House* 146–49 ■ *The Moonstone* 198 ■ *The Big Sleep* 236–37

I AM A CAT. AS YET I HAVE NO NAME. I'VE NO IDEA WHERE I WAS BORN

I AM A CAT (1905–1906), NATSUME SŌSEKI

IN CONTEXT

FOCUS
I-novel

BEFORE
1890 Mori Ōgai's short story *The Dancing Girl*, in which a Japanese student in Germany has a doomed relationship, heralds a trend for revelatory autobiographical writing.

1906 In Tōson Shimazaki's *The Broken Commandment* a fearful teacher struggles for self-realization as he tries to keep secret the fact he belongs to the outcast social class.

AFTER
1907 Tayama Katai's *Futon*, the confessional tale of his unconsummated passion for a student, is the first overtly factual and autobiographical example of an I-novel.

1921–37 Shiga Naoya's *A Dark Night's Passing* is an I-novel with poetic spirit depicting the inner struggle of a tormented man in search of serenity.

The "I-novel" is a Japanese literary genre that emerged at the beginning of the 20th century. Although called the I-novel, the genre has little in common with the Western concept of a novel; it is a form of confessional literature in which the story's contents are usually autobiographical. The genre takes its name from the first-person perspective, "I"; narrators are always sincere (and never unreliable). The Western practice of using multiple viewpoints to tell the narrative was considered misleading, because a writer could not tell the objective truth about anyone's perspective but their own.

Heartless humans

Natsume Sōseki (1867–1916) is arguably the greatest writer in modern Japanese history and his *I Am a Cat* is a major (and witty) example of the I-novel. The cat-narrator's tone is snooty and supercilious, as though he regards himself a nobleman, looking down upon the errant behaviour of humans. The autobiographical element of the I-novel comes through the cat's owner (Mr Sneaze) who, like all the humans in the book, is mercilessly mocked, and is based upon Sōseki himself. It is through the eyes of the cat that Sōseki paints his self-portrait.

I Am a Cat was first published in instalments in the literary magazine *Hototogisu*, which had mainly showcased haiku verse. Most of the instalments can stand on their own as short stories. ∎

Living as I do with human beings, the more I observe them, the more I am forced to conclude that they are selfish.
I Am a Cat

See also: *The Temple of the Golden Pavilion* 263

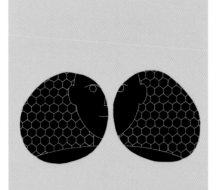

GREGOR SAMSA FOUND HIMSELF, IN HIS BED, TRANSFORMED INTO A MONSTROUS VERMIN
METAMORPHOSIS (1915), FRANZ KAFKA

IN CONTEXT

FOCUS
Existentialism

BEFORE
1864 Fyodor Dostoyevsky's *Notes from the Underground* is published; it is later celebrated as early existentialist writing.

1880 Dostoyevsky's *The Brothers Karamazov* focuses on the father–son relationship.

1883–85 Contempt for human pity and compassion, a typical existentialist theme, is a major focus in Friedrich Nietzsche's *Thus Spoke Zarathustra*.

AFTER
1938 Jean-Paul Sartre publishes *Nausea*, considered a great existentialist novel.

1942 *The Outsider* by Albert Camus explores people's futile search for meaning in life's disordered events.

1953 *Waiting for Godot* by Samuel Beckett depicts the absurd lives of two tramps.

The main proposition of existentialism is that anxiety forms the foundation of human feeling and thinking; this condition is triggered when we recognize the absurdity and meaninglessness of our existence. Existentialism has roots in 19th-century northern European philosophy – with key terms such as "angst", or anxiety, coined by Søren Kierkegaard, a Danish thinker whose works influenced Franz Kafka.

Confusion and anxiety are represented by an extreme metaphor in Kafka's disturbing story *Metamorphosis*, and staged in front of a cast of unsympathetic characters. While there are clearly literal discomforts associated with Gregor Samsa's waking form as a verminous, beetling insect, at the core of Kafka's tragic novella is the response of his family and acquaintances to his absurd predicament, as opposed to the impositions of changed physicality.

Hell is other people

Gregor is rendered utterly dysfunctional and can no longer work as a salesman or support his vulnerable family. Rather than offer compassion, his family appear hugely inconvenienced and disgusted. So Gregor as a beetle is treated as abject and alien, and Kafka deftly exposes the barbaric and inhumane response of the so-called civilized, rational world that they represent. In the words of the existentialist philosopher and writer Jean-Paul Sartre, "Hell is other people". His phrase perfectly describes Kafka's absurd depiction of a family in crisis.

Gregor is reduced to scuttling over the walls and ceiling of his room in the family apartment – or retreating under the sofa – to pass

For the first few days especially, there was no conversation that was not about him in one way or another, if only in private.
Metamorphosis

See also: *The Waste Land* 213 ▪ *The Trial* 242 ▪ *The Book of Disquiet* 244 ▪ *The Outsider* 245 ▪ *Waiting for Godot* 262

the hours. Although he ultimately abandons any attempt at dignity, and refuses to appeal to his family or assert his inner humanity, he is momentarily moved by his sister's violin playing and lured from his room to listen. With this episode, Gregor briefly refutes his outward "beastliness" and attempts to assert his authentic self, but this becomes another opportunity for the family (and their lodgers) to revile and abuse him – the hostile audience contributing further to his sense of shame and alienation.

Surrender to the absurd

Kafka's heroes do not usually conquer angst; instead, they continually seek empirical solutions to outlandish puzzles, often under extraordinary conditions. His longer works, such as *The Trial* and *The Castle*, describe unresolved quests, defined by paradox and instability of meaning and interpretation. *Metamorphosis*, although illogical and nightmarish, is a departure (arguably in a more "existential" direction) because even the drive to solve the puzzle and finish the quest is abandoned. Gregor experiences a kind of revelation through surrender in the denouement of the novella.

Interestingly, Kafka is not known to have declared himself an existentialist, although he acknowledged the influence of Kierkegaard and Dostoyevsky, two key figures in existentialism. It was Sartre and Camus who appropriated Kafka into the movement after his death. ∎

Franz Kafka

Franz Kafka was the eldest of six children of Ashkenazi Jewish parents in Prague. Born in 1883, he was educated in a German elementary school followed by the state *gymnasium* (selective school). He studied law at university in Prague, where he met Max Brod, who posthumously edited and published most of Kafka's works.

By 1908 Kafka was working in an insurance company but focusing on his writing. His work was interrupted by ill health and he was diagnosed with tuberculosis in 1917.

Kafka's personal life was troubled: his *Letter to His Father* portrayed an authoritarian father who alienates his son; and he had a series of unsuccessful relationships with women. In 1923 he moved from Prague to Berlin to live with a lover, but worsening ill health meant a return to his family in Prague, where he died in 1924.

Other key works

1913 *The Judgement*
1922 *A Hunger Artist*
1925 *The Trial*
1926 *The Castle*
1966 *Letter to His Father*

Metamorphosis in the novel

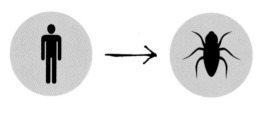

Gregor
The most obvious metamorphosis in Kafka's book is Gregor's physical transformation into an insect, though this is paralleled by the psychological changes as he learns to deal with his new state.

Grete
The book also charts the metamorphosis of Gregor's sister from a girl into a woman, and the change in her attitude towards caring for Gregor – from love and kindness to duty.

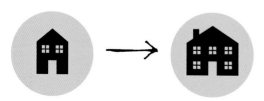

The Samsa family
During the course of the book, the fortunes of Gregor's family change from hopeless to hopeful.

DULCE ET DECORUM EST PRO PATRIA MORI
POEMS (1920), WILFRED OWEN

IN CONTEXT

FOCUS
World War I poets

BEFORE
1915 Rupert Brooke, a poet of war's noble sacrifice, writes in his sonnet "The Dead" that "dying has made us rarer gifts than gold" – a sentiment echoed in another sonnet, "The Soldier".

1916 While serving in the Foreign Legion, Alan Seeger, the "American Rupert Brooke", writes "I Have a Rendezvous with Death" – a high-flown, solemn, prophetic poem later admired by President Kennedy.

1916 A "sardonic rat" scurries among the dead and the wounded in Isaac Rosenberg's vivid, unrhyming poem "Break of Day in the Trenches".

1917 The archetype of the affable but incompetent leader of men is satirized by Siegfried Sassoon in "The General".

Poets of many nations wrote of their experiences of combat in World War I. They bore witness to the harrowing events; many of them died young. Among those most admired are the English poets: Siegfried Sassoon, Rupert Brooke, and Wilfred Owen.

The pity of war
Owen (1893–1918) worked as a tutor in France before joining the army. At first his work was patriotic: "Anthem for Doomed Youth" tells of men "who die as cattle" but closes with "bugles calling for them from sad shires" – a plaintive note of tribute. The slaughter on the Somme, and the influence of Sassoon, toughened up his verse. In "Dulce et Decorum Est", observing blood "gargling from the froth-corrupted lungs", Owen knew that a witness to the horror would not repeat to "children ardent for some desperate glory, / The old Lie: Dulce et decorum est /Pro Patria mori" ("It is sweet and fitting to die for one's country"). "The poetry," he said in a draft preface, "is in the pity."

Some poems focus on the surreal nightmare. In "The Show", his soul looks upon the aftermath of battle, where dying men crawl like caterpillars over the ground. In "Strange Meeting", the poet meets, in Hell, a loquacious stranger who claims to be the enemy he "jabbed and killed". Owen, when he was killed aged 25, was still learning his craft. He is valued for his moral and artistic integrity in powerful poems about man's inhumanity to man. ∎

What passing-bells for these who die as cattle?
– Only the monstrous anger of the guns.
"Anthem for Doomed Youth"

See also: *The Waste Land* 213 ▪ *Catch-22* 276

RAGTIME LITERATURE WHICH FLOUTS TRADITIONAL RHYTHMS
THE WASTE LAND (1922), T S ELIOT

IN CONTEXT

FOCUS
Modernist poetry

BEFORE
1861–65 In Massachusetts, Emily Dickinson privately writes her many masterpieces: short, unconventional poems of religious doubt, anticipating the visionary originality of Ezra Pound and T S Eliot.

1915–62 Ezra Pound's *Cantos*, a poetic epic, is akin to *The Waste Land* in its erudite, magpie complexity and direct, unsentimental language.

1915 Eliot's "The Love Song of J. Alfred Prufrock", the monologue of a disillusioned man, is a milestone on the way to full poetic Modernism.

AFTER
1923 *Harmonium*, a collection by the US poet Wallace Stevens, brings a vivid yet philosophical imagination to Modernism, spinning poems of elusive beauty.

Modernist poetry in early 20th-century Europe and the USA embodied a feeling that the prevailing poetic ethos, with its firm attachment to Romantic subjectivity and traditional forms, was ill suited to a modern cosmopolitan culture of revolutionized science, technology, and social values. The Modernist poets moved away from making personal statements towards a more intellectual objectivity, and gave up any attempt to imagine a pastoral idyll or turn away from the complexities of the city.

Rhythmical grumbling
T S Eliot (1888–1965) described his Modernist masterpiece *The Waste Land* as "just a piece of rhythmical grumbling". An American who transformed himself, in London, into an English man of letters, he wrote much of it while recuperating from a breakdown. But contemporaries such as the US poet Ezra Pound saw its pessimism, its fragmented forms, its unmarked quotations in

several languages, and its shifting voices as a brilliant reflection of the disorders of the post-war world and its metaphorical barrenness. The critic Clive Bell, brother-in-law of Virginia Woolf, saw the influence of the Jazz movement in the poem, calling it a "ragtime literature which flouts traditional rhythms".

The title of the poem refers to the Arthurian legend of the Fisher King – a king tasked with looking after the Holy Grail, whose impotence affects not just his ability to father children, but the fertility of his entire kingdom, which becomes an arid wasteland. Water and thirst, and death implied within growth, are major themes of Eliot's poem: from its very beginning, even the coming of spring holds no promise.

The poem creates the effect of looking through a rapidly turned kaleidoscope of spiritual (and psychological and social) anxiety. Both lyricism and magnificence feature in the quotations and pastiches – but only as ironic counterpoints to desolation. ■

See also: *Les Fleurs du mal* 165 ■ *Ulysses* 214–21 ■ *A Portrait of the Artist as a Young Man* 241

THE HEAVENTREE OF STARS HUNG WITH HUMID NIGHTBLUE FRUIT

ULYSSES (1922), JAMES JOYCE

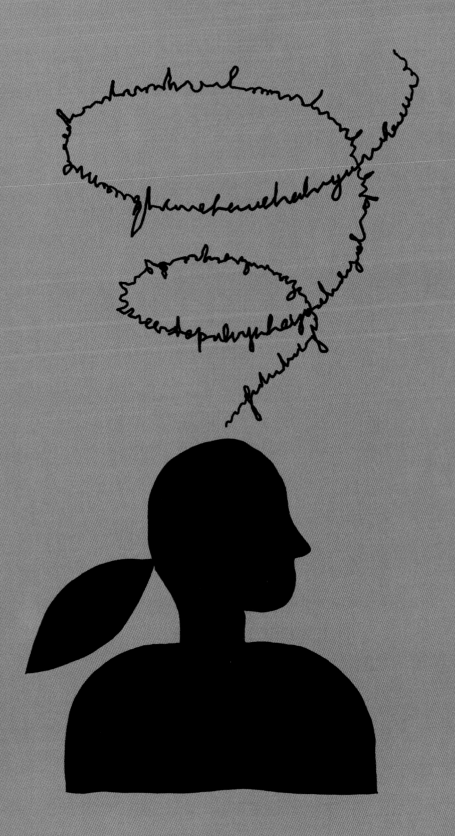

IN CONTEXT

FOCUS
Stream of consciousness

BEFORE
1913–27 Marcel Proust, in his seven-volume *In Search of Lost Time*, delves deep into memory and the free-floating associations that help to shape the content of consciousness.

1913–35 Fernando Pessoa labours on *The Book of Disquiet*, the existential meanderings of a Lisbon clerk – illuminating fragments of thought and art.

AFTER
1927 In *To the Lighthouse* Virginia Woolf moves back and forth between narrative omniscience and stream of consciousness.

1929 William Faulkner uses stream of consciousness in *The Sound and the Fury*, entering the minds of three very different brothers.

Literary critic and poet Ezra Pound declared 1922 to be the start of a new era, asserting that the old one had ended when James Joyce wrote the last words of his novel *Ulysses*. The "year that changed everything" was bookended by the publication of *Ulysses* and of T S Eliot's poem *The Waste Land*, two towering achievements of Modernist literature.

Exploding the genres of realist fiction and poetry, both works mined, out of the depths of their authors' astonishing originality and serious artistic and moral purpose, a new kind of literary ore. In the bleak years after World War I, Joyce, Eliot, and other writers set about forming a new culture out of the fragmented remains of the old. Literature would never be the same again.

Stream of consciousness
One approach Modernist writers adopted to disrupt narrative realism was stream of consciousness. In fiction, stream of consciousness is a representation of the flow of a character's thoughts, perceptions, and feelings. While long passages of introspection can be found in much earlier works such as the

Dislike that job. House of mourning. Walk. Pat! Doesn't hear. Deaf beetle he is.
Ulysses

epistolary novel *Pamela* (1740) by Samuel Richardson, fiction at the turn of the 20th century went further. Henry James and Marcel Proust moved towards greater subjectivity of viewpoint, in terms of both subject matter and its formal treatment.

The first full-blown use of interior monologue in fiction is thought to have been in a short novel, *Les Lauriers sont coupés* ("The laurels are cut down"), by Édouard Dujardin, published in 1887. Joyce famously picked up a copy of this book at a Paris railway station kiosk in 1903.

The style has been linked with the rise of psychology as a science, and indeed the phrase "stream of

James Joyce

Born in a suburb of Dublin, Ireland, in 1882, James Joyce was brought up in poverty after his father lost his job as a tax collector. Joyce read English, French, and Italian at University College Dublin, then moved to Paris, intending to study medicine. He returned to Dublin after his mother died, scraping a living reviewing and teaching. Joyce eloped with Nora Barnacle in 1904 and the couple moved to Zurich. Later, he got a teaching job in Trieste. His book of short stories, *Dubliners*, was published in 1914, the year before he began writing *Ulysses*. When sections of

this novel appeared in the US journal *The Little Review*, the magazine was put on trial for obscenity. In 1920, Joyce moved to Paris, where he lived for 20 years. Here he wrote his dream-like late masterpiece, *Finnegans Wake*. In 1940, Joyce fled the Nazi invasion and went to Zurich, where he died in 1941.

Other key works

1914 *Dubliners*
1916 *A Portrait of the Artist as a Young Man*
1939 *Finnegans Wake*

See also: *Odyssey* 54 ▪ *The Waste Land* 213 ▪ *In Search of Lost Time* 240–41 ▪ *A Portrait of the Artist as a Young Man* 241 ▪ *Mrs Dalloway* 242 ▪ *The Sound and the Fury* 242–43 ▪ *The Book of Disquiet* 244

Ulysses takes place on a single day, 16 June 1904, in Dublin, in the course of which its three protagonists cross paths with each other and a variety of other characters the city.

consciousness" was coined by the philosopher and psychologist William James (brother of Henry) in *The Principles of Psychology* (1890).

The term was first applied in a literary context to an early stream-of-consciousness novel in English, Dorothy Richardson's *Pointed Roofs* (1915), which used the technique to explore the idea of a feminine prose.

With *Ulysses* – the most famous and influential example of stream-of-consciousness writing – Joyce made the sustained literary leap out of traditional narrative techniques into conveying the mind of the character directly, unmediated by the author. Virginia Woolf, too, began experimenting with stream of consciousness soon after, notably in *Mrs Dalloway* (1925).

To register the complexity and subtlety of the interior mental process, from conscious to almost

Every life is many days, day after day. We walk through ourselves, meeting robbers, ghosts, giants, old men, young men, wives, widows, brothers-in-love.
Ulysses

unconscious thought, these writers followed loose, often metaphorical, associations of words and phrases, as well as inserting ungrammatical constructions and omitting definite or indefinite articles.

Joyce abandoned complete coherence for the realism of the interior monologue, although the flow of thoughts may indirectly evoke action. "Postal order stamp. Postoffice lower down. Walk now" suggests that Leopold Bloom, walking through the city in *Ulysses*, is reminding himself of what he needs to buy and where to buy it.

A June day in Dublin

The entire action of *Ulysses* takes place in and around Dublin on 16 June 1904 (now celebrated as "Bloomsday"), as three main characters cross paths: Stephen Dedalus, a teacher and would-be writer, aged 22; Leopold Bloom (usually just referred to as Bloom in the text), an advertising canvasser, half Hungarian-Jewish and half Irish, aged 38; and his wife Molly,

a singer, aged 34, whom Leopold rightly suspects of having an affair with a man-about-town known as "Blazes" Boylan. The novel teems with other characters, too, and a kaleidoscopic portrait of Dublin emerges out of the inner lives of Stephen, Bloom, and Molly, in a quarter of a million words of microscopically detailed invention.

The principal settings are a habitable defensive tower, a school, a beach, a house, a butcher's shop, a graveyard, a newspaper office, a library, a funeral parlour, a concert room, a tavern, a hospital, a brothel, and a cabman's shelter, as well as Dublin's city streets.

Laying bare the multiplicity of thoughts, emotions and actions (including bodily functions) that take Stephen, Bloom, and Molly through their day and night, *Ulysses* makes the private public on a scale never before undertaken in fiction.

The opening chapters form a bridge with Joyce's earlier, auto-biographical novel, *Portrait of the Artist as a Young Man*, which is »

The 18 episodes of *Ulysses* in Dublin

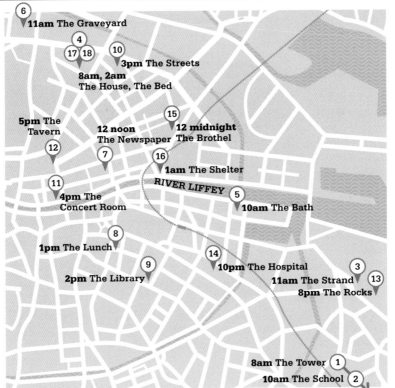

2 The School:
Stephen walks from the Tower, where he lives, to Mr Deasy's School in Dalkey to teach a lesson.

4, 17, 18 The House:
"Bloomsday" starts and ends at Leopold and Molly Bloom's house, No. 7 Eccles Street.

5 The Bath:
Wandering in a drowsily complacent state, Bloom picks up a letter, then heads to the Turkish baths.

6 The Graveyard:
Bloom and three friends share a carriage for the funeral procession from Paddy Dignam's House.

7 The Newspaper:
Stephen and Bloom cross paths, as Bloom chases advertising and Stephen places Mr Deasy's letter.

 The numbers on the map plot the events of 16 June 1904

11am The Graveyard
3pm The Streets
8am, 2am The House, The Bed
5pm The Tavern
12 noon The Newspaper
12 midnight The Brothel
1am The Shelter
RIVER LIFFEY
10am The Bath
4pm The Concert Room
1pm The Lunch
2pm The Library
10pm The Hospital
11am The Strand
8pm The Rocks
8am The Tower
10am The School

10 The Streets:
In this central episode, 19 characters pursue mini-odysseys through the streets of Dublin.

12 The Tavern:
Bloom is accosted by an Irish nationalist "citizen" when he stops for a drink in Barney Kiernan's pub.

14 The Hospital:
A group of drunken men, among them Bloom and Stephen, wait for Mina Purefoy to give birth.

15 The Brothel:
After a hallucinatory walk through Nighttown, Bloom and Stephen meet in a brothel.

16 The Shelter:
Bloom and Stephen take refuge in a cabman's shelter. Fellow feeling is soon undermined as the gulf between their views becomes apparent.

---

the story of Stephen Dedalus gaining the confidence to liberate his talents from the conformist pressures of the Catholic Church, his upbringing, and country. In *Ulysses*, Stephen is first shown in the morning, verbally jousting with cynical quasi-friend Buck Mulligan, in the tower where they live on Sandycove. He thinks back to his mother on her deathbed and guiltily reflects on his refusal, on atheistic principle, to pray for her. He then teaches a history lesson and walks on the beach.

The novel then shifts back in time to 8am and enters full "stream-of-consciousness" mode as the reader follows Leopold Bloom planning breakfast at home, shopping at the butcher's, and then cooking the meal and taking a tray upstairs to Molly. Joyce uses stream of

consciousness to varying degrees to relate the experiences of Stephen, Bloom, and Molly, although to move the action forward in any particular passage, he skilfully interweaves stream of consciousness and third-person narrative.

Bloom and the real world

Naturalism, or "scientific" realism, had become the lifeblood of the novel in mid-19th-century France, especially in the fiction of Émile Zola, who presented life's seamier aspects in meticulous detail. Later French writers such as Henri Barbusse, in *Under Fire* (1916), deployed brutal realism to describe the appalling horrors of World War I.

Ulysses, which Joyce began writing in 1915, belongs to this tradition of novelistic candour –

although Joyce's spiritual ancestor was less Zola, whose naturalism was pessimistic and didactic, than Zola's 16th-century compatriot François Rabelais – a writer whose broad comedy and fascination with the excesses of the carnival *Ulysses* parallels in certain sections.

Leopold Bloom is one of the most fully realized characters in all fiction. He is what the French call "*un homme moyen sensuel*" – an average man with the usual appetites – intelligent but far from intellectual. He has a genial character and shows a liking for comfort and a desire to avoid confrontation. When he is first introduced, the easy relationship he enjoys with his own bodily functions and with at least some people within his social milieu sets

The Martello Tower with its "gloomy, domed livingroom" is where Stephen Dedalus pursues a writer's life with "stately, plump Buck Mulligan" and "ponderous Saxon" Haines.

him apart from the cerebral, spiky Stephen, whose monologue on the beach in the third episode begins: "Ineluctable modality of the visible: at least that if no more." Compare the first sentence of Bloom's stream of consciousness: "Another slice of bread and butter: three, four: right. She didn't like her plate full."

Panoply of styles

As the novel progresses, many other prose styles interweave with stream of consciousness and naturalism. Episode 13, for instance, parodies sentimental women's fiction, beginning with the words, "The summer evening had begun to fold the world in its mysterious embrace". Bloom, relaxing at dusk on the beach, masturbates at the sight of a young woman knowingly revealing her legs. The narrative's formulaic, rose-tinted romanticism provides an ironic counterpoint to his seedy voyeurism.

In the following episode, when Bloom visits a maternity hospital, Joyce uses a sequence of different literary styles, a pastiche of English literature that draws on Anglo-Saxon, Chaucer, Samuel Pepys, and Thomas De Quincey. For some readers, this is Joyce at his most alienatingly erudite.

Episode 15 is a phantasmagorical play set in Dublin's red-light district, Nighttown, where Bloom's repressed masochistic fantasies and Stephen's guilt over his mother are reflected in vivid, dreamlike tableaux. In its dissolution of space and time and its rapid succession of hallucinations – for example, Bloom giving birth to "eight male yellow and white children", and the poet Tennyson appearing in a Union Jack blazer and cricket flannels – the fantasy is deeply unsettling. In a nightmarish scene, Bloom acts as Stephen's protector when he is gripped by a petrifying hallucination at a brothel.

In part, Joyce was inspired by Dada – a surrealist movement that rejected reason and logic, which the young artists of the Cabaret Voltaire founded in Zurich (Joyce's home at the time) in 1916. The influence is particularly evident in this episode. Like the Dadaists, Joyce set out to shock the public with a deliberate offensive against conventional standards of taste and propriety.

There follows an episode that takes the form of a catechism – an extended question-and-answer dialogue – that is used to convey an account of Bloom and Stephen repairing together to Bloom's house for cocoa. It is here that Bloom and Stephen come closest to empathy. The analytical, exhaustively cataloguing manner in which events are related acts as a counterpoint to the subtle affinity the two feel towards each other.

Molly Bloom's soliloquy

The final chapter of *Ulysses* is a masterpiece of stream-of-consciousness writing. It reveals the intimate thoughts of Molly Bloom in the night, lying in bed on the verge of sleep. Until this point, Molly has been seen through the eyes of her jealous husband, Leopold. The shift in viewpoint, to the feminine, is one of the most brilliant in modern literature.

Having depicted the city's patriarchal culture, in which women play an indispensable role as wives, mothers, and prostitutes – sources of emotional nourishment and physical satisfaction – without their voices being heard, Joyce »

Id have to get a nice pair of red slippers like those Turks with the fez used to sell or yellow and a nice semitransparent morning gown that I badly want like the one long ago in Walpoles only 8/6 or 18/6…
Ulysses

> Listen: a fourworded
> wavespeech: seesoo,
> hrss, rsseeiss, oos.
> **Ulysses**

now restores the balance by giving Molly her own voice. Allowing his female protagonist to have the last word (an affirmative "yes", repeating the connective "yes" she starts with) is a testament to Joyce's all-inclusive imagination. However, some feminist critics see Molly, in her passivity, as a creature of male misconceptions.

As Molly lies in bed, away from all stimuli, the interior monologue can attain its purest form, without narrative interruptions. Punctuation is abandoned. Recollections jostle together. Frank language, with earthy colloquialisms, gives way to a memory of her youth in Gibraltar and her later passionate courtship by Bloom, expressed in the style of romantic fiction. This style is not purely a literary device but part of the inner language of Molly's romantic, though fleshly, sensibility.

Myth and modernity

Linguistic experimentation is not the only literary technique that underpins this multi-layered book. The title, *Ulysses*, is the clue to an elaborate symbolic sub-structure. "Ulysses" is the Latin-derived name for Odysseus, the Greek king of Ithaca, who, in Homer's epic poem the *Odyssey*, spends 10 years after the Trojan War as a wandering adventurer, before returning home. Joyce identifies Leopold Bloom with Odysseus, and equates Stephen with the king's son, Telemachus, who in the first four books of the *Odyssey* searches in vain for his lost father. He associates Molly with Penelope, Odysseus's wife, who believes that her husband is still alive and will return to her.

Each of the 18 episodes of the novel (sometimes called chapters) corresponds with an adventure from Homer's epic. The first three episodes focus on Stephen, and follow a structure that echoes the *Odyssey*. In the third episode, Stephen questions the institution of fatherhood while thinking about a discussion in a library. The passage translates Telemachus's predicament as a son without a father into an abstract debate on modern notions of the father–son relationship.

In episode 12, the Cyclops, a one-eyed giant from whom Odysseus escapes in the *Odyssey*, takes the form of an aggressively xenophobic patriot who argues vociferously with Bloom. The narrow chauvinism of the "citizen" mirrors the Cyclops' limited vision. Later, the unnamed narrator tells of a chimney sweep who "near drove his gear into my eye".

The thematic value of the Homeric parallels is strongest in the mythic roles given to Stephen and Bloom. Stephen is unconsciously seeking a supportive father figure, so he can become a father himself, both of children and of art. Passages on the Holy Trinity, which contains

In *Odysseus and Circe* (1590) by Bartholomeus Spranger, the witch goddess uses her powers to seduce the hero – paralleled by Bella Cohen's teasing of Bloom in *Ulysses*.

the most complex of all father–son relationships, and on Shakespeare's *Hamlet* – torn apart by vengeful thoughts about his father's murderer, who is now his own stepfather – add layers of meaning to Stephen's quest. Conversely, Bloom (whose son, Rudy, died 11 years earlier, a few days after his birth) has a deep psychic need for a son. This adds poignancy to the Odysseus–Telemachus dynamic.

Bloom and Stephen, after several near-misses, encounter each other by chance at the Holles Street Maternity Hospital; the associations of the place with birth and parenthood are no accident. Bloom in due course saves Stephen from getting arrested after a fracas in Dublin's red-light area. When, later that night, they sit drinking cocoa together in Bloom's kitchen, Stephen glimpses the past in Bloom, while Bloom sees the future in Stephen. It is typical of Joyce's fictional subtlety that this mutual recognition is a fleeting suggestion rather than an obvious climax.

Joyce's Homeric framework, as well as providing a set of symbolic correspondences, also allowed him to imply that Bloom, the ordinary man and good citizen, could be credited with a heroic dimension.

He heard then a warm heavy sigh, softer, as she turned over and the loose brass quoits of the bedstead jingled.
Ulysses

Homeric parallels in *Ulysses*

HOMER'S *ODYSSEY*	JAMES JOYCE'S *ULYSSES*
Telemachus is the son of Odysseus and Penelope, who searches in vain for his lost father in an epic subplot.	**Stephen Dedalus**, an intellectual and artist lost in a maze of his own self-absorption, searches for a father figure.
Calypso is a beautiful goddess-nymph, who enthralls Odysseus and holds him captive for seven years.	**Molly Bloom**, later the dutiful wife, is portrayed in an early episode as the immortal nymph who enchants Leopold.
Odysseus travels to **Hades**, the underworld, to ask the spirit of blind prophet Tiresias the way home.	Bloom attends **Paddy Dignam's funeral**, his thoughts wandering in at times humorous and inappropriate ways.
Circe is a beautiful witch-goddess, who drugs Odysseus's men and turns them into swine. Odysseus becomes her lover.	Stephen and Bloom wander through Nighttown to visit a brothel operated by **Bella Cohen**, a modern-day Circe.
Penelope keeps suitors at bay while waiting for the return of Odysseus, missing and presumed dead at sea.	**Molly** dallies with a lover but, although bored with her husband, Leopold, she awaits his homecoming.

This is the heroism, or antiheroism, of the everyday, conducted largely within the mind, the arena of an individual's fears and longings. It is here that he combats jealousy, anger, boredom, shame and guilt, and cherishes the hope and love that give life its meaning.

Exile and belonging

After the closing paragraph of the novel, Joyce left a reminder of his own Odyssean journey as its writer: "Trieste–Zurich–Paris, 1914–1921". While aware of himself as an artist operating in a cosmopolitan milieu, he also felt the tug of exile. Living abroad made it possible for him to recreate Dublin in all its vulgarity and vibrancy as the home of his imagination. Back in 1904, when the book is set, political feelings were running high, after the failure of Home Rule – an attempt to make Ireland self-governing. In the year of *Ulysses*' publication (1922), after a bloody civil war, the Irish Free State was formed. Reflecting these political realities, the characters of Joyce's fictional Dublin are full of anxieties about their relationship with institutions: Irish nationalism, the British Empire, the Catholic Church, and the Irish Literary Revival. While *Ulysses* presents the details of individual experience with unprecedented frankness, it is also unflinching in its portrayal of a restless microcosm of Irish society.

However, all themes in *Ulysses* are subordinate to the living richness of its fictional world. The vitality of the novel comes from the life invested in it, which fights back against the book's elaborate literary artifices. At the core of this – the most self-consciously artful novel since the playful experiments of Laurence Sterne's *Tristram Shandy* in the mid-18th century – are the lives and loves of Dubliners, realized with amazing verisimilitude. ∎

WHEN I WAS YOUNG I, TOO, HAD MANY DREAMS

CALL TO ARMS (1922), LU XUN

IN CONTEXT

FOCUS
Baihua literature

BEFORE
1917 Hu Shi publishes "A Preliminary Discussion of Literature Reform" in *New Youth* magazine, calling for a new approach to literature that does not rely on old forms.

1918 Lu Xun publishes "Diary of a Madman", considered the first modern Chinese story.

1921–22 Lu Xun's "The True Story of Ah Q" (later included in *Call to Arms*) is serialized in *Beijing Morning News*.

AFTER
1931–32 "Turbulent Stream", by Ba Jin, is published in serial form, later appearing as a single volume, *The Family*. A novel about the clash of old and new ways, it was hugely popular with Chinese youth.

1935 Lu Xun publishes *Old Tales Retold*, recasting popular Chinese myths.

The Baihua literary and cultural movement in China, initiated in 1917 by the scholar and intellectual Hu Shi, went hand in hand with the May Fourth Movement – a political and cultural crusade that grew out of a student uprising in Beijing in 1919 and spearheaded a new sense of Chinese nationalism.

Followers of the movement rejected traditional beliefs, and promoted a shift towards Western ideas of democracy and modern science. They also encouraged a move away from writing in classical Chinese (understood by only a tiny minority) and towards the use of "baihua": a written vernacular language that was understood by everyone. Baihua language was soon used in Chinese newspapers and textbooks, revolutionizing the education of the peasantry.

New ways of thinking

Lu Xun (1881–1936) was the first modern author to write in the vernacular script. His work was championed by the Communist Party, which he supported, though he never became a member. *Call to Arms* is Lu Xun's first collection of writing, and brings together his two earliest and most famous stories: "Diary of a Madman" and "The True Story of Ah Q".

An ironic attack on traditional culture, "Diary of a Madman" tells of a villager – the "madman" – who believes that his friends and family are practising cannibalism, and also becomes convinced that the classic Confucian texts contain encouragement of the practice.

"The True Story of Ah Q" is a novella about an ignorant and deluded peasant who considers himself to be wise, and shows the backwardness and complacency of the old generation.

Both these stories mark the beginning of Baihua literature, embodying it not only in their use of vernacular language but also in addressing concerns of the May Fourth Movement, such as the outdated strictures of Confucian thought and the unthinking acceptance of rusty traditions. ■

See also: *Quan Tangshi* 46

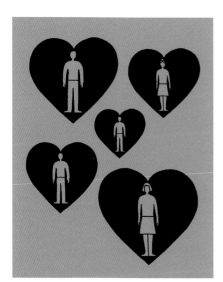

LOVE GIVES NAUGHT BUT ITSELF AND TAKES NAUGHT BUT FROM ITSELF
THE PROPHET (1923), KAHLIL GIBRAN

IN CONTEXT

FOCUS
Modern Arabic voices

AFTER
1935 Prolific writer and scholar Taha Hussein, the "Dean of Arabic Literature", tells of an Egyptian author's struggle between Arab and European culture in his novel *A Man of Letters,* played out between Cairo and Paris during World War I.

1956–57 Naguib Mahfouz's *The Cairo Trilogy* follows a Cairene family from the 1919 Egyptian Revolution against British colonial rule to near the end of World War II in 1944, highlighting the personal, social, and political struggle of a changing city and country.

1985 *The Sand Child*, written in French by Tahar Ben Jelloun, explores and critiques issues of traditional Islamic values, gender politics, and the construction of identity in a postcolonial Moroccan setting.

olonial empires began their inevitable decline in the aftermath of World War I, thanks partly to the war's impact on the centres of Western culture. Literary orientations, topics, and themes began to reflect the new shift in the balance between colonizers and colonized. Among the many postcolonial narratives to emerge, those emanating from the Arab world of North African and Middle Eastern countries came to international prominence.

Diversity of ideas

Lebanese writer, philosopher, and artist Khalil Gibran (1833–1931; also known as Kahlil) was one of the most acclaimed authors to emerge out of the blossoming pool of Arab intellectuals. His own Christian upbringing and his interest in the teachings of Islam, Sufism, and Judaism represented a break from the traditional link between geographical and spiritual beliefs, and were the major influences on his English collection of illustrated prose poems entitled *The Prophet*.

In this book, Gibran uses a style familiar in religious scripture and sermons to deliver short speeches spoken by the prophet Almustafa to a diverse crowd as he is about to depart by boat from the city of Orphalese. The 26 essays range from reflections on love, passion, children, and eating, to thoughts on justice, time, evil, and death. The essays emphasize human relationships and encompass themes of diversity and a universal love that is free from the bounds of a single belief system. ∎

These things move within you as lights and shadows in pairs that cling.
The Prophet

See also: *One Thousand and One Nights* 44–45

CRITICISM MARKS THE ORIGIN OF PROGRESS AND ENLIGHTENMENT

THE MAGIC MOUNTAIN (1924), THOMAS MANN

IN CONTEXT

FOCUS
Bildungsroman

BEFORE
1795–96 Johann Wolfgang von Goethe publishes *Wilhelm Meister's Apprenticeship*, often called the first Bildungsroman.

1798 German author Ludwig Tieck publishes *Franz Sternbald's Wanderings*, a Romantic novel with hallmarks of the Bildungsroman.

1849–50 Charles Dickens' partly autobiographical book *David Copperfield* is published.

1855 Swiss author Gottfried Keller publishes *Green Henry*, a crucial Bildungsroman, and also partly autobiographical.

1916 *A Portrait of the Artist as a Young Man*, by James Joyce, shows that the Bildungsroman has a place in Modernist literature.

Widely considered to be Thomas Mann's masterpiece, *The Magic Mountain* has many claims to greatness: it is regarded as one of the best German novels of all time; one of the finest works of the 20th century; a sublime dark comedy and rumination on death and disease; and a key work of Modernism. It is also a fine example of a Bildungsroman ("novel of formation"), a genre that had its roots in 18th-century Germany, and is still going strong today.

Although earlier examples are sometimes cited, many studies place the birth of the genre at the publication of Johann Wolfgang von

See also: *Jane Eyre* 128–31 ▪ *David Copperfield* 153 ▪ *Little Women* 199 ▪ *A Sentimental Education* 199 ▪ *Death in Venice* 240 ▪ *A Portrait of the Artist as a Young Man* 241 ▪ *To Kill a Mockingbird* 272–73 ▪ *Midnight's Children* 300–05

Goethe's novel *Wilhelm Meister's Apprenticeship* in 1795–96. It contains all of the key ingredients, being the story of a young artist's formation, or *Bildung*: his struggle to find expression and happiness, and his eventual acceptance of his place in society. Over the succeeding decades and then centuries, many other great writers felt a desire to tell a story roughly similar to their own: in France, Gustave Flaubert published *A Sentimental Education*; in England, Charles Dickens wrote *David Copperfield*; and the Irish writer James Joyce offered *A Portrait of the Artist as a Young Man*. The genre's influence spread across Europe and then the world.

Inspired by sickness

The Magic Mountain had its beginnings in Thomas Mann's visit to a high-altitude sanatorium in Davos, Switzerland, in 1912, where his wife was recovering from a lung infection. It was at first intended to be a slim volume to accompany the novella *Death*

in Venice, which he had published that year. However, it expanded in the telling, as, with the outbreak of World War I in 1914, Mann became very aware that the world he was describing was coming to a sudden and violent end. His views on both nationalism and bourgeois society were greatly changed by the conflict, in which he saw the values of so-called civilization driving society blindly towards mass death and destruction. The novel had thus taken on greater significance, and continued to grow

All interest in disease and death is only really another expression of interest in life.
The Magic Mountain

The "magic mountain" on which the Berghof is located is a symbol of the sanatorium's metaphorical distance from the rest of the world: a secluded place where even time flows differently.

in size. After the war Mann revised the text for many years, eventually publishing the novel in 1924, when it was hailed as a masterpiece.

The Magic Mountain tells the story of a young man called Hans Castorp, who goes to the Swiss Alps to visit his cousin Joachim in a sanatorium (a hospital dedicated to the treatment of people who have a chronic illness, often tuberculosis) called the Berghof. Hans has good prospects, and is about to take up a job in the shipbuilding industry.

With its clear air, spectacular surroundings, few visitors, and quiet, peaceful atmosphere, the hospital exists in its own small, enclosed world. Once he is there, Castorp himself begins to display symptoms of tuberculosis, and is persuaded to stay until he has recovered. He ends up remaining in the sanatorium for seven years. »

Ludovico Settembrini
represents humanism, intellect, and the
rational values of the Enlightenment.

**Mynheer
Peeperkorn**
symbolizes hedonism,
the pleasure principle,
and the superiority of
emotion over reason.

Hans Castorp
Hans represents the
typical blank slate of a
central character in a
Bildungsroman, who absorbs
the influences of those around
him. In his case, however, he
remains ambivalent,
passive, and unable to
commit himself.

Leo Naphta
stands for
radicalism,
irrationality,
and religious
fundamentalism.

Joachim Ziemssen
typifies faithfulness, duty, a committed
and uncomplicated response to life.

Clawdia Chauchat
embodies love, sex,
sensual pleasure.

The plot of the novel revolves around the various patients who he meets, and the relationships he develops with them.

An education in life

It is from the other patients in the sanatorium that Hans Castorp receives the education – in art, politics, love, and the human condition – that all Bildungsroman heroes must gain. Mann uses the characters as representatives of the different ideas and belief systems of pre-World War I Europe. We meet Leo Naphta, a Jew-turned-Marxist Jesuit; Ludovico Settembrini, an Italian secular humanist; and Mynheer Peeperkorn, a hedonistic Dutchman with a tropical disease. Each of these characters attempts to sway Castorp towards his own way of thinking, meaning that a great part of the book is taken up with philosophical debates. There is a woman, too, called Clawdia Chauchat, with whom Castorp falls in love, thereby receiving his necessary education in romance and erotic temptation.

Where most Bildungsromans involve a physical as well as an emotional journey, *The Magic Mountain* makes a point of staying geographically in one place – the Berghof; and the journey it offers is through Western (and to some extent Eastern) ideologies. It is almost as if the height of the mountain itself provides the young Castorp with a view across all of Europe at this crucial juncture.

The book serves as both a major example of a Bildungsroman and a parody of the genre. The essential elements of the Bildungsroman are all present: a young, impressionable hero who is setting out in life; an education process that is often difficult, but which he comes through in one piece; and at last, a venturing forth. Castorp must go through the experience of sickness and recovery to arrive at a true appreciation of life. Therefore the book unquestionably belongs to the genre. Yet Mann parodies or challenges it on almost every level.

Layers of parody

On one level, there are the various lessons that Castorp receives. Different characters offer views of the world that contradict each other, and it is not clear whether Mann approves of any of them. In earlier Bildungsromans, the lessons learned and the values gained by the central character are intended to be approved of, or agreed with, by the reader. So, for example, David Copperfield in Dickens' novel might learn not to take people at face value. *The Magic Mountain* rejects this formula. As a Modern novel it is aware that there are many ways of looking at the world, and none of them is necessarily

I, for one, have never
come across a perfectly
healthy human being.
The Magic Mountain

> It is love, not reason, that
> is stronger than death.
> *The Magic Mountain*

the right one. Considering this as Mann's viewpoint, the whole purpose of the book as a novel of education is revealed to be parody.

Deep down, the Bildungsroman genre had always been an earnest enterprise and it is this that Mann is poking fun at. For example, the narrator maintains an aloof attitude towards Castorp himself, thereby reminding the reader that he is a mediocre young man. And whereas the Bildungsroman hero should be fully formed by the end of the book, in fact Castorp emerges with no real sense that he has learned anything from the lessons in life and philosophy he has received over the course of seven years.

Adrift in time

Mann undercuts the purpose of the Bildungsroman in other ways, in particular as regards the theme of time and its relation to narrative progression. The passage of time is a crucial matter to those who are sick and dying, and yet in the hermetically sealed environment of the sanatorium time is something that is very hard to keep track of. The patients calculate the amount of time that has passed only in units of one month. Any past event, however long ago, is said to have happened "just the other day" – a habit Castorp himself eventually

adopts. It is important to our idea of a Bildungsroman that an education should be an ongoing process, a story told in sequence. Yet Mann deprives Castorp (and the reader) of this structure, or perspective on events. Incidents are loose in time, and we cannot pin them down: each successive chapter covers an increasing amount of time, from one day to six years.

The Magic Mountain is thus deeply disparaging towards its own genre. It contains all the contents of a Bildungsroman while showing them (in the cold light of Modernist thought) to be a sham, or that their benefits are at best impossible to calculate. It is not surprising, then, that the book has inspired relatively few imitators; it is too much like the last word in the genre, and perhaps too grand and brilliant in scope and sweep, for anyone to want to follow in its footsteps.

Writers have nonetheless continued to find new uses for the genre, exploring themes that range from postcolonialism and modern history (as in Salman Rushdie's *Midnight's Children*) to sensual and sensory awakenings (*Perfume* by Patrick Süskind). ∎

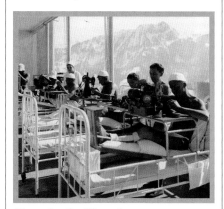

Chronically ill patients at high-altitude sanatoria in the Swiss Alps lived in a rarefied atmosphere, with events in the world "down there" barely impinging on their lives.

Thomas Mann

Thomas Mann was born to a wealthy family in Lübeck, northern Germany, in 1875. He first came to attention with his early masterpiece *Buddenbrooks*, published when he was just 26, a novel about the decline of a wealthy family much like Mann's own. In 1905 he married Katia Pringsheim, the daughter of a wealthy Jewish industrialist; they had six children, three of whom became writers. In 1929, Mann was awarded the Nobel Prize in Literature.

In 1933, Mann left Germany for Switzerland, and on the eve of World War II he moved to the USA, where he taught at Princeton University before settling in California and becoming an American citizen. During the war he made a number of anti-Nazi speeches recorded in the USA and broadcast from Britain to Germany. After the war he returned to Europe; he died in Switzerland in 1955, aged 80.

Other key works

1901 *Buddenbrooks*
1912 *Death in Venice*
1933–43 *Joseph and His Brothers*
1947 *Doctor Faustus*

LIKE MOTHS AMONG THE WHISPERINGS AND THE CHAMPAGNE AND THE STARS

THE GREAT GATSBY (1925),
F SCOTT FITZGERALD

IN CONTEXT

FOCUS
The Lost Generation

BEFORE
1920 F Scott Fitzgerald's short story "Bernice Bobs Her Hair" looks at the tension between traditional feminine values and the liberation of the Jazz Age, themes the author revives in *The Great Gatsby*.

1922 T S Eliot's *The Waste Land* prefigures Lost Generation writing in its exploration of the disintegration of culture – including empty sex and loss of spiritual meaning.

AFTER
1926 Ernest Hemingway, in *The Sun Also Rises*, delves into the themes of love, death, and masculinity.

1930–36 John Dos Passos explores the American Dream with the stories of 12 characters in his *U.S.A.* trilogy.

The author and literary hostess Gertrude Stein, talking with Ernest Hemingway, spoke of a "lost generation" of the young – those who had served in World War I. Hemingway claimed that Stein first heard the words from a garage owner who had serviced her car, an anecdotal detail that resonates suggestively with the garage scenes in *The Great Gatsby*. "Lost" in this context means disoriented or alienated, as opposed to disappeared. After Hemingway's use of it in the epigraph to his novel *The Sun Also Rises*, the phrase "Lost Generation" came to refer to a group of young American expatriate writers in the creative melting-pot of Paris in the 1920s, which included F Scott Fitzgerald, John Dos Passos, Ezra Pound, and Hemingway himself. World War I had left its mark, and they were restless and cynical, searching for meaningful experience in love, writing, drink, and hedonism.

Fitzgerald, one of the Lost Generation's most important writers, found himself seduced by the scintillating surfaces of the "Jazz Age" of the 1920s, while at

'Can't repeat the past?' he cried incredulously. 'Why of course you can!'
The Great Gatsby

the same time being keenly aware of its defective moral values and the emptiness of its promise of a better life for all. His most famous novel, *The Great Gatsby*, tells a personal story of Gatsby's doomed dream of love. However, at the same time it is a story about the doomed American Dream – its promise of a better world revealed as a sham.

New money, new values
Fitzgerald saw the Jazz Age as an era of miracle and excess. A new post-war prosperity was centred on Wall Street, where huge fortunes were made trading in stocks and bonds. The ideal of the self-made

F Scott Fitzgerald

Francis Scott Fitzgerald was born in 1896 in Saint Paul, Minnesota, USA. In 1917 he dropped out of Princeton University to join the army. He fell in love with Zelda Sayre, the daughter of a judge, marrying her after his first novel, *This Side of Paradise*, brought him success, at the age of 24. He supported the family (they had one daughter) by writing stories for popular magazines. His second novel, *The Beautiful and Damned*, confirmed his reputation as chief chronicler and critic of the Jazz Age. In 1924 he moved with Zelda to the French Riviera to write *The*

Great Gatsby. The couple later shuttled between France and the USA. Fitzgerald had a troubled relationship with alcohol; after *Tender Is the Night* came out in 1934, he struggled for two years with drink and depression. In 1937 he tried his hand at writing for Hollywood, and died of a heart attack there in 1940, aged 44.

Other key works

1922 *The Beautiful and Damned*
1922 *Tales of the Jazz Age*
1934 *Tender Is the Night*

See also: *The Waste Land* 213 ▪ *Of Mice and Men* 244 ▪ *The Grapes of Wrath* 244 ▪ *The Outsider* 245

man was an attractive antidote to the power of old money passed on by inheritance and marriage among the "best" families. The 1920s in the USA seemed to offer a new social mobility, healing class wounds and challenging snobbery. Those who had sought their fortunes in the West now came East again, to make their fortunes and to spend their wealth on magnificent homes, fine things, and high living – such was the dream, anyway. But the reality was that wealth for some led to the impoverishment of others, and at the same time gave rise to a culture of surface glitter that was morally and spiritually empty at its core. Fakery of all kinds abounded and snobbery still existed – it had just found new targets.

After the passing of the 18th Amendment in 1919, which prohibited the sale of alcohol, many entrepreneurs channelled their talents into bootlegging – the smuggling of illegal liquor, much of it sold in speakeasies (illegal bars). Racism was rife too; in the first chapter of *The Great Gatsby*, Tom Buchanan expresses the supremacist view that "if we don't look out the white race will be – will be utterly submerged".

Radiance and rottenness

Fitzgerald saw his novel as "a purely creative work – not trashy imaginings as in my stories but the sustained imagination of a sincere and yet radiant world". That radiance, reflected in a sensuous prose style suffused with a romantic glow, is seen in the dazzling glamour of fashionable East Coast society that Fitzgerald takes for his subject.

Gatsby's wild, opulent parties, depicted in this 1949 film adaptation of the book, brought together the old-moneyed socialites from East Egg and their brash West Egg neighbours.

Jay Gatsby owns a colossal mansion, in the style of a French hôtel de ville (city hall), in West Egg, on the shore of Long Island, outside New York. Gatsby is an enigma, an incomer from the Midwest around whom many rumours circulate – that he has killed a man; that his claim to an Oxford education is a lie; that he made his money bootlegging. Every Saturday he throws decadent parties, with hundreds of guests, as described by the novel's narrator, Nick Carraway, who rents a small house next door. There is hilarity and jazz in these revels, but also a great deal of drunkenness and falling out, especially between couples. Indeed, men and women speak to each other throughout the book in dialogue that is flippant and insincere.

Nick gets to know Gatsby and learns his secret: that for five years he has been obsessively in love with the beautiful socialite Daisy Buchanan, who happens to be

Nick's cousin, and who is now married to Tom, a wealthy college friend of Nick's. Daisy is the reason Gatsby bought his mansion on the opposite shore from the Georgian Colonial house she shares with Tom. All Gatsby's wealth, acquired from shady business dealings with a mafioso-style crook called Meyer Wolfshiem, is paraded with the sole intention of winning back his lost love, now that he finally has the capital to support her.

The importance of place

The novel's themes are mapped out in its highly symbolic topography. East Egg, home to Daisy and Tom as well as most of Gatsby's party guests, stands for traditional values and old money; West Egg where Gatsby lives, for fashionable »

Geography of *The Great Gatsby*

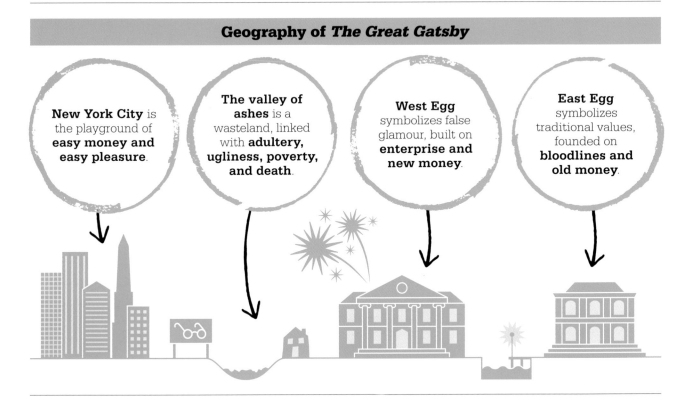

New York City is the playground of **easy money and easy pleasure**.

The valley of ashes is a wasteland, linked with **adultery, ugliness, poverty, and death**.

West Egg symbolizes false glamour, built on **enterprise and new money**.

East Egg symbolizes traditional values, founded on **bloodlines and old money**.

affluence, the nouveau riche. A short distance away is New York, teeming with dubious deals and clandestine pleasures. In between lies a patch of terrain where the bleakness underlying the glamour is depressingly apparent: the "valley of ashes". This desolate region recalls T S Eliot's Modernist

I was within and without, simultaneously enchanted and repelled by the inexhaustible variety of life.
The Great Gatsby

poem *The Waste Land*, whose title refers to the ancient myth of a kingdom blighted by a curse. It is here that Tom's mistress, Myrtle Wilson, lives with her sad, passive, garage-owning husband, near a giant billboard advertising an optician's business. The spectacles on the sign are ironic, as nobody is clear-sighted in Gatsby's world – not even Nick, who thinks of himself as "inclined to reserve all judgements" but in fact feels superior to everyone, including his cynical girlfriend, a professional golfer named Jordan Baker.

Colour and time
Jordan and Daisy are first seen in white dresses, but neither is as innocent as this choice of colour might suggest. Colour in *The Great Gatsby* is symbolic of the book's themes: Gatsby wears a pink suit and drives a yellow Rolls-Royce –

hues denoting his desperate need to make an impression. One of the book's most prevalent symbols is green, the colour of the light at the end of Daisy's mooring dock, which Gatsby gazes at yearningly from across the water. In the final pages, alone in Gatsby's empty garden, Nick has a vision of the "fresh, green breast of the new world", glimpsed by the first settlers to reach Long Island; he then muses on Gatsby's belief in that symbolic "green light, the orgastic future that year by year recedes before us". It is here, in the green light and the green land, that the novel's concerns with individual and national destiny converge.

At the end of the book, feeling that the East is haunted after the book's final tragedy and "distorted beyond my eyes' powers of correction", Nick returns to his Midwestern home. In his shifting, worldly, highly nuanced perceptions and sympathies, Nick is as much the novel's subject as Gatsby. The thought he leaves us with is that the past pulls us back irresistibly: dreams of progress are fool's gold.

Belated acclaim

When he was planning his novel in 1923, Fitzgerald wrote that he wanted to produce "something extraordinary and beautiful and simple and intricately patterned". He achieved this ambition with panache, but the book initially received mixed reviews and sold poorly. By the time of his death Fitzgerald thought of himself as a failure: during the last year of his life only 72 copies of his nine books were recorded as sales in his royalty statements.

Nowadays, *The Great Gatsby* and Fitzgerald's subsequent work, *Tender is the Night*, are widely regarded as among the greatest US novels ever written. *Tender is the Night* follows a narrative that

So we beat on, boats against the current, borne back ceaselessly into the past.
The Great Gatsby

fictionalizes strands in Fitzgerald's deeply troubled life, including adultery, mental illness, and an acute sense of personal and creative failure.

The Great Gatsby is the more acclaimed of the two novels. It is particularly admired for its forensic exposure of a flawed milieu; its finely judged prose, combining first-person informality with

superbly cadenced description; its brilliantly telling dialogue, capable of revealing a moral vacuum in the briefest of exchanges; and its structural accomplishment – for example, in the placing of Jordan's account of Gatsby's back-story, which is both a flashback (telling of past events) and a flash-forward (because Tom tells of Jordan's revelations out of sequence).

Like the rest of the Lost Generation, Fitzgerald may have been reacting to the mood of his times – disillusionment, a loss of moral bearings, and the focus on the material rather than the spiritual – but his novel transcends the moment of its creation. This is in part because of its continuing relevance in today's climate of celebrity, corporate greed, and a world economy driven by inflated asset prices. But the book is also timelessly important because every aspect of it, aesthetically, bears witness to Fitzgerald's unassailable mastery of his art. ∎

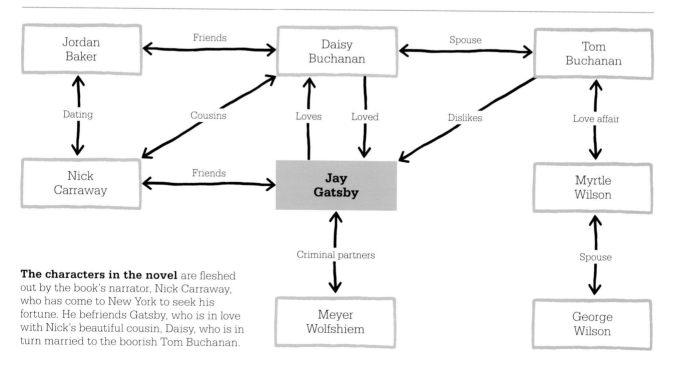

The characters in the novel are fleshed out by the book's narrator, Nick Carraway, who has come to New York to seek his fortune. He befriends Gatsby, who is in love with Nick's beautiful cousin, Daisy, who is in turn married to the boorish Tom Buchanan.

THE OLD WORLD MUST CRUMBLE. AWAKE, WIND OF DAWN!
BERLIN ALEXANDERPLATZ (1929), ALFRED DÖBLIN

IN CONTEXT

FOCUS
Weimar-era experimentalism

BEFORE
1915 *Metamorphosis*, a key early anti-realistic text by Franz Kafka, influences several other modern German-language writers.

AFTER
1931–32 Austrian author Hermann Broch's trilogy *The Sleepwalkers* experiments with form, changing genre according to the plot.

1930–43 Austrian Robert Musil's novel *The Man Without Qualities* is structured as a tour of ideas through which the central character attempts to define himself.

1943 Herman Hesse's use of Jungian psychoanalysis and Eastern mysticism in *The Glass Bead Game* results in a combination similar to the later genre of Magic Realism.

Although the 15 years after the end of World War I saw hyperinflation and mass unemployment in Germany, it was also a time of a great flourishing in the arts and sciences, known as Weimar culture. Many leading intellectuals were Jewish, and the period came to an end with Hitler's ascent to power in 1933 and the rise in anti-Semitism, when thousands of Jews fled Germany.

New forms for a new world
While the Weimar era lasted, German-language literary experimentalism was ambitious in its attempts to express the complexities of the modern world, and *Berlin Alexanderplatz* by Alfred Döblin (1878–1957) was a key work. It is the story of a low-level pimp, Franz Biberkopf, who struggles to make his way in the criminal underclass after being released from prison. The characters speak in the almost untranslatable argot of the slums of inter-war Berlin, and the novel is a dazzling exercise in literary montage. At times it takes the form of newspaper stories, street ballads, speeches, and extracts from fictional books. The narrative incorporates stream of consciousness and a mixture of first- and third-person viewpoints. Through this complex experimental technique, 1920s Berlin itself is given vivid expression, leading *Berlin Alexanderplatz* to be seen as one of the great *Großstadtromane*, or "big city novels", which focus on life in urban areas. ∎

German fellow-citizens, never has a nation been betrayed more ignominiously and more unjustly than the German people.
Berlin Alexanderplatz

See also: *Metamorphosis* 210–11 ▪ *The Magic Mountain* 224–27 ▪ *The Man Without Qualities* 243

SHIPS AT A DISTANCE HAVE EVERY MAN'S WISH ON BOARD

THEIR EYES WERE WATCHING GOD (1937), ZORA NEALE HURSTON

IN CONTEXT

FOCUS
The Harlem Renaissance

BEFORE
1923 Jean Toomer publishes his first novel, *Cane* – a key Modernist work evoking black life in the South. Of mixed race, Toomer preferred to be termed an "American writer" rather than a "black writer", but was a central figure in the Harlem Renaissance.

1923 Aged 21, Countee Cullen wins an award from the Poetry Society of America for his poem "The Ballad of the Brown Girl", about a doomed interracial romance. He becomes a key figure in the Harlem Renaissance.

1934 Harlem Renaissance writer Langston Hughes publishes his first short story collection, *The Ways of White Folks*, focusing on race relations; the title is intended to be mocking.

The Harlem Renaissance of the 1920s and '30s – or the "flowering of Negro Literature", as the US author and Civil Rights activist James Weldon Johnson put it – was an important awakening of African-American cultural pride and identity. The movement centred on Harlem, New York City, USA, and began in 1924 when *Opportunity* magazine held a party to introduce black writers to white publishers, giving them access to mainstream exposure.

Emerging out of a burgeoning urban black middle class, the Harlem Renaissance also embraced theatre, music, and a new political awareness. Although the Great Depression brought the movement to an end, it marked a significant step forward in self-respect for black America, and laid the groundwork for the Civil Rights Movement after World War II.

A defiant voice

Zora Neale Hurston (1891–1960), was a Harlem Renaissance writer and a prominent figure in both African-American and women's literature. Her best-known novel, *Their Eyes Were Watching God*, is about a poor black woman, Janie Crawford, in the Southern states of the USA in the early 20th century. The story is book-ended by her return to Eatonville, Florida – the USA's proud first all-black city – where Hurston herself grew up.

Like other Harlem Renaissance texts, the novel differs from earlier works about African-American life by being honest and realistic rather than overtly sentimental. Hurston's innovative use of the rural Southern black dialect is a notable feature of the text. The book also focuses on Janie's marriages to three husbands, each of whom dominates her life and undermines her status, and against whom she rebels.

Their Eyes Were Watching God is an early and defiant voice on several crucial issues that have lost none of their relevance or resonance in the modern world – notably racism, poverty, and gender inequality. ∎

See also: *Narrative of the Life of Frederick Douglass* 126–27 ∎ *Invisible Man* 259 ∎ *Beloved* 306–09

DEAD MEN ARE HEAVIER THAN BROKEN HEARTS

THE BIG SLEEP (1939), RAYMOND CHANDLER

IN CONTEXT

FOCUS
Hard-boiled fiction

BEFORE
1930 *The Maltese Falcon*, by US author Dashiell Hammett, introduces the sleuth Sam Spade, whose strong ethical values were an inspiration for Chandler's Philip Marlowe.

1934 *The Postman Always Rings Twice*, by US writer James M Cain, gains notoriety for its sex and brutal violence.

AFTER
1943 Another novel by Cain, *Double Indemnity*, tackles the theme of a femme fatale plotting to kill her husband, in this case the motive being to claim on life insurance.

1953 In Chandler's *The Long Goodbye*, which has Marlowe as its hero, two characters, Roger Wade, a hard-drinking writer, and Terry Lennox, another alcoholic, are partly autobiographical.

Hard-boiled detective fiction brought realism, sex, violence, and fast, colloquial dialogue to the crime genre. It began with the short story form, especially those stories published in the popular pulp magazines of the 1920s to 1940s, the leading exponent being *Black Mask*. Raymond Chandler's most illustrious predecessor was Dashiell Hammett, whose first hard-boiled detective story, *Red Harvest*, came out a decade before Chandler's *The Big Sleep* and was originally serialized in *Black Mask*.

The hard-boiled detective, although clever, is a man of action. Battling organized crime and police corruption, he gets dragged into violence. Guns are among the hazards he faces, and in certain situations he needs to carry one, and sometimes use it. These experiences harden him into cynicism – hence the phrase "hard-boiled". Yet at the same time, he has his principles. Chandler's detective, Philip Marlowe, ordering a young woman to get dressed in *The Big Sleep* after refusing her advances, looks down at his

Raymond Chandler

Born in Chicago, USA, in 1888, Raymond Chandler was taken to England at the age of 12 by his divorced mother. He was schooled at Dulwich College, South London, and later studied international law in France and Germany. Returning to the USA in 1912, he lived in California, working, among other jobs, as a tennis-racket stringer. He joined the Canadian Army after World War I broke out, and served in France. In 1924 he married Cissy Pascal, a woman 18 years his senior. He started writing in earnest after losing his job at an oil company in the Great Depression. His first published story appeared in *Black Mask* magazine in 1933. *The Big Sleep* was his first novel; he went on to write six others. In 1959, the year before he died, he became president of the Mystery Writers of America.

Other key works

1940 *Farewell, My Lovely*
1949 *The Little Sister*
1953 *The Long Goodbye*

See also: *Bleak House* 146–49 ▪ *The Moonstone* 198–99 ▪ *The Hound of the Baskervilles* 208 ▪ *The New York Trilogy* 336

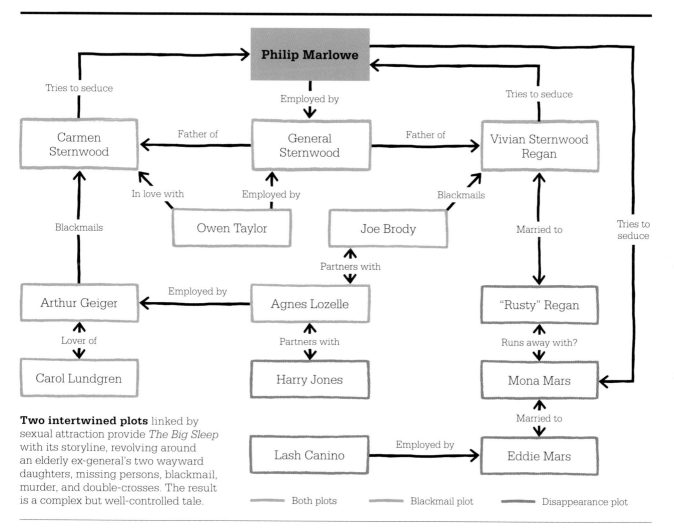

Two intertwined plots linked by sexual attraction provide *The Big Sleep* with its storyline, revolving around an elderly ex-general's two wayward daughters, missing persons, blackmail, murder, and double-crosses. The result is a complex but well-controlled tale.

chessboard and sees that he has made a mistake with a knight move. "Knights," he says, "have no meaning in this game." But they do: Marlowe, for all his faults, is a modern knight, among the kings and queens of crime and their pawns. He is loyal to clients, hates liars, cheats, and thugs, and fights back with wit and courage.

New uses for pulp

Part of Chandler's achievement was to apply literary sophistication to pulp-fiction subjects. *The Big Sleep* is told by Marlowe in the first person, and the language is sharply idiomatic – colloquial not only in the dialogue but also the narration. But the prose has a jewel-like precision, with terse, beautifully crafted sentences. There are witty or amusingly exaggerated similes, such as doors "which would have let in a troop of Indian elephants", but they are not overdone.

The story has a tight plot, with one situation flowing naturally into the next. Two-thirds of the way in, Marlowe has solved the mystery for his client; however, he spends the rest of the book tying up a loose end, and putting himself in further danger to discover how deep into evil an arch-villain has fallen. Throughout, Marlowe remains one step ahead of everybody else, and able, like the chess knight, to outwit his enemies by unexpected moves. The big sleep of the title is death, and is the subject of a poignant coda in which Marlowe, showing self-understanding far beyond Sherlock Holmes, implicates himself as "part of the nastiness". ▪

IT IS SUCH A SECRET PLACE, THE LAND OF TEARS

THE LITTLE PRINCE (1943), ANTOINE DE SAINT-EXUPÉRY

IN CONTEXT

FOCUS
Writers in exile

BEFORE
1932 The Austrian-Jewish writer Joseph Roth writes *The Radetzky March*, which details Austria–Hungary's decline, a year before he leaves Germany for Paris. He remains in exile for the rest of his life.

1939 Bertolt Brecht's anti-war play *Mother Courage and Her Children* is written a few years after he flees Nazi persecution.

1941 Published just before his suicide in Brazilian exile, Austrian author Stefan Zweig's novella *The Royal Game* criticizes the brutality of the Third Reich's Nazi regime.

AFTER
1952 Holocaust survivor Paul Celan produces a collection of poems, *Poppy and Memory*, after settling in Paris following horrific wartime experiences in his native central Europe.

M any writers were forced to flee their homelands before and during World War II, and a sombre, wistful, and elegiac tone is often evident in the literature produced in exile by such writers, who include Joseph Roth, Bertolt Brecht, Stefan Zweig, and Paul Celan. Also among this exodus was Antoine de Saint-Exupéry, who wrote *The Little Prince* in New York after he had left France, following its occupation by the Nazis.

Like many of the great literary works from this era, *The Little Prince* is not strictly a "war" novel but it is shaped by the political and social context that the war brought

Here is my secret, very simply: you can only see things clearly with your heart. What is essential is invisible to the eye.
The Little Prince

about. Saint-Exupéry's book has been read in numerous ways: as a general moral and philosophical fable; as a children's fairy tale; as an autobiographical story that has been re-imagined as fantasy; and as a direct reflection of its times. These interpretations have all been made of other works of exile literature, which commonly lament a lost way of life.

State of dislocation
Given its genesis in a time of displacement, it is not surprising that the title character of Saint-Exupéry's novel is an alien boy who falls to Earth in the eerie landscape of the Sahara Desert. The narrator, a pilot who has crash-landed, encounters the boy there.

Abandonment, wandering, escape, and instability characterize the narrative of *The Little Prince*, which presents us with a seemingly simple children's story. But like all good examples of such fiction, it is a tale for both old and young. Saint-Exupéry takes from classic children's literature the idea that the state of childhood is one of transition, where difference predominates. The prince is literally and metaphorically an alien wandering the Earth – a

See also: *Mother Courage and Her Children* 244–45 ▪ *Poppy and Memory* 258 ▪ *One Day in the Life of Ivan Denisovitch* 289

child lost in an adult world. But as a character, his alienness is infused with a moral philosophy that celebrates dissimilarity and questions the world of adults which has led to war – and, in Saint-Exupéry's case, exile from home. Like a child's painful maturation into the unknowable realm of adulthood, the state of exile is a process of losing and relearning one's place in the world.

Tolerating difference

This strangeness of the adult world coupled with the novel's celebration of the little prince's alienness, has also been read as a political critique. The baobab trees, which infest the home planet of the little prince, have been interpreted as a reference to the contemporary "sickness" of Nazism and its equally grasping

nature as it moved across Europe destroying all in its path, including Saint-Exupéry's beloved France.

The narrator warns about "some terrible seeds on the little prince's planet. … And a baobab, if you tackle it too late … will bore right through a planet with its roots." In contrast, the novel positions the humanist philosophy of rationality, compassion, and respect for difference against this spreading disaster. The alien boy advises us all that "eyes are blind. One must look with the heart".

The Little Prince is a timeless yet timely exploration of the value of human life. Like other writers in exile, Saint-Exupéry explores loss and change against a backdrop of upheaval and alienation, which fosters kindness towards others and a toleration of difference. ▪

Antoine de Saint-Exupéry

Born to a French aristocratic family in 1900, Antoine de Saint-Exupéry had a strict upbringing in a château near Lyon. During his national service, he became an aviator.

Before World War II, he was a commercial pilot who pioneered airmail routes in Europe, South America, and Africa. When war broke out, he joined the French Air Force and flew reconnaissance missions until 1940. During these years he produced many well-known works, but *The Little Prince* was not written until he and his wife, Consuelo Suncin, fled heartbroken into exile after France's defeat and its armistice with Germany.

Vilified by his government and depressed by his stormy marriage, Saint-Exupéry flew his last flight in 1944, over the Mediterranean, where it is believed he was shot down. His posthumous reputation has recovered him as one of France's literary heroes.

Other key works

1926 *The Aviator*
1931 *Night Flight*
1944 *Letter to a Hostage*

The rise of the Nazis saw the emergence of writer-refugees whose homelands became hostile environments due to politics (Marxist Brecht left for Denmark), antisemitism (Jews Roth and Zweig went to Paris and London, respectively), and war (Saint-Exupéry fled occupation, while wartime internee Celan chose post-war exile).

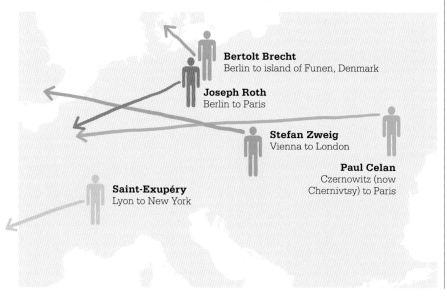

Bertolt Brecht
Berlin to island of Funen, Denmark

Joseph Roth
Berlin to Paris

Stefan Zweig
Vienna to London

Paul Celan
Czernowitz (now Chernivtsy) to Paris

Saint-Exupéry
Lyon to New York

FURTHER READING

THE CALL OF THE WILD
(1903), JACK LONDON

The masterpiece of the US writer London (1876–1916), *The Call of the Wild*, a popular and unashamedly emotional tale of survival, is set during the 1890s Klondike Gold Rush in Alaska. The main character is a dog, half Saint Bernard, half Collie, purloined from a California ranch and set to work as a sled-dog in faraway Alaska. He suffers abuse by his owners and aggression from a rival dog before finally turning feral. Shedding civilization and relearning primitive ways, he becomes leader of a wolf pack.

They were savages, all of them, who knew no law but the law of club and fang.
The Call of the Wild
Jack London

NOSTROMO
(1904), JOSEPH CONRAD

Poland-born novelist Conrad (see p.197), a mariner for 20 years, took British citizenship in 1886 and wrote in English. *Nostromo*, subtitled "A Tale of the Seaboard", is an analysis of politics, revolution, and corruption that plays out in a fictional republic of South America, and an important examination of postcolonial global capitalism. Fused with these themes is a tale of adventure that traces the fortunes of the eponymous hero, a man of principle. This is a dark work, full of betrayal and disillusion. Much of the story – even the climax – is conveyed by flashbacks.

ETHAN FROME
(1911), EDITH WHARTON

The most popular work of US author Wharton (1862–1937), *Ethan Frome* is narrated by a visitor to a New England town who is intrigued by one of its residents, Ethan Frome, a dour and monosyllabic farmer. Switching from the first person to an extended third-person flashback, the novel tells the tragic tale of the secret love of Frome for his wife's cousin, and the tragic outcome of a snowy "smash-up" that occurred 24 years earlier. The themes of passion, thwarted emotions, resentment, and frustration are magnified against the harsh rustic environment.

DEATH IN VENICE
(1912), THOMAS MANN

The most famous novella by German Nobel Laureate Mann (see p.227), *Death in Venice* is about a famous author suffering from writer's block, who takes a short holiday in the Italian city of the title, where he becomes obsessed by a 14-year-old boy. Cholera has been detected and there are health warnings in place, creating an atmosphere of dissolution. The book is a Freudian reflection on both the degenerative force of illicit homoerotic passion across the generations, and of the profound poignancy of ageing.

SONS AND LOVERS
(1913), D H LAWRENCE

A partly autobiographical exploration of the working-class family and romantic relationships, *Sons and Lovers* is often seen as Lawrence's finest work. Set in the mining region where Lawrence was brought up, the book tells the story of a young budding artist, Paul Morel, who has romantic involvements with an unyielding, religiously minded girlfriend and a married woman – both of whom are overshadowed by Paul's mother, with whom he shares a close, suffocating bond. Paul's father is violent and uneducated, which adds to family tensions. The book is an unsentimental portrait of childhood, adolescence, the clash between generations, and familial possessiveness and grief, set within a closely observed social setting. The mother's unfulfilled life and final fatal illness are poignantly depicted.

IN SEARCH OF LOST TIME
(1913–1927), MARCEL PROUST

Published in seven volumes over 15 years, *In Search of Lost Time*, or *Remembrance of Things Past*, is the masterpiece of French writer Marcel Proust (1871–1922). In a

D H Lawrence

Born in 1885, David Herbert Lawrence was the son of a coal miner and the first from his village in Nottinghamshire, England, to win a scholarship to the local high school. His early promise led to university and a teaching career, but his writing talent – his first story was published in 1907 – persuaded him to quit teaching in 1912. He eloped to Germany with married aristocrat Frieda Weekley in the same year. Marked by a spontaneous, vivid realism, Lawrence's writing subverted prevailing social, sexual, and cultural norms, earning him censorship and – at the time of his death in 1930 – a tarnished reputation.

Key works

1913 *Sons and Lovers* (see left)
1915 *The Rainbow*
1920 *Women in Love*

famous early scene, the taste of a madeleine cake releases memories of boyhood holidays for the first-person narrator. Proust's leisurely, analytical prose outlines detailed accounts of the inner lives of both himself and the characters of the work, including love and jealousy, homosexuality, artistic ambition, and many varieties of vice and virtue. The experience of living in wartime Paris is vividly conveyed. Throughout, social nuances are subtly registered. Eventually the narrator learns that the beauty of the past lives on in the memory – time is regained. He then sets about writing his life's story. This autobiographical dimension is one of the work's many fascinations.

A PORTRAIT OF THE ARTIST AS A YOUNG MAN
(1916), JAMES JOYCE

The first novel by Irish writer Joyce (see p.216), *A Portrait of the Artist as a Young Man* traces the early years of a character who would later reappear in Joyce's 1922 masterpiece, *Ulysses*. Stephen Dedalus rebels against the norms of Ireland and Catholicism, and sets out to forge his own destiny – as a writer in Paris. The book uses stream-of-consciousness narrative in a way that foreshadows the author's later work.

THE HEARTLESS
(1917), YI KWANG-SU

A South Korean journalist and independence activist, Yi Kwang-su (1892–1950) was the author of the first modern Korean novel, *The Heartless*. It tells the story of a young teacher of English in Seoul, torn between two women in the period of Japanese occupation: one is traditionalist and working as a *kisaeng* (geisha), the other is inclined to liberated Western values. The protagonist's predicament is used to dramatize social tensions in Korea, but the book also explores personal, sexual awakening as well as cultural ambiguities.

SIDDHARTHA
(1922), HERMANN HESSE

Hugely popular in the 1960s due its exploration of Eastern spirituality, *Siddhartha* by Swiss writer Hesse (1877–1962) describes the spiritual life of a young Brahmin in ancient India. The title is Sanskrit, meaning

"he who has attained his goals". The hero opts not to join the order newly created by the Buddha, but to discover his own form of insight. Sidetracked by wealth and erotic desire, he finally gains wisdom and love in the consciousness of the world's unimprovable completeness. The book fuses spiritual thinking with psychoanalysis and philosophy.

A PASSAGE TO INDIA
(1924), E M FORSTER

English author E M Forster (1879–1970) sets *A Passage to India* during the period of the British Raj in India, amid the stirrings of the movement for independence. The book's central event is an alleged and unspecified attempt at sexual impropriety in a cave complex, by a young Muslim Indian doctor against a British woman with whom he is on friendly terms. The case against the doctor, which leads to a trial, brings to the surface tensions between colonized and colonizing nations. Forster questions the underlying principles of British imperialism, in the process puncturing the romantic delusions of those seduced by the

In England the moon had seemed dead and alien; here she was caught in the shawl of night together with earth and all the other stars.
A Passage to India
E M Forster

image of the British Raj. He also shows the marginalization of women in a milieu where male friendships are strong and mutually supportive.

THE TRIAL
(1925), FRANZ KAFKA

Written in 1914–15, *The Trial* is the most complete of three unfinished novels by Jewish Czech writer Franz Kafka (see p.211), who wrote in German. Its account of Joseph K, arrested and prosecuted by an inscrutable authority without being told the nature of his crime, has been interpreted as an archetypal metaphor for modern alienation, and for the dehumanizing effect of elaborate, inflexible bureaucracies – and, by extension, of totalitarian states. The latter interpretation makes Kafka a prescient author, anticipating Fascism and Nazism.

Someone must have been telling lies about Joseph K, for without having done anything wrong he was arrested one fine morning.
The Trial
Franz Kafka

MRS DALLOWAY
(1925), VIRGINIA WOOLF

Mrs Dalloway, written by Woolf when she was at the height of her powers, lays bare the consciousness of a well-to-do woman spending a day in London. Clarissa Dalloway's thoughts turn to a party she will be hosting that evening, but also range back in time, to her youth and the experience of her marriage to a reliable but unsatisfying man. The other major character is a traumatized soldier who spends time in the park with his Italian wife, before making a tragic decision. Technically the novel is accomplished and original, shifting between direct and indirect speech, and juggling between omniscient narration, stream of consciousness, and soliloquy.

THE COUNTERFEITERS
(1926), ANDRÉ GIDE

Seen as a precursor to the 1950s *nouveau roman* novel form, *The Counterfeiters* by French author Gide (1869–1951) draws a parallel between counterfeit gold coins and the authenticity of human feelings and relationships. Structured as a story-within-a-story, the book is complicated by multiple plot lines and viewpoints in an attempt at a literary form of Cubism, an art style in which the concept of a single point of perspective was abandoned. Centred around young men in fin-de-siècle Paris, one of the themes is the possibilities for fulfilment within homosexual relationships.

DOÑA BARBARA
(1929), RÓMULO GALLEGOS

Rómulo Gallegos (1884–1969) wrote *Doña Barbara* two decades before becoming the first democratically elected president of his native Venezuela. The novel – named after its charismatic female character,

Virginia Woolf

Foremost of the writers in the "Bloomsbury Set" of influential intellectuals and artists, Woolf was born in 1882 in London. She started writing as a girl and her first novel, *The Voyage Out*, appeared in 1915. She married, happily, in 1912, but is also known for her love affair with talented gardener Vita Sackville-West. Woolf soon established herself as a leading intellectual and writer, taking fiction in a new direction – inwards. But she was prone to depression and mood swings. She committed suicide by drowning near Lewes, Sussex, in 1941, aged 59. Many feminist thinkers since her death have revered her as an inspiration.

Key works

1925 *Mrs Dalloway* (see left)
1927 *To the Lighthouse*
1931 *The Waves*

who exerts mysterious power over men – examines the tension between primitive and civilized impulses, and between the sexes. Set in the rural cattle-ranching Llanos prairie region, the story is told using evocative, vernacular language. There are magical realist elements that anticipate the fiction of Gabriel García Márquez.

THE SOUND AND THE FURY
(1929), WILLIAM FAULKNER

An ambitious and enigmatic novel comprising four counterpointed perspectives, *The Sound and the Fury* is a masterpiece by Nobel Laureate Faulkner, arch-chronicler of the US South. The setting is Jefferson, Mississippi. The first section is a disjointed narrative told by Benjy, a 33-year-old, cognitively disabled man. The second section is narrated by his older brother, a suicidal Harvard student 18 years earlier; the third, by Benjy's hard-nosed younger brother; and the last section is narrated by one of the family's female black servants. Using stream of consciousness and radical time shifts, Faulkner creates a complex jigsaw of imagination and insight, and writes with an unparalleled understanding of race, grief, family dysfunction, and the decay of old Southern values.

THE MAN WITHOUT QUALITIES
(1930, 1933, 1943), ROBERT MUSIL

Unfinished and written in three volumes (the third was published posthumously), *The Man Without Qualities* was the life's work and masterpiece of Austrian novelist Musil (1880–1942). Eschewing plot-driven momentum, Musil presents a complex social vision and exposes modern values and political folly. Set in the twilight of the Austro-Hungarian Empire, which is satirized with heavy irony, the rambling story encompasses many characters in its more than 1,000 pages: a black page, an aristocrat, the murderer of a prostitute, and a hero who serves as a detached commentator on a collapsing society.

BRAVE NEW WORLD
(1932), ALDOUS HUXLEY

English writer Aldous Huxley (1894–1963) presents in *Brave New World* – whose ironic title comes

from a line in Shakespeare's *The Tempest* – a vision of a dystopian future, set in London around the year 2540. A world totalitarian state represses individual freedom and self-expression, including emotions. Genetic engineering and brainwashing are used as tools of control, and recreational drugs ("soma") and sex are freely available. Consumerism is rampant ("ending is better than mending"), while spiritual values have shrivelled to nothing. Even the terms "mother" and "father" are outlawed. A rebellious spirit, John the Savage, sets himself against the system and does battle with the World Controllers. The book is admired for its prophetic insights as well as for its moral outlook and vivid writing.

JOURNEY TO THE END OF THE NIGHT
(1932), LOUIS-FERDINARD CÉLINE

Radically experimental in style and treatment, *Journey to the End of The Night* is a partly autobiographical novel by French writer Dr Louis-Ferdinand Auguste Destouches

(1894–1961), who wrote under the pseudonym Céline, which was also his grandmother's first name. Characterized by black-comedic invective, the mood is darkly pessimistic, even misanthropic. The story traces the protagonist Ferdinand Bardonee's journeys from France at the start of World War I, via colonial Africa to the USA and back to Paris. Focusing on human stupidity, Céline has challenging things to say about war, empire, and the ruling classes.

TROPIC OF CANCER
(1934), HENRY MILLER

Banned by censors for its explicit and deliberately shocking sexual content, *Tropic of Cancer* was the debut novel of US writer Miller (1891–1980). A sprawling, plotless, semi-autobiographical masterpiece, it describes life and love at the extremes of existence in 1930s' Paris. Publication in the USA and UK was delayed until censorship laws were overturned in the 1960s. The book inspired a new wave of writers, such as the US "Beat Generation".

William Faulkner

An American Nobel Prize winner, Faulkner chronicled the South of his country. He was born in 1897, in New Albany, Mississippi. In 1902 his family moved to Oxford, Mississippi, where his father was business manager of the university. This was where Faulkner would spend most of his life, and the surrounding Lafayette County was the inspiration for his fictional Yoknapatawpha County, the setting for most of his novels. He first wrote poetry, and it was

not until 1925 that he tackled a novel. He also trained in Canada as a pilot in the Royal Air Force. Faulkner's books often depict the decline of the upper echelons of society, addressing controversial themes such as slavery; but he also wrote about the poorer classes. He died in 1962, aged 64.

Key works

1929 *The Sound and the Fury* (see left, opposite page)
1930 *As I Lay Dying*
1931 *These 13* (short stories)
1936 *Absalom, Absalom!*

THE BOOK OF DISQUIET
(WRITTEN c.1913–35; PUBLISHED 1982), FERNANDO PESSOA

Described by Portuguese author Pessoa (1888–1935) as a "factless autobiography", *The Book of Disquiet* was only published 47 years after his death. A modernist masterpiece, it is a fluid, kaleidoscopic, and unfinished mosaic of fragments that combine glimpses of self-revelation with reveries and maxims of literary criticism and philosophy. Pessoa filtered his writing through the use of heteronyms – invented authorial personae – and this highly original book gives a spellbinding insight into the process. Although a study in loneliness and despair, the story has a brilliant inventiveness that makes it engaging.

OF MICE AND MEN
(1937), JOHN STEINBECK

Steinbeck's most popular book and widely praised at the time of its publication, *Of Mice and Men* is set in 1930s' California during the Great Depression. It follows two itinerant ranch workers whose dream is to have a small farm of their own. An incident involving a ranch-owner's daughter propels the story into tragedy. Steinbeck's themes include the hardship of penury, our desperate wish for comfort in loneliness, and the way aggressive self-interest can flourish in the weak as well as the strong.

NAUSEA
(1938), JEAN-PAUL SARTRE

A major work of existentialism, *Nausea* was the first novel by French philosopher Jean-Paul Sartre (1905–80), who was later awarded – but declined to accept – the 1964 Nobel Prize. In a seaside town an introverted historian is captivated by the idea that his intellectual and spiritual freedoms are circumscribed by the objects and situations that impinge upon him. The consequence is nausea, which turns into a profound angst and self-loathing that undermine his sanity. He begins to feel that relationships are empty: the struggle to make sense of the world can only be conducted within himself. Eventually the protagonist views reality's indifference to his life as liberating, since he is now free to create his own version of meaning, with all the responsibility it brings.

THE GRAPES OF WRATH
(1939), JOHN STEINBECK

Like *Of Mice and Men* (see left), Steinbeck's masterpiece *The Grapes of Wrath* is set in the 1930s during the Great Depression. It focuses on the suffering of the Joads, an Oklahoma Dust Bowl family who drive a saloon car converted into a truck along Route 66 to California to find work. Like many other economic migrants, they flee drought, dispossession, and unpaid debts. This powerful novel, which conveys the resilience of the human spirit under stress through poetic prose and sharp characterization, publicized the exploitation of migrant workers in the USA during the 1930s and drew attention to the cause of social improvement. While the Joads are imperfect, they gradually exhibit a capacity for empathy: the final scene (controversial at the time of the book's publication), features an act of great compassion by the family's teenage daughter, Rose of Sharon.

MOTHER COURAGE AND HER CHILDREN
(1941), BERTOLT BRECHT

An important antiwar play, *Mother Courage and Her Children* is set during the Thirty Years' War of 1618–48, although its ramifications are contemporary with the time of the author: German poet, theatre

---

John Steinbeck

A Nobel Prize winner, John Steinbeck explored in fiction the relationship between humankind and the land. Born, in 1902 in Salinas, California – most of his stories were set in the central and southern regions of the state – he was the son of a library treasurer. He majored in English at Stanford University but left in 1925 without a degree. His first successes as a writer date from the early 1930s, and in 1940 he won the Pulitzer Prize for Fiction for *The Grapes of Wrath*. As well as writing fiction Steinbeck served as a war reporter, covering World War II in 1943 and the Vietnam War in 1967. He returned to California in 1944 and concentrated on local themes in his fiction. He died in New York, where he was living at the time, in 1968, aged 66.

Key works

1937 *Of Mice and Men* (see above)
1939 *The Grapes of Wrath* (see above)
1952 *East of Eden*

director, and playwright Bertolt Brecht (1898–1956). By presenting the central figure, Mother Courage, without sentimentality, Brecht focuses his audience's attention on issues and broad themes, discouraging any identification with character. The play shows his trademark "estrangement effect", drawing attention to theatrical artifice through placard captions, bright lighting, and other effects.

THE OUTSIDER
(1942), ALBERT CAMUS

French author, journalist, and philosopher Albert Camus (1913–60) denied that *The Outsider* is an "existentialist" novel, although its plot is saturated in the bleakness associated with this philosophy. In the book, a French Algerian, unmoved by his mother's funeral, later unfeelingly shoots dead an Arab – someone he has never met. Convicted and imprisoned, he appears to be indifferent to his deprivations. However, the incident does awaken some self-awareness. The story, told from his viewpoint, is an example of the literature of the "absurd", focusing on our attempt to find meaning where none exists.

My mother died today.
Or maybe yesterday,
I don't know.
The Outsider
Albert Camus

THE FOUNTAINHEAD
(1943), AYN RAND

A study of the triumph of individual artistic vision when confronted by traditionalist pressures to conform, *The Fountainhead* by Russia-born US author Ayn Rand (1905–82) tells the story of a modernist architect, who is thought to have been based on Frank Lloyd Wright. The novel combines uncompromising ethical individualism (in its subject matter) with romantic realism (in its treatment). More than seven years in writing, it became a rallying cry for the right-wing, anticommunist philosophy of Objectivism – a movement that Rand herself founded – which was based on reason, freedom, and personal talent and achievement.

FICCIONES
(1944), JORGE LUIS BORGES

An enigmatic short story collection, *Ficciones* reveals Borges' ability to draw the reader into his fantastical, complex imagination with stories that are as enchanting as fairy tales. The 17 pieces are exuberant, yet finely controlled. The prose has jewel-like precision, while the characteristic tone is one of profound metaphysical anxiety. The first story revolves around an encyclopedia entry for a country that cannot be located. Other stories tell of the reviewing of a non-existent book that in the process brings it into being, an ancient society ruled by chance, the infinite Library of Babel, and a person with perfect memory. Certain symbols that are used in the book – particularly the mirror and the labyrinth – later become Borges' trademarks.

Jorge Luis Borges

The Argentinian writer Borges, known for his intellectually intriguing stories, is a major figure of Spanish-language literature. Born in Buenos Aires in 1899, as a teenager he travelled with his family to Europe, and studied French and German in Geneva. He returned to Argentina in 1921. In 1955 he became director of the national library and professor of English Literature in Buenos Aires. He went blind at the age of 55 but never learned Braille, which may have been a factor in his vivid symbolism. As well as fiction he wrote poetry and essays. He died in Geneva in 1986.

Key works

1935 *A Universal History of Infamy*
1944 *Ficciones* (see left)
1967 *Book of Imaginary Beings*

ANIMAL FARM
(1945), GEORGE ORWELL

Animal Farm shows that satirical allegory can be as effective as realism in revealing the evils of totalitarianism. English author Orwell (see p.252) uses a tale of talking animals to dramatize the communist politics of the Russian Revolution and Stalinism. The human owners of the farm are ousted in a coup orchestrated by the pigs, Napoleon and Snowball. Initial idealism falls prey to "human" weakness, and hypocrisy sets in. Entertaining yet chilling, this is one of the most influential political books of the 20th century.

POST-W
WRITIN
1945–1970

AR
G

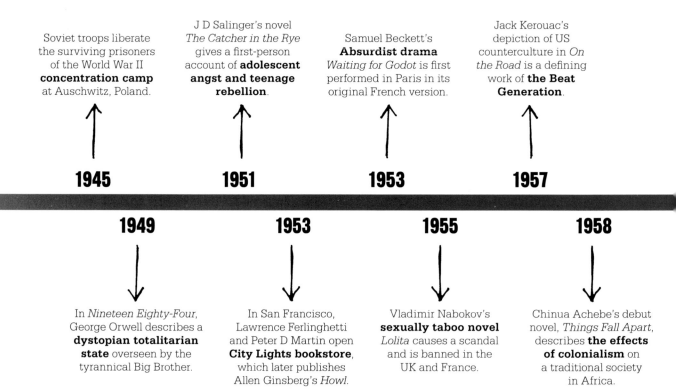

Soviet troops liberate the surviving prisoners of the World War II **concentration camp** at Auschwitz, Poland.

J D Salinger's novel *The Catcher in the Rye* gives a first-person account of **adolescent angst and teenage rebellion**.

Samuel Beckett's **Absurdist drama** *Waiting for Godot* is first performed in Paris in its original French version.

Jack Kerouac's depiction of US counterculture in *On the Road* is a defining work of **the Beat Generation**.

1945

1951

1953

1957

1949

1953

1955

1958

In *Nineteen Eighty-Four*, George Orwell describes a **dystopian totalitarian state** overseen by the tyrannical Big Brother.

In San Francisco, Lawrence Ferlinghetti and Peter D Martin open **City Lights bookstore**, which later publishes Allen Ginsberg's *Howl*.

Vladimir Nabokov's **sexually taboo novel** *Lolita* causes a scandal and is banned in the UK and France.

Chinua Achebe's debut novel, *Things Fall Apart*, describes **the effects of colonialism** on a traditional society in Africa.

In 1945, much of the world was reeling from three decades of turmoil: two cataclysmic world wars, separated by a global Great Depression. In what proved to be a short-lived period of hope, many people struggled to make sense of the destruction and rebuild a better world. But as old empires and powers declined, new ones arose, resulting in the "clash of cultures" between the West and the Communist Eastern bloc. The following decades were dominated by this Cold War, and the ever-present danger of nuclear war.

Aftermath of World War II

Literature in the post-war period was inevitably influenced by experiences of war. Jewish writers, and especially Holocaust survivors such as poet Paul Celan, attempted to come to terms with the horrors of the death camps. German authors, including Günter Grass, tackled the shameful legacy of Nazism. In Japan, a generation of writers examined the social and political changes following the nuclear attack on Hiroshima.

The negative effects were also felt in those countries that had been victorious in war. In England, George Orwell, who was also a veteran of the Spanish Civil War, argued that the defeat of Nazism had not removed the threat of totalitarianism. In *Animal Farm* and *Nineteen Eighty-Four* he portrayed dystopian societies that darkly satirized Stalin's Soviet Russia, capturing the pessimistic mood of the Cold War. This mood was also felt keenly in France, where the experience of war and the existential threat of the nuclear bomb manifested itself as nihilism rather than cynicism. Instead of trying to find some sense in life, writers such as Paris-based Irishman Samuel Beckett, in his play *Waiting for Godot*, pointed out its absurdity, depicted with a grim humour. In addition to this "Theatre of the Absurd", black humour could be found in US novels such as Joseph Heller's *Catch-22*.

New voices

The unsettled atmosphere of the era after the war also inspired new, postmodern writing techniques which reflected this uncertainty: narratives could be paradoxical, fragmented, or presented out of chronological order, often from multiple perspectives, or that of an unreliable narrator.

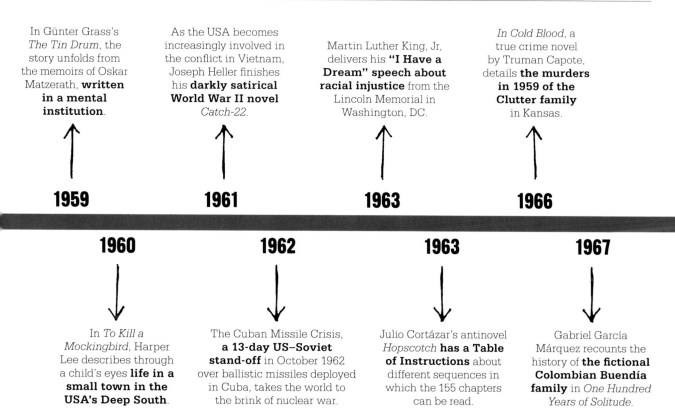

In Günter Grass's *The Tin Drum*, the story unfolds from the memoirs of Oskar Matzerath, **written in a mental institution**.

As the USA becomes increasingly involved in the conflict in Vietnam, Joseph Heller finishes his **darkly satirical World War II novel** *Catch-22*.

Martin Luther King, Jr, delivers his **"I Have a Dream" speech about racial injustice** from the Lincoln Memorial in Washington, DC.

In Cold Blood, a true crime novel by Truman Capote, details **the murders in 1959 of the Clutter family** in Kansas.

1959   **1961**   **1963**   **1966**

1960   **1962**   **1963**   **1967**

In *To Kill a Mockingbird*, Harper Lee describes through a child's eyes **life in a small town in the USA's Deep South**.

The Cuban Missile Crisis, **a 13-day US–Soviet stand-off** in October 1962 over ballistic missiles deployed in Cuba, takes the world to the brink of nuclear war.

Julio Cortázar's antinovel *Hopscotch* **has a Table of Instructions** about different sequences in which the 155 chapters can be read.

Gabriel García Márquez recounts the history of **the fictional Colombian Buendía family** in *One Hundred Years of Solitude*.

These techniques, developed by European writers such as Jean-Paul Sartre and Günter Grass, were an inspiration to the new generation of South American authors, who were establishing a distinctive style. Among them were Julio Cortázar, whose experimental "antinovel" *Hopscotch* subverted many literary conventions, and Gabriel García Márquez, who popularized the style known as Magic Realism, inspired by the surreal short stories of Argentinian Jorge Luis Borges.

New literary movements were also emerging elsewhere, as many countries – especially in Africa – achieved national independence from European colonial control. Foremost among these countries was Nigeria, where Chinua Achebe provided an indigenous voice to a people rebuilding their nation.

In the USA, too, writers continued to assert their identity. As the Civil Rights Movement gathered momentum in the 1950s and 1960s, African-American authors such as Ralph Ellison described how black people were marginalized, while Harper Lee's *To Kill a Mockingbird* looked at race from the perspective of someone from the Deep South. Social issues of all types also provided the subject matter for New Journalism, the blend of fact and fiction pioneered by Lee's friend Truman Capote.

Youth culture
Perhaps the most vociferous manifestation of post-war culture came with the younger generation, and was most noticeable in the USA. An anti-establishment youth culture emerged as a reaction

against the older generation that had taken them into two world wars and had continued on an aggressive path with military involvement in Korea and Vietnam. These young people also reacted to Cold War uncertainties and the nuclear threat with hedonistic dissent. J D Salinger was one of the first to describe teenage angst and rebellion, followed by the writers of the Beat Generation, whose work was inspired by the freedom of modern jazz and the brashness of rock 'n' roll. Experimental writing by Jack Kerouac, Allen Ginsberg, and William S Burroughs pushed the boundaries not only of form, but also of content: their sometimes explicitly sexual material resulted in legal action and bans on books in some places, before the more relaxed attitudes of the 1960s. ■

BIG BROTHER IS WATCHING YOU

NINETEEN EIGHTY-FOUR (1949),
GEORGE ORWELL

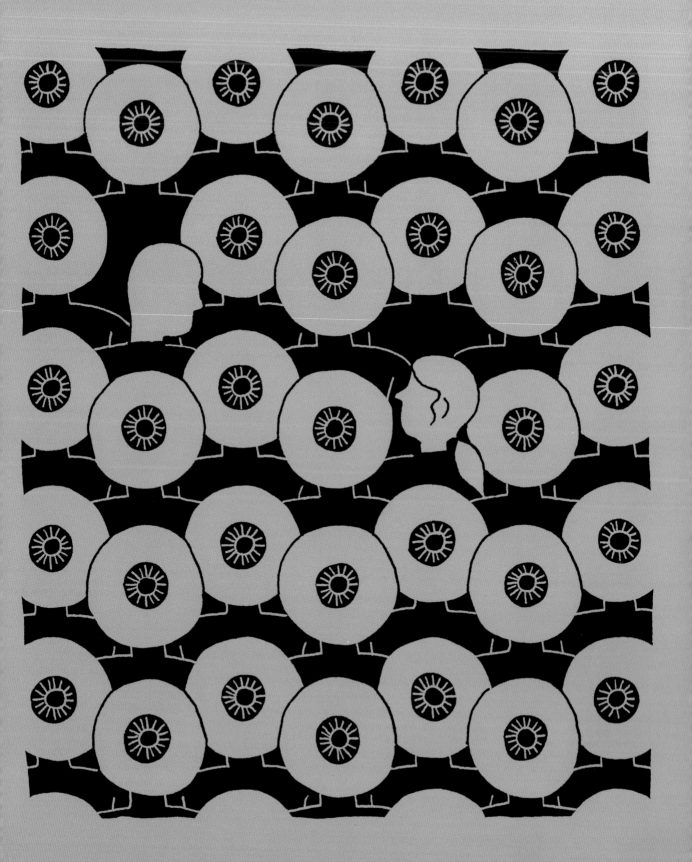

IN CONTEXT

FOCUS
Dystopia

BEFORE
1516 English humanist Sir Thomas More's *Utopia* first imagines an ideal society, and its opposite – a dystopia.

1924 Russian writer Yevgeny Zamyatin's *We* describes the One State, where people live for the collective good.

1932 In English writer Aldous Huxley's *Brave New World* individuality is suppressed.

AFTER
1953 In *Fahrenheit 451* by US novelist Ray Bradbury, books are banned and burned.

1962 English novelist Anthony Burgess's *A Clockwork Orange* depicts a world full of violence.

1985 *The Handmaid's Tale*, by Canadian author Margaret Atwood, is set in a USA run by a totalitarian Christian regime.

D ystopian literature is a genre that portrays the nightmarish vision of a society that is the polar opposite of a utopia (an ideal, perfect world). Ever since the appearance of Thomas More's *Utopia* in 1516, dystopias have been evoked over the centuries by a wide range of writers to focus on topics such as dictatorships (both communist and fascist), poverty, torture, the oppression of populations, and the control of people's minds.

Authors use these dystopian worlds to explore central human concerns, creating visions of the possible consequences of things happening in ways that are unrestrained. Margaret Atwood's *The Handmaid's Tale* (1985), for instance, sees a world run by a military regime, in which women have been stripped of their rights and are appreciated purely for their reproductive value.

Turning points

Dystopias focus primarily on imagined futures, and often on the fear of what may arise from new technologies and social change. For example, in the 20th century,

He who controls the past controls the future. He who controls the present controls the past.
Nineteen Eighty-Four

the threat posed by the destructive force of the atomic bomb and the scenario of dramatic climate change have both provided powerful sources for dystopias.

George Orwell's *Nineteen Eighty-Four* is the best-known modern dystopia. Orwell's fear of rising Stalinism is the starting point for the novel. Although Orwell believed in a democratic socialism, he saw the emerging USSR – in which one political party had consolidated complete control – as anything but socialist. He had also witnessed the splintering of anti-Franco forces in the Spanish Civil

George Orwell

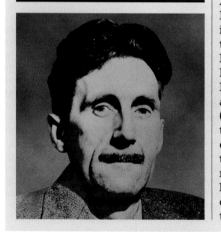

George Orwell was born as Eric Arthur Blair in India in 1903 to British parents. He was schooled in England before heading back to the East, to enrol with the Indian Imperial Police in Burma. In 1928, he moved to Paris, returning to London in 1929 to write *Down and Out in Paris and London* (1933). In 1936, Orwell travelled to Wigan, northern England, to experience the poverty forged by the Depression. That same year he married Eileen O'Shaughnessy before going to fight in Spain's civil war and getting shot through the throat. Orwell returned to

England in 1937 and in 1941 he joined the BBC, only to resign in 1943. He returned to writing with *Animal Farm* (1945), which proved an immediate success. His wife died unexpectedly that same year, and Orwell isolated himself on Jura, a Scottish isle, where he wrote *Nineteen Eighty-Four* (1949). He died of tuberculosis in 1950, aged 46.

Other key works

1934 *Burmese Days*
1937 *The Road to Wigan Pier*
1938 *Homage to Catalonia*

See also: *Candide* 96–97 ▪ *Gulliver's Travels* 104 ▪ *Brave New World* 243 ▪ *Fahrenheit 451* 287 ▪ *Lord of the Flies* 287 ▪
A Clockwork Orange 289 ▪ *The Death of Artemio Cruz* 290 ▪ *The Handmaid's Tale* 335

War in 1936, when pro-Stalin communists turned on those who were supposed to be their allies.

Orwell had already painted a bleak vision of such treachery in his novella *Animal Farm* (1945). He also had a template of sorts for his new work: the world outlined by Russian writer Yevgeny Zamyatin's *We* (1924), in which individual freedom no longer exists.

Nineteen Eighty-Four depicts a totalitarian society manipulating its citizens through propaganda, flipping truths into lies for the sake of maintaining political power. This dystopian society is far darker – one without the hope that the revolution in *Animal Farm* had first promised, and one in which individual lives have become mere cogs in an overarching system.

The end of history

Nineteen Eighty-Four's opening words – "It was a bright cold day in April, and the clocks were striking thirteen." – alert the reader to the fact that even the very nature of the day's temporal construction has shifted. Winston Smith, the novel's protagonist, is entering his apartment building. He is a citizen of London, capital of Airstrip One (once known as Great Britain), a province of Oceania, one of the three cross-continental states that exist following a global nuclear war. Posters fill the wall space with the image of a face – "a man of about forty-five, with a heavy black moustache and ruggedly handsome features", and whose "eyes follow you about when you move. BIG BROTHER IS WATCHING YOU, the caption beneath it ran". Big Brother is the leader of the Party that governs Oceania.

The world Smith inhabits is ruled by an elite. The masses ("the proles"), who make up 85 per cent of the population, are controlled by four paradoxical ministries: the Ministry of Peace, which oversees war; the Ministry of Love, which deals with policing; the Ministry of Plenty, which controls the economy, including rationing for the population; and the Ministry of Truth, or Minitrue, which deals with news and the education of the masses, issuing propaganda to control the thoughts of the people.

One of the chief conduits of control is Newspeak, the language of the Ministry of Truth, which dictates the truth of the past as well as the present. History is revised and rewritten to fit the changing diktats of the state. And Winston Smith himself works in the Ministry of Truth: editing historical records, and burning the original documentation by posting it into a "memory hole". History, as the reader understands it, has stopped: "Nothing exists except an endless present in which the Party is always right."

The all-seeing government

A network of telescreens, cameras, and covert microphones operate to spy and eavesdrop on the »

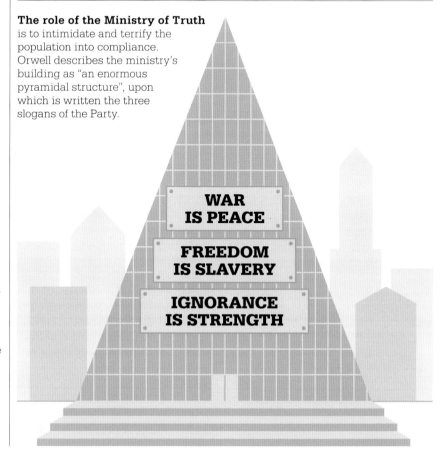

The role of the Ministry of Truth is to intimidate and terrify the population into compliance. Orwell describes the ministry's building as "an enormous pyramidal structure", upon which is written the three slogans of the Party.

WAR IS PEACE

FREEDOM IS SLAVERY

IGNORANCE IS STRENGTH

"Newspeak" is a sinister, curtailed form of everyday English ("Oldspeak") devised by the all-powerful state. In time, "Oldspeak" will be replaced by Newspeak, a stark, simple language, purified to express meanings and to meet the ideological needs of Ingsoc, or English Socialism. Because thought requires words, the state will have inhibited "thoughtcrimes", and personal ideas and feelings of dissent will have become unthinkable.

Duckspeak:
a form of brainless speaking that enables rubbish to be uttered convincingly.

Goodthink:
approved views that give ideological conformity to the Party.

Doubleplusgood:
something that is simply the best.

Doublethink:
a system of thought in which control in the present means amending the past.

Thoughtcrime:
the criminal act of a belief that questions the ruling Party.

Unperson:
someone erased by the state from the historical records.

Blackwhite:
blind, uncritical belief in spite of the facts.

Bellyfeel:
gut-instinct acceptance of Party ideas.

---

population: these are run by the Thought Police, who supervise the protection of the ruling Party.

Everyman's rebellion

Orwell immerses his readers in this hideous totalitarian world before revealing that Winston Smith is engaged in a vital act of rebellion. In his tiny flat, dominated by the instrument of Party control (the telescreen), Smith is starting to write his own history in a diary he has acquired second-hand – a

crime of self expression. He knows it will be an act that he cannot ever step back from and, moreover, that "he was a lonely ghost uttering a truth that nobody would ever hear". And yet he continues to write.

Winston Smith is the everyman hero of the novel – his surname's commonality suggesting that there is nothing special or unusual about him. That quality makes his act of subversion so incendiary: if every Smith or Jones were to rise up against society, then revolution would follow. The use of a name that feels ordinarily English echoes Eric Blair's own adoption of the pseudonym "George Orwell", which he did shortly before publication of his first book, *Down and Out in Paris and London* (1933), to avoid any embarrassment to his family.

Orwell's characterization of the ordinary Smith as a rebel, one who makes his own stand for genuine truth against the machinery of the Party, creates an unlikely champion. In Julia, he finds a fellow dissenter and a lover. Younger than Smith, Julia is an apparent firebrand for

the Junior Anti-Sex League, but passes Smith a note with the simple message "I love you". Their affair is an act of rebellion itself, a sex crime. Yet their covert love cannot last for long, hidden beneath the facade of their obedience to Big Brother and the rules of Oceania.

Enemies of the state

The state's acknowledged enemy is Emmanuel Goldstein, the Party's former leader who now heads a resistance movement called

In the end the Party would announce that two and two made five, and you would have to believe it.
Nineteen Eighty-Four

If you want a picture of the future, imagine a boot stamping on a human face – forever.
Nineteen Eighty-Four

> You want it to happen to the
> other person. You don't give
> a damn what they suffer.
> All you care about is yourself.
> **Nineteen Eighty-Four**

The Brotherhood. Goldstein is a despised figure (like Leon Trotsky was in Stalin's USSR – the two even have the same goatee beards), who is used to unite the citizenship of Oceania via the daily ritual act of "Two Minutes Hate", during which abuse is flung at Goldstein's image on the telescreens.

In a second-hand bookshop, Smith opens a text "with no name or title on the cover". The book is *The Theory and Practice of Oligarchical Collectivism* by Emmanuel Goldstein. Orwell inserts full pages from this book into the text of *Nineteen Eighty-Four* to draw the reader closer to the rebel-protagonist and to reveal the political philosophies and social theories that have led to the present. This book within a book thus serves as a device to fill in some of the background, explaining the establishment of Oceania and the other superstates, Eurasia and Eastasia, in the global reorganization following World War II, and to expose the truth that each

A Soviet poster depicts Stalin as the revered leader. Orwell's dystopia was shaped by his experience in Spain, where the Stalinist faction was ruthless in its pursuit of total control.

superstate has a similar ideological construct based on keeping their population compliant.

The persuasiveness of the passages from Goldstein's book reveal the seductive power of words and language. One of *Nineteen Eighty-Four*'s greatest legacies is the plethora of words and phrases that have seeped from "Newspeak" into English. Big Brother, sex crime, thoughtcrime, and Room 101 are just a handful of the most common linguistic creations found in Orwell's work.

Mastering manipulation

The ways in which the state can manipulate and control its citizens are key themes of *Nineteen Eighty-Four*. In a totalitarian system, individual choices and lifestyles largely become the dictates of an overarching body of governance.

Oceania's ruling organization shows that it is determined to maintain its grip on power by weakening personal relationships and eradicating trust and mutuality. Orwell traces the psychological and physical methods by which the state can coerce, either covertly or overtly, and try to crush human feelings and break a person's spirit. As Julia remarks: "Everybody always confesses. You can't help it." The experience of Winston Smith reveals how the state apparatus acts on a single, human individual, making the reader not only feel his pain but also his burning desire to fight back against the machine in whatever ways he can.

A modern message

Initial critical reception of *Nineteen Eighty-Four* was extremely positive, referencing the originality of the bleak vision. Since then, the text has reached across the globe, been translated into some 65 languages, and found new audiences in a major film version directed by Michael Radford and released in 1984, with John Hurt playing Winston Smith.

The central concern at the heart of the dystopia depicted in *Nineteen Eighty-Four* is the danger of allowing those who rule us to gain too much control. In a globalized modern era of mass surveillance, Orwell's warning resonates more than ever. ∎

I'M SEVENTEEN NOW, AND SOMETIMES I ACT LIKE I'M ABOUT THIRTEEN

THE CATCHER IN THE RYE (1951), J D SALINGER

IN CONTEXT

FOCUS
Birth of the teenager

BEFORE
1774 *The Sorrows of Young Werther*, by German writer Johann Wolfgang von Goethe, follows the passions of a sensitive young artist.

1821 English poet John Keats dies, aged 25. His early verse is criticized as "adolescent".

1916 Irish writer James Joyce publishes *A Portrait of the Artist as a Young Man*, a coming-of-age novel that depicts rebellion and anti-Catholic sentiment.

AFTER
1963 US writer Sylvia Plath publishes *The Bell Jar*, a coming-of-age story with a twist – its teenage protagonist descends into madness.

1982 In *Ham on Rye*, by US author Charles Bukowski, the first-person male narrator remembers his teen years.

Numerous authors, from Johann Wolfgang von Goethe and John Keats to James Joyce and F Scott Fitzgerald, explored the precarious state of adolescence long before the birth of the "teenager" in 1950s' America. Teenagers, though, with their wild new music and their thrill-seeking, represented a challenge to conservative society and culture, and were treated with nervous dismissal: adults considered this generation to be morally lax and directionless. Teenagers kicked back with assertions of hypocrisy, considering themselves outsiders in an uncaring world; and this is the territory of Salinger's writing.

I'm the most terrific liar you ever saw in your life. It's awful.
The Catcher in the Rye

The Catcher in the Rye is narrated by 17-year-old Holden Caulfield. He is liberal with his parents' money, and relentless in his commentary on the human condition, sexuality, and morality. He has little regard for authority and seems careless about his self-destructive trajectory.

Teenage disaffection
But Holden Caulfield is much more than a teenage rebel. His frank admissions of deceptions, imperfections, and contradictions reveal a bemused individual who is hankering after childhood innocence, suffering grief, and growing painfully aware of the contradictions of adult life. He is a compelling antihero – an ambivalent, vulnerable figure – who can be sensitive and witty as well as immature and vulgar. Caulfield's casual disregard for honesty and disdain for societal norms are mitigated by a genuine confessional impulse and surprising tolerance for some of the diverse characters he encounters throughout the course of the novel.

Caulfield is also an easy victim. He is bullied in his dormitory at school, and ripped off by a pimp working the elevator in the New

See also: *The Sorrows of Young Werther* 104 ▪ *The Magic Mountain* 224–27 ▪ *A Portrait of the Artist as a Young Man* 241 ▪ *The Bell Jar* 290

Holden's journey through New York

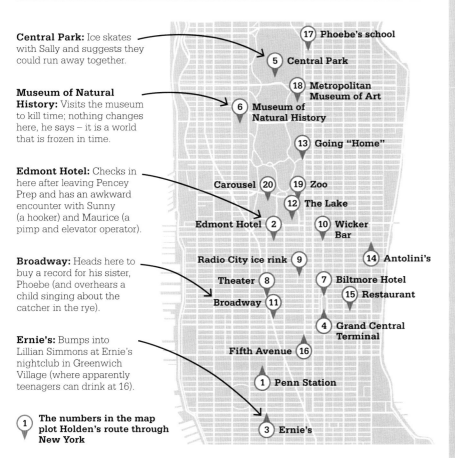

Central Park: Ice skates with Sally and suggests they could run away together.

Museum of Natural History: Visits the museum to kill time; nothing changes here, he says – it is a world that is frozen in time.

Edmont Hotel: Checks in here after leaving Pencey Prep and has an awkward encounter with Sunny (a hooker) and Maurice (a pimp and elevator operator).

Broadway: Heads here to buy a record for his sister, Phoebe (and overhears a child singing about the catcher in the rye).

Ernie's: Bumps into Lillian Simmons at Ernie's nightclub in Greenwich Village (where apparently teenagers can drink at 16).

① The numbers in the map plot Holden's route through New York

⑰ Phoebe's school
⑤ Central Park
⑱ Metropolitan Museum of Art
⑥ Museum of Natural History
⑬ Going "Home"
Carousel ⑳   ⑲ Zoo
⑫ The Lake
Edmont Hotel ②   ⑩ Wicker Bar
Radio City ice rink ⑨   ⑭ Antolini's
Theater ⑧   ⑦ Biltmore Hotel
Broadway ⑪   ⑮ Restaurant
④ Grand Central Terminal
Fifth Avenue ⑯
① Penn Station
③ Ernie's

J D Salinger

Jerome David Salinger was born in 1919 to wealthy parents in New York City. Like his main protagonist Holden Caulfield in *The Catcher in the Rye*, Salinger attended several schools before graduating. After spending a year in Europe, he studied at Columbia University, taking a writing course led by Whit Burnett, editor of *Story* magazine, who became his mentor early in his writing career.

Salinger was drafted into the US Army in 1942 and continued to write despite suffering from a "nervous condition". *The Catcher in the Rye* thrust Salinger onto the world stage as a literary celebrity. However, he resented the attention and became reclusive and far less productive. By the time of his death in 2010, *The Catcher in the Rye* remained Salinger's only full-length novel.

Other key works

1953 *Nine Stories*
1955 *Raise High the Roof Beam, Carpenters*
1959 *Seymour: An Introduction*
1961 *Franny and Zooey*

York hotel. In his confusion about women and sex, he unconsciously seeks out kindness and familiarity. Having paid for a prostitute he asks if they can simply "talk". He strikes up a conversation with two nuns, despite his atheism, and they insist he is "a very sweet boy".

Inevitably, Salinger's dirty realism caused controversy. Some critics dismissed the novel as puerile and maudlin. But Salinger gained cult status in the years following its publication, further fuelled by his reclusive lifestyle.

Death and grief are prevailing themes in *The Catcher in the Rye*. After Holden's brother dies, he smashes his hands in rage; his classmate is bullied and comes to a tragic end; and the very title of the book refers to stopping (catching) children running through fields before they fall off a cliff. It is likely that the loss of numerous young soldiers in World War II influenced Salinger to write this compelling first-person narrative, which remains an enduring portrait of the teenager in crisis. ■

258

DEATH IS A GANG-BOSS AUS DEUTSCHLAND
POPPY AND MEMORY (1952), PAUL CELAN

IN CONTEXT

FOCUS
Literature after Auschwitz

BEFORE
1947 In her poetry collection *In den Wohnungen des Todes* ("In the Apartments of Death") Berliner Nelly Sachs describes her own sufferings and those of the European Jews.

1947 Italian writer Primo Levi's *If This is a Man* is a first-hand account of his incarceration in Auschwitz.

1949 German sociologist Theodor Adorno says that "to write poetry after Auschwitz is barbaric", a condemnation not of the right to expression but of the society that had allowed Auschwitz to happen.

AFTER
1971 *The Nazi and the Barber*, a novel by German Holocaust survivor Edgar Hilsenrath, adopts the perspective of an SS officer who assumes a Jewish identity to escape prosecution.

After the World War II concentration camp of Auschwitz was liberated on 27 January 1945, and the scale of the atrocities of the Jewish Holocaust became known, some thought the events so horrific that conventional bounds of literature would be unfit to describe them. To Jewish authors, however, some form of expression was essential.

A mournful heritage
The poet Paul Celan (1920–1970) was born Paul Antschel into a family of German-speaking Jews in Romania. He survived a ghetto and an internment camp to become, under the pen name Celan, a major post-war German-language poet. But, haunted by his experiences, he eventually committed suicide.

Poppy and Memory, which contains more than 50 poems, was Celan's second collection and established his reputation. It includes his most famous poem, "Todesfuge" ("Death Fugue"). Written in a musical rhythm, the poem features Death, in the guise of the camp commandant, making prisoners dance by their own graves. The collection also includes another of his best-known poems, "Corona", which has been read as a reflection on the attempt to achieve true love without it becoming an escape from the truth of the world.

Elsewhere in *Poppy and Memory*, haunting images of the Holocaust recur: ash, hair, smoke, mould, bitterness, shadows, death, memory, and forgetting. In exploring these themes, Celan expresses the mournful heritage of organized mass murder. ∎

Black milk of morning we drink you at night.
"Todesfuge"

See also: *The Little Prince* 238–39 ▪ *The Tin Drum* 270–71 ▪ *One Day in the Life of Ivan Denisovich* 289 ▪ *Death of a Naturalist* 277

I AM INVISIBLE, UNDERSTAND, SIMPLY BECAUSE PEOPLE REFUSE TO SEE ME
INVISIBLE MAN (1952), RALPH ELLISON

IN CONTEXT

FOCUS
The Civil Rights Movement

BEFORE
1940 Richard Wright's *Native Son* discusses the criminal roles that white society creates for African-Americans.

1950 African-American writer Gwendolyn Brooks wins the Pulitzer Prize for Poetry with her collection *Annie Allen*. It charts a woman's move from individual freedom to more engaged ideas of progress.

AFTER
1953 In *Go Tell It on the Mountain*, James Baldwin reflects on his own life and involvement with the Church as an African-American, showing both its positive side and its oppressive hold.

1969 Maya Angelou's *I Know Why the Caged Bird Sings* expresses the author's changing responses to the violence of racism.

The African-American Civil Rights Movement of the late 1950s and 1960s sought to end racial segregation and discrimination in the USA through protest and civil disobedience. Authors such as James Baldwin, Maya Angelou, Richard Wright, and Ralph Ellison engaged with the movement, writing about the systematic disenfranchisement, overt racial discrimination, and state-sanctioned violence that pervaded the USA.

An isolated activist
Born in Oklahoma in 1914, Ralph Ellison first studied music at Tuskagee Institute in Alabama, but later moved to New York to pursue courses in the visual arts. Here, he met Richard Wright and was influenced both by his writing and his communist affiliations. Following service in the merchant navy in World War II, Ellison became disillusioned with left-wing ideology and began writing *Invisible Man*, a book concerned with political and social protest. Ellison found a new form for the protest novel, removed from earlier Realist and Naturalist works. His style was idiosyncratic, both in structure and narrative, describing events based on his experience of being a black man, and what that meant in a personal and public perspective in US society.

The book's narrator is invisible, unnamed, and completely alone: society chooses either not to see him, or to ignore him. He lives underground, mirroring the segregation of African-Americans at the time. In his isolation, the narrator reflects passionately on the path his life has taken – from public speaker in his youth, to disgraced college student and mistreated worker in a white factory in Harlem, to involvement with the politically ambiguous Brotherhood. The narrator muses over the injustices he has suffered in life, but finally he concludes that he must live a life that is true to his nature and his wider responsibilities: he is ready to emerge into the world. ∎

See also: *Les Misérables* 166–67 ▪ *Their Eyes Were Watching God* 235 ▪ *I Know Why the Caged Bird Sings* 291

LOLITA, LIGHT OF MY LIFE, FIRE OF MY LOINS. MY SIN, MY SOUL

LOLITA (1955), VLADIMIR NABOKOV

IN CONTEXT

FOCUS
Banned books

BEFORE
1532–64 François Rabelais' *Gargantua and Pantagruel* is condemned for obscenity by the College of Sorbonne, Paris.

1759 Although banned by government and Church authorities for its satirical content, Voltaire's *Candide* becomes a bestseller.

1934 *Tropic of Cancer*, Henry Miller's account of life as a writer in Paris, is banned in the USA for sexual content.

AFTER
1959 Narrated by a junkie, William Burroughs's *Naked Lunch* is banned in Boston in 1962; the decision is overturned in 1966.

1988 Salman Rushdie's *The Satanic Verses* is banned in more than 10 countries for perceived blasphemy against Islam.

Literary history is punctuated with books that were either banned or censored because they were thought to corrupt public morals or cause political or religious offence. In the first half of the 20th century, literary experimentation pushed the boundaries of taste and shocked a conservative audience. In response to this, censors trawled through works such as Irish writer James Joyce's *Ulysses* to identify obscenities, and removed sexual references from English author D H Lawrence's *Lady Chatterley's Lover*. But after the unexpurgated *Lady Chatterley* was tried on grounds of obscenity in 1960 and acquitted, restrictions on the publication of pornographic literature in the UK were effectively abandoned. Across the world, book censorship eased, but it never disappeared entirely.

Accepting the unacceptable

Few now would be offended by books that were censored in the past, and yet Vladimir Nabokov's controversial novel *Lolita* retains its power to disturb as well as enchant. Banned after its 1955 publication in France and republished in London in 1959, the novel is founded on narrator Humbert Humbert's obsession with a certain type of underage seductress: the "nymphet", a slender, silky-skinned pubescent girl, aged between 9 and 14 years. The title of the novel has become part of the English language as a reference to a young temptress.

Reading *Lolita* creates a state of mental confusion as the reader warms to a narrator who subverts all normal reactions to his appalling story. In Humbert's claustrophobic fantasy, readers lose perspective, seduced by an urbane European professor, with a well-prepared defence peppered with apologies, literary allusions, wordplay, and treacherous wit.

The spell of obsession

As an adolescent on the French Riviera, Humbert fell in love with the young Annabel – the template for his obsession. Years later, in the USA, he "broke her spell by incarnating her in another": Dolores Haze, dubbed Lolita, the 12-year-old daughter of his landlady. The devastating consequences are played out after Humbert marries the mother to gain access to the girl, the object of his fantasy. A vague plan to murder his new wife becomes unnecessary after she is

See also: *Gargantua and Pantagruel* 72–73 ▪ *Madame Bovary* 158–63 ▪ *Ulysses* 214–21 ▪ *Nineteen Eighty-Four* 250–55 ▪ *The Tin Drum* 270–71 ▪ *Howl and Other Poems* 288 ▪ *American Pyscho* 313 ▪ *The Satanic Verses* 336

Literature is often perceived as a threat by authorities because of its ability to convey ideas that have the potential to change minds and challenge prevailing ideologies. Some surprising titles have been banned over the years by nations, states, or libraries for their political content, sexual explicitness, and offensiveness to religion.

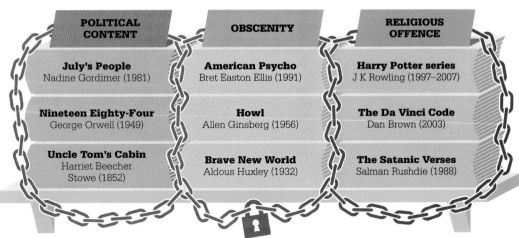

POLITICAL CONTENT	OBSCENITY	RELIGIOUS OFFENCE
July's People Nadine Gordimer (1981)	**American Psycho** Bret Easton Ellis (1991)	**Harry Potter series** J K Rowling (1997–2007)
Nineteen Eighty-Four George Orwell (1949)	**Howl** Allen Ginsberg (1956)	**The Da Vinci Code** Dan Brown (2003)
Uncle Tom's Cabin Harriet Beecher Stowe (1852)	**Brave New World** Aldous Huxley (1932)	**The Satanic Verses** Salman Rushdie (1988)

mown down by a car; the bereaved stepfather then collects Dolores from summer camp and begins his attempt to live out his dream.

In love with language
In an "erotic novel" that offers almost nothing salacious, part two is a continuation of the author's real love affair – with language. In his highly wrought, ornate, and lyrical prose, Humbert pieces together his year-long road trip with Dolores across the continent, "putting the geography of the United States into motion". The details of his despotic infatuation (the quarrels, close calls, and bribes) intermittently surface in a surreal, cinematic account that spools across page after page of wry observation on US culture. Arriving back on the East Coast after a year, Humbert enrols Dolores at school, and the fabric of his fantasy begins to fall apart.

Style, structure, and imagery are not found in pornographic books, as Nabokov reminds us in a defensive afterword to a novel that excels on all three counts. Humbert Humbert is the ultimate unreliable narrator, shielded by a fictional foreword writer who wraps up the loose ends before the story has even begun. There are no alternative accounts, only the posthumous voice of Humbert, defending the indefensible to his readers. ∎

Vladimir Nabokov

Born into an aristocratic family in St Petersburg, in April 1899, Vladimir Nabokov spent his childhood in Russia and grew up trilingual in English, French, and Russian. After the Russian Revolution of 1917, the family was exiled to England in 1919, where Nabokov studied at Trinity College, Cambridge. Following a further move to Berlin, Nabokov's father, a journalist and politician, was assassinated at a political rally. Living in Berlin and in Paris, Nabokov wrote novels, short stories, and poems in Russian, while working as a tennis coach and tutor. He married Véra Slonim in 1925; they had one son, Dmitri. After fleeing to the USA during World War II, Nabokov wrote *Lolita* in English. He taught at Wellesley College and Cornell University and, as an authority on butterflies, held a position at the Museum of Comparative Zoology at Harvard. He died in Montreux, Switzerland, in 1977.

Other key works

1937 *The Gift*
1962 *Pale Fire*

HE LEAVES NO STONE UNTURNED, AND NO MAGGOT LONELY
WAITING FOR GODOT (1953), SAMUEL BECKETT

IN CONTEXT

FOCUS
The Absurd

BEFORE
1942 The narrator of Albert Camus' novel *The Outsider* expresses a typical Absurdist belief: "I laid my heart open to the gentle indifference of the universe."

AFTER
1959 *Les Nègres,* a play by French writer Jean Genet, shocks audiences by using black actors whited up.

1959 In *Rhinocéros* by Romanian playwright Eugène Ionesco, characters turn into rhinoceroses and wreak havoc, indicating the absurdity of a world where ordinary people change into fascist monsters.

1960 English writer Harold Pinter's play *The Caretaker* owes a great debt to Beckett in its lack of plot and its oblique dialogue, full of tangents and offbeat implications.

The Theatre of the Absurd, in which the acclaimed Irish writer Samuel Beckett (1906–1989) played a major role, subverted the norms of art and life by entertaining the idea that any meaning in the universe would always elude our attempts to discover it. "He leaves no stone unturned," said English playwright Harold Pinter admiringly of Beckett, "and no maggot lonely". In both his plays and his fiction, Beckett gave voice to the inarticulate – damaged souls, without hope and with only pathetic consolations, facing the brute truths of existence.

Words in orbit
The play *Waiting for Godot* (originally written in French, like much of Beckett's work) features two tramps, Vladimir and Estragon. Their dialogue is a tragicomic dance of ideas, and the action defies common sense. Another character, Lucky, led on a rope by his master, Pozzo, says nothing initially but later spews out a surreal 700-word unpunctuated monologue with phrases that have no meaning. The speech stops only when Vladimir pulls off Lucky's hat, causing him to break off mid-sentence – an example of Beckett's debt to vaudeville comedy and, more specifically, to comedians Laurel and Hardy. The tramps are waiting for Godot, but this character never turns up, and has been seen as a stand-in for God, often referred to but also absent – an analysis that irritated Beckett, although he conceded its plausibility. ∎

Joyce was a synthesizer, trying to bring in as much as he could. I am an analyser, trying to leave out as much as I can.
Samuel Beckett

See also: *Metamorphosis* 210–11 ▪ *The Trial* 242 ▪ *Nausea* 244 ▪ *The Outsider* 245

IT IS IMPOSSIBLE TO TOUCH ETERNITY WITH ONE HAND AND LIFE WITH THE OTHER
THE TEMPLE OF THE GOLDEN PAVILION (1956), YUKIO MISHIMA

IN CONTEXT

FOCUS
Post-war Japanese writers

BEFORE
1946 Haruo Umezaki's collection of short stories *Sakurajima* is published. The tales, which made his name, touch on aspects of Japanese life in World War II, such as *kamikaze* pilots.

1951 Shōhei Ōoka's most famous novel, *Fires on the Plain*, is published. Like Umezaki's *Sakurajima*, it reflects the author's wartime experiences, including Japan's defeat by US forces on Leyte island in the Philippines.

AFTER
1962 Kōbō Abe's novel *The Woman in the Dunes* is a bleak and disturbing tale about an amateur entomologist who is held captive in an escape-proof shack at the bottom of a pit of sand in a remote village.

In the decades leading up to World War II, Japan was an aggressive military state, occupying parts of China. Its strict code of literary censorship tightened even further during wartime. The relaxing of these restrictions at the end of the war saw a flowering of literary voices.

Freedom and diversity

Many of the "first generation" of post-war writers (those whose first work was published in 1946–47) focused on the subject of wartime experiences. However, with the appearance of a second generation (1948–49), and a third (1953–55), the only theme that united the authors was the freedom that allowed them to flourish. This resulted in a period of intense creativity and productivity.

Yukio Mishima (1920–1970), was of the second generation, and *The Temple of the Golden Pavilion* is often said to be his finest work. It tells the fact-based story of an ugly, stuttering young monk who comes to hate all beauty, especially the

It is no exaggeration to say that the first real problem I faced in my life was that of beauty.
The Temple of the Golden Pavilion

550-year-old Zen temple in Kyoto, decorated in gold leaf. Initially, it represents to the monk the transitory nature of life and beauty, but comes to dominate his thoughts as a bullying presence, and one that he cannot escape. The novel was extremely popular – a compelling study of madness that leads to destruction, but also a meditation on beauty itself, of which one of the most beautiful aspects is Mishima's prose. ■

See also: *The Love Suicides at Sonezaki* 93

HE WAS BEAT – THE ROOT, THE SOUL OF BEATIFIC
ON THE ROAD (1957), JACK KEROUAC

IN CONTEXT

FOCUS
The Beat Generation

BEFORE
1926 Ernest Hemingway's *The Sun Also Rises* depicts modern Americans travelling through Europe on a quasi-spiritual journey.

1952 John Clellon Holmes's novel *Go* includes the first use of the term "beat" to define the people of the Beat movement.

1953 Lawrence Ferlinghetti opens City Lights Bookshop in San Francisco; it becomes a haunt for the Beat writers.

1956 Allen Ginsberg's first collection of poetry *Howl and Other Poems* is published, launching him as the leading Beat poet.

AFTER
1959 William S Burroughs' *Naked Lunch* uses a radically disjointed, non-linear style extending the narrative form of the Beat Generation.

In the post-war United States, a generation of middle-class youth became increasingly reluctant to follow the societal pathways of their parents based on materialistic goals. Instead, they adopted a meandering, spontaneous form of existence in their quest to find true meaning in life. Some of them became known as "Beats": a collective of poets and writers who sought kicks, spiritual refuge, and excess in drink, drugs, and sex; they also delighted in jazz.

The birth of Beat

An **idealistic youth culture** turns away from mainstream US society in the 1940s.

Jack Kerouac, Neal Cassady, and others take to the roads of North America **seeking the meaning of life**.

The Beat Generation record their thoughts and adventures in **"spontaneous prose"**.

"Beat" writing forges a path into **mainstream literature** in both poetry and prose.

See also: *The Red Room* 185 ▪ *The Catcher in the Rye* 256–57 ▪ *Howl and Other Poems* 288 ▪ *Fear and Loathing in Las Vegas* 332

The term "beat" simultaneously held notions of being "beatific"; of being "beaten" by the punishing intensity of a hobo existence; and of a life lived to a jazz "beat". In the 1950s, tales of the Beat movement's free lifestyle and reckless ways shocked mainstream society, and their writings signalled a radical reinvigoration of US literature. The appearance of Jack Kerouac's novel, *On the Road*, in 1957 framed him as the leading Beat novelist.

On the Road details a series of journeys that Kerouac took between 1947 and 1950. In the book they are narrated by Sal Paradise (identified with Kerouac himself) who is often accompanied on his travels by Dean Moriarty (the writer Neal Cassady). A number of other Beat Generation writers also appear in the book, disguised by name only, such as Allen Ginsberg ("Carlo Marx") and William S Burroughs ("Old Bull Lee").

The book has five parts. The first sees Sal Paradise setting off for San Francisco in July 1947. Sal meets Dean Moriarty and the two launch on a riotous road trip, hitchhiking and riding buses on a meandering adventure: partying, meeting friends, and looking for girls before finally returning to New York. The subsequent parts tell of a series of hedonistic charges through North America.

Spontaneous prose

The narrative form of *On the Road*, which Kerouac referred to as "spontaneous prose", was inspired by an 18-page typed letter that he received in December 1950 from his friend Neal Cassady. According to Kerouac, the key to the prose was to write swiftly and "without consciousness", in a semi-trance, allowing the mind to flow freely, associating sights, sounds, and senses in a narrative of absolute immediacy. For example, as Sal and Dean reach Chicago, Kerouac writes "Screeching trolleys, newsboys, gals cutting by, the smell of fried food and beer in the air, neons winking – 'We're in the big town, Sal! Whooee!'" The long, fluid, descriptive sentences

Kerouac typed *On the Road* onto rolls of tracing paper that he had glued together to avoid having to change paper and interrupt his creative flow. The final manuscript was 120-foot long.

and stream-of-consciousness style mirrored the intensive pace of Sal's alcohol-infused, vagrant existence, while imitating the improvisational character of jazz music. Kerouac wrote *On the Road* in a frenetic three-week period in April 1951, fuelled by caffeine and drugs. The result was a manuscript in wildly creative, original prose – or "spontaneous bop prosody", as Ginsberg called it – that came to define the Beat Generation. ▪

Jack Kerouac

Jack Kerouac was born to French-Canadian parents in Lowell, Massachusetts, USA, in 1922. He attended Columbia University where he met Allen Ginsberg, Neal Cassady, and William S Burroughs who would become fellow leading lights of the Beat Generation. Kerouac dropped out of university in his second year then joined the merchant navy, before turning to writing as a profession. From 1947, he became increasingly attracted to the whisky-drinking hobo lifestyle and began wandering across the USA and Mexico, often visiting various other Beat writers. Those voyages across the North American landscape were relayed in his various *roman à clef* writings, friends' faces only thinly veiled as protagonists. Kerouac's alcoholism led to cirrhosis and his death in 1969.

Other key works

1950 *The Town and the City*
1957 *On the Road*
1958 *The Subterraneans*
1958 *The Dharma Bums*
1972 *Visions of Cody* (published posthumously)

WHAT IS GOOD AMONG ONE PEOPLE IS AN ABOMINATION WITH OTHERS

THINGS FALL APART (1958), CHINUA ACHEBE

IN CONTEXT

FOCUS
Nigerian voices

BEFORE
1952 Amos Tutuola tells a Yoruba folklore story in English in *The Palm-Wine Drinkard*.

1954 Cyprian Ekwensi gains international attention with *People of the City*.

AFTER
1960 Wole Soyinka's play *A Dance of the Forests* critiques present-day corruption through the nation's mythological past.

2002 Helon Habila depicts a new generation living in Lagos under a military regime in *Waiting for an Angel*.

2006 *Half of a Yellow Sun*, set during the Biafran War, confirms Chimamanda Ngozi Adichie as an exceptional new voice and wins the 2007 Orange Prize for Fiction.

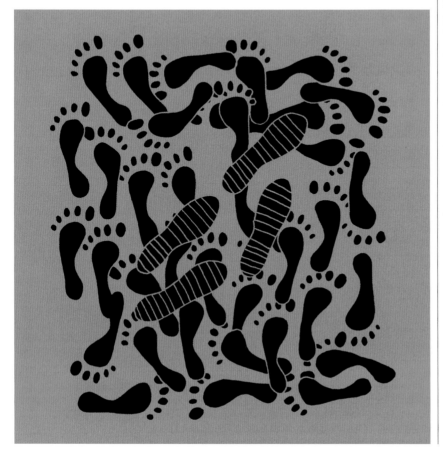

Published in 1958, Chinua Achebe's slim volume of less than 150 pages, *Things Fall Apart*, is one of the earliest novels to offer a mode of expression to indigenous writers in Nigeria, and was an instrument in the formation of a dazzling canon of literature. This multi-layered story of a fictionalized tribal village and its cataclysmic contact with British colonizers in the late 19th century has since become the world's most widely read African novel, selling more than 12 million copies in over 50 languages. The story told in *Things Fall Apart* has a resonance for all of the world's traditional cultures torn apart by invasion.

See also: *Heart of Darkness* 196–97 ▪ *Disgrace* 322–23 ▪ *Half of a Yellow Sun* 339

The Igbo people celebrate different festivals throughout the year. In *Things Fall Apart*, the Feast of the New Yam is held just before the yam harvest to give thanks to the Earth goddess, Ani.

The novel's title is taken from W B Yeats's poem "The Second Coming", which was written in the aftermath of World War I. Yeats's apocalyptic imagery of the world caught up in anarchy, and the arrival of an ambiguous messiah – some unformed, slouching beast – presages the novel's "first coming" of white Christian colonizers who invade and break apart tribal cultures.

Nigerian reality

Early in *Things Fall Apart*, we learn that "Among the Igbo the art of conversation is regarded very highly, and proverbs are the palm-oil with which words are eaten"; perhaps it is unsurprising that some of the villagers of Umuofia are won over by the colonizers' hymns and Bible stories. Achebe wins over his audience in much the same way, drawing readers into a classic novel with a three-part structure,

compelling plot, and tragic hero, but infused with the myths and oral tradition of Nigerian culture.

When Achebe published his pivotal work, Nigeria was in a state of political flux in the lead-up to independence in 1960. He wrote the novel partly as a response to the representation of Africa in the books he studied at college. In 2000 he described how Anglo-Irish writer Joyce Cary's novel *Mister Johnson* (1939), set in Nigeria, was held up as a fine example of writing about Africa, although native Nigerians saw in it an undercurrent of distaste and mockery. He also maintained that Joseph Conrad's lurid description of natives in *Heart of Darkness* (1899) typified the racism endemic in literature about Africa shown by European writers.

Achebe's reply was to write a textured, immersive story of the downfall of a traditional society – a rich, close community of Igbo people (formerly Ibo, as the novel refers to them). In place of Conrad's indistinguishable hordes of black "savages", Achebe peoples his village of Umuofia with vibrant characters that leap from the page.

Set in pre-colonial southern Nigeria in the 1890s, *Things Fall Apart* portrays a civilized society that has rich traditions of culture, commerce, religion, and justice. The people's social courtesies and greetings – such as the breaking and sharing of kola nuts – the bargaining of terms of betrothal, and the importance of women's chastity and obedience in this patriarchal society would not seem out of place in a Jane Austen novel. In Umuofia, life revolves around the seasons as villagers plant, tend, and harvest the crop of yams, observe the "Week of Peace", and enjoy celebrations marked with palm-wine feasts, wrestling matches, storytelling, and songs.

A self-made man

The protagonist, Okonkwo, is a famous wrestler and warrior, a quick-to-anger husband of three wives, and the proud owner of a large compound. Having inherited nothing from his idle, cowardly, and indebted father – whom he strives to resemble as little as possible – Okonkwo works the fields as a »

The white man is very clever … He has put a knife on things that held us together and we have fallen apart.
Things Fall Apart

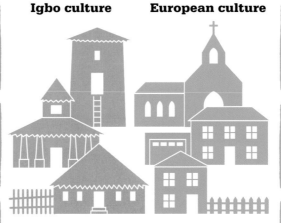

Igbo culture   **European culture**

Decentralized government with multiple small diverse groups and no overall ruler.

Belief in the Earth goddess, and numerous other deities and ancestor spirits.

Community elders manage grievances and settle disputes with the aim of making peace.

European colonizers saw Africans as primitive, making little attempt to understand their customs and cultures. The imposition of alien values and institutions led to profound transformations in traditional African communities at all levels.

One central government ruling over a single large political entity.

Belief in one God and in Jesus Christ, his son on Earth, as the saviour and redeemer of humankind.

Formal courts settle disputes, according to written laws, with the aim of upholding rights.

sharecropper to become wealthy, building up the storehouses of yams and coffers of cowries that signify prosperity. His second wife, Ekwefi, is a tribal beauty who leaves her first husband because of her passion for Okonkwo; their only child, Ezinma, is a spirited tomboy with such an understanding of her father and the subtleties of village

Masks were worn by Igbo men for magical purposes during certain rituals, especially at funerals and festivals, or, as in *Things Fall Apart*, by the *egwugwu* to administer justice.

life that Okonkwo concludes more than once that she should have been born a boy.

Questions and answers
In Igbo culture, the wishes of the gods are passed on by *egwugwu* – masked village elders representing the clan's ancestral spirits – and include brutal acts of sacrifice: these will become the crack in their culture that allows ingress and collapse. This may be a "land of the living […] not far removed from the domain of the ancestors", but there are few who adhere as slavishly to the murderous will of the gods as Okonkwo. His warrior ideology begins to set him apart from others who are starting to ask questions even before the white men arrive. Ekwefi resolves to defend her daughter from the gods; Obierika, Okonkwo's friend, questions the practice of abandoning twins at birth – "but although he thought for a long time he found no answer".

The first white man to arrive in the neighbouring village of Mbanta supplies an answer. He tells the

tribe that they worship "gods of deceit who tell you to kill your fellows and destroy innocent children. There is only one true God …" As the missionary's converted interpreter struggles to explain to the crowd about Jesu Kristi, the son of God, Okonkwo asks if God also has a wife. The missionary ploughs on with an incomprehensible account of the Holy Trinity, which seems to be little different from the multiple gods of the Igbo tribes, and just as reliant on blind faith.

Two sides of the story
Achebe exposes the brutality of colonization, including massacres and imprisonments, but also describes the work of Mr Brown, a gentle missionary, who listens as well as preaches, winning hearts and minds by combining religion with education, gifts, and medicine. Okonkwo's eldest son, Nwoye, is among those of the tribe who are drawn to the poetry of the new religion and moved by the "gay and rollicking

tunes of evangelism". For Nwoye, Christian hymns not only have the "power to pluck at the silent and dusty chords in the heart of an Ibo man", but seem to answer "a vague and persistent question that haunted his young soul".

The power of language

Asked why he chose to write in English rather than his native Igbo, Achebe replied that it would be foolish not to use a language he had spent a lifetime acquiring and one that could be put to active use as "a counterargument to colonization". Achebe maintained that written Igbo, devised by the missionaries at the turn of the century, was a mix of dialects that had lost all the rhythm and music of the spoken language. The point is illustrated in his novel when the white man's Igbo interpreter is mocked by the local villagers for his different dialect – his way of saying "myself" translates as "my buttocks".

Achebe followed *Things Fall Apart* with two novels that form a trilogy built around the country's turbulent half-century under British rule. *No Longer at Ease*, set in the period just before Nigeria gained independence, tells the story of

An abominable religion has settled among you. A man can now leave his father and his brothers. ... I fear for you; I fear for the clan.
Things Fall Apart

Okonkwo's grandson Obi, who returns from university abroad and struggles with ideals in a society built on bribery and corruption. Achebe then turns back the clock in *Arrow of God*, to continue the story of the destruction of Igbo culture in the colonial years.

Described as the "father of modern African literature", Achebe opened the door to African writing in English. In an article in *The New Gong Magazine*, columnist Henry Chukwuemeka Onyema suggests that *Things Fall Apart*'s "singular achievement ... was that it told us about ourselves through our own eyes". Onyema describes the 1960s in Nigeria as a "literary ferment", as writers sought to define the newly independent nation and to make sense of its contradictions. Among them was playwright and novelist Wole Soyinka, who was awarded the 1986 Nobel Prize in Literature.

Confronting oppression

Later generations of Nigerian writers continued to grapple with the aftermath of colonialism, civil war, and cultural conflict. In 1991, Ben Okri was awarded the Booker Prize for *The Famished Road*, in which a spirit-child faces down death to become part of the lives of real people. Women writers such as Chimamanda Ngozi Adichie have also found a voice engaging with Nigeria's turbulent political history and exploring the place of women in a male-dominated culture. In Adichie's debut novel, *Purple Hibiscus* (2003), the narrator is a 15-year-old girl struggling to emerge from the repression of a patriarchal Catholic upbringing. Other writers have explored a wide range of modern-day issues – such as homosexuality, prostitution, and environmental degradation – from a Nigerian perspective. ■

Chinua Achebe

Born in 1930 in the small town of Ogidi, southeast Nigeria, to Protestant parents, Chinua Achebe spoke Igbo at home and English at school. He graduated from University College, Ibadan, in 1952, and within 12 years had written the three novels that were to become the foundation of his oeuvre. Achebe married Christie Chinwe Okoli in 1961, and they had four children.

An early career in radio ended with the outbreak of the Biafran War. Achebe went on to teach in the USA and Nigeria, and wrote stories, poetry, essays, and children's books. In 1990 a car crash left him confined to a wheelchair for the remainder of his life. In 1992 he became Professor of Languages and Literature at Bard College, New York, and in 2009 he moved to Brown University, Rhode Island. In 2007 Achebe was awarded the Man Booker International Prize for fiction. He died in March 2013, aged 82.

Other key works

1960 *No Longer at Ease*
1964 *Arrow of God*
1966 *A Man of the People*
1987 *Anthills of the Savannah*

EVEN WALLPAPER HAS A BETTER MEMORY THAN HUMAN BEINGS
THE TIN DRUM (1959), GÜNTER GRASS

IN CONTEXT

FOCUS
The unreliable narrator

BEFORE
1884 The naive boy hero in Mark Twain's *The Adventures of Huckleberry Finn* fails to understand the significance of events that is clear to readers.

1955 Humbert Humbert's narrative is assembled from notes made in an asylum and presented after his death in Vladimir Nabokov's *Lolita*.

AFTER
1962 Delinquent teenager Alex confesses all in "Nadsat", a futuristic teen-speak, in Anthony Burgess's novel *A Clockwork Orange*.

1991 Bret Easton Ellis's serial killer speaks through a yuppie archetype in *American Psycho*.

2001 Yann Martel's narrator stretches credulity in *Life of Pi*, with his tale of life adrift with a tiger – and then offers a different option.

The term "unreliable narrator" refers to first-person narrators who undermine the authority of their own stories. Realist novels tend to offer a rational speaking voice telling a story that meets a reader's expectations. But what if the narrator gives the reader reason to doubt, because he or she is insane, or has a distorted perception of the world, or is very young, or lying?

Texts of the 20th century are littered with slippery speakers, from Humbert Humbert in Vladimir Nabokov's novel *Lolita* to Patrick Bateman in Bret Easton Ellis's *American Psycho*. But unreliable narrators have been around for centuries, and include Jonathan Swift's naive Gulliver and Mark Twain's ingenuous Huckleberry Finn. Executed well, novels with unreliable narrators engage the reader differently: that element of doubt both stretches credulity and draws the reader in.

In the midst of history

Günter Grass has been described as "the conscience of a nation" for his darkly satirical portrait of the rise of Nazi sympathies in ordinary families and the aftermath of the

… I stuck to my drum and didn't grow a finger's breadth from my third birthday on.
The Tin Drum

war in *The Tin Drum*. Anyone seeking an example of an unreliable narrator need look no further than the stunted hero of the novel, Oskar Matzerath. Oskar introduces himself from his bed in a "mental hospital" where he has been held following his trial for murder. He explains that until the age of 20 he was just three feet tall, having arrested his own growth on his third birthday by sheer force of will.

History is happening all around, but the spotlight focuses on the fierce, tiny figure of Oskar, with his constant companion – a tin drum – and a scream that can break glass. He has two possible fathers: his mother's lover, or her

See also: *Tristram Shandy* 104–05 ▪ *The Adventures of Huckleberry Finn* 188–89 ▪ *Lolita* 260–61 ▪ *A Clockwork Orange* 289 ▪ *American Psycho* 313

husband, who runs a grocery store in the Free City of Danzig (now Gdansk, Poland), which is under German control. Oskar is a witness to real events in history in Danzig and Düsseldorf but, self-absorbed and obsessed with his own needs, he is no hero. Over the years he is implicated in a string of deaths.

Unlikely truths

Sometimes the narration slips into the third person, or is passed to Oskar's jailer to allow another perspective. The tone varies: a slaughter of nuns on a Normandy beach is scripted like a drawing-room farce, while Oskar's poetic voice both enchants and revolts as he describes a fisherman hauling up a horse's head writhing with

eels. He diverts us down the blind alleys of his obsessions with art, circus dwarfs, nurses, and the scents of women he seduces. He offers a rational history of Danzig, then conjures up a nightclub called the Onion Cellar where people chop raw onions to make themselves cry.

What does Oskar represent? Perhaps he is the devil, using his scream to cut holes in shop windows to tempt passers-by to steal, or seducing women by ingenious means. Or perhaps he embodies Grass's perception of Germany – immune to suffering during Nazism and quick to bury the past. What is certain, however, is that through Oskar's grim magical fantasy the author found a way to drum history into memory. ∎

Günter Grass

Born in 1927 in Danzig (now Gdansk, Poland) to a German father and Kashubian mother, Günter Grass attended the Conradinum Gymnasium and was a member of the Hitler Youth. In late 1944, at the age of 17, he was drafted into the Waffen-SS (the Nazi elite military wing), as he revealed controversially in 2006.

After the war, Grass worked as a miner and farm labourer, and studied art, before working as a sculptor and writer in Paris and Berlin. He published his first poetry and plays in 1955, but his breakthrough came in 1959 with *The Tin Drum*, which was followed by two further novels that made up the Danzig Trilogy. In 1999 he was awarded the Nobel Prize in Literature, one of many awards during his career. Grass was heavily involved in German politics, supporting the Social Democratic Party and opposing reunification. He died in 2015 aged 87.

Other key works

1961 *Cat and Mouse*
1963 *Dog Years*
1999 *My Century*
2002 *Crabwalk*

Unreliable narrators come in different guises: some are liars or conceal facts, others are unstable, confused, or manipulative. They may be immature or unaware, reporting events that the reader perceives differently.

	To Kill a Mockingbird **CHILD** *The Adventures of Huckleberry Finn*	
One Flew over the Cuckoo's Nest	**The Tin Drum**	*A Clockwork Orange* *The Catcher in the Rye* *Life of Pi*
American Psycho **MENTALLY UNSTABLE/MAD**		*Midnight's Children*　*The Blind Assassin* **LYING/CONFUSED** *Heart of Darkness*　*Tristram Shandy*
The Sound and the Fury		*Wuthering Heights*
The Turn of the Screw		**CONCEALED FACTS** *The Moonstone*

I THINK THERE'S JUST ONE KIND OF FOLKS. FOLKS.
TO KILL A MOCKINGBIRD (1960), HARPER LEE

IN CONTEXT

FOCUS
Southern Gothic

BEFORE
1940 Carson McCullers'
debut novel *The Heart Is a
Lonely Hunter* encapsulates
the elements of Southern
Gothic in a story of social
misfits in Georgia in the 1930s.

1955 *Cat on a Hot Tin Roof*,
by playwright Tennessee
Williams, is set on a cotton
plantation in the Mississippi
Delta and challenges Southern
social conventions with its
portrayal of the favourite
son as a repressed gay
man and alcoholic.

AFTER
1980 *A Confederacy of
Dunces*, by John Kennedy
Toole, is set in New Orleans
and follows the antics of
slob and misfit Ignatius J
Reilly. Toole is posthumously
awarded the Pulitzer Prize
for Fiction for the book a
year after its publication.

Building on the traditions
of 18th-century Gothic
literature, with its elements
of fantasy and the grotesque,
mid-20th-century writers of
the American Deep South, such
as Tennessee Williams, Flannery
O'Connor, and Carson McCullers,
established a literary genre known
as Southern Gothic. These writers
used the characteristics of the
traditional Gothic style to inspect
the unsettling realities and twisted
psyches beneath the surface of
Southern respectability. With their
damaged or eccentric characters,
macabre settings, and sinister

You never really understand
a person until you consider
things from his point of
view – until you climb into his
skin and walk around in it.
To Kill a Mockingbird

situations, the texts in this genre
examine Southern social issues
such as racism, poverty, and crime.

Harper Lee's classic novel *To
Kill a Mockingbird* incorporates
a coming-of-age theme into the
Southern Gothic genre, and
highlights racial prejudice in the
American South in the years before
the Civil Rights Movement. It also
explores the behaviour of those who
live in a small Southern community.

Challenging convention
The story is set in the mid-1930s in
Maycomb, an Alabama town where
"a day was twenty-four hours long
but seemed much longer". The
narrator is a young girl, Scout, aged
nearly six at the start of events. She
is a tomboy, who questions social
conventions. Scout lives with her
widowed father, lawyer Atticus
Finch (a morally upright man
who strives to teach his children
the values of understanding and
compassion), her brother Jem,
and their black cook, Calpurnia.

Scout describes daily life in
Maycomb, their neighbours, her
friendship with an unusual boy
called Dill, and her school, creating
a picture of an apparently timeless
society in the Deep South. Heat

See also: *The Adventures of Huckleberry Finn 188–89* ■ *The Sound and the Fury 242–43* ■ *Invisible Man 259* ■ *In Cold Blood 278–79*

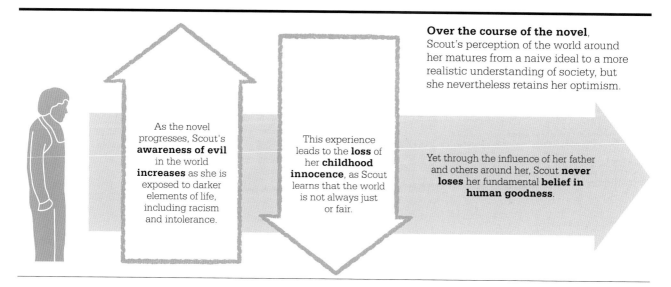

Over the course of the novel, Scout's perception of the world around her matures from a naive ideal to a more realistic understanding of society, but she nevertheless retains her optimism.

As the novel progresses, Scout's **awareness of evil** in the world **increases** as she is exposed to darker elements of life, including racism and intolerance.

This experience leads to the **loss** of her **childhood innocence**, as Scout learns that the world is not always just or fair.

Yet through the influence of her father and others around her, Scout **never loses** her fundamental **belief in human goodness**.

bakes the streets, refined ladies gossip at missionary teas, poor white children arrive at school with no shoes, and black people live segregated lives as land workers or domestic servants. In Southern Gothic tradition, however, there are oddities in the community – in particular the reclusive Boo Radley, who lives in a supposedly haunted house, and about whom the children weave fantastical tales.

When Atticus agrees to take on the defence of a local black man, Tom Robinson, who is falsely accused of raping a white woman, Scout describes the tensions and violence created by Atticus's determination to defend Robinson, in spite of the fact that, as he admits, it is a lost cause. Following the trial there is a murderous attack on the children, which reveals Boo Radley to be guardian, not a monster. The novel ends with Scout older, wiser, and reflecting on human behaviour within her small community.

Published as the Civil Rights Movement was accelerating, *To Kill a Mockingbird* was an almost instant bestseller. Despite its gentle tone, the novel, like others in the genre, exposed the darkness underpinning the gentility of a Southern community forced to face the reality of racial hatred. ■

Harper Lee

Born in the town of Monroeville, Alabama, on 28 April 1926, Harper Lee was a loner and a tomboy. Her father was a lawyer, and her best friend was the author Truman Capote (she would later help him to research *In Cold Blood*).

Lee attended the University of Alabama, where she edited the university magazine. Although she started law school, she wanted to write, and in 1949 dropped out and moved to New York. In 1956 close friends offered to fund her for a year so that she could write. Taking inspiration from events and people in her childhood, she started *To Kill a Mockingbird*, which she completed in 1959.

The tremendous success of *To Kill a Mockingbird* gained Lee many literary awards, including the Pulitzer Prize in 1961. She accepted a post on the National Council of the Arts but largely retired from public life from the 1970s. It was believed that Lee had only ever written one book but in 2015 *Go Set a Watchman*, her second novel, was published: although a sequel, it was written before *To Kill a Mockingbird*.

NOTHING IS LOST IF ONE HAS THE COURAGE TO PROCLAIM THAT ALL IS LOST AND WE MUST BEGIN ANEW
HOPSCOTCH (1963), JULIO CORTÁZAR

IN CONTEXT

FOCUS
The antinovel

BEFORE
1605 *Don Quixote*, by Miguel de Cervantes, is regarded as the first modern novel, but its literary features and episodic structure are at odds with later definitions of the genre.

1939 *At Swim-Two-Birds* by Irish author Flann O'Brien has multiple characters and plots that lose linear structure.

AFTER
1973 *The Castle of Crossed Destinies*, by Italian author Italo Calvino, has multiple plots; each is determined by a randomly chosen sequence of tarot cards.

2001 *Bartleby & Co.*, by Spanish writer Enrique Villa-Matas, revolves around unwritten texts, fragmented notes, footnotes, literary allusions, and comments on authors both real and fictional.

One of the distinguishing features of the novel is generally thought to be the sequential, linear organization of its narrative segments: chapters, more or less in sequence, are presumed or expected to hold equal status with each other, from a narrative perspective.

The antinovel – first named as such by French writer Jean-Paul Sartre in the mid-20th century – subverts this assumption, marking a radical departure from the conventional novel with respect to plot, dialogue, and structure. In the

References to jazz appear throughout *Hopscotch*, not only in its subject matter but also in its jazz-infused language, non-linear structure, and improvisational approach.

case of Argentine writer Julio Cortázar's *Hopscotch*, the novel is subverted even from a physical point of view. The reader of an antinovel is forced to suspend all narrative expectations and to engage with the text in ways that a traditional work of fiction does not require. As the reader of *Hopscotch* is told in the book's Table of Instructions, "In its own way, this book consists of many books, but two books above all".

An open-ended book

Hopscotch can be read as a straightforward novel – the first book – one chapter after the other (ending at Chapter 56), or as a second story, skipping from the so-called "Expendable Chapter" 73 to 1, back and forth, all the way to 58 and 131, where the reader gets caught in an endless loop of the latter two. The author also allows the reader to explore the novel in any other sequence, and to ignore the Expendable Chapters entirely.

Even in the more linear option, the plot moves in an erratic fashion, capturing a series of fragments as it follows the main character, Horacio Oliveira, initially in 1950s Paris. We discover Oliveira's intellectual interests and his passion for jazz –

See also: *Don Quixote* 76–81 ▪ *Tristram Shandy* 104–05 ▪ *The Outsider* 245 ▪ *If on a Winter's Night a Traveller* 298–99

Hopscotch invites the reader to experiment with different pathways through its pages. There is a "normal" first book of 56 chapters, and a second making use of 99 "Expendable Chapters". Each book can be read separately, and there also several alternative options.

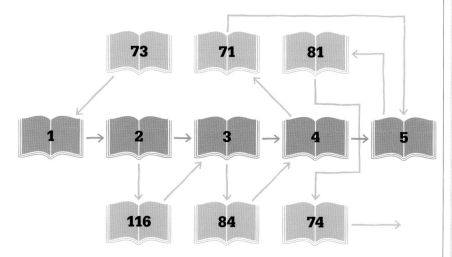

First book

Expendable Chapters

Julio Cortázar

Julio Cortázar was born to Argentinian parents in Belgium in 1914. His family moved to Switzerland at the beginning of World War I, but settled in Buenos Aires, Argentina, in 1919.

Cortázar became qualified as a teacher at an early age, and began his university studies in philosophy and language in Buenos Aires, but these were interrupted owing to financial difficulties.

In 1951 he emigrated to France, where he worked as a translator while constantly travelling and writing short stories. He became engaged in political causes, supporting the left-wing movements in Cuba and mainland Latin America, which he visited several times from the 1960s onwards. Around the same time, his novels, including *Hopscotch*, started being published. Cortázar died in 1984, aged 69, and is buried in Paris.

a form of music that was a clear influence on Cortázar's style, with its staccato, syncopated rhythm. We hear of Oliveira's discussions with fellow members of the vaguely defined Serpent Club, their reverence for mysterious author Morelli, and Oliveira's love of (but troubled relationship with) La Maga. Eventually, he heads to Argentina, where he finds work in an asylum.

Narrative strategies

The second book takes Argentina as its stage. In some Expendable Chapters, Cortázar's belief that the reader should be aware of the workings of a novel – as participant and even conspirator – can be detected, ultimately destroying the status of the text itself as a novel.

Cortázar's depiction of mental deterioration, disconnected and alienating human interaction, and

forced travel across countries is mirrored in the effects that the book as an object demands of the reader. In this way the author successfully draws attention to the text's fictional constructs, as well as to the expectations that we have of the novel form. ■

[A] chess world where you moved about like a knight trying to move like a rook trying to move like a bishop.
Hopscotch

Other key works

1960 *The Winners*
1967 *Blow-Up and Other Stories*
1968 *62: A Model Kit*
1973 *A Manual for Manuel*

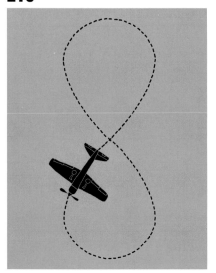

HE HAD DECIDED TO LIVE FOREVER OR DIE IN THE ATTEMPT
CATCH-22 (1961), JOSEPH HELLER

IN CONTEXT

FOCUS
American black humour

BEFORE
1939 *The Day of the Locust* by Nathanael West satirizes the grotesque vanity of Hollywood and its hangers-on during the Great Depression.

1959 Philip Roth's fiction collection *Goodbye, Columbus* humorously deals with the dark or taboo side of subjects such as sex, religion, and cultural assimilation.

AFTER
1966 Thomas Pynchon's *The Crying of Lot 49* explores the failure of communication and the absurd and disordered nature of the world.

1969 The search for meaning in increasingly fractured times is satirized in Kurt Vonnegut's *Slaughterhouse-Five*, inspired by the author's experience of the fire-bombing of Dresden and the absurdity of war.

With a fascination for the morbid and the taboo, black humour uses farce to make light of controversial or serious issues. Such humour often comes from despair or horror and frequently highlights the futility of life. Many dark, satirical novels came out of the USA in the latter half of the 20th century, when the nation assumed leadership of the West after the shattering of Europe through two world wars, and the onset of the Cold War nuclear age.

The madness of sanity
Catch-22, the satirical novel by US writer Joseph Heller (1923–99), is set in World War II, although the book can be read as a commentary on the ongoing Vietnam War.

It follows the exploits of Captain Yossarian and his fellow airmen, who serve on bombing missions. Unmoved by patriotism, Yossarian is furious that his life is at risk; convinced he is surrounded by crazed idiots, he tries to avoid his missions by faking illness. Yet he and his comrades are in a "Catch-

Anything worth dying for ... is certainly worth living for.
Catch-22

22" situation (which refers to a military code of practice): they can apply for discharge on the grounds of insanity, but the very process of claiming madness using the correct protocol proves their sanity and so they must continue to fly.

The madness of war so clearly seen by Yossarian is underscored through Heller's use of paradox, absurdity, and the kind of circular reasoning exemplifed by Catch-22 itself. True to the conventions of black humour, the novel is by turns bleak, hilarious, and tragic. ∎

See also: *The Crying of Lot 49* 290 ▪ *Slaughterhouse-Five* 291 ▪ *American Psycho* 313

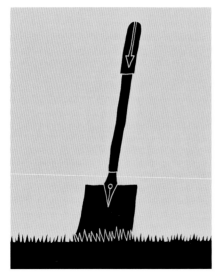

EVERYDAY MIRACLES AND THE LIVING PAST
DEATH OF A NATURALIST (1966), SEAMUS HEANEY

IN CONTEXT

FOCUS
Post-war poetry

BEFORE
1945 Anglo-American poet
W H Auden's *Collected Poetry*
includes work on public
politics and the start of his
religious imagery, reflecting
the crisis of modern society.

1957 In *The Hawk in the Rain*,
English poet Ted Hughes
explores love and war through
and alongside the symbolic
lives of animals, showing a
world of struggle mirroring
the one of humanity.

1964 English poet Philip
Larkin's *Whitsun Weddings*
is a series of poems conscious
of the decline of established
familial and social relations.

1965 US poet Sylvia Plath's
Ariel, published posthumously,
sees a shift to a dark and
unsettling flow of imagery,
borrowing from the horrors
of war crimes.

The political, cultural, and personal landscape of the generation of poets that sprang up after World War II was one scarred by the war's atrocities and filled with guilt. Writers and other artists had a troubled relationship with the past, whether public or personal. In the work of poets such as W H Auden, Ted Hughes, and Philip Larkin, personal relationships often stood in for wider interactions, and the memory of the war insinuated itself in imagery, references, poetic forms, and style.

Memory and change
The first major poetry collection by Irish poet Seamus Heaney (1939–2013), the successful and acclaimed *Death of a Naturalist*, explores the schism between childhood and adulthood, past and present as a version of the division between a pre-war and a post-war world. Themes and imagery invoke nature, family, human labour, and rural Irish landscapes in poems such as "Blackberry Picking" and "Churning Day". While there is no progression of a narrative in the collection, the 34 poems all revolve around similar elements of style and thematics, with natural imagery used to highlight the effects of the war upon external and internal spaces. In the second poem, "Death of a Naturalist", a boy encounters frogs that Heaney likens to grenades of mud, rupturing the childhood connection with nature.

The past is also incarnated in Heaney's family members, his father in particular. In "Digging" he shows their now outmoded link to manual labour and expertise in older ways of life, recalling his father digging for potatoes and his grandfather digging turf. Yet their labour, after all, is perhaps not too different from his own, as Heaney almost apologetically recognizes writing as a link to his earthier, more "useful" forebears.

Heaney was awarded the Nobel Prize for Literature in 1995, "for works of lyrical beauty and ethical depth, which exalt everyday miracles and the living past". ∎

See also: *The Waste Land* 213 ▪ *The Bell Jar* 290 ▪ *Crow* 291

THERE'S GOT TO BE SOMETHING WRONG WITH US. TO DO WHAT WE DID
IN COLD BLOOD (1966), TRUMAN CAPOTE

IN CONTEXT

FOCUS
New Journalism

BEFORE
Early 1900s Investigative journalists such as Lincoln Steffens and Ida M Tarbell blend literary techniques and journalism in articles that expose corrupt business and government practices.

1962 Journalist Gay Talese uses interviews, dialogue, and observation in a factual but literary article on boxer Joe Louis in *Esquire* magazine.

AFTER
1970 Tom Wolfe challenges traditional journalism with *Radical Chic and Mau-Mauing the Flak Catchers*, reporting in a lively observational style.

1972 Hunter S Thompson publishes the drug-fuelled *Fear and Loathing in Las Vegas*, the genesis of "gonzo journalism", in which the writer plays an integral part in the story.

The term "New Journalism" was introduced by critics in the 1960s to describe the work of US writers such as Truman Capote, Norman Mailer, Tom Wolfe, and Gay Talese, who used literary techniques to relate non-fictional stories and present factual reporting dramatically. Capote's theory that journalism could be forced to yield a new art form, the "nonfiction novel" (which he expounded in a 1966 interview in *The New York Times*), lay at the heart of his book *In Cold Blood*.

In 1959 Capote had read a newspaper report that offered an ideal subject on which to exercise his theory: a wealthy Kansas farmer, Herbert Clutter, and members of his family had been shot dead for no apparent reason. Assisted by his friend, author Harper Lee, Capote visited the scene and began researching the murder. *In Cold Blood* was published seven years later.

Murder in Kansas
The book describes the murder, which occurred on 15 November 1959. There were four victims: 48-year-old Clutter, a church-going, hard-working man; his wife, Bonnie; his daughter, Nancy; and his son, Kenyon. The family were well respected and popular – their brutal slaying shocked the community. A local man said they were "gentle, kindly people, people I knew – *murdered*".

In contrast the two murderers, Richard "Dick" Hickock and Perry Smith, were ex-convicts – misfits on parole from the Kansas State Penitentiary. Dick's promise to Perry was that they would "blast hair all over them walls". The two were caught and arrested in Las Vegas on 30 December 1959. Capote immersed himself in his subject, spending time with friends

I thought that Mr Clutter was a very nice gentleman … I thought so right up to the moment that I cut his throat.
In Cold Blood

See also: *To Kill a Mockingbird* 272–73 ▪ *The Armies of the Night* 291 ▪ *Fear and Loathing in Las Vegas* 332

Blending fact and fiction

Journalism
- Accurate and thoroughly researched.
- Focuses on narrative – telling the story.
- Brevity and concise form are valued.

New Journalism
- Creates a connection with the reader.
- Blends reporting with a distinct literary "voice".
- Examines emotions, motivations, and characters.
- Retains factual accuracy.

Fiction
- Literature created from the imagination of the author.
- May be based on real events.

and relatives of the victims, local residents, police, prison warders, psychiatrists, and the murderers themselves. He did not record interviews, but scribbled down quotes and impressions afterwards.

Truth and embellishment
The end result is a remarkable work in which Capote constructs scene after scene, building up characters and allowing participants to tell their stories in their own words. The book was first serialized in *The New Yorker* magazine, and was an instant success. US journalist Jack Olsen said it was the first book to make true crime a "successful, commercial genre". Even so, Capote was accused of having falsified or exaggerated events. He denied this falsification, though there is some evidence of embellishment.

Tom Wolfe wrote that *In Cold Blood* had given New Journalism "an overwhelming momentum", and he went on to codify the features of the form in his 1973 book, *The New Journalism*. He stated that Capote's novel incorporated all the form's key techniques: first-hand witnessing of events; real dialogue; third-person narrative; and detailed description of minute life details, such as how the killers brushed their teeth. This created a near-factual reportage presented in the style of a novel, enabling readers to gain an understanding of events and characters that was all the more powerful for being based on real events. ∎

Truman Capote

Born Truman Streckfus Persons in New Orleans on 30 September 1924, Capote had a troubled childhood. His parents divorced when he was four, and he was raised by relatives. He then rejoined his mother and her second husband, Joseph Capote, attending school in New York City and Greenwich, Connecticut. His career began with a string of short stories published in magazines such as *Harper's Bazaar* and *The New Yorker*. His first novel, *Other Voices, Other Rooms*, was published in 1948 and established him as a significant writer. Capote was a controversial figure. A socialite, heavy drinker, and sometime drug user, he enjoyed a flamboyant lifestyle and lived openly as a gay man, which was unusual at that time. In later life he became reclusive, and died in Los Angeles on 25 August 1984.

Other key works

1945 "Miriam" (short story)
1951 *The Grass Harp*
1958 *Breakfast at Tiffany's*
1986 *Answered Prayers: The Unfinished Novel* (published posthumously)

ENDING AT EVERY MOMENT BUT NEVER ENDING ITS ENDING

ONE HUNDRED YEARS OF SOLITUDE (1967), GABRIEL GARCÍA MÁRQUEZ

IN CONTEXT

FOCUS
The Latin American Boom

BEFORE
1946–49 Guatemalan Miguel Angel Asturias blends modernist techniques with surrealism and folklore in *Mr President* and *Men of Maize*.

1962 In *The Death of Artemio Cruz*, Carlos Fuentos layers memory, poetic imagery, stream of consciousness, and multiple perspectives to explore corruption in Mexico.

1963 Argentinian Julio Cortázar allows readers to choose their own path through his radically experimental work *Hopscotch*.

AFTER
1969 The shattered society of 1950s' Peru is revealed at lightning speed in a discussion between two men of different classes in Mario Vargas Llosa's *Conversation in the Cathedral*.

Time was not passing ... it was turning in a circle ...
One Hundred Years of Solitude

A s its name suggests, the Latin American Boom was an explosion of literary creativity that occurred in South America in the 1960s. Although Jorge Luis Borges had ignited a slow-burning fuse some 20 years before with *Ficciones* – a puzzle box of short stories that broke all literary conventions – the Boom years saw the publication of stellar works that gained worldwide attention for authors such as Gabriel García Márquez, Julio Cortázar, and Mario Vargas Llosa. These intellectuals engaged with the political struggles of Latin America.

Their writing was fuelled by the counterculture of the 1960s, and their narratives frequently make use of innovative and experimental techniques such as non-linear time, shifting perspectives, and magic realism – a technique regarded by many to be an invention of South American literature.

Isolation

Often considered the masterwork of the Boom, Colombian García Márquez's *One Hundred Years of Solitude* brings together Bible stories, ancient myths, and South American traditions of magic, resurrection, and regeneration in a metaphorical commentary on the continent's history.

The story spans one century and seven generations of a single family, the Buendías. Macondo, the town that they found, represents the history of Colombia at large. At the story's opening, Macondo is a small village of adobe houses, wedged between mountains and swamp. Its isolation from the modern world is complete; no route stretches back over the mountains. Established by José Arcadio Buendía and his wife Úrsula Iguarán, it is a utopia where everyone is younger than 30 years old and no one has yet died.

José Arcadio and Úrsula have two sons – a lusty giant, also called José Arcadio, and his anxious, prescient brother Aureliano. Their names, physical traits, and personalities are repeated down the generations, while characters such as Pilar Ternera, the village prostitute, both enrich the gene pool and complicate it, by coupling with and bearing children for multiple Buendías.

Through all this complexity, the beating heart of Macondo is always the matriarch Úrsula, whose long life allows her to protect and maintain the Buendía family in every new generation after each invasion of incomers and the episodes of insanity that follow them.

Invasion

Each generation is faced with its own fresh catastrophe, many of which parody an episode in Latin American history or reflect the continent's rich tradition of myth and legend. Although he is an artist at heart, Aureliano is soon caught up in civil wars that ravage the country for years. He becomes a famous colonel, renowned throughout the land as much for his poetry as his military exploits.

The house in Aractaca, Colombia, where Gabriel García Márquez grew up is now a pilgrimage site for fans of the author, who come to visit the place that inspired the creation of Macondo.

See also: *Ficciones* 245 ▪ *Hopscotch* 274–75 ▪ *Pedro Páramo* 287–88 ▪ *The Death of Artemio Cruz* 290 ▪ *The Time of the Hero* 290 ▪ *Midnight's Children* 300–05 ▪ *The House of the Spirits* 334 ▪ *Love in the Time of Cholera* 335 ▪ *2666* 339

All Aureliano's victories come to nothing however, as the country remains convulsed by conflict, a parody of the bloody struggles that wracked Latin America in the 19th century. The wars bring death and violence to the previously peaceful Macondo, and Aureliano's nephew Arcadio becomes a dictatorial governor until he is shot by a firing squad. The town has been changed forever, and the opening of a new railway exposes Macondo to the influence of the outside world for the first time.

At first the villagers are enthralled by the wonders of modernity – they cannot understand how an actor who dies in one movie, can come back to life to appear in another – but Macondo soon becomes an outpost of US economic imperialism. The American Fruit Company turns the town into a banana plantation, controlled by a small encampment of Americans. When the workers go on strike for better conditions, they are massacred in an episode that forms the violent catalyst of the town's final decline. »

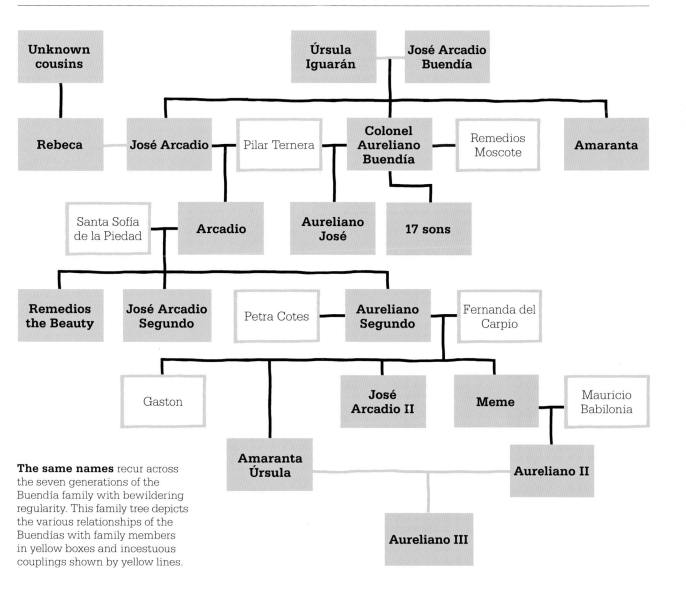

The same names recur across the seven generations of the Buendía family with bewildering regularity. This family tree depicts the various relationships of the Buendías with family members in yellow boxes and incestuous couplings shown by yellow lines.

The misery inflicted on Macondo represents the centuries of pain caused by Western economic exploitation. Even a rain storm that lasts for four years, 11 months, and two days, fails to wash the town clean. It does, however, cause an exodus, leaving Macondo empty apart from a handful of Buendías living out their final days in the town.

Bible stories and myths

Márquez draws on South America's mixed heritage of myths and Bible tales to tell the story of a paradise destroyed through its loss of innocence. In Macondo "the world was so recent that many things lacked names". The novel's exploration of the history of human progress therefore begins with an idiosyncratic Buendía creation myth.

The family's founding marriage is a union between the cousins José Arcadio and Úrsula, and the story of a previous Buendía incest that produced a child with a pig's tail becomes an ever-present anxiety. As it turns out, this fear was entirely justified; the final Aureliano is born with the feared affliction. There are several Inca creation myths founded on incest between brother and sister, and the natural progression of family from Adam and Eve in the Bible would have progressed along similar lines. Some 17th-century arrivals in South America believed that the Garden of Eden was sited in eastern Bolivia. The first Conquistadors thought they had discovered a people descended from the son of Noah, a survivor of the Great Flood, or possibly from the lost tribes of Israel.

Deluge myths were widespread among indigenous South American people. These bubble to the surface in the great rain towards the end of *One Hundred Years of Solitude.*

Science and magic

Magic is not sprinkled lightly across this novel; it is woven into the fabric of its lilting, poetic text. At first, the villagers are mystified by modern phenomena such as false teeth and photographs. But even when the modernization of Macondo is well underway, the forces of magic carry just as much weight as reason and science. Remedios the Beauty, a woman too beautiful to be looked upon, rises to heaven in a cloud of bedsheets. After the first José Arcadio descends into

The last that remained of a past whose annihilation had not taken place because it was still in a process of annihilation.
One Hundred Years of Solitude

madness, he becomes literally bonded to the chestnut tree in his garden, and when he is taken indoors the smell of mushrooms and wood-flower fungus follows him. As Úrsula ages and her sight fades, "the lucidity of her old age allows her to see", and she develops her other senses: using odours to remember sights, she tracks a child's movements by sprinkling a little rosewater on his head; and she distinguishes colour by texture.

García Márquez said that he discovered the key to handling the narrative voice in his novel

Gabriel García Márquez

Born in Columbia in 1928, Gabriel José García Márquez was raised by his grandparents in Aractaca, a town resembling the fictional Macondo of *One Hundred Years of Solitude*. This upbringing shaped his anti-imperialist beliefs. During The Violence, a 10-year period of political repression in Colombia, García Márquez became a reporter in Barranquillo.

Although Garcia Márquez's journalism flourished, his liberal views meant that he had to leave Colombia and work as a foreign correspondent in Europe. After reporting on the Cuban revolution in 1959, he worked in Bogotá and New York for Prensa Latina, the Cuban news agency. His second full novel, *One Hundred Years of Solitude* was written in Mexico City and earned the author worldwide acclaim. Márquez authored 22 books and was awarded the Nobel Prize in Literature in 1982. He died in Mexico City in 2014.

Other key works

1985 *Love in the Time of Cholera*
2004 *Memoirs of My Melancholy Whores*

in his grandmother's stories and from an aunt who had a knack for offering fantastical explanations with the conviction of the truth.

Resurrection

In *One Hundred Years of Solitude* the dead continue to exert an influence on the living and the grave is a door to multiple realities beyond our own. Early in the story José Arcadio Buendía throws a spear through the throat of Prudencio Aguilar, a neighbour who insults him. José Arcadio is then haunted by the man's spirit until he is on his own deathbed. The two men make plans for a bird-breeding farm in the afterlife so that they will have "something to do on the tedious Sundays of death".

The fixation on death persists when distant relative Rebeca arrives at the Buendía house dragging a bag of her parents' bones. She eats earth and lime, the stuff of the grave, while she awaits their proper burial.

Circular time

Fractured or non-linear time is a key feature of the Latin American Boom's postmodernist approach to literature. The opening lines set this up in a very memorable way: "Many years later, as he faced the firing squad, Colonel Aureliano Buendía was to remember that distant afternoon when his father took him to discover ice."

Time is cyclical in the story: present, past, and future events are commingled in the 100-year span of the Buendía family. The setting, too, is circular. All of the action takes place within concentric spheres: first, the modern world that is encroaching on Macondo; then the village itself; the Buendía's house; and finally the mysterious laboratory that is established in the heart of the house and which

remains untouched by the passing of time. Rescued from the firing squad, Aureliano retreats there to fashion tiny gold fishes, which he then melts down and makes all over again in an attempt to live forever in the present moment – a bitter reflection of the futile repetitions of the story and of human history.

When the last Buendía is drawn to the laboratory to finally unravel the scrolls which document and prophesy Macondo's 100-year history, and which were delivered to the first José Arcadio by the gypsy Melquíades, he finds prehistoric plants and luminous insects have

Races condemned to one hundred years of solitude did not have a second opportunity on earth.
One Hundred Years of Solitude

A banana plantation is established in Macondo, and the American Fruit Company's economic imperialism leads to a massacre and reflects the USA's exploitation of Latin America.

removed "all trace of man's passage on earth from the room". As he reads he finds himself "deciphering the instant that he was living, deciphering it as he lived it, prophesying himself in the act of deciphering the last page of the parchments, as if he were looking into a speaking mirror". In this extraordinary metafictional moment the narrator, character, and reader arrive at the point at which past, present, and future combine and fall into the void beyond which the words stop on the page.

One Hundred Years of Solitude has sold more than 30 million copies and is regarded as a masterpiece of a literary boom that reverberated across two decades. Márquez's postmodern vision spoke to both Latin America and the wider world in its depiction of a planet that is doomed to repeat a cycle of endless environmental catastrophe, warfare, and infighting over and over for generation after generation. ∎

FURTHER READING

PAROLES
(1946), JACQUES PRÉVERT

Paroles ("Words") is the first poetry collection by the French poet and screenwriter Prévert (1900–77). Comprising 95 poems of varying length, it reveals multiple elements of his trademark writing style, such as wordplay, prose poems, puns, and mini dialogues. The collection covers a variety of subjects and themes, entwining everyday life in post-war Paris with sentiments of antiwar protest, critiques of both religion and politics, and a reflection of the role of art in society.

CRY, THE BELOVED COUNTRY
(1948), ALAN PATON

The masterpiece of South African author Paton (1903–88) focuses on Stephen Kumalo, a black Anglican priest in Johannesburg who is in search of his son, who has been involved in the murder of a white activist for racial justice. It also tells the story of the activist's father, and how his own prejudices and views are changed by his son's death and writing, and by meeting Kumalo. Paton's narrative reveals the changing reality of South Africa on the verge of apartheid.

SNOW COUNTRY
(1948), YASUNARI KAWABATA

Japanese novelist Yasunari Kawabata (1899–1972) is a Nobel Laureate. One of his most famous novels, *Snow Country*, tells of doomed love amid the mountains of western Japan. Shimamura – a bored, wealthy businessman – meets Komako, a beautiful but forlorn geisha at a hot spring resort. The landscape becomes a metaphor for feelings – including hopelessness and isolation. Kawabata's focus on the personal, with no mention of the fighting in World War II, which was raging at the time of writing, may have been a conscious artistic response to the conflict.

The train came out of the long border tunnel – and there was the snow country. The night had turned white.
Snow Country
Yasunari Kawabata

THE LAGOON AND OTHER STORIES
(1951), JANET FRAME

A collection of short stories, this was the first publication by New Zealand author Frame (1934–2004). To varying extents, the texts in the collection question their own status as fiction, explore the author's agency and identity, and experiment with narrative voice. The book's publication and critical reception – including a highly regarded literary prize – were crucial in saving Frame from a lobotomy and a series of atrocious practices in mental institutions, where she had been committed.

Ernest Hemingway

Born in Illinois, USA, in 1899, Hemingway discovered his affinity for writing early in life as a reporter for *The Kansas City Star*. He later served as a volunteer ambulance driver in World War I in Italy, from where he returned wounded in 1918. His first novel, *The Sun Also Rises,* was written while working as an overseas correspondent in Paris. Establishing himself in Europe, Hemingway saw increasing success from his short stories and novels and travelled widely to pursue – among other interests – his love of hunting, a subject that would appear in many of his stories. He returned to journalism to report on the Spanish Civil War (1936–39) and the Normandy landings (1944), and won the Nobel Prize in 1954. Hemingway committed suicide in Idaho in 1961.

Key works

1929 *A Farewell to Arms*
1940 *For Whom the Bell Tolls*
1952 *The Old Man and the Sea* (see opposite)

THE OLD MAN AND THE SEA
(1952), ERNEST HEMINGWAY

Written during Hemingway's stay in Cuba in 1951, *The Old Man and the Sea* was the last piece of fiction to be published during the author's lifetime. The story is as simple as the writing style, depicting the struggle of old fisherman Santiago with a marlin off the coasts of Cuba and Florida. Nevertheless, the work is deeply emotional and powerful, as both the Pulitzer and Nobel commissions acknowledged in their awards to Hemingway. Multiple interpretations of the book have been suggested, such as that it is a reflection on the author's career, that it has an allegorical religious significance, or that it is a personal story based on people Hemingway encountered during his life.

FAHRENHEIT 451
(1953), RAY BRADBURY

One of the most famous novels by the US writer of speculative fiction Ray Bradbury (1920–2012), *Fahrenheit 451* is a key example

A book is a loaded gun in the house next door … Who knows who might be the target of the well-read man?
Fahrenheit 451
Ray Bradbury

of dystopian fiction. In a world in which knowledge and books are banned, Guy Montag, a fireman (in *Fahrenheit 451*, a fireman is a person who is in charge of setting fire to books) slowly rediscovers his own humanity and individuality. The story highlights the conflict between mindlessly following orders and questioning established power structures, and the role that books and knowledge can play in that ongoing struggle.

LORD OF THE FLIES
(1954), WILLIAM GOLDING

Despite its initial lack of success, *Lord of the Flies* has since become a classic and fundamental text of dystopian, allegorical, political, and satirical writing. The story begins with a group of boys stranded on an otherwise unpopulated island, and follows their unsuccessful, violent, and ultimately savage attempts to impose different types of self-government and order on the group. The story takes place in the shadow of a rotting pig's skull surrounded by insects – the eponymous Lord of the Flies of the title. Although Golding's first novel has often been challenged for its controversial exploration of human nature, utilitarian themes, and violence, it is nevertheless a fascinating insight into political, psychological, and philosophical thought of its time.

THE LORD OF THE RINGS
(1954–1955), J R R TOLKIEN

English writer and academic Tolkien (1892–1973) helped to redevelop the fantasy genre with the three-volume sequel to his children's book *The*

William Golding

Golding was born near the British town of Newquay, Cornwall, in September 1911. He grew up in a political household in Wiltshire: his father, Alec, was a science master, a socialist, and a rationalist, while his mother, Mildred Curnoe, was a female suffrage activist. Golding studied natural sciences, then English literature at Oxford. He served in the Royal Navy during World War II, and published his first work of fiction, *Lord of the Flies*, in 1954. He kept writing until his death in 1993, and was awarded both the Booker and Nobel prizes.

Key works

1954 *Lord of the Flies* (see left)
1955 *The Inheritors*
1980, 1987, 1989 *To the Ends of the Earth: A Sea Trilogy*

Hobbit (1937). Taking inspiration from events in the world wars, his childhood in South Africa, and his studies in Icelandic and Germanic literatures, he developed the epic tale of *The Lord of the Rings*. The story follows multiple characters as they journey through *The Fellowship of the Ring*, *The Two Towers*, and *The Return of the King*, in a life-or-death quest to end the spread of evil forces across Middle-earth.

PEDRO PÁRAMO
(1955), JUAN RULFO

Influencing writers such as Gabriel García Márquez and José Saramago, *Pedro Páramo* by Mexican author

Yasar Kemal

Born in Gökçedam, Turkey, in 1923, Kemal experienced childhood hardships that may have contributed to his later urge to speak out on behalf of the dispossessed. He was blinded in one eye as a child, and suffered the tragedy of witnessing his father's murder at the age of five. He first met with literary acclaim with his short stories and novels, which he wrote in the 1950s and 60s while working as a journalist. He also wrote ballads and children's books. Kemal was awarded 38 literary prizes throughout his career, and was nominated for the Nobel Prize in 1973. He died in 2015.

Key works

1954 *The Drumming Out*
1955 *Memed, My Hawk*
(see right, above)
1969 *They Burn The Thistles*

Juan Rulfo (1917–86) is a surreal, supernatural, and enigmatic story of grief, haunting memories, and deeply fraught relationships. Through non-linear storytelling, the blurring of events, dreams, and hallucinations, the reader is dragged into the confusion of the narrator Juan Preciado. He tells of his return to the ghost town of Comala after his mother's death to fulfil her last wish – to find his father, Pedro Páramo. Juan is shocked to discover the extent of Páramo's influence in the town. As the narrative unfolds, Páramo is revealed as protagonist and antagonist of the story, holding the power of life and death over Comala and its inhabitants.

MEMED, MY HAWK
(1955), YASAR KEMAL

Kemal's first full novel, *Memed, My Hawk* – originally titled *Ince Memed* ("Memed, the Slim") – was the first Turkish-language book to achieve international fame. The first volume in a series of four, it follows the troubled story of young Anatolian Memed, who runs from his abusers with his loved one Hatche, loses her, and joins a band of brigands. He returns to his mother and hometown to challenge the abusive landowner who caused Hatche's death, and discovers that his story has only just begun.

THE DEVIL TO PAY IN THE BACKLANDS
(1956), JOÃO GUIMARÃES ROSA

A major work of South American literature, *The Devil to Pay in the Backlands*, by Brazilian writer João Guimarães Rosa (1908–67), is narrated by ex-mercenary Riobaldo as a long and continuous tale, with no section breaks. It is the story of the narrator's life, his encounters with turncoat ranchers and other brigands, and the devil himself, as they all cross paths, literally and metaphorically, in the outback of the Brazilian state Minas Gerais.

HOWL AND OTHER POEMS
(1956), ALLEN GINSBERG

The first and most significant collection by US poet Ginsberg (1926–97), and the most influential for the Beat Generation movement. Containing among other poems the epic "Howl", Ginsberg's pieces are raw and emotional, and openly condemn consumer capitalism, homophobia, racism, and cultural hegemony in the US. The book's publisher was charged with obscenity, but won the case, which only served to increase demand for the book and boost circulation both in the USA and across the world.

DOCTOR ZHIVAGO
(1957), BORIS PASTERNAK

The internationally acclaimed novel *Doctor Zhivago* by Russian writer Pasternak (1890–1960) is a thought-provoking investigation of the Russian Communist Party between the revolution of 1905 and World War I. It had to be published in Italy due to censorship by the Russian government, which also removed the Nobel Prize awarded to Pasternak. The story is told through multiple characters – centred around Yuri Zhivago – as they adapt to the new political reality of their country. It deals with the regime's misguided attempts to impose conformity and its misreadings of socialist ideals, as well as the characters' struggles in their attempts to deal with and overcome the alienation, loneliness, and coldness of communist Russia.

LA JALOUSIE
(1957), ALAIN ROBBE-GRILLET

An experimental French *nouveau roman* (new novel), *La Jalousie* by Robbe-Grillet (1922–2008) features a narrator who is effectively absent – although his presence is implied – from the events he describes. He spies, out of jealousy, on his wife through a "jalousie", a type of window. Scenes are repeated multiple times, with some of the details changed. Ambiguous and

> She begins serving: the Cognac … then the soda, and finally three transparent ice cubes, each of which imprisons a bundle of silver needles in its heart.
> ### *La Jalousie*
> **Alain Robbe-Grillet**

fragmented, the work is an example of the author's experimentation with the novel form; the reader is left to interpret the story for themselves.

A HOUSE FOR MR BISWAS
(1961), V S NAIPAUL

The first novel by Trinidad-born British writer Naipaul (1932–) to achieve international acclaim, *A House For Mr Biswas* draws on the author's experiences of growing up in the Caribbean. Mohun Biswas strives towards his goal of owning his own house, to provide a home for his family and escape from his overbearing in-laws. The book lays bare the inequalities of colonialism, and exposes the tensions between individual and familial life.

THE TIME REGULATION INSTITUTE
(1962), AHMET HAMDI TANPINAR

Tanpinar (1901–62) wrote *The Time Regulation Institute* as a critique of the excessive bureaucracy in modern governmental procedures, basing many of his observations on his native Turkey. This major Turkish-language novel recounts the protagonist's personal struggles (as well as those of the secondary characters he interacts with) to adapt to the Eurasian post-war reality, and to be at peace with the changing nature of modern times.

ONE DAY IN THE LIFE OF IVAN DENISOVICH
(1962), ALEKSANDR SOLZHENITSYN

An active critic of the totalitarian government ruling over his native Russia, Solzhenitsyn (1918–2008) wrote this, his first literary work, to openly condemn Stalin's rule. The book recounts a day in the life of a wrongly condemned labour-camp prisoner, Ivan Denisovich, and the nature of the punishments, hardships, and horrors that he endures. The underlying message, however, is one of solidarity, loyalty, and humanity among the prisoners, who only survive from day to day by working together.

ONE FLEW OVER THE CUCKOO'S NEST
(1962), KEN KESEY

One Flew Over the Cuckoo's Nest by US writer Kesey (1935–2001) is a novel set in a mental institution in Oregon, and is based on the author's own time as a staff member at a similar facility. Although the novel has been well received in most quarters, it has also been subject to bans. Kesey's best-known book, it highlights the humanity – and in some cases, cruelty – behind the individuals, from patients to staff, in the mental-care system. It is often seen as a critique of this type of institution, as well as of other systems of control in US society.

A CLOCKWORK ORANGE
(1962), ANTHONY BURGESS

In this dystopian novel, Burgess (1917–93) takes his observations of the changing youth cultures present in Britain in the 1960s to disturbing extremes. The reader follows the teenage narrator Alex in his exploits of "ultraviolence", depravity, and drug use, told in both English and the Russian-influenced teen slang known as "Nadsat". Also described are the authorities' attempts to reform Alex through an experimental type of aversion therapy, no matter the cost to his mental state; the final chapter, cut from US editions until the 1980s, seems to show some redemption for Alex. The satirical novel spawned an extremely successful and equally controversial cinematic adaptation in 1971 by Stanley Kubrick, which helped to increase the popularity of and interest in the book.

> If he can only perform good or only perform evil, then he is a clockwork orange … an organism lovely with colour and juice but … only a clockwork toy to be wound up by God or the Devil.
> ### *A Clockwork Orange*
> **Anthony Burgess**

THE DEATH OF ARTEMIO CRUZ
(1962), CARLOS FUENTES

One of the novels that helped bring Latin American literature to wider international recognition, *The Death of Artemio Cruz* by Mexican author Fuentes (1928–2012) is a recollection of the life of fictional main character Artemio Cruz, as he lies on his deathbed. Through the memories of Cruz, the reader joins his greedy family, overbearing priest, and not-too-loyal assistant in revisiting over 60 years of Mexican history, politics, and religion, including the country's foreign policies, corruption, and betrayals.

THE BELL JAR
(1963), SYLVIA PLATH

This semi-autobiographical novel by US poet Sylvia Plath (1932–63) retells events in the author's life, and was initially published under a pseudonym. The text is made up of multiple flashbacks to protagonist Esther's earlier life, as she interns for a renowned magazine in New York one summer. Esther, in search of her own identity as a woman, descends into a worsening mental state, eventually ending up in a mental hospital and being treated with electroshock therapy.

I felt very still and very empty … moving dully along in the middle of the surrounding hullabaloo.
The Bell Jar
Sylvia Plath

THE TIME OF THE HERO
(1963), MARIO VARGAS LLOSA

The heavily censored literary début of Peruvian Nobel Prize winner Mario Vargas Llosa (1936–), *The Time of the Hero* is an experimental work of fiction. Employing multiple perspectives and a complex, non-linear chronology, the story is set in a real-life military academy in Lima. It exposes the techniques used to train cadets, turning them into loyal, silent, hyper-masculine drones, never questioning or challenging imposed structures of authority. In turn, these practices are not solely seen as issues of the academy, but also of more general military structures, and of a state that relies on military power to maintain control – such as in Peru from the 1930s to the 1980s. The authorities attempted to prevent the novel's publication, condemning it as a plot by neighbouring Ecuador to denigrate the nation of Peru.

THE CRYING OF LOT 49
(1966), THOMAS PYNCHON

Written by New Yorker and author of speculative fiction Pynchon (see p.296), this novella was hailed as both a prime example and a harsh parody of postmodern fiction and psychoanalysis. It follows Oedipa Maas and her discovery of a worldwide conspiracy rooted in a centuries-old feud between two postal services, one real ("Thurn und Taxis"), one fictional ("Trystero").

The text is littered with cultural and social references to popular music, literature, and art.

WIDE SARGASSO SEA
(1966), JEAN RHYS

A powerful novel by Dominica-born British writer Jean Rhys (1890–1979), *Wide Sargasso Sea* explores feminist and postcolonial themes through relationships of power, especially between men and women. The story, a prequel to Charlotte Bronte's *Jane Eyre* (1847), follows white Creole Antoinette and her troubled life in Jamaica, as she is controlled, oppressed, then dismissed as a mad woman by her English husband, before being forced to relocate to England under the name of Bertha.

We stared at each other, blood on my face, tears on hers. It was as if I saw myself. Like in a looking-glass.
Wide Sargasso Sea
Jean Rhys

THE MASTER AND MARGARITA
(1966–67), MIKHAIL BULGAKOV

Written by Russian author Bulgakov (1891–1940) between 1928 and 1940 but only published almost 30 years later, *The Master and Margarita* is set both in 1930s' Moscow and – as told in a novel by lead character the

"Master" – in Jerusalem at the time of Christ. Through both story lines, the book can be seen as a historical validation of religious tenets, a critique of overly bureaucratic rules, and a satire of the Soviet authorities, catalyzed in the characters of Professor Woland – an anarchic but scholarly manifestation of Satan – and his devilish entourage.

THE ARMIES OF THE NIGHT
(1968), NORMAN MAILER

Pulitzer Prize-winning novel *The Armies of the Night: History as a Novel/The Novel as History*, by journalist, playwright, novelist, and film-maker Norman Mailer, was a key work in the rise and acceptance of creative non-fiction in the literary landscape. The text is a historicized, political, journalistic recollection of an anti-Vietnam War rally in Washington, DC, in 1967, interspersed with self-reflections, novelizations, and personal thoughts on the subject matter and the author himself.

SLAUGHTERHOUSE-FIVE
(1969), KURT VONNEGUT

Written by US author Vonnegut (1922–2007), *Slaughterhouse-Five or The Children's Crusade: A Duty-Dance with Death* is a key example of speculative fiction and surreal political satire. It meshes together time-travel and its paradoxes, alien creatures, and semi-autobiographical notes about the author's service in World War II, including the bombing of Dresden. The result is a critique of the horrors of war, the publishing industry, and the status of literature, and is a thoughtful, almost comic, meditation on death and mortality.

THE FRENCH LIEUTENANT'S WOMAN
(1969), JOHN FOWLES

This popular and highly acclaimed novel by British author John Fowles (1926–2005) is often labelled as a postmodern historical fiction. It tells the story of naturalist Charles Smithson and Sarah Woodruff, a former governess, in a style that comments upon Victorian romances, while dealing with topics such as gender issues, history, science, and religion. The narrator, who also becomes a character, allows for multiple possible endings to the story, destabilizing the linear narrative of the texts it is imitating.

I KNOW WHY THE CAGED BIRD SINGS
(1969), MAYA ANGELOU

The first book of a seven-volume autobiography, *I Know Why the Caged Bird Sings* by Maya Angelou (1928–2014) – the African-American Pulitzer Prize winner and activist – expresses the author's changing responses to the violence of racism. A powerful and influential literary work as well as a candid memoir of Angelou's early life in Arkansas from ages three to 16, the book explores issues of childhood, trauma, and motherhood, and proclaims the power of belief in one's self, and of literature and the written word.

CROW
(1970), TED HUGHES

Often regarded as the most important collection of the British poet Ted Hughes (1930–98), *Crow: From the Life and Songs of the Crow* was inspired by US artist Leonard Baskin's illustrations of the bird. The poems – some of which are traditional in style, while others take more experimental forms – follow the character of Crow, weaving elements of world mythologies and religions into an ongoing epic folktale. While the tale is incomplete – Hughes was unable to continue after the suicide of his lover Assia Wevill in 1969 – the ambitious collection is a noteworthy philosophical and literary reflection on mythology and the natural world.

Norman Mailer

Born in New Jersey, USA, in 1923, Mailer grew up in New York. He joined Harvard University at the age of just 16, initially to study aeronautical engineering, but soon became interested in writing. One of his stories won a competition in 1941, which led him to pursue writing seriously – an ambition that he argued (unsuccessfully) should exempt him from military service. His first novel *The Naked and the Dead* (1948) is based on his war experience in the Philippines. In 1955 he co-founded the political arts magazine *The Village Voice*. A cultural commentator and critic, Mailer also wrote biographies of Picasso, Lee Harvey Oswald, and Marilyn Monroe. His creative non-fiction, political activism, and two Pulitzer prizes ensured his fame. He died in 2007.

Key works

1957 "The White Negro"
1968 *The Armies of the Night* (see left, above)
1979 *The Executioner's Song*

CONTEM
LITERAT
1970–PRESENT

PORARY
URE

The photograph "Earthrise" taken from the **Apollo 8 manned spacecraft** orbiting the moon, a year before the first moon landing, becomes an iconic image of our planet.

1968

Chairman Mao Zedong, China's communist leader, dies, **bringing to an end the Cultural Revolution** that began in 1966.

1976

Salman Rushdie's *Midnight's Children* tells the story of the **partition of India** in the style of magic realism.

1981

The **fall of the Berlin Wall** symbolizes the end of the Cold War.

1989

1973

Thomas Pynchon's long and complex novel *Gravity's Rainbow* combines **science and philosophy** with elements of high and low culture.

1979

In the postmodern novel *If on a Winter's Night a Traveller*, by Italo Calvino, alternate **passages are written in the second person** – "you", the reader.

1987

Toni Morrison examines **the psychological effects of slavery** in her novel *Beloved*.

1990

St Lucian poet Derek Walcott publishes *Omeros*, reinterpreting Homer's *Iliad* in a **postcolonial setting**.

Towards the end of the 20th century, the world was becoming a smaller place. The accelerating pace of technological advances, particularly in transport and communications, brought about a globalization of trade and cultures on a scale never seen before. Political changes, most noticeably the liberalization of eastern European communist bloc countries and the lifting of the Iron Curtain, also helped to foster ever-greater international links.

At the same time as nations around the globe developed their own distinct postcolonial cultures, Europe and North America became influenced by multiculturalism, which led to a realization within the West that its culture could no longer be considered a benchmark for the rest of the world.

This was a period in which the first generation of writers to have been born in nations that had gained independence from the European empires came of age. Many writers admired the new techniques of postmodernism that some South American authors had adopted as a style, and especially the genre of magic realism. The English language still dominated the literary world, however, and it was people from the old British Empire who came to prominence in the first wave of postcolonial literature.

New national voices

India produced authors such as Salman Rushdie and Vikram Seth who, writing in English, portrayed the experiences of the new India after independence and partition. Local voices also emerged in other former outposts of empire, including the Caribbean poet Derek Walcott and the novelist V S Naipaul. In Canada, Australia, and South Africa, where many people had resettled from the UK, British influence on writing waned and literature began to appear that was recognizably of those nations.

New styles of writing were also emerging in East Asia, as writers sought to establish a national identity in a modern China after the upheaval of the Cultural Revolution, and in a Korea that was now divided into an authoritarian north and a liberal south by the 38th parallel.

Multiculturalism

While European culture was losing its monopoly in its old colonies, it was also being influenced by

Vikram Seth's lengthy novel *A Suitable Boy* uses four families to explore the **internal conflicts of India** after independence.

1993

J M Coetzee's novel *Disgrace* details the fall from grace of a college lecturer in **post-apartheid South Africa**.

1999

Love, jealousy, and betrayal feature in Margaret Atwood's *The Blind Assassin*, which offers a **new twist on Gothic fiction**.

2000

The Guest, by Hwang Sok-yong, deals with the aftermath of fanatical hatred and civil strife in **the Korean War**.

2001

In his novel *Extremely Loud and Incredibly Close*, Jonathan Safran Foer uses several experimental techniques to shed light on the **9/11 attacks**.

2005

1995

In his allegorical novel *Blindness*, Portuguese author José Saramago describes the **social turmoil** that follows an imagined epidemic.

2000

White Teeth, by Zadie Smith, tells the story of two families in **multicultural, 20th-century London**.

2001

Jonathan Franzen's *The Corrections* examines the hidden **dysfunctions of a traditional family** in the US Midwest.

2001

Terrorists crash three passenger planes into the Pentagon and **the "twin towers" of the World Trade Center** in New York.

---

rising numbers of immigrants from around the world. Many cities in Europe became cosmopolitan centres, attracting not only people in search of a new life and a better standard of living, but also writers and artists who still regarded Europe as an intellectual centre.

Ironically, many writers who had helped to establish a literary style in their homeland, such as Rushdie, Seth, and Naipaul, had chosen to settle in England, where their presence inspired younger writers, many of whom were the offspring of immigrants from the Indian subcontinent, Africa, the Caribbean, and elsewhere. Such authors described the complex experiences of living in multicultural cities, with Zadie Smith exploring the integration of immigrants into British society.

In the USA, however, issues of race and cultural assimilation had a longer history. US society had long been based on the model of its European settlers' homelands, while a quite separate culture had developed among the African-American descendants of slaves. Even after many of the political goals of the Civil Rights Movement had been achieved, racial tensions persisted and this was reflected in a distinctive body of literature by writers such as Toni Morrison.

International literature

Alongside the development of new national voices, a global trend of adopting postmodern stylistic techniques gave much of the era's literature an international appeal. The counterculture of the 1960s broke down the barriers between "serious" and "popular" culture, while sophisticated computing and telecommunications technologies were the inspiration for novels such as US author Thomas Pynchon's *Gravity's Rainbow*. Magic realism in particular had become a widely accepted genre, yet new writing continued to draw upon older forms, such as in the allegorical satire of José Saramago and the metafiction of Italo Calvino.

While English is now a second language for numerous people across the world, many novels are also available in translation. The modern readership is international, and authors – no longer restricted by regional boundaries – are quick to reflect on ideas and issues that have global resonance, such as the dysfunctions in modern society and the threat posed by terrorism. ∎

OUR HISTORY IS AN AGGREGATE OF LAST MOMENTS

GRAVITY'S RAINBOW (1973), THOMAS PYNCHON

IN CONTEXT

FOCUS
The encyclopedic novel

BEFORE
1851 Herman Melville's *Moby-Dick* is the first great encylopedic American novel.

1963 Thomas Pynchon's debut novel *V.* anticipates *Gravity's Rainbow* in its panoramic and information-packed scope.

AFTER
1996 Dealing with addiction, family relationships, tennis, entertainment, advertising, Quebecois separatism, and film theory, the encyclopedic novel *Infinite Jest*, by US writer David Foster Wallace, has 388 endnotes.

1997 Using baseball – and one baseball in particular – as its central conceit, US author Don DeLillo's complex novel *Underworld* stretches from the 1950s to the 1990s and involves both fictional and historical characters.

The term "encyclopedic novel" refers to a capacious, complex work of fiction that includes swathes of specialized information on subjects ranging from science to the arts to history. It attempts to create, through a virtuoso effort of imagination, a fictional world beyond the reach of linear storytelling. In his novel *Moby-Dick*, Herman Melville combined, among other things, biblical and Shakespearean references, facts about whales, and realistic descriptions of life on board a ship. In *Gravity's Rainbow*, set at the end of World War II, Thomas Pynchon interweaves wartime secret operations with pop culture, surrealism, perverse eroticism, rocket science, and mathematics.

Determinism and disorder

Within a formidably complex plot, with shifts in time and around 400 characters, the novel is a display of prodigious erudition. Its themes include paranoia, determinism, death, and entropy – a term from thermodynamics that indicates a steady decline into disorder.

Thomas Pynchon

Born in 1937 in Long Island, New York, Thomas Pynchon counts among his ancestors the founder of Springfield, Massachusetts, USA. Pynchon attended the high school in Oyster Bay, and went on to study engineering physics at Cornell University, but left before graduating to serve in the US Navy. He returned to Cornell to study English. In the early 1960s Pynchon worked as a technical writer at Boeing in Seattle; he would later draw upon his experiences there in his fiction (especially *Gravity's Rainbow*). He spent some time in Mexico before moving to California. After *Gravity's Rainbow* his fiction became less stylistically challenging and more humanistic and political. Pynchon is known for being protective of his privacy, and shy of media coverage.

Other key works

1966 *The Crying of Lot 49*
1984 *Slow Learner* (stories)
2006 *Against the Day*
2013 *Bleeding Edge*

See also: *Moby-Dick* 138–45 ▪ *Les Misérables* 166–67 ▪ *War and Peace* 178–81 ▪ *Ulysses* 214–21 ▪ *Catch-22* 276 ▪ *Infinite Jest* 337

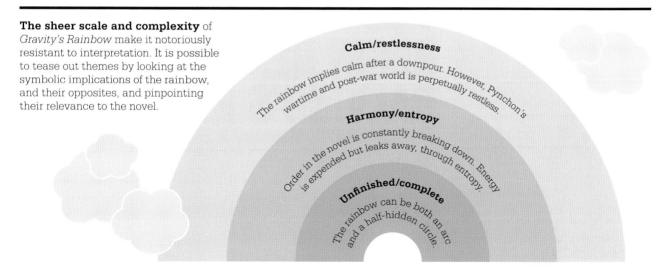

The sheer scale and complexity of *Gravity's Rainbow* make it notoriously resistant to interpretation. It is possible to tease out themes by looking at the symbolic implications of the rainbow, and their opposites, and pinpointing their relevance to the novel.

Calm/restlessness
The rainbow implies calm after a downpour. However, Pynchon's wartime and post-war world is perpetually restless.

Harmony/entropy
Order in the novel is constantly breaking down. Energy is expended but leaks away, through entropy.

Unfinished/complete
The rainbow can be both an arc and a half-hidden circle.

The central symbol in the book is the German V-2 rocket, an image both of transcendence and of a frightening, unknown future. The book's opening words describe the sound of a V-2 hitting London: "A screaming comes across the sky." Symmetrically, at the end of the novel, a rocket is about to detonate. In between, numerous plots and subplots propel the characters through a succession of wildly improbable scenarios, in which paranoia and fear of death are often rendered with black humour.

The book's main plot lines revolve around the quest by several characters to uncover the secret of a V-2 rocket numbered 00000. One such character is an American GI, Tyrone Slothrop, whose sexual encounters in London occur at the precise sites where V-2 rockets will fall. Slothrop later rescues a Dutch girl named Katje, who is a double-agent, from an octopus conditioned to attack her. The octopus has been trained by Laszlo Jamf, who had conducted Pavlovian experiments on Slothrop as a child and is the

inventor of an "erotic" plastic from which a capsule in rocket 00000 is made. When the rocket is launched, a young boy, Gottfried, is strapped inside this capsule: he is the sex slave of the book's Nazi arch-villain, who by sacrificing Gottfried seeks to transcend his mortality.

Such bizarre scenes are shot through with a profusion of ideas, including allusions to science and philosophy. The reader, like Slothrop, struggles to find meaning.

Paranoid truth-seeking
All systems by which we might make sense of our lives, whether they are scientific, mystical, religious, or political, are described at a certain point in the novel as paranoid. Against human attempts at rationalization, Pynchon posits a complex reality in which events occur according to inscrutable laws – while perhaps entertaining the idea that true paranoia lies in precisely such a world view.

In his short story "The Secret Integration" (1964), white schoolchildren with a black

imaginary friend experience adult racism, after which their dreams "could never again be entirely safe". *Gravity's Rainbow* traces a parallel loss of innocence on a massive scale, and Pynchon no doubt relished the idea that reading itself could no longer be entirely safe after his virtuoso feat of fictional black magic. ▪

The V-2 rocket is a key presence in *Gravity's Rainbow*, which features a project to assemble one, while embracing a profusion of chaos, perversity, and paranoia.

YOU ARE ABOUT TO BEGIN READING ITALO CALVINO'S NEW NOVEL

IF ON A WINTER'S NIGHT A TRAVELLER (1979), ITALO CALVINO

IN CONTEXT

FOCUS
Metafiction

BEFORE
1615 In the second part of the novel *Don Quixote*, by Spanish writer Miguel de Cervantes, the eponymous fictional hero is aware that the first part had been written about him.

1759–67 Anglo-Irish novelist Laurence Sterne's fictional autobiography *Tristram Shandy* contains so many digressions that the author is not born until Volume III.

1944 Argentine writer Jorge Luis Borges' *Ficciones* plays with the nature of fiction in a series of enigmatic and mesmerizing short stories.

AFTER
1987 US author Paul Auster's *The New York Trilogy* twists the form of the detective novel and makes the reader question the tropes of the genre.

The term metafiction was coined by US writer William H Gass in 1970 and refers to a fictional form of writing in which a series of literary tools are employed by writers to draw attention to how fiction and reality interrelate, emphasizing the nature of the text as a constructed work, an artefact of the author. While largely associated with the fiction of postmodern writers, many examples exist from earlier eras, including the 17th-century epic of Cervantes', *Don Quixote*, and the 18th-century hilarity of Laurence Sterne's *The Life and Opinions of Tristram Shandy*.

A novel about novels and points of view, Calvino's book interweaves excerpts of imagined books from different contemporary fiction genres; the titles of these 10 books form a complete sentence.

If on a winter's night a traveller

OUTSIDE THE TOWN OF MALBORK

Leaning from the steep slope

WITHOUT FEAR OF WIND OR VERTIGO

Looks down in the gathering shadow

IN A NETWORK OF LINES THAT ENLACE

See also: *Don Quixote* 76–81 ▪ *Ficciones* 245 ▪ *Hopscotch* 274–75 ▪
The French Lieutenant's Woman 291 ▪ *Midnight's Children* 300–05

Italo Calvino's *If on a Winter's Night a Traveller* is acknowledged as one of the metafiction novel's finest modern incarnations, with a mesmerizing narrative plot that not only challenges traditional narrative forms but also asks the reader to interrogate the actual process of reading.

As with the finest examples of metafictional texts, the opening words of *If on a Winter's Night a Traveller* immediately demand that the reader undertake a process preparatory to actually commencing the "story": "You are about to begin reading Italo Calvino's new novel, *If on a winter's night a traveller*. Relax. Concentrate. Dispel every other thought. Let the world around you fade."

The self-reflection by Calvino in the first sentence is a typically metafictional device. Half the first chapter is a guide to "you" preparing for the very real task of reading this book; it is a somewhat mesmeric world – reminiscent of the metafictional playfulness of Jorge Luis Borges' work – as though Calvino has some insight into the processes of each reader's mind as they embark on reading his book.

A fantasy of fictions

After the meditative beginning, Calvino proceeds to plunge the reader into what appears to be a more traditional narrative plot. A character ("you") keeps starting a book, but due to various circumstances cannot continue; in his quest to finish the books he meets a female reader who he ("you") falls in love with. He also discovers a conspiracy to render all books false and meaningless. This rather strange narrative tale is fractured by further metafictional reflection: the reader is questioned about their reaction to the book, and thereby invoked as one of the novel's protagonists.

A distinct structural form runs through the novel. Each chapter is in two parts: the first is written in second-person form ("you") and concerned with the very process of reading; the second part, being the beginning of a new book, is seemingly an original narrative. The influence of the Oulipo – a group of French writers who experimented with new and demanding literary forms, which Calvino joined in 1968 – is evident in these structural constraints.

A narrative maze

If on a Winter's Night a Traveller introduces the reader to imaginary writers of fictional works that do not exist, to fabricated biographies, and even to countries that are invented – all are common traits of metafiction. The reader is guided into a narrative maze by a masterful storyteller – one who delights in playing eccentric postmodern games. The experience is utterly captivating. ▪

One reads alone, even in another's presence.
If on a Winter's Night a Traveller

Italo Calvino

Italo Calvino was born in Cuba in 1923 and was two when he moved to Italy with his parents, who were returning home. Having settled in Turin during World War II, Calvino fought for the Italian Resistance, before turning to journalism at the war's end, writing for the communist paper *L'Unità*. Not long after the war, in 1947, his first novel, *The Path to the Spiders' Nests*, was published.

Calvino left the Italian Communist Party in 1957, after the Soviet invasion of Hungary. In 1964, he married Esther Judith Singer, resettled in Rome, and focused on the short stories that would form the collection *Cosmicomics*.

Calvino moved with his family to Paris in 1968, where he joined the group of innovative writers known as Oulipo, short for Ouvroir de littérature potentielle ("workshop of potential literature"). He died in 1985 from a cerebral haemorrhage.

Other key works

1957 *The Baron in the Trees*
1959 *The Nonexistent Knight*
1965 *Cosmicomics*
1972 *Invisible Cities*

TO UNDERSTAND JUST ONE LIFE YOU HAVE TO SWALLOW THE WORLD

MIDNIGHT'S CHILDREN (1981), SALMAN RUSHDIE

IN CONTEXT

FOCUS
Magic realism goes global

BEFORE
1935 *A Universal History of Infamy* by Jorge Luis Borges is published, often considered the first work of magic realism.

1959 Günter Grass writes *The Tin Drum*, founding magic realism in German literature.

1967 *One Hundred Years of Solitude* by Gabriel García Márquez takes magic realism to new heights of wonder.

AFTER
1982 Chilean-American author Isabel Allende's first novel, *The House of the Spirits*, becomes a global bestseller.

1984 British writer Angela Carter writes the magic realist *Nights at the Circus*.

2002 Haruki Murakami publishes the dreamlike novel *Kafka on the Shore*.

Magic realism is a literary style in which magical or surreal elements appear in an otherwise realistic and traditional narrative structure and setting. Originally used to describe the work of certain German artists in the 1920s, the term was then applied to literature, in particular to the works emanating from Latin America in the mid-20th century. The Cuban Alejo Carpentier and the Argentinian Jorge Luis Borges are often considered the precursors of the form, while the Colombian Gabriel García Márquez brought it to its peak in the boom years of the 1960s and '70s. From Latin America, magic realism spread around the world, with a number of US and European writers adopting the style, or elements of it, in their work. In Salman Rushdie's *Midnight's Children*, magic realism merges with postcolonial themes and Indian references to give the novel its unique flavour.

Aspects of magic

Magic realist writers depict bizarre, inexplicable, or overtly supernatural events alongside ordinary events in the real world in such a way that

Memory's truth ... selects, eliminates, alters, exaggerates, minimizes, glorifies, and vilifies also; but in the end it creates its own reality.
Midnight's Children

the strange phenomena seem completely normal. Plots are often labyrinthine, and the world may be depicted in exaggerated detail or colour, adding to the surreal complexity of the novel's vision. In some respects, magic realism requires the reader to take on a more active role than in other forms of fiction, because the elements of the novel are disconcerting, and may impact on the sense of reality experienced by the reader.

Much magic realism also contains a metafictional aspect, which makes the reader question

Salman Rushdie

Salman Rushdie was born in Bombay (now Mumbai) in 1947 to Muslim parents of Kashmiri descent, who moved to Karachi in Pakistan soon after the Partition of India. He was educated in India and Britain, attending Cambridge University, before becoming an advertising copywriter. *Midnight's Children*, Rushdie's second novel, brought him worldwide attention, winning the Booker Prize in 1981 and the Best of the Bookers in 2008, and establishing Rushdie as a leading light of the Indian diaspora. The appearance of *The Satanic Verses* (1988) drew

great controversy when Iranian leader Ayatollah Khomeini issued a *fatwa* (religious ruling) calling for the assassination of Rushdie for blasphemy. Rushdie went into hiding in Britain. In 2000, he settled in New York and has continued to write on matters of religion and society. He has been married four times and was knighted in 2007.

Other key works

1983 *Shame*
1988 *The Satanic Verses*
2005 *Shalimar the Clown*

See also: *The Tin Drum* 270–71 ▪ *One Hundred Years of Solitude* 280–85 ▪ *A Suitable Boy* 314–17 ▪ *The House of the Spirits* 334 ▪ *Love in the Time of Cholera* 335

Magic realism goes global

In the first half of the 20th century, Latin American writers such as Jorge Luis Borges lead **the construction of a new style** of literature that merges the realistic with the fantastical.

From the mid-20th century, the **style is named magic realism** and gains popularity across the globe, from Colombia to Germany to Japan.

Postcolonial, hybrid layers deepen the scope of the form, as **ever more complex and fantastical** examples are offered by late 20th-century figures such as Salman Rushdie.

the way in which they read the work. Metafiction often includes a self-referential narrator, and stories within stories: both devices are present in *Midnight's Children*. These manipulations of reality – magic tricks within the narrative – make demands on the reader and ensure their role is an active one.

The birth of a nation

Politically, magic realist texts often embody an implicit critical position against the dominant ruling elite, and as such they are generally subversive in their stance. In *Midnight's Children*, the fusion of Rushdie's magic realism with postcolonial issues weaves new and vibrant threads into an already complex genre.

Rushdie sets the work partly in the vast, sprawling city of Bombay (now Mumbai) – once a jewel in Britain's colonial crown and now at a crucial moment of history. Events

take place as monumental political shifts are happening with the removal of British authority over India after some 200 years.

At the beginning of the novel, the main protagonist Saleem Sinai is approaching his 31st birthday and is convinced that he is dying. The book is ostensibly the story of Saleem's life – as well as the lives of his parents and grandparents – narrated by Saleem himself to his companion, Padma; but it is also the story of the creation of modern India. In the opening lines of the book Saleem recounts: "I was born in the city of Bombay … on August 15th, 1947. … On the stroke of midnight.". As Saleem says, "at the precise instant of India's arrival at independence, I tumbled forth into the world." He then goes on to explain, in broad hints that cannot yet be fully understood by the reader, the premise of the book: "I had been mysteriously handcuffed to history, my destinies indissolubly chained to those of my country." »

Mumbai is a densely populated city, teeming with all forms of human life. Rushdie uses rich, vivid language to evoke its myriad elements – squalor, beauty, pathos, despair, and humour.

India's Independence Day on 15 August 1947 was a time of celebration, yet chaos soon struck, as Muslims and Hindus migrated between the new nations of India and Pakistan.

As the narrative unfolds, it soon becomes clear that every political event appears to be driven by – or be driving – one or more events in the life of Saleem.

Saleem's arrival at the exact moment of India's independence is wildly celebrated by the Indian media. India's first prime minister, Jawaharlal Nehru, sends him a letter congratulating him on the "happy accident" of his moment of birth, and identifies him with the nation – a role that Saleem adopts, seeing himself as an important historical figure. His life is seen as closely tied to the fate of the newly born India; the bloodshed that ensues directly after Partition and the fierce conflicts that occur over the following years are echoed by the concurrent violence within his own family. Saleem's narration of his family's story, and of the

historical events of India and Pakistan, represents his attempt to understand all the elements that make him who he is.

The many and the one
Saleem is marked by his large, cucumber-like, and constantly dribbling nose. At the age of 10, he discovers that he has telepathic powers (a not uncommon trait of magic realist protagonists).

… perhaps, if one wishes to remain an individual in the midst of the teeming multitudes, one must make oneself grotesque.
Midnight's Children

This gift allows him to discover that there were a total of 1,001 "Midnight Children", who were born in the hour after midnight on India's Independence Day. They all have marvellous superpowers, with those who were born nearest to the actual second of Partition having the greatest powers. By the time Saleem discovers their existence, 420 of the children have already died, and only 581 remain.

Saleem befriends another of the children, Parvati, who can perform magic; another of their number, Shiva, who is at once Saleem's counterpart and nemesis, has incredibly strong knees and a gift for warfare. Parvati and Shiva are named after Hindu gods, thereby illustrating the religious underpinning of India as a cultural entity and adding a further layer of allegory to the novel.

Using his telepathic powers to broadcast their thoughts, Saleem arranges a nightly "conference" of the Midnight Children. There are the same number of children – 581 – as there are members in the lower house of the Indian parliament, adding political symbolism to their meetings. Their conference is a model of successful pluralism, reflecting the way the new Indian government sought to collate the disparate elements of its vast country. Rushdie implies that troubles arise when such multiplicity becomes suppressed.

The rush of history
As the tale of *Midnight's Children* unfolds, so Rushdie shifts his story across the subcontinent, employing the narrative of his characters' tales to tell the history of India, and so too of Pakistan and Kashmir.

In 1962, border tensions between China and India erupted into war; it was short-lived, but

India was defeated and in the novel, public morale "drains away". In Saleem's life, as conflict with China intensifies, his nose gets ever more blocked until, on the day the Chinese army halts its advance, he has an operation to drain his sinuses. Once again, the events in Saleem's life seem to be entwined with the wider events of history.

However, with his nose finally clear, Saleem finds that he has lost his mind-reading powers. In compensation, for the first time in his life he has a sense of smell. And this itself is another kind of superpower, as he can detect not only smells but also emotions and lies – "the heady but quick-fading perfume of new love, and also the deeper, longer-lasting pungency of hate".

Memory, truth, destiny

The novel is a kaleidoscope of Saleem's memories, and yet the distinction between true and untrue is never clear, even making allowances for the outright magical elements that form part of the book's tapestry. Some characters are overt liars, while in many cases Saleem admits that he has embroidered certain things in order to convey an emotional truth rather than a strictly factual one.

Early on in the narrative, Saleem confesses that he was switched at birth with another baby who was born at the same time. This baby was Shiva, while Saleem's real parents, far from being the relatively rich Muslims who brought him up, are a colonial Englishman, William Methwold,

Saleem's friends Shiva and Parvati are named respectively after the great Hindu god of destruction and the goddess of love, and these attributes are reflected in their roles in the book.

> Who what am I?
> My answer: I am the sum total of everything that went before me, of all I have been seen done, of everything done-to-me.
> *Midnight's Children*

and a poor Hindu woman who died in childbirth. So, paradoxically, the "destiny" he is fulfilling was that of another child; yet because he was brought up as Saleem Sinai, he considers that that is who he is: it is his truth.

Even historical facts cannot be regarded as unassailable. Saleem notes that he recorded the wrong date for the death of Mahatma Gandhi, and yet he is content to let the error stand: "in my India,

Gandhi will continue to die at the wrong time." In this novel, the truth is malleable, subjective, and far from absolute.

The end of the book returns to the present day, as Saleem finishes telling his story to Padma. Despite his own prophecy that his body will crack apart, he agrees to marry her on his 31st birthday – which is also Independence Day. To the last, his history is intermingled with India's.

Magical mystery tour

For the reader, *Midnight's Children* is a complex and mesmerizing journey, a mystery tour through the back streets to the heart of modern India. Time speeds up and slows down or is non-linear. Fate is frequently invoked, futures are foretold, prophecies are listened to and expected to come true. The bizarre and the magical are commonplace and real. Weaving together all these elements of magic realism, Rushdie creates a dense and vibrant tapestry full of violence, politics, and wonder to tell the tale of the early years of independent India. ∎

FREEING YOURSELF WAS ONE THING; CLAIMING OWNERSHIP OF THAT FREED SELF WAS ANOTHER

BELOVED (1987), TONI MORRISON

IN CONTEXT

FOCUS
Contemporary African-American literature

BEFORE
1953 James Baldwin's *Go Tell It on the Mountain* captures the pain of life in a racist society.

1976 Alex Haley's novel *Roots: The Saga of an American Family* traces family history back to slavery.

1982 Alice Walker reveals the hardships of African-American women's lives in the 1930s in *The Color Purple*.

AFTER
1997 Junot Díaz's sizzling prose paints a picture of the Dominican-American diaspora in his story collection *Drown*.

1998 Edwidge Danticat recounts the 1937 massacre of Haitian cane workers in *The Farming of Bones*.

By the end of the 20th century, African-American writing had grown from the slave narratives of 150 years earlier into a major canon of American literature. From educational works such as Booker T Washington's *Up From Slavery* (1901), through the vibrant literature of the 1920s Harlem Renaissance, it reached a high point with Ralph Ellison's philosophical novel *Invisible Man* (1952). During the late 1950s and the 1960s, young black writers were fuelled by the Civil Rights and Black Power movements.

Toni Morrison's novel *Beloved* emerged during a new flourishing of black writing that began in the

See also: *Narrative of the Life of Frederick Douglass* 126–27 ▪ *Their Eyes Were Watching God* 235 ▪ *Invisible Man* 259 ▪ *I Know Why the Caged Bird Sings* 291 ▪ *Roots: The Saga of an American Family* 333

1970s, when authors such as Alex Haley, Maya Angelou, and Alice Walker sought new ways to explore race, identity, and the legacies of slavery. This affirmation of the power of black writing has continued into the present day with "hyphenated American" authors, including Dominican-American Junot Díaz and Haitian-American Edwidge Danticat.

Memory and history

In her early novels – *The Bluest Eye*, *Sula*, and *Song of Solomon* – Morrison focused on the African-American experience within her own lifetime, offering an original voice on themes such as moral and spiritual revival, white standards of beauty, and sisterhood. Her Pulitzer Prize-winning novel *Beloved* is regarded as one of the most influential works in African-American literature. Dedicated to the "Sixty Million and more" who are believed to have died on slave ships and in captivity, it reclaims the ascendancy of memory and history in black identity, resolving symbolically issues that are still swept aside in present-day reality.

Not a house in the country ain't packed to its rafters with some dead Negro's grief.
Beloved

Freed slaves, such as these men photographed during the US Civil War, were technically free, but they were still affected by segregation and the psychological aftermath of slavery.

Inspired by the real-life case of Margaret Garner, a fugitive slave who killed her baby after she was recaptured by marshals in Cincinnati, Ohio, *Beloved* is a piece of social history with a strong political agenda, but it undermines expectations of its genre with its use of expressionist fantasy and rhetorical stylization. Morrison also asserts her roots and her pride in African folklore by incorporating the cultural focus, origins, and mythology of black Americans into the novel. She employs the rhythms and speech patterns of African-American discourse, not as a simple pastiche of black speech but in a lyrical, incantatory voice, often making use of poetic repetitions at the beginning and the end of interior monologues: "Beloved is my sister", "She's mine, Beloved. She's mine", "I am Beloved and she is mine". The author invents a feminine style of narrative built around motherhood, sisterhood, Afro-Christian revivalism, tribal rites, and ghosts. She asks the

reader to engage with a retelling of history that is built on an easy intimacy with the supernatural.

The book begins in 1873 in Cincinnati, Ohio. Slavery has been abolished but racism is still rife. Sethe, a former slave, and her 18-year-old daughter Denver live in a home haunted by a spiteful baby spirit named 124, after the number of their house on Bluestone Road. Sethe's two sons ran away years ago and her mother-in-law, Baby Suggs, is dead. The arrival of Paul D, who lived as a slave with Sethe at Sweet Home, Kentucky, starts a process that unlocks the past.

The past in the present

Morrison's time-travelling story slips back and forth between Sethe's present and events 20 years earlier, when slaves fleeing north » were subject to Fugitive Slave laws that allowed owners to cross into free states to reclaim their property. Piece by piece a story emerges. Sethe and her husband, Halle, planned a break for freedom, unable to endure their treatment at the hands of the new governor of Sweet Home, known as "schoolteacher". Heavily pregnant, Sethe sent her two small boys and baby daughter on ahead. When Halle failed to arrive at their agreed meeting place, Sethe travelled on alone, giving birth to her new daughter on the way, with the help of a white girl called Amy Denver. After reaching safety in Cincinnati, she found temporary happiness with her mother-in-law Baby Suggs, a freed slave. A horrific event – the details of which are revealed later in the novel – is triggered by the arrival of schoolteacher with a posse to take Sethe and her children back to the farm.

Moral complexity

Good and evil are not binary opposites in this story. At its core is a terrible action committed out of profound love. The supposedly "free" society that sympathetic white folks offer to released slaves is built on unchallenged racism

> I never talked about it. Not to a soul. Sang it sometimes, but I never told a soul.
> *Beloved*

Slavery is a psychological as well as a physical condition. While slaves are bound in literal chains – shackles, gags, iron neck collars – the psychological chains that Sethe is left with as an ex-slave mean that every area of her life is infected.

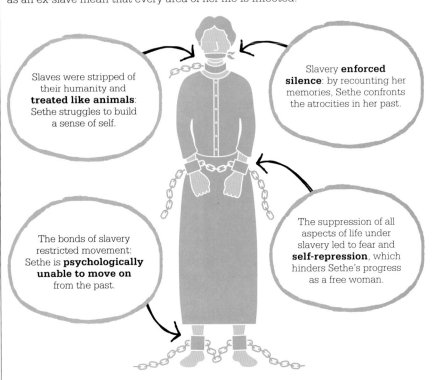

Slaves were stripped of their humanity and **treated like animals**: Sethe struggles to build a sense of self.

Slavery **enforced silence**: by recounting her memories, Sethe confronts the atrocities in her past.

The bonds of slavery restricted movement: Sethe is **psychologically unable to move on** from the past.

The suppression of all aspects of life under slavery led to fear and **self-repression**, which hinders Sethe's progress as a free woman.

and segregation. The absurd notion of "good" and "bad" slave owners is addressed by Paul D as he re-examines life at Sweet Home under the benign Mr Garner: on other farms male slaves were gelded to make them manageable, but Garner's men "are men". After Garner's death, the much harsher regime instituted by schoolteacher enabled them to know the real condition of their slavery for the first time, and Paul D realizes they had only been men on home soil by virtue of Garner's protection. "One step off that ground and they were trespassers among the human race."

Remembered pain

Self-repression brought on by years of sociopolitical repression is a major theme in the novel. Buried memories are the emotional shards that make self-determination so hard, and which are drawn out as a psychological necessity. Morrison suggests that black Americans can begin living in the present only by confronting the past. The fragments of earlier events in Sethe's and Paul D's lives slowly come to the surface throughout the novel, coalescing into a horrific account of slavery conditions in the South – tales that are too terrible to relate as a consecutive narrative.

"Rememory" is the invented word that Sethe uses for the kind of remembering that takes former slaves deeper into the past to the appalling places that are always waiting to reclaim them. Sethe's rememories include the time that schoolteacher instructed his nephew to list her human and animal characteristics, and the occasion when his boys pinned her down and drank her breast milk. Paul D keeps his memories in a rusted "tobacco tin buried in his chest where a red heart used to be". Baby Suggs remembers the births of seven children from different fathers and losing them all.

Beloved

The embodiment of the hurtful past is Beloved, a young woman in unspoiled shoes and a silk dress who insinuates herself into the household after Paul D drives away the baby poltergeist. This attention-seeking woman with baby-smooth skin is violently selfish and has an inexplicable knowledge of Sethe's past. Sethe is slow to recognize what for Denver is obvious. Beloved is a revenant (a person who has died but come back to life): Sethe's dead baby grown to womanhood and craving the love she has been denied. She is the

African folklore traditions connect with the American present in *Beloved*: the character of Beloved herself appears to embody the belief that the dead return to Earth in the form of spirits.

personification of Sethe's guilt, both destroyer and enabler, who coaxes out stories that have been too difficult to articulate. Her own story in child-speak recalls the cramped hold of slave ships and bodies tipped into the sea. Beloved seems to embody the suffering of the 60 million and more, but nothing is certain.

The true element to be "beloved" is a sense of self. Reclaiming self, a central theme in Morrison's work, is an imperative as there is nothing in the landscape for ex-slaves to own. Robbed of normal family life, mated, traded, and their offspring sold on, slaves are defined by their enslavement. Starting with these first tentative steps taken in freedom, the events in the novel presage the long road ahead. In the 1950s the protagonist of Ellison's *Invisible Man* was still in search of a self, and we can hear the first notes of Martin Luther King's Civil Rights rhetoric in Baby Suggs' sermon in the forest: "in this here place, we flesh; flesh that weeps, laughs; flesh that dances on bare feet in grass. Love it." Pride in race, sex, and self is the healing medicine, because, as Paul D tells Sethe, "you your best thing". ∎

Toni Morrison

Toni Morrison is one of the USA's most powerful literary voices, and the first African-American woman to win the Nobel Prize in Literature (1993), among her numerous other awards. Born Chloe Anthony Wofford in 1931 into a working-class Ohio family, she grew up with a love of reading, music, and folklore. She gained a BA degree from Howard University and an MA from Cornell. She was married for a short time to Jamaican architect Harold Morrison, with whom she had two sons. Morrison wrote her first four novels while working as an editor in New York. Her fifth, *Beloved*, was widely acclaimed and adapted into a film. From 1989 to 2006 Morrison held a professorship at Princeton University. In 2005 she wrote the libretto for *Margaret Garner*, an opera based on the story that inspired *Beloved*. She continues to write, and to speak against censorship and repression of history.

Other key works

1970 *The Bluest Eye*
1977 *Song of Solomon*
2008 *A Mercy*
2012 *Home*

HEAVEN AND EARTH WERE IN TURMOIL
RED SORGHUM (1987), MO YAN

I n the *xungen*, or "roots-seeking", movement that arose in Chinese literature during the mid-1980s, writers tried to reconnect with folk culture. The movement took its name from a 1985 essay by Han Shaogong, "The Roots of Literature", which called on writers to seek out forgotten sources of creativity. While some *xungen* authors examined China's ethnic minorities, others took a fresh look at the indigenous values within Daoism and Confucianism.

For decades, Chinese writing had been on a strict diet of realism. In harking back to folk influences, the *xungen* authors also introduced elements of the supernatural. The new work brought Chinese writers to the attention of the literary world again for the first time in decades.

Redefining modernity
One of the movement's most famous books is *Red Sorghum* by Guan Moye (1955–), better known by his pen name Mo Yan ("Don't Speak"). *Red Sorghum* is named after a rare wheat crop, whose colour symbolizes vitality, bloodshed, and stability. Set in northwest China's rural Shandong Province, the book follows one family from 1923 to 1976, through the Japanese occupation, the Communist Revolution, and the horrors of the Cultural Revolution.

As a true "roots-seeking" novel, *Red Sorghum* incorporates mythical and folkloric elements, and its break with the chronological structures that accompanied the realistic tradition gave new energy to Chinese literary modernism. ∎

Lines of scarlet figures shuttled along the sorghum stalks to weave a vast human tapestry.
Red Sorghum

See also: *Romance of the Three Kingdoms* 66–67 ▪ *Call to Arms* 222 ▪ *Playing for Thrills* 336

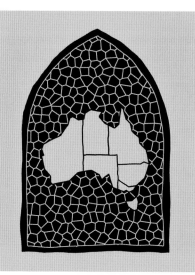

YOU COULD NOT TELL A STORY LIKE THIS. A STORY LIKE THIS YOU COULD ONLY FEEL
OSCAR AND LUCINDA (1988), PETER CAREY

IN CONTEXT

FOCUS
Australian writing

BEFORE
1957 Patrick White – one of the most influential modern Australian writers – uses religious symbolism in *Voss,* a story of a visionary explorer's encounter with Australia in the mid-19th century.

1982 Thomas Keneally's *Schindler's Ark* mixes fact and fiction to explore the impact of an individual on historical events.

AFTER
2001 Peter Carey is awarded a second Booker Prize for his novel *The True History of the Kelly Gang,* an imaginative take on the legendary Australian hero Ned Kelly.

2006 Indigenous writer Alexis Wright explores the dispossession of Aboriginal lands by white people in her novel *Carpentaria.*

Australian writers have attracted international interest since the middle of the 20th century. Novelists have moved from traditional themes such as "mateship" (the egalitarian bonds forged by mutual reliance in a harsh environment), national pride, and rural survival, to create works that are provocative and often disturbing. The areas explored by these books include fantasy, beliefs, and personal relationships, while being rooted in the Australian experience.

One of the leading writers and creators of this modern genre is Australian novelist and former advertising copywriter, Peter Carey (1943–). His *Oscar and Lucinda,* which won the Booker Prize in 1988, is a rich and complex novel set in the mid-19th century, with events taking place in England and New South Wales.

Guilt and faith
The protagonists of the book are Oscar Hopkins and Lucinda Leplastrier. The former is a young clergyman who grapples with his faith – an ungainly, uncomfortable individual, brought up in an English seaside community. The latter is an independent-minded young woman, who grew up in an "earth-floored hut in New South Wales" surrounded by the works of Dickens, Balzac, and other literary greats. Becoming an heiress after her mother's death, Lucinda buys an old glassworks in Sydney, where she is regarded as odd because of her aloofness and strange behaviour.

The pair meet on board ship travelling from Britain to Australia and from then on their lives are interlinked, coming together in an extraordinary project to build and transport a glass church through the Australian bush.

While on one level *Oscar and Lucinda* is a historical novel, it is also steeped in fantasy and unreality – Peter Carey described it as "a science fiction of the past". Its rich and complex characters, descriptive storytelling, and broad-ranging themes of faith, belief, and sexuality ensured its influence on modern Australian literature. ∎

See also: *The Three Musketeers* 122–23 ∎ *The Lagoon and Other Stories* 286

A HISTORICAL VISION, THE OUTCOME OF A MULTICULTURAL COMMITMENT
OMEROS (1990), DEREK WALCOTT

IN CONTEXT

FOCUS
Caribbean writing

BEFORE
1949 Cuban writer Alejo Carpentier publishes his novel *The Kingdom of this World*, which negotiates Caribbean history and culture.

1953 *In the Castle of My Skin*, by Barbadian writer George Lamming, is one of the region's key autobiographical novels and wins the Somerset Maugham award in 1957.

1960 In *Return to My Native Land*, Martinican poet Aimé Césaire discusses *négritude*, or black consciousness, as a form of identity for people whose ancestors had been dislocated from Africa.

AFTER
1995 *To Us, All Flowers Are Roses: Poems* confirms Lorna Goodison as one of the finest Jamaican poets of the post-war generation.

History and memory have always been a part of the Caribbean literary landscape, and writing from the region has highlighted the struggle to find a truthful voice that reflects the reality of alienation in a colonial situation. Caribbean authors – contingent on who their islands' previous colonial owners were – write in Spanish, French, English, or Dutch. Each writer negotiates the known fragments of his or her own history within the particular postcolonial situation.

Intertwined narratives
A towering figure in this literary landscape is St Lucian author Derek Walcott (1930–). In 1992 he was awarded the Nobel Prize for Literature for "a poetic oeuvre of great luminosity, sustained by a historical vision, the outcome of a multicultural commitment".

Walcott's magnificent and hugely ambitious 300-page poem *Omeros* (the Greek name for Homer) endorses the judges' claim. Epic in length, it references Homer's *Odyssey* and *Iliad*, while also celebrating the landscape, people, and language of St Lucia. The poem follows Dante's *The Divine Comedy* in its use of *terza rima*, a three-line poetic form, or tercet, in which the second line rhymes with the first and third lines of the next tercet. At the same time, Walcott honours the tone and rhythm of the local Caribbean patois from the very beginning of the poem. While some of the characters' names, such as Achille and Hector, are classical in origin, they are also not unusual names for St Lucian fishermen.

Omeros interweaves time and place to interrogate topics such as slavery, American-Indian genocide, and expatriates in the Caribbean. Walcott fuses stories from Africa, the USA, London, and Ireland with St Lucian events to create a mosaic narrative of collective memory.

Island life, memories of Africa, and the vestiges of colonialism remain the focus for Caribbean writers as they attempt to make sense of their disjointed histories. ∎

See also: *Iliad* 26–33 ∎ *Odyssey* 54 ∎ *The Divine Comedy* 62–65 ∎ *Ulysses* 214–21 ∎ *A House for Mr Biswas* 289

I FELT LETHAL, ON THE VERGE OF FRENZY
AMERICAN PSYCHO (1991), BRET EASTON ELLIS

IN CONTEXT

FOCUS
Transgressive fiction

BEFORE
1973 The protagonists of English writer J G Ballard's controversial novel *Crash* are a group of car-crash victims who are sexually aroused by car accidents.

1984 Foreshadowing later transgressive fiction, US writer Jay McInerney's satire *Bright Lights, Big City* places the reader as the central character in a hollow world.

AFTER
1992 Brutal and shocking, Irish writer Patrick McCabe's *The Butcher Boy* plunges the reader into the violent fantasy world of schoolboy Francie Brady.

1996 Tyler Durden, the antihero in US writer Chuck Palahniuk's transgressive *Fight Club*, is an anarchic, masochistic nihilist.

The explicit treatment of taboo topics such as rape, incest, paedophilia, drugs, and violence characterizes trangressive fiction, a genre that came to the fore in the 1990s. Writers such as Charles Bukowski, William S Burroughs, J G Ballard, and Kathy Acker had paved the way in previous decades with novels that variously described weird sexual acts, body mutilation, drug use, and extreme violence.

To transgress is to go beyond established moral boundaries, and *American Psycho*, a black comedy by US author Bret Easton Ellis (1964–), does this with relish. Its scenes of violence, particularly against women, have led to calls for the book to be banned.

Psychotic dream

Its true transgression, however, lies perhaps in the suggestion that the pursuit of the American Dream is akin to a mental disorder. The book is set in Manhattan during the 1980s Wall Street boom and the narrator, Patrick Bateman, is both a yuppie and a homicidal sociopath. He inhabits a morally bankrupt, drug-dependent world that revolves around designer clothes and exclusive clubs and restaurants; he expounds his love of a rock band in the same tone as he ponders how to dispose of a corpse. Forced to view the world through his eyes, the reader is urged to question a society in which everything has become commodified. ∎

I have all the characteristics of a human being: blood, flesh, skin, hair; but not a single, clear, identifiable emotion, except for greed and disgust.
American Psycho

See also: *Lolita* 260–61 ▪ *A Clockwork Orange* 289 ▪ *Crash* 332

QUIETLY THEY MOVED DOWN THE CALM AND SACRED RIVER

A SUITABLE BOY (1993), VIKRAM SETH

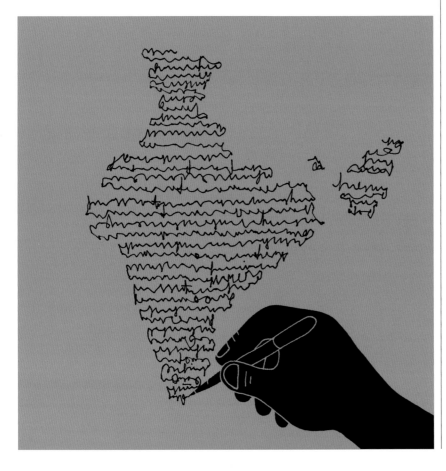

O ver the last few decades Indian English writing has carved a niche as a recognizable literary genre that has gained increasing international attention. In the 1950s and '60s some Indian writers – notably R K Narayan, one of the first Indian English novelists to be recognized outside India – made a deliberate choice to write about the Indian experience in English rather than in one of the numerous Indian languages or dialects. Most of these earlier Indian English novelists were writing from within India, portraying everyday experiences. Since the 1980s, however, a new generation of

See also: *Midnight's Children* 300–05 ▪ *Interpreter of Maladies* 338

Indian English novelists has emerged, most of whom have chosen to focus on the themes of postcolonial India, including the impact of imperialism, religious tensions, and the caste system.

Intertwined stories

Salman Rushdie was one of the first of the so-called Indian diasporic novelists – Indian writers living outside India. His Booker Prize-winning *Midnight's Children*, with its blend of Hindu myth, Bombay cinema, magic realism, and hybrid use of English peppered with Indian terms, is the starting point of what has been described as a renaissance in Indian English literature, mainly produced by diasporic authors. Several writers followed Rushdie, including Vikram Seth, whose novel *A Suitable Boy* was published in 1993.

Towns along the river Ganges pulsate with life and colour, providing a vibrant backdrop to the interweaving stories and multiple realities of the India evoked by Seth's narrative.

Epic in scale, *A Suitable Boy* is one of the longest novels in the English language. Set in the early 1950s – soon after India's independence and partition in 1947 – the novel follows the fortunes of four families over a period of 18 months. Three of the families, the Mehras, Chatterjis, and Kapoors – all of whom are middle-class, educated Hindus – are related to one another by marriage. The fourth family, the aristocratic, Muslim Khans, are friends of the Kapoors.

The novel opens in the fictional town of Brahmpur, on the river Ganges between Banares (also known as Varanasi) and Patna, although events also take place in Calcutta, Delhi, and Kanpur. These places are described with immense richness, and often with wit. Seth re-creates, in magnificent, almost photographic, detail the India of the early 1950s, bringing to vivid life the river Ganges, the crowded, bustling streets and markets, the country's extremes of wealth and poverty, and its wonderfully varied landscapes. Central to »

Vikram Seth

The son of a businessman and a judge, Vikram Seth was born in 1952 in Calcutta, India. After leaving the Doon School, he completed his schooling in Tonbridge, England, and went on to Oxford University, where he graduated in Philosophy, Politics, and Economics (PPE). He received a master's degree in economics from Stanford University, USA, and later spent some time in China, where he studied classical Chinese poetry. He now lives in England but keeps close contact with India.

Seth's written works include poetry, a children's book, and three novels. In 2009 he announced that he was working on a sequel to *A Suitable Boy*, entitled *A Suitable Girl*. Initially due to finish the novel in 2013, he commented on BBC's radio programme *Desert Island Discs* in 2012 that the pace of work was slow: "The sound of deadlines pushing past is one of the sounds that authors are most familiar with."

Other key works

1986 *The Golden Gate*
1999 *An Equal Music*
2005 *Two Lives* (biography)

'You too will marry a boy I choose,' said Mrs Rupa Mehra firmly to her younger daughter.
A Suitable Boy

the text is the determination of Mrs Rupa Mehra to arrange the marriage of her younger daughter Lata, a 19-year-old university student, to a "suitable boy".

The personal and political

The novel begins with a wedding: that of Lata's elder sister Savita to Pran Kapoor, a young university professor from a prominent family. Although he suffers from asthma, he qualifies as a "suitable boy". Lata, an independent-minded young woman whose thoughts and actions in many ways mirror the changes occurring in India at the time, has mixed feelings about the marriage of her beloved sister, questioning how a woman can marry a man she does not know.

As the novel progresses, Lata herself falls in love with three young men: Kabir, a Muslim student; Amit, an internationally celebrated poet; and Haresh, a determined businessman in the shoe trade. It is not until the last moment that the reader learns which of the three Lata chooses; significantly, it is a decision that she makes for herself, taking account of her mother's wishes, social realities, and her own feelings about love and passion.

And yet *A Suitable Boy* is much more than just a romantic plot, incorporating numerous subplots, both personal and political, and a large and finely drawn cast of characters. These range from the widowed Mrs Rupa Mehra, with her tireless meddling in the lives of her four children, to the young Muslim idealist Rasheed; from the strong-minded Malati, Lata's best friend, to the young mathematical genius Bhaskar; and from the politician Mahesh Kapoor to the musician Ishaq. Real historical figures, such as India's first prime minister, Jawaharlal Nehru, are also added to the literary mix.

A Suitable Boy provides a detailed account of the social and political events taking place in post-partition India during the formative years of the Nehru period (1947–64). Woven into the text are key issues such as the value of work, the process of change, the injustice of poverty, and the direction being taken by India. It describes the run-up to the post-independence election of 1952, in which the Kapoor family is closely involved. Religious intolerance, in particular Hindu–Muslim tensions, is revealed in the reactions to Lata's love for Kabir and to Pran's younger brother Maan's relationship with a Muslim singer-courtesan, Saeeda Bai; and, more violently, in a near-riot between Hindus and Muslims over plans to erect a Hindu temple near a mosque. The author also depicts the iniquities of the caste

Lata has a tough choice to make: should she choose the Muslim student, the internationally acclaimed poet, or the businessman as her partner? Her plight echoes that of post-partition India: should it opt to overcome religious factionalism, to strive for a sophisticated internationalism, or to settle for economic stability?

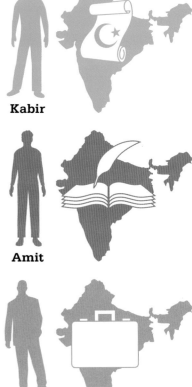

Kabir

Amit

Haresh

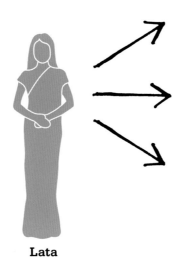

Lata

Marriage lies at the heart of *A Suitable Boy* and is used to explore key issues – from religion, class, gender, and politics to national and personal identity.

compared to Jane Austen – but although *A Suitable Boy*, like Austen's novels, deals with family events and is realistic and perceptive, it is unmistakably an Indian novel, written in English, and a landmark of the genre.

There have been fierce debates concerning the validity of Indian English literature, and in particular a questioning of why leading Indian novelists, most of whom live outside India, should even be writing in English. In Rushdie's words, "the ironic proposition that India's best writing since independence may have been done in the language of the departed imperialists is simply too much for some folks to bear". Nevertheless, the popularity of the Indian English genre continued to grow into the 21st century, with writers such as Arundhati Roy, Jhumpa Lahiri, Amitav Ghosh, and Kiran Desai making significant contributions, either setting their novels in India or focusing on the experience of rootlessness and alienation in the diaspora. ∎

system, poverty, and the status of lower-caste Indians, such as the *jatav*, who scrape their living in the evil-smelling tanneries. Certain parts of the plot revolve around land reforms and the abolition of the *zamindari* system, which aimed to remove property from large aristocratic landholders. The novel explores the roles of women in 1950s India, too, comparing Lata's dependence on her family with the independence of her friend Malati and the Muslim custom of purdah, in which women are segregated and wear form-covering clothes such as the burqa.

Real-life concerns
Unlike Rushdie's magical India, Seth's novel focuses on the matters of real life: work, love, family, the intricacies of lawmaking, political intrigue, the academic world, and religious tensions. These are presented in beautifully written and lyrical prose that is compelling, eminently readable, and often amusing. It presents the English language as it is spoken by the people of India – embellished with scatterings of Hindu and Muslim terms, many of which do not translate into English. The Indian

English novelist Anita Desai has observed that it was only after Rushdie "that Indian writers finally felt capable of using the spoken language, spoken English, the way it's spoken on Indian streets by ordinary people", something that Seth also captures perfectly.

Language of imperialists?
Vikram Seth is a skilled and renowned poet as well as a novelist, so it is perhaps unsurprising that his text includes superbly poetic passages. Many of these draw the reader into the world of Urdu poetry, Indian music and singing (*ghazals*), and myths and legends as sung and played by Saaeda Bai and her musicians. Equally haunting are descriptions of a tiger hunt, the stinking pools of the tanning works, the Indian countryside, and the Kumbh Mela festival. The novel also includes the flippant couplets nonchalantly tossed out by the Chatterjis; and a contents page that comprises 19 rhyming couplets, one for each part of the book.

It took Seth more than eight years to write his monumental novel; it was a huge success and was awarded the Commonwealth Writers' Prize. He has been

They agreed with each other violently and disagreed with each other pleasurably.
A Suitable Boy

IT'S A VERY GREEK IDEA, AND A PROFOUND ONE. BEAUTY IS TERROR
THE SECRET HISTORY (1992), DONNA TARTT

IN CONTEXT

FOCUS
The campus novel

BEFORE
1951 US writer Mary McCarthy's *The Groves of Academe* is published. It is considered one of the first academic or "campus" novels.

1954 The influential book *Lucky Jim*, by English writer Kingsley Amis, develops the campus genre further through a plot that follows a young history lecturer making his way in a post-war world.

1990 The Booker Prize-winning novel *Possession: A Romance*, by English novelist A S Byatt, details a postmodern historical mystery set in an academic world.

AFTER
2000 *The Human Stain* by US writer Philip Roth follows the complex life story of a retired classics professor and the shifting world of US academia.

When US author Donna Tartt (1963–) published her novel *The Secret History*, it was recognized as a striking addition to the campus-novel genre, which it both borrows from and extends. Academic novels developed in the 1950s, when the concerns of post-war society were linked with the literary and cultural debates taking place on Western campuses. These novels, set within the confined space of a university, often satirize academic life and the pretentiouness of scholars.

The allure of civilization

The Secret History follows a group of six Classics students at an elite New England university. Using this setting to focus on various literary and cultural debates, Tartt expands on her 1950s predecessors' use of a university environment to question the role of literature, identity, and the genre itself.

Tartt's novel is an anti-detective story that complicates the 19th-century detective genre. The book opens with a murder-mystery plot, but it is the motive, not the identity of the perpetrator, that mystifies the reader and is gradually revealed as the plot unfolds. Tartt uses the premise of a hidden murder among the six students to explore wider ideas. Borrowing from Greek tragedy, she compels her reader to question whether the "tragic flaw" in character, a feature of that genre, does indeed exist. She explores this question through the plot to interrogate how and why we use the literary past in the present.

A philosophical murder

For Tartt's student characters, the literary is all too real: it is taken to an explicitly literal extreme in the form of a murder that pays homage to the philosophical idea that "Death is the mother of beauty", as one student, Henry, declares. Whether the murder is indeed to be interpreted as a playful and self-conscious literary device that draws from academic theory, or perhaps as a critique of theory itself, is something that Tartt leaves for her reader to decide. ∎

See also: *Oedipus the King* 34–39 ▪ *Disgrace* 322–23

WHAT WE SEE BEFORE US IS JUST ONE TINY PART OF THE WORLD
THE WIND-UP BIRD CHRONICLE (1994–1995), HARUKI MURAKAMI

IN CONTEXT

FOCUS
Writing for the world

BEFORE
1987 The hero of Murakami's *Norwegian Wood*, a nostalgic tale of friendship, love, and loss, is a former college student interested in US literature.

1988 Banana Yashimoto's *Kitchen* tells a wistful story of a young Japanese woman, for whom the consumer opulence of Western-style cooking provides an emotional refuge.

AFTER
1997 Ryu Murakami's *In the Miso Soup* is a crime story set among the hostess bars of Tokyo, with conversational references to real-life Americans such as Whitney Houston and Robert de Niro.

2002 *Kafka on the Shore* shows Murakami exploring metaphysical fantasy – in a Japan where Westernized culture and Shintoism meet.

From the late 20th century, globalization – in particular the spread of US popular culture around the world – has created a forum in which writers have been able to free their fiction of localized traditions, as if writing for a universal readership.

US influences are particularly evident in Japanese culture – stemming, in part, from the US occupation of Japan (1945–52). Japanese author Haruki Murakami (1949–) has a cultural background that seems half American: he translated F Scott Fitzgerald and Truman Capote into Japanese, and ran a jazz club in Tokyo.

East meets West
Murakami's novel *The Wind-Up Bird Chronicle* calls on American influences, as well as cultural motifs from Europe. For example, it begins with its hero, Toru Okada, listening to Rossini while cooking pasta; later in the novel, a baseball bat is used as a weapon. The book itself is a complex quest narrative with its roots in Western culture.

As Orpheus visits the Underworld to bring back Eurydice in Greek myth, so Okada descends into a well to recover his wife Kumiko after she disappears.

Yet this is still a Japanese story at its core. Murakami evokes the alienation of modern urban Japan, while at the same time probing Japanese history. For instance, Lieutenant Mamiya's tales of wartime exploits in Manchuria and a Soviet prison camp address Japan's violent war record. ■

Is it possible … for one human being to achieve perfect understanding of another?
The Wind-Up Bird Chronicle

See also: *Playing for Thrills* 336

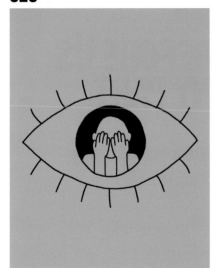

PERHAPS ONLY IN A WORLD OF THE BLIND WILL THINGS BE WHAT THEY TRULY ARE
BLINDNESS (1995), JOSÉ SARAMAGO

IN CONTEXT

FOCUS
Allegorical satire

BEFORE
1605 In *Don Quixote*, Miguel de Cervantes explores the inability to see the world as it really is, in his main character's delusional quest to enact a knight's saga.

1726 Anglo-Irish writer Jonathan Swift's *Gulliver's Travels* exaggerates moral and political corruption in tales of fantastical cultures.

1945 In *Animal Farm,* English author George Orwell traces the parallels between the degeneration of politics in human society and a cast of rebellious farm animals.

AFTER
2008–10 US writer Suzanne Collins publishes *The Hunger Games*, using allegorical satire to indicate the power of media as a political tool in contemporary US society.

José Saramago's harrowing novel *Blindness* (originally published in Portuguese as *Ensaio Sobre a Cegueira*, "Essay on Blindness") is an example of allegorical satire – a type of narrative that has a parallel subtext that is often moral or political in nature. In allegorical satire, events are used explicitly or implicitly as metaphors to ridicule aspects of society, politics, or life. In *Blindness*, the satire is inspired by Portugal's Estado Novo (New State), an authoritarian regime that ruled the country from 1933 to 1974, although the novel's actual settings, characters, and times are left ambiguous. Under scrutiny is the lack of morality, kindness, and empathy typical of any right-wing capitalist society.

What if we were all blind?
The novel describes events after people in a city of an unnamed country start going blind – not a dark blindness, but a milky, pearl-white blindness. The affliction spreads via human contact or

The world of the blind

Society is affected by **metaphorical blindness**: lack of empathy, reason, and morality.

→

Members of society are affected, as a result, by **literal blindness**.

↓

New societies form in blindness, as the old ones descend into darkness.

←

Society seeks to incarcerate, quarantine, and **contain the affected**.

See also: *The Divine Comedy* 62–65 ▪ *The Canterbury Tales* 68–71 ▪ *Don Quixote* 76–81 ▪ *Candide* 96–97 ▪ *Gulliver's Travels* 104 ▪ *Animal Farm* 245 ▪ *Lord of the Flies* 287

Portugal's repressive Estado Novo regime is an unspoken presence in Saramago's text; the book's title and contents gesture to a parallel theme of a dark and sinister political blindness.

presence and is incurable. The government transfers those affected to a guarded asylum, and leaves them to fend for themselves, with food and cleaning equipment as their only aids.

As a form of society, based on solidarity, begins to emerge among the blinded – fuelled by need, survival, and a return of human empathy – we see the main characters grow as members of a community. Saramago describes the physical and psychological struggles of the newly blinded as a parallel to people who have lost sight of reason, humanity, and the very idea of human society: "These blind internees [...] will soon turn into animals, worse still, into blind animals." The arrival of a group of organized blind thugs becomes an added element of oppression, with obvious political connotations

of the violence and terror of a totalitarian regime. Saramago gives his narrative unstoppable force by minimizing punctuation and switching between tenses and perspectives. This creates a sense of being propelled through the story, thus echoing the themes of the narrative.

Blindness and insight
The reader is given an added perspective on the bleak situation through the eyes of the doctor's wife, one of the first internees, but one who feigns blindness to be with her husband. This

device allows for an enhanced understanding of the bonds being created, the habits being abandoned, and the ideologies being formed and re-formed in the story. It is through the doctor's wife that the characters discover one another, and find hope and the strength to survive the white blindness, the cruelty of the thugs, and the harshness of the asylum. It is thanks to her humanity and her empathy – symbols of the type of society towards which people should be striving – that, ultimately, they start to rebuild a life outside the asylum. ▪

José Saramago

José de Sousa Saramago was born in Portugal in 1922, the son of poor rural workers. His parents could not afford to send him to school, so he trained as a mechanic; only later did his talent for writing lead him into work as a translator, journalist, and editor. A politically engaged man, Saramago found that his first novel, *Land of Sin* (*Terra do Pecado*, 1947), was not well received by the conservative Catholic regime of Estado Novo (New State), which blocked the book's production. He resurfaced in 1966 with *Possible Poems*

(*O Poemas Possìveis*) and, after writing more novels, received the Nobel Prize for Literature in 1998. He moved to Spain following the Portuguese government's censorship of one of his books in 1992. He lived there until his death in 2010.

Other key works

1982 *Baltasar and Blimunda*
1984 *The Year of the Death of Ricardo Reis*
1991 *The Gospel According to Jesus Christ*
2004 *Seeing*

ENGLISH IS AN UNFIT MEDIUM FOR THE TRUTH OF SOUTH AFRICA
DISGRACE (1999), J M COETZEE

IN CONTEXT

FOCUS
South African literature

BEFORE
1883 Olive Schreiner explores patriarchal and gender issues against a colonial backdrop in *The Story of an African Farm*.

1948 The bestselling *Cry, the Beloved Country* by Alan Paton exposes South Africa's politics of oppression to the world.

1963–90 Thousands of books are banned as "undesirable" in South Africa.

1991 Writer and activist Nadine Gordimer is awarded the Nobel Prize in Literature.

AFTER
2000 Writer NoZakes Mda experiments with a complex mix of Xhosa history, myth, and colonial conflict in his novel *The Heart of Redness*.

2003 Damon Galgut's *The Good Doctor* picks apart the promise of political change.

An extraordinary canon of literature has evolved in South Africa from a society in which the black majority was oppressed for decades by colonialism and apartheid – a tyrannical system of segregation. Writing during and after apartheid falls very broadly into two camps: authors such as Nobel prizewinner Nadine Gordimer produced complex novels that are a testimony to history, rooted in social realism and the politics of their era. In comparison, J M Coetzee appears almost socially irresponsible in producing texts that "rival history". His stories are characterized by ambiguity and elusiveness, with a

Repentance belongs to another world, to another universe of discourse.
Disgrace

Postmodern preoccupation with the language of their production and the authority of the speaking voice.

Power relations
Coetzee's novel *Disgrace* centres on the downfall of David Lurie, a professor in classics and modern languages who is reduced to teaching "communications". A cipher for the lost certainties of whites from old European stock in the new South Africa, Lurie finds that communication fails him. He cannot engage his students, nor use poetry to seduce Melanie, a student whom he effectively rapes during an affair.

After Lurie is plunged into disgrace and dismissed from his job, the story shifts to the Eastern Cape, where his daughter Lucy runs a smallholding. Lurie sees glimpses of an idealized rural past, but struggles with the changing order between white landowners and their black employees and neighbours. He fills his time helping to dispatch neglected animals in a rural veterinary clinic.

The professor speaks several European languages, but cannot engage with Lucy's neighbour Petrus. "Pressed into the mould

See also: *The Story of an African Farm* 201 ▪ *Cry, the Beloved Country* 286 ▪ *A Dry White Season* 333–34

of English, Petrus's story would come out arthritic, bygone." He has no African words to reason with the three black youths who attack the farm and rape his daughter, nor can he unveil her neighbour's complicity. Later, at a celebration of Petrus's new status as landlord, a guest takes centre stage to narrate in the Xhosa language a future that only the blacks can understand.

An uncertain future

Disgrace, published five years after the first free elections in South Africa, sits in stark contrast to post-apartheid "honeymoon" literature, suffused with the optimism of the new nation. Condemned by some for its violent storyline, the novel is finely balanced in its portrayal of a state of disgrace that has no cultural boundaries. In the end, there is a parity between the attack on Lucy and the professor's sexual abuse of black prostitutes and the student Melanie, who is assumed to be of mixed race. While Lurie, in his arrogance, refuses to speak at his hearing, Lucy's silence about her ordeal suggests a realization that life has to be stripped back to the basics because there are no words available to repair or heal. ▪

J M Coetzee

Novelist, linguist, essayist, and translator John Michael Coetzee was born in 1940 to English-speaking Afrikaner parents. Coetzee spent his early life in Cape Town and Worcester in the Western Cape. After graduating in the 1960s, he worked as a computer programmer in London. He has a PhD in English, Linguistics, and Germanic languages from the University of Texas.

From 1972 Coetzee held posts at the University of Cape Town, finishing in 2000 as Distinguished Professor of Literature, and taught frequently in the USA. He has won a raft of literary awards, including the Booker Prize (twice) and the 2003 Nobel Prize in Literature. Coetzee now lives in South Australia and is an advocate for animal rights.

Other key works

1977 *In the Heart of the Country*
1980 *Waiting for the Barbarians*
1983 *Life & Times of Michael K*
1986 *Foe*
1990 *Age of Iron*

Professional disgrace
The professor's faltering academic career is completely destroyed by his sexual harassment of a student.

Sexual disgrace
Lurie's sex life with prostitutes and sordid casual seductions contrasts with the Byronic romances that haunt his imagination.

The novel's title
reaches further than the disgrace of the unrepentant David Lurie. Inhuman acts, shame, and humiliation threaten to engulf a new and fragile society.

Treatment of animals
Shameful animal neglect and maltreatment – a common theme in Coetzee's novels – is reflected in the grim work of the veterinary clinic.

Racial violence
Lucy's rape and the ongoing coercion and threat to her safety typify the tension between black people and the wealthy white minority.

Apartheid
The many strands of disgrace underpinning the novel suggest the wider disgrace of South Africa's history of colonialism and apartheid.

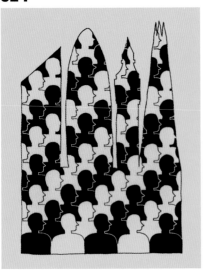

EVERY MOMENT HAPPENS TWICE: INSIDE AND OUTSIDE, AND THEY ARE TWO DIFFERENT HISTORIES
WHITE TEETH (2000), ZADIE SMITH

IN CONTEXT

FOCUS
Multiculturalism

BEFORE
1979 A Black Power group takes over the basement in *Moses Ascending*, Trinidad-born Sam Selvon's tales of a West Indian landlord in London.

1987 Michael Ondaatje, a Sri Lanka-born Canadian writer, weaves native cultures into rich storytelling about the lives of immigrant labourers in Toronto in *In the Skin of a Lion*.

1991 Renan Demirkan's semi-autobiographical account of conflicting loyalties in a Turkish family in Germany, *Schwarzer Tee mit drei Stuck Zucker* ("Black Tea with Three Sugars"), becomes a bestseller.

AFTER
2004 *Small Island*, English author Andrea Levy's story of the lives of two couples, sheds light on the migrant experience in post-war Britain.

Immigration has been a major part of the cultural fabric of the USA, Canada, and the UK for generations, but recent decades have seen a surge of new writing that reflects both the diversity of their populations and the ubiquity of English. The need to assimilate into a new culture tends to suppress migrant voices, so it is often the second generation in immigrant families who are strongly motivated to write stories that reflect the fusion of their cultures. This in part explains the slower emergence of multicultural writing in the rest of Europe and around the world, but as other nations become more diverse, new voices start to be

Do you think anybody is English? Really English? It's a fairy-tale!
White Teeth

heard. In Germany, for instance, Renan Demirkan has paved the way for Turkish German writing.

In the UK, multicultural literature goes back to major waves of immigration from the Commonwealth in the 1950s, and often brings a troubled, xenophobic space into sharp focus, revealing the lives of people of multiple ethnic groups in major cities. As elsewhere, many mixed-race and second-generation immigrant authors penned first novels that dwell on the integration of diaspora communities. Zadie Smith's award-winning book *White Teeth* offers a fresh, youthful perspective on the complex inheritance of multicultural families in North London.

Melting-pot Britain
White Teeth stretches back to the last days of World War II, when the English white working-class Archie Jones is paired with a Bangladeshi Muslim wireless engineer called Samad Iqbal in a British Army tank unit in Greece. The friendship, crossing class and colour lines, continues after the war. The bond is cemented by long afternoons in an Arab-run Irish pub, marital discord, and late-in-life fatherhood

See also: *Cry, the Beloved Country* 286 ▪ *A House for Mr Biswas* 289 ▪ *Interpreter of Maladies* 338 ▪ *Life of Pi* 338 ▪ *The Kite Runner* 338 ▪ *Half of a Yellow Sun* 339

In *White Teeth*, the network of relationships among whites, first-generation immigrants, and their British-born children reflects the changing nature of British society.

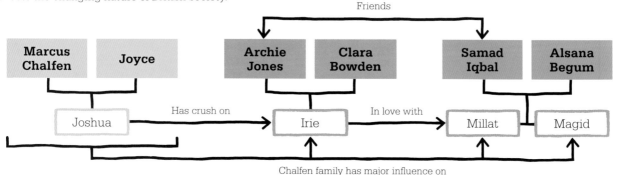

for both men. Samad has twin boys, Magid and Millat, through his arranged marriage with Alsana; Archie and his Jamaican-born wife Clara have a daughter named Irie.

Samad, now a "curry shifter" in a local restaurant, decides to send his son Magid back to Bangladesh to have him raised with a respect for his Muslim heritage; but when Magid returns years later, it is as a secular scientist. By ironic contrast, his twin, wild-child Millat, joins a Muslim fundamentalist group. Irie is drawn to her mother's homeland through her grandmother. Millat, Magid, and Irie struggle, as their parents do, with the feeling that they belong nowhere, in contrast to those that have lived in Britain for generations and enjoy the luxury of history and entitlement. "There was England, a gigantic mirror, and there was Irie, without reflection."

Smith has an ear for dialogue, and eyes everywhere – cataloguing assaults on immigrant communities, comprehensive schools awash with hash, and the chattering middle classes – as epitomized by the intellectual white Chalfen family, who exert an inexorable influence on Irie, Millat, and Magid.

Set in part during the Thatcher years – the 1980s – the book is dotted with cultural references, from Salman Rushdie's *fatwa* to street crews in Nike gear. Smith has criticized her undergraduate novel, but it remains a feisty chronicle of a time that demanded new definitions of what it was to be British. ▪

Zadie Smith

Zadie Smith was born in North London in 1975 to an English father and a Jamaican mother. Originally named Sadie, she changed her name to Zadie aged 14. Smith wrote her acclaimed first novel *White Teeth* during her final year at King's College, Cambridge. Moving to the USA, she studied at Harvard and taught creative writing at Columbia University School of Fine Arts before taking her current post at New York University. She divides her time between New York and London, with her husband, writer Nick Laird, and their two children.

Smith has received nearly 20 nominations and awards for her writing. In recent years she has branched into short stories and critical essays. In an article in *The Guardian* newspaper she was asked to give her 10 golden rules for writing fiction, which included: "Tell the truth through whichever veil comes to hand – but tell it."

Other key works

2002 *The Autograph Man*
2005 *On Beauty*
2012 *NW*

THE BEST WAY OF KEEPING A SECRET IS TO PRETEND THERE ISN'T ONE

THE BLIND ASSASSIN (2000), MARGARET ATWOOD

IN CONTEXT

FOCUS
Southern Ontario Gothic

BEFORE
1832 Considered the first Canadian novel, *Wacousta* by John Richardson is full of menace and Gothic terror.

1967 Timothy Findley's *The Last of the Crazy People* is published. Five years later the author coins the term Southern Ontario Gothic to describe his novel.

1970 Robertson Davies' *Fifth Business* is an early example of Southern Ontario Gothic, looking at the dark underbelly of an Ontario community.

AFTER
2009 Intrigue, murder, and fear infuse Alice Munro's Gothic short-story collection *Too Much Happiness*.

2013 Hilary Scharper's *Perdita*, which she describes as "Ecogothic", is a modern Canadian ghost story.

The Gothic fiction of the 18th and 19th centuries typically featured such elements as haunted castles, tyrannical villains, endangered heroines, mysteries, and ghosts. In the late 20th century, Canada, and Southern Ontario in particular, developed its own take on this tradition. Novelists including Alice Munro, Robertson Davies, and Margaret Atwood appropriated aspects of Gothic fiction such as the supernatural and the grotesque, and the genre's dark imagery, and applied them to contemporary Canadian life. Frequently, such literature attempts to make sense of Canadian national identity in a

Darkness moved closer …
Back into the long
shadows cast by Laura.
The Blind Assassin

postcolonial context, and can be seen as a reflection of settlers' anxieties about their history.

Narrative complexity
Margaret Atwood relocates the fascination with fear and terror that fed the European Gothic to her own home territory, exploring the darker side of human nature and the destructive potential of buried secrets. Her book *The Blind Assassin* is a notable example of Southern Ontario Gothic, playing on notions of sacrifice and betrayal, truth and lies, conspiracy and romance, and the boundaries between the living and the dead.

The novel is a multi-layered story told through the eyes of 83-year-old Iris Chase Griffen, writing her memoirs in the form of a letter to her granddaughter. Within the story of Iris's life another novel is nestled, also called *The Blind Assassin*, about two lovers, and purportedly written by Iris's sister, Laura. And within that novel is yet another story, a pulp science-fiction tale related by the man in Laura's novel. All these stories are punctuated by newspaper reports that add a further, supposedly factual, dimension to the narrative.

See also: *Frankenstein* 120–21 ▪ *Dracula* 195 ▪ *Wuthering Heights* 132–37 ▪ *The Handmaid's Tale* 335 ▪ *Selected Stories* (Alice Munro) 337

The main story, recounted in Iris's memoir, revolves around Laura and Iris Chase in the 1920s and '30s. Gothic motifs are updated: the haunted castle becomes Iris's family home, Avilion, a mansion built by her rich grandfather, complete with attics and turrets; there is a cruel male villain in Iris's domineering husband, Richard; and Iris and Laura themselves are versions of the victimized heroine.

Haunted by the real

The novel is realistic in tone, yet symbolically the supernatural is never far away. The structure of flashbacks means that characters we know to be dead appear almost as if they are ghosts speaking to the present from the past. Laura, whose suicide the reader learns about in the very first sentence, haunts Iris through memories and secrets that are slowly uncovered.

Southern Ontario is itself a dark and brooding character in the book. It may be likened to the underworld of classical literature: ominous stretches of water must be crossed in order to enter it, and it has its own villainous gatekeeper, in the form of Richard. The protagonists wander here in search of meaning.

Overall, Atwood's reworking of Gothic tropes and her skilful interweaving of different genres creates a novel in which, despite the darkness, each element illuminates the whole. ∎

The structure of *The Blind Assassin*, with its stories within stories and multiple narrators, echoes Gothic literature, while the third tale – although set on the planet Zycron – contains the familiar Gothic elements of romance, betrayal, and murder.

The first narrative is Iris Chase Griffen's memoirs, in which she reconstructs the past and re-evaluates her own life and that of sister.

The second narrative is a novel also called *The Blind Assassin*, ostensibly by Laura Chase, which tells the story of a political fugitive and his socialite lover.

The third narrative is a dark science-fiction fantasy about a blind assassin and a mute sacrificial virgin.

Margaret Atwood

The Canadian novelist, poet, and essayist Margaret Atwood was born in 1939 in Ottawa, Ontario. For much of her childhood, she spent half the year in the wilderness, where her father studied insects. During this time she would write poems, plays, and comics, and while still at school she decided to become a writer. The US writer Edgar Allan Poe was among her favourite authors and his dark influence can be seen in much of her fiction.

Atwood's first publication was a collection of poems in 1966, but she is best known as a novelist. Her first novel to be published was *The Edible Woman* in 1969. Her passion for environmental issues and human rights comes through in her dystopian novels such as *The Handmaid's Tale* and the trilogy begun with *Oryx and Crake*. She has received many distinguished literary prizes, including the Booker Prize for *The Blind Assassin*.

Other key works

1985 *The Handmaid's Tale*
1988 *Cat's Eye*
1996 *Alias Grace*
2003 *Oryx and Crake*

THERE WAS SOMETHING HIS FAMILY WANTED TO FORGET

THE CORRECTIONS (2001), JONATHAN FRANZEN

IN CONTEXT

FOCUS
Dysfunction in the modern family

BEFORE
1951 In J D Salinger's *The Catcher in the Rye*, Holden Caulfield is lonely and alienated yet consumed by thoughts of his family.

1960 The first novel of John Updike's "Rabbit" series is published, dramatizing family turmoil in contemporary USA.

1993 In *The Virgin Suicides*, Jeffrey Eugenides tracks the unexplained suicides of five teenage sisters.

AFTER
2003 In *We Need to Talk about Kevin*, Lionel Shriver tackles the subject of parenting a child who becomes a mass murderer.

2013 Theo Decker, the narrator of Donna Tartt's *The Goldfinch*, describes a family shattered by alcoholism and loss.

The title of Jonathan Franzen's *The Corrections* echoes that of William Gaddis's *The Recognitions* (1955), which features a restless son searching for authenticity and contemplating his relationship with his father, who is losing his mind. As in *The Corrections*, the scope of *The Recognitions* extends to a wider cast of characters and tells the story of a single family by weaving narrative threads to garner multiple viewpoints. Since the late 20th century, the theme of the dysfunctional family has often been at the heart of work by great US male novelists, such as John Updike, Philip Roth, and Don DeLillo. As well as Gaddis, many of them would likely feature in Franzen's literary ancestry.

The Corrections tells the stories of the Lamberts: Alfred and Enid and their adult children Gary, Chip, and Denise. This is a family tested by individual needs set against differing notions of the familial unit, values, and rights – all played out against a backdrop of a US economy dominated by capitalist-driven high-tech and financial sectors. As the saga unfolds, the text achieves acute political and social insights, touching on wide-ranging themes, from financial misdoings and gun death to food and children's literature.

Suspense and narrative drive come from the family's attempt to have "one last" Christmas together and the unfolding brutality of degenerative disease. The personal lives of the main characters are all marked by instability, whether it be professional, romantic, or mental.

Generational change

Through his depiction of two generations, Franzen is able to reflect societal change over the period of a lifetime. Alfred, the repressed patriarch, identifies with

He became agitated whenever they were going to see their children.
The Corrections

See also: *The Catcher in the Rye* 256–57 ▪ *White Teeth* 324–25

Emotional
There are shifts in the character traits of damaged individuals, leading to personal growth.

Financial
Seeking to profit from the anticipated wonder-drug Corecktall, Gary fails to notice gradual changes in the investment markets.

Parental
Discipline is used to stifle the spontaneous affection that the children naturally demonstrate for their father, Alfred.

Types of correction
The Corrections reveals a network of associations relating to the key word of the title, unfolding a plot that poses profound questions about the extent to which we are able fix our selves and our lives.

Pharmaceutical
A pill, Corecktall, that is a symbol of vain hope, doing "nothing and everything".

Textual
Changes that Chip needs to make to his screenplay.

Family rumours
Long-held myths, built from incomplete information, are dispelled and truths revealed.

Jonathan Franzen

Jonathan Earl Franzen's father was a civil engineer and his mother, Irene, was a "homemaker" (not unlike the Lamberts in *The Corrections*). Franzen grew up in Chicago and graduated in German from Swarthmore College, Pennsylvania, USA, in 1981.

He married Valerie Cornell at the age of 23; they divorced 14 years later. He is now in a relationship with the writer Kathryn Chetkovich, and lives in New York and California.

In 2001 Franzen sparked a feud with US talk-show host Oprah Winfrey when he voiced unease at the choice of *The Corrections* for her book club, fearing that men would be put off reading it. He continues to write on a range of topics, including the pitiful state of Europe and the impermanence of e-books.

Franzen won the National Book Award for Fiction in 2001 with *The Corrections*, which was also a finalist for the Pulitzer Prize for Fiction.

Other key works

1992 *Strong Motion*
2006 *The Discomfort Zone: A Personal History* (essays)
2010 *Freedom*

a past order. His sections are punctuated with quotes from Schopenhauer and illuminated by recalled scenes from Midwest America in the mid-20th century, when he worked as a rail engineer. Gary, Chip, and Denise inhabit a much less tractable world; their experiences distil the pressures and vicissitudes of the increasingly troubled late 20th century.

Genetics aside, there is a common link between all of them: despite neuroses and flaws, they all have hope of improvement. Even Alfred, unwavering in his self-belief and certainty that family ties and emotion have to be sacrificed to fully contribute to civilization, reflects, while Enid is pregnant with their youngest child, Denise: "A last child was a last opportunity to learn from one's mistakes and make corrections, and he resolved to seize this opportunity."

Franzen later published a memoir called *The Discomfort Zone*, which included an intimate exploration of the impact of his mother's death. This eclectic collection reveals that the notion of family still dominates his work. ▪

IT ALL STEMS FROM THE SAME NIGHTMARE, THE ONE WE CREATED TOGETHER
THE GUEST (2001), HWANG SOK-YONG

IN CONTEXT

FOCUS
The 38th parallel

BEFORE
1893 Literature in Korea emerges from the cultural shadow cast by classical Chinese literature. The first Western work of fiction printed in Korean is John Bunyan's *The Pilgrim's Progress*, which precedes even a translation of the Bible, published in 1910.

1985 Hwang Sok-yong's *The Shadow of Arms* is an account of black-market trading during the war in Vietnam (another East Asian country split between north and south).

1964–94 Park Kyong-ni's epic 16-volume historical novel *The Land* depicts the struggles of Koreans under Japanese oppression.

AFTER
2005 North and South Korean authors attend a joint literary congress for the first time.

After Japan's surrender at the end of World War II, a line of latitude that crosses the Korean Peninsula, the 38th parallel, was chosen as the dividing line between Soviet and US occupation zones, and is still roughly in effect as the border between North and South Korea.

The post-war generation of South Korean writers embraced a traditionalist movement that looked back at an idealized past. But this nostalgia was rejected by the writers of the 1960s, who sought to engage with the psychological damage of recent Korean history: the Japanese occupation (1910–45), the Korean War (1950–53), and communist rule in the north.

Evils from abroad

In his novel *The Guest*, Hwang Sok-yong (1943–) deals with the real-life Korean War massacre at Sinchon, in what is now North Korea. The novel's Korean-born protagonist, a Christian minister living in the USA, returns to visit the site, along with the ghost of his

Ever since we were children we have known that the Guest is a Western disease.
The Guest

brother. He discovers the truth of the atrocity: it was not perpetrated by US forces, but was a result of fighting between Christian and communist Koreans themselves.

Christianity and communism are seen as foreign "guests" that have turned Koreans against each other; and the Korean word for guest refers also to smallpox, another plague from the West that ravaged the country. The novel's 12-part structure mirrors that of a shamanistic ritual to cure smallpox, known as a "guest exorcism". ∎

See also: *The Heartless* 241

I REGRET THAT IT TAKES A LIFE TO LEARN HOW TO LIVE

EXTREMELY LOUD AND INCREDIBLY CLOSE (2005), JONATHAN SAFRAN FOER

IN CONTEXT

FOCUS
Post 9/11 America

BEFORE
2001 Jonathan Franzen's
The Corrections, published
on 11 September 2001,
foreshadows the concerns
of US literature after 9/11.

AFTER
2007 Don DeLillo's *Falling
Man* is published, detailing
the effects of the World Trade
Center attacks on the life of a
middle-class survivor.

2007 Mohsin Hamid's *The
Reluctant Fundamentalist*
depicts the way in which
a middle-class Pakistani-
American financial analyst is
drawn towards radicalization.

2013 Thomas Pynchon's
Bleeding Edge is published,
a lively novel touching on
financial malfeasance during
the dotcom boom, in which
9/11 takes place more than
halfway through the story.

The terrorist attacks in New York and Washington on 11 September 2001 caused a huge change in the political and cultural landscape, which literature was sure to tackle sooner or later. But at first many authors struggled with its enormity; after the attacks, leading novelists Martin Amis, Ian McEwan, and Don DeLillo all commented on how the nature of their job felt as if it had changed and become more difficult in ways they did not yet understand. Authors chose different methods to try to make sense of the topic.

A new way of looking

In *Extremely Loud and Incredibly Close*, Jonathan Safran Foer (1977–) explores the after-effects of 9/11 through a young boy, Oskar Schell. Nine months after the attacks, in which his father was killed, Oskar suffers from a depression, which he says is like wearing "heavy boots". Finding a key left by his father, he embarks on a quest around New York to discover what the key is for, meeting many curious characters

along the way. The novel contains unusual stylistic choices: pages are black, or several in a row are left white; words are circled in red; and many photographs appear – of objects, famous personalities, and the Twin Towers themselves. Through such techniques, Safran Foer tries to make us look afresh at 9/11, to find a new way of seeing something so terrible that has also become so familiar. ∎

There are so many times when you need to make a quick escape, but humans don't have their own wings, or not yet, anyway.
Extremely Loud and Incredibly Close

See also: *The Corrections* 328–29 ∎ *The Reluctant Fundamentalist* 339

FURTHER READING

L'HOMME RAPAILLÉ
(1970), GASTON MIRON

The masterwork of Gaston Miron (1928–96) – writer, poet, publisher, and luminary of Quebec literature – *L'homme rapaillé* ("The Man Made Whole") is a major selection of the author's poems. Lyric love poetry sits side by side with explorations of the political and social predicament of the French-speaking Québecois population in Canada – Miron called for separatism, and his poems are a celebration of Quebec's language, history, and people. He also saw poetry as an endless process of self-discovery, hence his refusal to authorize a definitive collection.

FEAR AND LOATHING IN LAS VEGAS
(1972), HUNTER S THOMPSON

Mixing autobiographical elements and surreal invention, this influential work, subtitled *A Savage Journey to the Heart of the American Dream*, describes journalist Raoul Duke's long weekend with his Samoan attorney Dr Gonzo to report on a motorcycle race, along with a visit to a narcotics officers' convention. US writer Thompson (1937–2005) – for whom Raoul Duke was an author surrogate, a character based on and speaking for the author – used this narrative framework to critique the failure of 1960s' counterculture, such as the reliance on drugs. The trip turns into a psychedelic odyssey of excess, comic yet brutal, with drugs consumed in such quantities that at one point people appear as giant reptiles. Thompson blends fact and fiction using the journalistic mode he pioneered, which came to be known as "Gonzo journalism" after the book's fictional attorney.

CRASH
(1973), J G BALLARD

Depicting the dark side of our fascination with speed, *Crash* is a controversial novel about car-crash sexual fetishism and "symphorophilia" (being aroused by disasters or accidents); its shock value is typical of science-fiction writer Ballard. The protagonist is Dr Robert Vaughan, a TV scientist and "nightmare angel of the highways", whose fantasy is to die in a collision with movie star Elizabeth Taylor. Unflinching in showing a fusion of sex and death, the text paints a dystopian picture of the close co-existence between humans and machines in a high-tech future world. People use technology and technology, in a sense, uses people, to the point that machines become an intermediary in human relations.

HISTORY
(1974), ELSA MORANTE

Morante (1912–85) and her husband Alberto Moravia, both half-Jewish Italians, hid from persecution during World War II in the mountains south of Rome. Her experiences were reflected 30 years later in her most famous novel, *History*, which traces the impact of politics and conflict on local farming communities in the countryside around Rome. The central character is Ida Mancuso, a widowed schoolteacher whose prime concern is the survival of her son, the offspring of a rape. A major theme is the extra challenges war brings to the poor, already familiar with hardship even in peacetime.

J G Ballard

An exponent of the New Wave of science fiction, J G Ballard specialized in depicting futuristic dystopias, although one of his most popular novels, *Empire of the Sun*, is more conventional. Ballard was born in 1930 in Shanghai, China. As a teenager he spent two years of the war interned by the Japanese. He studied medicine (at King's College, Cambridge), with the aim of training as a psychiatrist, but in 1951, during the second year of his studies, he won a short-story competition. He moved to London to study literature later the same year. His first fiction was influenced by psychoanalysis and surrealist art. Working as a copywriter and encyclopedia salesman before joining the Royal Air Force, he became a full-time writer from 1962. Ballard died in 2009, aged 78, in London.

Key works

1971 *Vermilion Sands*
1973 *Crash* (see above)
1991 *The Kindness of Women*

THE AESTHETICS OF RESISTANCE
(1975–1981), PETER WEISS

A three-volume historical novel dealing with the fight against the Nazis by left-wing students in Berlin, as well as charting anti-fascist movements elsewhere in Europe, *The Aesthetics of Resistance* proposes that the model for political resistance is to be found in the stand taken by the artist. The title of this highly acclaimed work refers to its meditations on painting, sculpture, and literature. Its author Weiss (1916–82), German-born but with Swedish nationality, was also a dramatist, painter, and film-maker.

ROOTS
(1976), ALEX HALEY

Beginning in the 18th century with the semi-fictional story of a teenage African boy who is kidnapped and sold into slavery in the American South, *Roots* traces the lives of the next six generations, culminating with US writer Haley (1921–92), who undertook a decade of extensive research into his own ancestry. A major theme is the triumph of

Through this flesh, which is us, we are you, and you are us!
Roots
Alex Haley

the human spirit over oppression. The book, and the television series based upon it, led to a surge of interest in African-American history and genealogy.

LIFE A USER'S MANUAL
(1978), GEORGES PEREC

Focusing on the inhabitants of a Paris apartment building, *Life A User's Manual*, by Frenchman Perec (1936–82) is a fictional web whose main thread is a resident's project to paint 500 watercolours of the places he visits, have them turned into jigsaws that he must solve on his return to Paris, before returning each image to the place it depicts. His art teacher – a fellow resident – plans to paint the lives of all the tenants. Perec was a member of the Oulipo group, who together practised writing under a set of constraining principles, and was fascinated by literary playfulness.

THE BLOODY CHAMBER AND OTHER STORIES
(1979), ANGELA CARTER

Author of "magical realist" tales, Angela Carter based all ten stories in her influential work *The Bloody Chamber and Other Stories* on folktales, including Little Red Riding Hood, Beauty and the Beast, and Puss in Boots. The psychological themes underlying the original narratives are intensified and modernized, although without any loss of their inherent Gothic folklore atmosphere. Rape, incest, murder, torture, and cannibalism all feature, showing the dark side of humanity. Stereotypes of feminity, including the innocence of girlhood and the notion of a happy marriage, are

Angela Carter

Known for fiction that fused feminism and magical realism, Angela Carter was born in 1940, in Eastbourne, England, and studied English at Bristol University. In 1969 she left her husband and spent two years in Tokyo, where she claims to have learned her feminist principles. She was writer in residence in the 1970s and '80s at various UK universities, and also taught in the USA and Australia. Her *Nights at the Circus* was a joint winner of the James Tait Black Memorial Prize in 1984. Carter was also a journalist and worked in radio and cinema. She died in 1992 in London, aged 51.

Key works

1967 *The Magic Toyshop*
1979 *The Bloody Chamber and Other Stories* (see left, below)
1984 *Nights at the Circus*

each subversively reinterpreted. Metamorphosis plays a significant part in these stories, both in the form of magic (such as men turned into wolves), and also in physical and moral transformations – for instance, with reference to menstruation and deception.

A DRY WHITE SEASON
(1979), ANDRÉ BRINK

The underlying metaphor of *A Dry White Season* is the equation of climatic and moral drought. This acclaimed novel is set in Afrikaner South Africa just before the political changes took place that overturned apartheid and brought renewal to

Milan Kundera

Born in Brno, Czechoslovakia, in 1929, Kundera studied music as a child and much of his work bears a musical signature. He studied literature and then film in Prague, becoming a lecturer after graduating. Initially a member of the Czech Communist Party, he was barred following the Soviet takeover of 1968, losing his teaching positions. Kundera emigrated to France in 1975 and has lived there ever since, taking citizenship in 1981. He labels himself as a novelist, although his works skilfully blend the philosophical, ironic, political, comedic, and erotic.

Key works

1967 *The Joke*
1979 *The Book of Laughter and Forgetting*
1984 *The Unbearable Lightness of Being* (see right)

the country. Through its protagonist, a white, male, mild-mannered schoolteacher, author André Brink (1935–2015) – himself a white South African – explores racial intolerance and the price for taking a principled stand against an unjust system.

SO LONG A LETTER
(1979), MARIAMA BÂ

Written in French by Senegalese writer Mariama Bâ (1929–81), *So Long a Letter* captures the feelings of a recently widowed Muslim schoolteacher. After spending the last four years of her marriage emotionally abandoned, she now has to share grieving for her late husband with his second, younger wife. The form of the novel is a letter written by the widow to her friend, an émigré to the USA. Personal and social oppression are seen as two sides of the experience of many women in Senegalese society.

THE HOUSE OF THE SPIRITS
(1982), ISABEL ALLENDE

The House of The Spirits was the first – and most successful – novel of Chilean-American writer Isabel Allende (1942–), the granddaughter of former socialist president of Chile Salvador Allende, who was deposed in a coup that features in the novel. The book began life as a letter to her 100-year-old grandfather and turned into a complex, epic saga tracing three generations of family life, against a background of social and political turbulence in an unnamed country (recognizably Chile). The book has elements of magical realism: one of the two sisters, Clara, possesses powers of telekinesis and clairvoyance, which she consciously develops – spirits

… I wait for better times to come, while I carry this child in my womb, the daughter of so many rapes or perhaps of Miguel, but above all, my own daughter …
The House of the Spirits
Isabel Allende

visit her house in abundance. Allende depicts love, betrayal, vengeance, and ambition in a country torn apart, but offering possible salvation in the prospects of the female blood-line.

THE UNBEARABLE LIGHTNESS OF BEING
(1984), MILAN KUNDERA

Set around the Prague Spring of 1968, a brief period of political reform in Soviet Czechoslovakia, *The Unbearable Lightness of Being* is Kundera's most famous work. The title refers to a philosophical dilemma: Friedrich Nietzsche's idea of eternal return, or heaviness, as opposed to the ancient Greek philosopher Parmenides' notion of life as light. It tells of a surgeon who pursues his belief in "lightness" through a promiscuous love life, which also serves as a distraction from his country's fragile and unstable politics. He falls in love with a waitress and marries her, but cannot give up his mistresses. Kundera asks whether life can have weight, or meaning, since return to the past is impossible.

NEUROMANCER
(1984), WILLIAM GIBSON

One of the earliest and most influential works of "cyberpunk" – a science-fiction subgenre usually featuring an antihero in a dystopian high-tech future – *Neuromancer* by American-Canadian author Gibson (1948–) tells of a damaged, suicidal computer hacker. Having been injected with a Russian toxin that prevents him from accessing cyberspace, he is commissioned by an enigmatic employer to do a special job; being cured will be his pay-off. The book combines a futuristic vision with elements of hard-boiled noir.

THE LOVER
(1984), MARGUERITE DURAS

Set in French Indochina in the 1930s, *The Lover* draws upon the real-life experiences of its French author, Marguerite Duras (1914–96). It details the intense affair between a 15-year-old girl from a poor family and a wealthy Chinese man of 27, yet beyond this it is also concerned with female empowerment, the relationship between mother and daughter, emerging adolescence,

Don DeLillo

Born in New York City in 1936, Don DeLillo garnered a cult following with his early works, entering the mainstream with *White Noise*. Growing up in an Italian Catholic family in the Bronx, he discovered a thirst for reading during a summer job as a parking attendant. He worked as an advertising copywriter after graduating in Communications Arts in 1958 but, disillusioned with the job, he quit in 1964 in order to write fiction. DeLillo's novels have been described as postmodern in tone and focus on the USA's material excess and empty culture as recurring themes.

Key works

1985 *White Noise* (see right)
1988 *Libra*
1991 *Mao II*
1997 *Underworld*
2011 *The Angel Esmeralda*

and the taboos that surround foreignness and colonialism. Alternating between first- and third-person narration and present and past tense, the novel uses a spare, poetic prose style.

THE HANDMAID'S TALE
(1985), MARGARET ATWOOD

A dystopian vision of the near future, *The Handmaid's Tale* by Canadian writer Atwood (see p.327) depicts a US in which the establishment of a Christian theocracy has led to the loss of women's freedoms. Caste and class become organizing principles of society, allowing Atwood to comment on present-day inequalities. The narrator is Offred, a "handmaid" – a concubine for reproductive purposes in an era of rampant sexually transmitted diseases. Her master develops feelings for her and gives her privileges, as well as access to some of the regime's secrets. She later becomes implicated in a growing resistance movement. The power of this highly controversial work of fiction comes from its devastating critique of patriarchy by exaggeration of its features.

LOVE IN THE TIME OF CHOLERA
(1985), GABRIEL GARCÍA MÁRQUEZ

A tender exploration of love's difficulties and ambiguities, *Love in the Time of Cholera* by Nobel Prize-winning Colombian novelist Márquez (see p.282) deftly navigates the twists and turns of human feeling. Two versions of love are presented, each enshrined in a male character: one passionate, and the other pragmatic. The

> … she would not bury herself alive inside these four walls to sew her shroud, as native widows were expected to do.
>
> **Love in the Time of Cholera**
> **Gabriel García Márquez**

passionate one, Florentino Ariza, proposes to his youthful sweetheart 50 years after first declaring his love and being rejected in favour of Dr Juvenal Urbino, the pragmatist. A central question in the book is, which kind of love is likelier to bring happiness? Cholera features literally in the narrative, but also serves as an imaginative analogy for infatuation. Other themes in the work include acceptance of ageing and the continuation of romantic love among the elderly, even as the body grows more infirm.

WHITE NOISE
(1985), DON DELILLO

In his bestselling novel *White Noise*, author and playwright Don DeLillo tells of how the chair of Hitler Studies at a US university is forced to confront his own mortality after a chemical spill creates an "Airborne Toxic Event". The book is a darkly amusing examination of consumerism, intellectual pretensions within academia, and the dominance of the media. It also examines cohesion, trust, and love within the family unit – which is described as the "cradle of the world's misinformation".

THE NEW YORK TRILOGY
(1985–1986; 1987), PAUL AUSTER

Auster plays with identity, illusion, and the absurd in his three hugely successful interlocking novels: *City of Glass*, *Ghosts*, and *The Locked Room*. This is film-noirish crime fiction, with elements of postmodern experimentalism. The links between an author and his or her subject are teasingly explored: in the first book the protagonist is a writer of detective stories who is caught in complications after being

Paul Auster

Novelist, essayist, translator, and poet, Auster primarily writes about ideas of the self, identity, and meaning – and sometimes the author himself features in his books. Born in 1947 in Newark, New Jersey, Auster moved to Paris in 1970 to translate contemporary French literature. Returning to the USA four years later, he continued his translation work, wrote poetry, and began writing a series of existentialist mystery novels, which were collected as *The New York Trilogy*. Auster has also written screenplays, two of which became films that he directed himself.

Key works

1982 *The Invention of Solitude*
1985–87 *The New York Trilogy* (see above)
1990 *The Music of Chance*
2005 *The Brooklyn Follies*

mistaken for a private eye; in the last, an author who is suffering from writer's block obsessively tries to track down a successful novelist who has disappeared. In immersing themselves in writing fiction, letters, poems, or reports, the characters become alienated from reality. A major theme running through the trilogy is the operation of chance and coincidence in our lives.

THE SATANIC VERSES
(1988), SALMAN RUSHDIE

In this deeply controversial book, two Indian survivors of a terrorist attack on a jet bound for London become symbols of the angelic and the wicked, and experience miraculous transformations. The novel's title, *The Satanic Verses*, refers to passages in the holy book of Islam, the Qu'ran, that allow intercessory prayers to pagan deities. British-Indian author Salman Rushdie (see p.302) was subjected to a *fatwa* (death order) by the Supreme Leader of Iran for allegedly blaspheming against Muhammad – one of the characters is partly modelled on the Prophet.

PLAYING FOR THRILLS
(1989), WANG SHUO

Wang Shuo (1958–) is a Chinese writer working in the "hooligan" style, typified by using Beijing dialect to show mocking indifference to establishment values. His much celebrated *Playing for Thrills* is a satirical novel of urban alienation, centred on a murder. It is narrated by the chief suspect, Fang Yan, a man who enjoys card-playing, drinking, and womanizing. Along with its "tough-guy" protagonist, the book

is populated by criminal and low-life characters, and is reminiscent of hard-boiled detective fiction.

THE ENGLISH PATIENT
(1992), MICHAEL ONDAATJE

In his Booker Prize-winning *The English Patient*, Sri-Lanka born Canadian author Michael Ondaatje (1943–) shows how the lives of four characters intersect in an Italian villa in 1945. A nurse, a thief, and a Sikh sapper are preoccupied by a plane-crash victim who lies injured upstairs. The narrative spirals into the past to reveal an affair in the North African desert and other dangerous secrets. Lies and half-truths mask identities, and physical and emotional damage are inflicted by both war and love.

The desert could not be claimed or owned – it was a piece of cloth carried by winds, never held down by stones, and given a hundred shifting names ...
The English Patient
Michael Ondaatje

TEXACO
(1992), PATRICK CHAMOISEAU

This key novel by Martinique author Chamoiseau (1953–) takes its name from a real-life shantytown suburb – itself named after an oil company due to its industry connections. The founder of this community, whose father was a freed slave, tells her family story, beginning in the early 1820s. The narrative is punctuated by excerpts from her notebooks, diaries, and letters. At the heart of the book is the struggle between colonizer and colonized, and between official history and oral storytelling, both of which are mirrored in the interplay of languages: French and Creole.

THE ROCK OF TANIOS
(1993), AMIN MAALOUF

Lebanese author Amin Maalouf (1949–), who writes in French, won the Prix Goncourt for *The Rock of Tanios*. The novel is set in the late 1880s, when Lebanon was caught in the conflict between Europe and the Ottoman Empire. It tells the story of Tanios, the illegitimate son of a sheikh, who flees his homeland with his adoptive father to escape political enemies. Tanios is soon embroiled in the wider conflict and becomes an unlikely intermediary between the Western and Middle Eastern powers.

GREEN GRASS, RUNNING WATER
(1993), THOMAS KING

American-Canadian novelist and broadcaster King (1943–), who is part Cherokee, writes about Native American culture in spare, colloquial prose. *Green Grass, Running Water* is set in the Blackfoot territory of Alberta, Canada. The novel's structure is complex, with four plot lines each interspersed with a different creation myth. One strand features figures from Native

> ## What that Coyote dreams, anything can happen.
> ### *Green Grass, Running Water*
> #### Thomas King

American and Christian traditions, as well as from literature (such as Robinson Crusoe). Both comic and satirical, the work touches on the cultural and political aspects of Native American land issues.

SELECTED STORIES
(1996), ALICE MUNRO

Canadian author Alice Munro has written novels, but it is her short stories that are regarded as her supreme achievement, as can be seen in this collection from eight of

her books. Mostly set in Huron County, southwestern Ontario, they typically show a mastery of structure, switching back and forth in time. They also feature a preoccupation with moral ambiguity and messiness in relationships, and also with the responsibility people assume for parents, children, and in-laws at different times of life.

INFINITE JEST
(1997), DAVID FOSTER WALLACE

A torrent of zany humour and surreal incident, *Infinite Jest* is the masterpiece of Wallace (1962–2008), a US writer whose suicide cemented his cult status. An ambitious novel that explores addiction, recovery, and the American dream, the book is set in a dystopian near future. Multi-layered and non-chronological in style, it features a huge cast of characters, such as the residents of a Boston halfway house, students at a nearby tennis academy, and a gang of homicidal Quebec terrorists in wheelchairs. The addictions it examines include entertainment, sex, nationalism, and drugs.

Alice Munro

A writer of exquisitely crafted, compelling, and emotionally rich stories, Alice Munro has developed and advanced the art of short-story writing over the course of six decades. Born in Ontario, Canada, in 1931, she had her first writing published in 1950 while studying English and Journalism at the University of Western Ontario. Her first collection of short stories, *Dance of the Happy Shades*, appeared in 1968, featuring the lives of women in small-town Ontario

(although Munro had moved from her home province ten years earlier). Writing an impressive range of short stories and novels over the decades since, she has pioneered a narrative style that is simultaneously rich in imagery yet also lyrical, sparse, and intense in its description of the complexities of ordinary lives.

Key works

1978 *Who Do You Think You Are?*
1996 *Selected Stories* (see above)
1998 *The Love of a Good Woman*
2004 *Runaway*

Jhumpa Lahiri

Jhumpa Lahiri's father emigrated to the UK from India, and Jhumpa was born in London in 1967. Her family moved to the USA – the country that she considers her home – when she was two years old. After her school years she attended Boston University, where she was awarded multiple degrees, and went on to teach creative writing there. Renowned for her restrained, poignant prose, Lahiri has achieved acclaim with both her short stories and novels, writing on themes informed by her experience as a second-generation Indian American.

Key works

1999 *Interpreter of Maladies* (see right)
2003 *The Namesake*
2008 *Unaccustomed Earth*
2013 *The Lowland*

MY NAME IS RED
(1998), ORHAN PAMUK

An intellectual murder mystery centred around 16th-century miniaturists, *My Name is Red* won international acclaim for its author, Turkish Nobel Laureate Orhan Pamuk (1952–). The book exhibits a postmodern consciousness of its own artistry: characters know they are fictional, and the reader is frequently referenced. The narration switches viewpoint, often between unexpected narrators – there are passages narrated by a coin and the colour red. The novel's themes include artistic devotion, love, and tensions between East and West.

INTERPRETER OF MALADIES
(1999), JHUMPA LAHIRI

Jhumpa Lahiri's first work of fiction, *Interpreter of Maladies* was initially rejected by several publishers, but went on to win the Pulitzer Prize. A collection of eight short stories, the unifying theme is the experience of first- and second-generation Indian immigrants in America. Among the other subjects explored are loss, disappointed expectations, the disconnection between different generations of immigrants, and the struggle to find a place in the West for the traditional culture of India, where two of the stories are set. In many of them, food plays a major role as a focus of human interaction.

AUSTERLITZ
(2001), W G SEBALD

Often writing in an intentionally elaborate form of his native tongue, German author Sebald (1944–2001) lived in England for the latter part of his life. *Austerlitz* is typical of his work in its melancholy reflections

> No one can explain exactly what happens within us when the doors behind which our childhood terrors lurk are flung open.
> ### Austerlitz
> **W G Sebald**

on loss, memory, and dissolution, through memoir, history, and observation. The book's title is the name of the central character, who was sent to England and placed with foster parents. Later, after discovering his Czech identity and becoming an architectural historian, he explores his troubled past.

LIFE OF PI
(2001), YANN MARTEL

In his acclaimed novel *Life of Pi*, Canadian author Martel (1963–) follows the voyage of an Indian teenage boy, the son of a zookeeper, who for 227 days drifts on a lifeboat in the Pacific Ocean following a shipwreck, with only a Bengal tiger named Richard Parker as his companion. The boy, en route to Canada, develops wisdom through adversity. His experiences (including delirium, blindness, meerkats, and carnivorous algae) provide the occasion for urgent and thought-provoking reflections on spirituality, religions, and zoology.

THE KITE RUNNER
(2003), KHALED HOSSEINI

Portraying themes of betrayal, guilt, sin, atonement, and friendship, *The Kite Runner* begins in Afghanistan in 1975. A 12-year-old boy plans to win a kite-flying competition with the help of his best friend, but an act of violence mars the day of the contest. Exiled in California after the Soviet invasion of 1979, he eventually returns to a land under Taliban rule. Khaled Hosseini (1965–) was inspired to write this part-autobiographical novel after reading that kite-flying had been banned in his homeland.

2666
(2004), ROBERTO BOLAÑO

The last, unrevised, labyrinthine novel by the Chilean writer Bolaño (1953–2003), *2666* (whose title is never fully explained) focuses on a mysterious writer, Archimboldi. Partly set on the Eastern Front of World War II, the story mainly takes place in a Mexican town notorious for around 300 serial homicides of women. After detailing the murders in a relentless series of police reports, Bolaño rewards readers for their stamina with a vivid historical reconstruction that illuminates the enigma at the novel's core.

Metaphors are our way of losing ourselves in semblances or treading water in a sea of seeming.
2666
Roberto Bolaño

HALF OF A YELLOW SUN
(2006), CHIMAMANDA NGOZI ADICHIE

Adichie named her masterpiece *Half of a Yellow Sun* – which traces the Nigerian Civil War (1967–70) through its impact on three main characters – after the symbol on the Biafran flag. Themes include conflict's human cost, politics and identity in postcolonial Africa, and the relationship between Africa and the West. Writing with feminist overtones, Adichio also questions the ethics of Western journalism and the function of the academic establishment, as well as the effectiveness of relief aid.

WIZARD OF THE CROW
(2006), NGUGI WA THIONG'O

Set in an imaginary African dictatorship, *Wizard of the Crow* is a madcap satire of totalitarian politics. Author Ngugi wa Thiong'o (1938–), a prisoner of conscience in his native Kenya, emigrated to the USA after his release. In a parody of corrupt governments, the plot involves a despotic ruler who wishes to climb to heaven by building a modern-day Tower of Babel. Hope is found in multiple voices of dissent – such as a group that causes chaos with plastic snakes. Influenced by oral traditions, the book operates by broad strokes of caricature, with some scatological touches.

THE RELUCTANT FUNDAMENTALIST
(2007), MOHSIN HAMID

Presented as a monologue that takes place in a Lahore (Pakistan) café, *The Reluctant Fundamentalist* captures the experiences of a Pakistani man who comes home from the USA after a failed love affair and 9/11, turning his back on a well-paid business job. In Pakistan his disillusionment with US capitalism forms into more radical views. Pakistani author Hamid (1971–) uses the storyline of the narrator's girlfriend's inability to free herself from a past relationship as a metaphor of the USA's nostalgic attachment to past glories.

WE NEED NEW NAMES
(2013), NOVIOLET BULAWAYO

Set initially in a Zimbabwean shanty named Paradise, the coming-of-age novel *We Need New Names* depicts lives scarred by violence, poverty, disease, and injustice. The young female narrator, sent to live with her aunt in the Midwestern USA, is faced with a new source of discontent: the exclusiveness of the American Dream. The novel is especially memorable for its depiction of the loyalty and vitality of childhood friendships in Zimbabwe, where author NoViolet Bulawayo (1981–) was born and raised.

Chimamanda Ngozi Adichie

Born in 1977 in southeastern Nigeria, Chimamanda Ngozi Adichie studied medicine and pharmacy at the University of Nigeria in Enugu, where her father was professor of statistics and her mother was the first female registrar. She studied communications and political science in the USA, later obtaining a Master's in African Studies from Yale. An author of novels, short stories, and poetry, she won the 2007 Orange Prize for Fiction for *Half of a Yellow Sun*. Adichie divides her time between the USA and Nigeria, where she teaches creative writing.

Key works

2003 *Purple Hibiscus*
2006 *Half of a Yellow Sun* (see left)
2013 *Americanah*

GLOSSARY

aesthetic Concerning beauty and the appreciation of beauty; as a noun, used to denote the set of principles and ideas that define an artistic movement ("a classical aesthetic").

Aestheticism A movement, originating in the late 19th century in England, which valued "art for art's sake", and rejected the idea that art or literature should offer a moral message or social purpose. Leading proponents included playwright Oscar Wilde, artist James Whistler, and poet and artist Dante Gabriel Rossetti.

alexandrine A poetic line consisting of 12 syllables split into six iambic feet (an unstressed syllable followed by a stressed syllable).

allegory A work of art or literature that contains a veiled meaning or message, often conveyed symbolically. For example, a tale about squabbling farmyard animals can be an allegory for a country's corrupt political leaders.

alliteration The use of several words in a row or close together that begin with the same consonant or sound, often for deliberate poetic effect.

antihero The **protagonist** of a literary work who embodies a noticeably different moral code from the conventional (or role model) hero, because they are either unheroic or actively villainous.

antinovel A term coined by the mid-20th century **Existentialist** philosopher and writer Jean-Paul Sartre to refer to a **novel** in which the conventions of the form are deliberately ignored or subverted. A key development of **Postmodern** literature, an antinovel may have some features in common with **metafiction**.

ballad A form of popular verse that narrates a story, often set to music, and widespread throughout Europe from the Middle Ages until the early 19th century.

Bildungsroman A "**novel** of formation" that tells of the early struggles and emotional education of a young **protagonist**, who grows and matures during the process. The **genre** originated in Germany in the late 18th century. Many Bildungsromans are regarded as partly autobiographical.

Byronic hero A hero having the qualities for which the English Romantic poet Lord Byron was famed, including rebelliousness, passion, defiance, contempt for conventional morality, and possibly an appetite for self-destruction.

canto From the Italian meaning "song", a section of a long (or especially **epic**) poem, comparable to a chapter in a **novel** or long work of **non-fiction**.

chanson de geste A form of **epic poem** of the 11th to 13th centuries that incorporates legends about historical figures such as Charlemagne, and which was sung or recited at court. Often considered to be the beginning of French literature. The term is from the Old French, "song of heroic deeds".

classic In its literary sense, a work widely accepted as being of lasting value and worthy of study.

comedy One of the two types of **drama** created in ancient Greece (the other being **tragedy**), whose purpose is laughter, entertainment, and **satire**. In contrast to tragedy, comedy tends to have a happy ending and to deal with ordinary people and with the mundane aspects of life.

conceit An elaborate or unlikely **metaphor**, especially popular in Elizabethan **poetry**, comparing two things that are not obviously similar. English poet John Donne famously compares parting lovers to the arms of a compass, apart but still connected.

couplet Two successive lines of verse that go together, often rhyming. When occurring at the conclusion of a poem (such as a Shakespearean **sonnet**), it can form a summing-up of the poem's sentiment or message.

drama A work intended to be acted out on a stage before an audience, originating in Athens in the 6th and 5th centuries BCE. The main **genres** were originally **tragedy** and **comedy**. The term comes from the Greek word meaning "action".

dystopia The opposite of **utopia**: a vision (usually in **novel** form) of a future in which society is dominated by a totalitarian state, or has broken down, often through environmental disaster or war. Life in a dystopia usually involves fear and hardship.

epic poem A long **narrative** poem, detailing the adventures of a historic or legendary hero. Epic poems are the oldest literary texts in the world, and probably originated in an oral tradition.

epistolary novel A type of **novel** popular in 18th-century European literature in which the **narrative** is told entirely via letters or other documents written by the characters.

Existentialism A theory of philosophy that emerged in Europe in the late 19th century, focusing on the individual's experience of the world and the importance of individual agency and responsibility. Existentialist literature often contains elements of anxiety, loneliness, and paranoia in characters' reactions to a meaningless universe.

fable A simple story with a moral message, often featuring animal characters and mythical elements.

fairy tale A short tale featuring **folkloric** fantasy characters and wonderful events, and set in a magical, timeless, and usually rural world.

fiction A work that is entirely invented, consisting of a made-up **narrative** and imaginary characters. A work of fiction may be wholly fantastical or embedded in the real world. In a wider sense, fiction is the **genre** consisting of **novels** and stories.

folklore The traditional beliefs, legends, and customs of a culture, passed down by oral tradition for many hundreds (or even thousands) of years.

folktale A popular or traditional tale handed down from generation to generation by oral transmission; another name for a **fairy tale**.

frame narrative An outer **narrative** that introduces a story (or stories) contained within it – generally via a character who narrates the main, inner story. The frame provides context and structure, and sometimes incorporates many different stories, as in Giovanni Boccaccio's *The Decameron* and Geoffrey Chaucer's *The Canterbury Tales*.

genre A style or category of literature (or art or music), such as **tragedy**, **comedy**, history, spy fiction, **science fiction**, **romance**, or crime.

Gothic A **genre** that explores the limits of the imagination, originating in England and Germany in the late 18th and early 19th centuries. Its features include gloomy, macabre settings (such as castles, ruins, or graveyards), supernatural beings (such as ghosts and vampires), and an atmosphere of mystery and horror.

haiku A Japanese form comprising a short poem with three lines of five, seven, and five syllables respectively, and traditionally dealing with the natural world. It flourished from the 17th to the 19th centuries and became popular in Western literature in the 20th century.

hard-boiled fiction A type of urban crime fiction originating with the US pulp-fiction detective magazines of the 1920s, often with a sardonic private investigator as the **protagonist**, and featuring gangsters, prostitutes, guns, sex, and violence, as well as fast, colloquial dialogue.

Harlem Renaissance A flourishing of black American writing (also art and music) that came out of the new black middle class in 1920s' Harlem, New York. Lasting from around 1918 to the early 1930s, it helped establish a black cultural identity in the USA.

humanism During the Renaissance, an intellectual movement springing from a revived interest in classical Greek and Roman thought; today, a largely secular, rationalist system of thought that emphasizes human rather than divine agency.

legend A traditional story, linked to historical events, people, or locations, and operating within the realms of the possible (as opposed to a **myth**, which incorporates supernatural elements), although the exact dates and details may have been lost.

magic realism A **Postmodern** style of artistic expression that in literature takes the form of a traditional **realist narrative** into which bizarre or supernatural elements are introduced, forcing the reader to re-evaluate the reality of the surrounding **fiction**.

metafiction A type of **Postmodern** writing that uses techniques to remind the reader of the artificiality of a fictional work (for example by including the author as a character,

or by having characters who are aware that they are in a story), to draw attention to the relationship between **fiction** and real life.

metaphor A figure of speech that adds an extra layer of meaning to an object by equating it with something else.

metre In poetry, the rhythm of a piece of verse, dictated by the "feet" (stressed syllables) in a line.

Modernism In literature, a movement that lasted from the late 19th to the mid-20th century. It broke with traditional forms and expanded the limits of **poetry** and **fiction** with experimental methods that sought a new level of psychological truth, such as **stream of consciousness**.

motif A theme that returns several times throughout a work, and which may reflect on and enhance the other themes or central message of a work.

myth A symbolic account of gods or superhuman beings existing in a time apart from ordinary human history, used to explain the customs, rituals, and beliefs of a people or culture. Often mentioned in the same phrase as, but different from, **legend**.

narrative An account of a series of connected events, whether **fictional** or **non-fictional**.

narrative voice The way in which a **narrative** is communicated to the reader, for example via a first-person or an omniscient narrator.

Naturalism A literary movement that went further than **realism** in trying to recreate human behaviour in exact and precise detail. It also tried to show how people (especially the poor) are formed by their environments and social pressures, and it was often criticized for concentrating on human misery. It originated in France in the mid-19th century, and is perhaps best exemplified by the novels of Émile Zola.

neoclassicism A fascination with the ideals of classical Greece and Rome that was prevalent in the arts in Europe during the Enlightenment (1650–1800). In literature, neoclassicism developed most fully in France, with playwrights Molière and Jean Racine writing **comedies** and **tragedies** respectively that adhered to the classical **unities**. In Britain, major proponents included poet Alexander Pope and satirist Jonathan Swift.

New Journalism A form of **non-fiction** writing that uses stylistic devices from **fiction** to achieve a heightened literary effect, dramatizing events rather than sticking to objective journalistic truth. Key practitioners included Hunter S Thompson, Truman Capote, Norman Mailer, and Joan Didion. The name derives from the 1973 book by US author Tom Wolfe.

non-fiction A work of **prose** in which nothing is made up, and which is about and based on facts and real events (as opposed to **fiction**).

novel A sustained work of **prose fiction**, usually of several hundred pages, and typically containing characters and a **plot**. The novel form developed gradually from the 16th century onwards.

novella A work of **prose fiction** that is shorter than a **novel**, but longer than a short story. A novella can touch on themes almost as broad in scope as a full novel, although it retains some of the compact unity of the short story.

novel of manners A literary style that examined (often satirically) the values and contradictions of society through the domestic scenarios of the middle and upper classes, and in which literary **realism** was a key element. Developed partly in reaction to the **Gothic** novels of the late 18th century and the excesses of **Romanticism**.

ode A usually **rhyming** lyric poem written as an address to (often in praise of) a person, place, or thing. It originated in ancient Greece, where it was performed accompanied by music.

parody A work that mocks its target by humorously, satirically, or ironically imitating and exaggerating its least effective elements.

pathetic fallacy First coined by Victorian critic John Ruskin in 1856, the term describes a literary device by which human emotions are attributed to nature or the environment, in such a way that nature seems to offer a reflection of a character's inner state.

picaresque novel From the Spanish word *pícaro*, meaning "rogue" or "rascal", an episodic **prose narrative** about a disreputable but likeable hero.

plot The main story, or the sequence and interrelationship of crucial events, in a work of literature.

poetry Literary writing of concentrated expression, intended to evoke a greater resonance than **prose**. Poetry uses a wide variety of devices, including **alliteration**, **rhyme**, **metaphor**, and rhythm, to achieve its effects. Different forms of poetry include the **epic**, the **ballad**, the **sonnet**, and, more recently, the less structured form of free verse.

postcolonial literature A branch of writing, especially **novels**, that developed in former colonies around the world in the mid-20th century, dealing with the aftermath of colonization and examining issues such as oppression and freedom, cultural identity, and diaspora.

Postmodernism In literature, a movement that began after World War II, developing from the experimentation of the **Modernist** era. Postmodernist works exhibit differing approaches, but often mock previous traditions by **parody**, pastiche, and the mixing of elements of high and low art; they use techniques of **metafiction** to draw attention to a work's artificiality.

prose The ordinary, natural form of written or spoken language, as opposed to the more structured, rhythmic forms of **poetry**.

protagonist The chief character in a story or **narrative**; the person to whom the story happens.

realism The accurate depiction of life as it is lived by ordinary people. Often specifically referring to the literary approach that was adopted in France (particularly in the **novels** of Gustave Flaubert) in the 19th century, which stressed material facts and sociological insight in reaction to the emotional nature of **Romantic** literature.

rhyme A repetition of the same sound in two or more words; when this occurs at the end of lines in a poem it creates an effect, which poets use to achieve various ends (for example to enhance meaning, to round off a poem, or simply for harmony).

rhyme scheme The pattern of the **rhymes** in a poem. Certain types of poem have strict rhyme schemes, such as *terza rima*, the Shakespearean **sonnet**, and the Keatsian **ode**.

roman à clef A work in which real people and events are presented in fictionalized form. From the French meaning "**novel** with a key".

romance In the 16th to 18th centuries, a work of **fiction** that contained extraordinary adventures or fanciful elements. In contemporary fiction, a **genre** whose **narrative** and **plot** focus on romantic love.

Romanticism In literature, a Europe-wide literary movement that began in the late 18th century, in which writers rejected the Enlightenment ideals of objective reason, and wrote only from their own personal perspective. Rationality and restraint were replaced by inspiration and subjectivity. Themes included intense emotional experiences and the sublime beauty of nature.

saga A **narrative** from Iceland or Norway written in the Middle Ages, mainly in the Old Norse language, and principally dealing with the founding of Iceland (family sagas), the kings of Norway (kings' sagas), and legendary or heroic exploits (sagas of antiquity). Although written in **prose**, the saga shares characteristics with the **epic**.

satire Born out of the **comedies** of ancient Greece, this is a literary form that uses such elements as irony, sarcasm, ridicule, and wit to expose or attack human failings or vices, often with the intent of inspiring reform.

science fiction Writing that explores the possibility of scenarios that are at the time of writing technologically impossible, extrapolating from present-day science; or that deal with some form of speculative science-based **conceit**, such as a society (on Earth or another planet) that has developed in wholly different ways from our own.

slave narrative A **non-fiction narrative** told by a slave who has escaped captivity or been granted freedom. Necessarily quite rare (because education was denied to slaves), they were used by anti-slavery campaigners to bring the slaves' plight to wider public attention, helping to end European trading in slaves and the abolition of slavery in North America.

soliloquy A device in a play in which a character speaks his or her innermost thoughts aloud, which has the effect of sharing them directly with the audience.

sonnet A type of poem created in medieval Italy, having 14 lines of a set number of syllables, and following a specific **rhyme scheme**. The two most common types are the Petrarchan (or Italian) and the Shakespearean (or English) sonnet.

speculative fiction First used in 1947 by US **science fiction** writer Robert A Heinlein as a synonym for science

fiction, the term now signifies a loose genre of work that deals with the question "What if?" through **science fiction**, horror, fantasy, mystery, and other genres, sometimes all at the same time.

stream of consciousness A key experimental technique used by **Modernist** writers, which tries to portray a character's thoughts, feelings, and perceptions as they actually occur, often jumbled and unfinished, instead of in formal, composed sentences. Its proponents include James Joyce, Virginia Woolf, and William Faulkner.

Sturm und Drang "Storm and stress", a German literary movement of the late 18th century that overturned Enlightenment conventions, and revelled in extremes of individuality, violence, and passionate expression. The young Johann Wolfgang von Goethe and Friedrich von Schiller were two of its main exponents.

terza rima A form of **poetry** that uses three-line verses with an interlocking **rhyme scheme**, so that the first and third lines **rhyme** with each other, and the middle line rhymes with the first and third lines of the next verse. Developed (although not invented) by the Italian poet Dante Alighieri.

tragedy One of two types of play created in ancient Greece (the other being **comedy**), in which events move towards a catastrophic conclusion, and which shows characters brought low and experiencing terrible suffering, often because of a **tragic flaw**.

tragic flaw In Greek **tragedy**, the element of a **protagonist's** character that leads to his or her downfall.

Transcendentalism A 19th-century movement in the USA whose adherents saw a divine beauty and goodness in nature that they tried to express through literature. Its most famous writers were Henry David Thoreau and Ralph Waldo Emerson.

troubadour A travelling composer and singer in the courts of medieval Europe. The troubadours were usually artists of noble birth who sang tales about courtly love, rather than tales of bloody and heroic deeds.

trouvère A composer of epic poems in northern France, operating roughly from the 11th to the 14th centuries.

unities, the The three rules that governed the structure of **neoclassical** drama, following Aristotle's notes on ancient Greek drama. They are unity of action (a single **plot** or storyline), unity of time (a single day), and unity of place (a single location).

utopia A theoretical perfect society in which all people live a harmonious existence. Taken from the name of the 1516 work by the English humanist and statesman Sir Thomas More.

vernacular The language of a specific country; ordinary language as it is actually spoken, as opposed to formal literary language.

Victorian literature British literature written during the reign of Queen Victoria (reigned 1837–1901), which often consisted of long and highly ambitious **novels** depicting broad cross-sections of society and often containing a moral lesson. Key authors were Charles Dickens, George Eliot, and William Makepeace Thackeray.

Weimar Classicism A German literary movement that lasted from the 1780s to 1805, named after the German city of Weimar, home of its principal authors, Johann Wolfgang von Goethe and Friedrich von Schiller. These authors used the structure of classical Greek **drama** and **poetry** to create works of aesthetic balance and harmony.

world literature Literature that has developed an audience and had an influence beyond its original culture and language.

INDEX

Numbers in **bold** refer to main entries.

38th parallel **330**
2666 (Bolaño) **339**

A

Abe, Kōbō, *The Woman in the Dunes*
263
Abu al-Alahijah 44
Abu Nuwas 44
Achebe, Chinua **269**
Things Fall Apart 248, **266–69**
Acker, Kathy 313
Adichie, Chimamanda Ngozi **339**
Half of a Yellow Sun 266, **339**
Purple Hibiscus 269, 339
The Adventures of Caleb Williams
(Godwin) 166
The Adventures of Huckleberry Finn
(Twain) 145, 157, **188–89**, 270
The Adventures of Pinocchio (Collodi)
168
Aeneid (Virgil) 19, **40–41**, 62
Aeschylus 18, 37, **54**
Oresteia **54–55**
Aestheticism 157, **194**
The Aesthetics of Resistance (Weiss)
333
"The Afternoon of a Faun" (Mallarmé)
165
Against Nature (Huysmans) 194
"The Agony" (Herbert) 91
Ah Cheng, *Romances of the
Landscape* 310
Al-Mu'allaqat 44
Alas, Leopolda, *La Regenta* **201**
The Alchemist (Jonson) 75
Alcott, Louisa May, *Little Women*
169, **199**
Alencar, José de, *The Guarani* **164**
Alfonso X **57**
Cantigas de Santa María **57**
Alice's Adventures in Wonderland
(Carroll) 156, **168–71**
allegorical satire 295, **320–21**
Allende, Isabel, *The House of The
Spirits* 302, **334**
Almayer's Folly (Conrad) 197
Amadis of Gaul (Montalvo) **102–03**
American black humour **276**
American Psycho (Ellis) 261, 270, **313**
American voices **188–89**
Amis, Kingsley, *Lucky Jim* 318
Amis, Martin 331
Andersen, Hans Christian, *Fairy
Tales* 45, **151**, 169
Angelou, Maya 307
I Know Why the Caged Bird Sings
259, **291**

Anglo-Saxon literature 19, **42–43**,
48, 219
Animal Farm (Orwell) **245**, 248, 252,
253, 320
Anna Karenina (Tolstoy) 149, 178,
200
Annals (Ennius) 40
Annie Allen (Brooks) 259
antinovel 249, **274–75**
Antony and Cleopatra (Shakespeare)
87, 89
Apuleius, *The Golden Ass* 40, **56**
Ariel (Plath) 276
Ariosto, Ludovico, *Orlando Furioso*
63
Aristophanes 90
The Clouds 36
Wasps **55**
Wealth 39
Aristotle, *Poetics* **39**, 90
The Armies of the Night (Mailer) **291**
Ars Amatoria (Art of Love) (Ovid) 57
Arthurian chivalric romance 19,
50–51
As You Like It (Shakespeare) 85, 88, 89
Asbjørnsen, Peter Christen,
Norwegian Folktales 116
Asturias, Miguel Angel
Men of Maize 282
Mr President 282
At Swim-Two-Birds (O'Brien) 274
Atwood, Margaret 14, **327**
The Blind Assassin 271, 295,
326–27
The Edible Woman 327
The Handmaid's Tale 252, 327, **335**
Auden, W H 117
Collected Poetry 277
Auschwitz, literature after **258**
Austen, Jane 14, 90, **119**, 131, 317
Pride and Prejudice 12, 108,
118–19
Auster, Paul **336**
The New York Trilogy 298, **336**
Austerlitz (Sebald) **338**
Australian writing **311**
The Awakening (Chopin) **203**

B

Ba Jin, *The Family* 222
Bâ, Mariama, *So Long a Letter* **334**
Baif, Jean Antoine de, *Mimes,
Lessons, and Proverbs* 74
Baihua literature **222**
Baldwin, James, *Go Tell It on the
Mountain* 259, 306
Ballard, J G **332**
Crash 313, **332**
Empire of the Sun 332

"The Ballad of the Brown Girl"
(Cullen) 235
Balzac, Honoré de **151**
The Black Sheep **152**
The Chouans 122, 151
La Comédie humaine 156, 160
Old Goriot **151**
banned books 243, **260–61**, 322
Bao Town (Wang) 310
Barcas trilogy (Vicente) **103**
Barrett Browning, Elizabeth 131
Barrie, J M, *Peter Pan* 169
Bartleby & Co. (Villa-Matas) 274
Bartleby, the Scrivener (Melville) 140
Bashar ibn Burd 44
Bashō, Matsuo, *The Narrow Road to
the Interior* 61, **92**
Baudelaire, Charles 157
Les Fleurs du mal **165**
Beat Generation 243, 248, 249,
264–65, 288
The Beautiful and Damned
(Fitzgerald) 230
Beckett, Samuel, *Waiting for Godot*
210, 248, **262**
Bel Ami (Maupassant) 160
The Bell Jar (Plath) 185, 256, **290**
Beloved (Morrison) 145, 294, **306–09**
Ben Jelloun, Tahar, *The Sand Child* 223
Beowulf 14, 19, **42–43**
Berlin Alexanderplatz (Döblin) 207,
234
"Bernice Bobs Her Hair" (Fitzgerald)
230
Bhagavad Gita (Vyasa) 24, **25**
The Big Sleep (Chandler) 207,
236–37
Bildungsroman 128, 206–07, **224–27**
The Black Sheep (Balzac) **152**
Blake, William **105**
*Songs of Innocence and
Experience* **105**, 110
Bleak House (Dickens) 109, 134,
146–49, 166, 195, 208
Bleeding Edge (Pynchon) 296, 331
The Blind Assassin (Atwood) 271,
295, **326–27**
Blindness (Saramago) 295, **320–21**
The Bloody Chamber (Carter) 116,
333
The Bluest Eye (Morrison) 307, 309
Boccaccio, Giovanni 14, 71
The Decameron 60, 68, 72, **102**
Bolaño, Roberto, *2666* **339**
The Bonfire of the Vanities (Wolfe)
149
Book of Changes 18, **21**
The Book of Disquiet (Pessoa) 216,
244
Book of Odes (*Shijing*) 46
The Book of Songs (Heine) 111

Borges, Jorge Luis **245**
A Universal History of Infamy 302
Ficciones **245**, 282, 298, 299
"Pierre Menard, Author of the
Quixote" 81
Bradbury, Ray, *Fahrenheit 451* 252, **287**
Brave New World (Huxley) **243**, 252,
261
Brecht, Bertolt, *Mother Courage and
Her Children* 238, **244–45**
Bright Lights, Big City (McInerney) 313
Brink, André, *A Dry White Season*
333–34
Broch, Hermann, *The Sleepwalkers*
234
The Broken Commandment
(Shimazaki) 209
Brontë, Charlotte **129**
Jane Eyre 109, 118, **128–31**, 137
Villette 128
Brontë, Emily 131, **134**
Wuthering Heights 69, 109, 128,
132, **134–37**, 192, 271
Bronze Age **20**
Brooke, Rupert, "The Dead" 212
Brooks, Gwendolyn, *Annie Allen* 259
The Brothers Karamazov
(Dostoyevsky) 149, 178,
200–01, 210
Brown, Dan, *The Da Vinci Code* 261
Buddenbrooks (Mann) 194, 227
Bukowski, Charles 313
Ham on Rye 256
Bulawayo, NoViolet, *We Need New
Names* **339**
Bulgakov, Mikhail, *The Master and
Margarita* **290–91**
Bunyan, John, *The Pilgrim's Progress*
330
Burgess, Anthony, *A Clockwork
Orange* 252, 270, **289**
Burroughs, William S 265, 313
Naked Lunch 260, 264
Buson, Yosa 92
The Butcher Boy (McCabe) 313
Butler, Octavia E, *Kindred* 126
Byatt, A S, *Possession: A Romance* 318
Byron, Lord 120, 124, 185
Don Juan 110

C

Cain, James M
Double Indemnity 236
The Postman Always Rings Twice
236
The Cairo Trilogy (Mahfouz) 223
Calderón de la Barca, Pedro, *Life is a
Dream* 78
Call to Arms (Lu) 207, **222**

The Call of the Wild (London) **240**
Calvino, Italo 295, **299**
   The Castle of Crossed Destinies 274
   If on a Winter's Night a Traveller 69, 294, **298–99**
Camões, Luís de, *The Lusiads* 62, **103**
campus novel **318**
Camus, Albert 177, 211
   The Outsider 211, **245**, 262
Candide (Voltaire) 61, **96–97**, 260
Cane (Toomer) 235
cantar de gesta poetry 48
Cantar de Mio Cid **56–57**
The Canterbury Tales (Chaucer) 60, **68–71**
Cantigas de Santa María (Alfonso X) **57**
Cantos (Pound) 213
Cao Xueqin, *Dream of the Red Chamber* 66
Capote, Truman **279**, 319
   In Cold Blood 249, 273, **278–79**
The Caretaker (Pinter) 262
Carey, Peter
   Oscar and Lucinda **311**
   The True History of the Kelly Gang 311
Caribbean writing 294, **312**
Carpentaria (Wright) 311
Carpentier, Alejo 302
   The Kingdom of this World 312
Carroll, Lewis **171**
   Alice's Adventures in Wonderland 156, **168–71**
Carter, Angela **333**
   The Bloody Chamber 116, **333**
   Nights at the Circus 302
The Castle (Kafka) 211
The Castle of Crossed Destinies (Calvino) 274
The Castle of Otranto (Walpole) 120
Castle Rackrent (Edgeworth) 122
Cat on a Hot Tin Roof (Williams) 272
Catch-22 (Heller) 249, **276**
The Catcher in the Rye (Salinger) 248, **256–57**, 271, 328
Celan, Paul, *Poppy and Memory* 238, **258**
"Cendrillon" (Perrault) 117
Cervantes, Miguel de 14, **78**
   Don Quixote 51, 61, 67, **76–81**, 274, 298, 320
Césaire, Aimé 196
   Return to My Native Land 312
Chamoiseau, Patrick, *Texaco* **336–37**
Chandler, Raymond **236**
   The Big Sleep 207, **236–37**
Chansons de geste **48**, 50, 52
Charlie and the Chocolate Factory (Dahl) 171
Chateaubriand, Francois-René, *René* **150**
Chaucer, Geoffrey 14, 57, **71**, 219
   The Canterbury Tales 60, **68–71**
   Troilus and Criseyde 69

Chekhov, Anton **203**
   Uncle Vanya **203**
Children's and Household Tales (Grimm) 45, 108, **116–17**, 168–69
China's four great classical novels 61, **66–67**
Chopin, Kate, *The Awakening* **203**
The Chouans (Balzac) 122, 151
Chrétien de Troyes 48, **50**
   Lancelot, the Knight of the Cart 19, **50–51**
Christie, Agatha 207
   The Mysterious Affair at Styles 208
Chūshingura (Imuzo, Sosuke, and Shoraku) 93
Civil Rights Movement 235, **259**, 272, 273, 295, 306, 309
Clarissa (Richardson) 100, **104**
classical Arabic literature **44–45**
classical Greek drama 18–19, **34–39**
Claude's Confession (Zola) 191
Clelia (Scudéry) 185
A Clockwork Orange (Burgess) 252, 270, **289**
Cloud Atlas (Mitchell) 69
The Clouds (Aristophanes) 36
Coetzee, J M **323**
   Disgrace 295, **322–23**
Coleridge, Samuel Taylor
   Lyrical Ballads 108, **110**
   The Rime of the Ancient Mariner 144
Collected Poetry (Auden) 277
Collins, Suzanne, *The Hunger Games* 320
Collins, Wilkie **198**, 207
   The Moonstone 146, 149, **198–99**, 208, 271
Collodi, Carlo, *The Adventures of Pinocchio* 168
colonial literature 157, **196–97**, 248
The Color Purple (Walker) 306
The Comedy of Errors (Shakespeare) 88, 89
comedy of manners 13, 61, **90**
Conan Doyle, Sir Arthur 69, 157, 207
   The Hound of the Baskervilles 206, **208**
   The Lost World 184
   Sherlock Holmes stories 149
A Confederação dos Tamoios (Magalhães) 164
A Confederacy of Dunces (Toole) 272
Confucianism 18, **21**
Conrad, Joseph **197**
   Almayer's Folly 197
   Heart of Darkness 157, **196–97**, 267, 271
   Lord Jim **203**
   Nostromo **240**
contemporary African-American literature 294, 295, **306–09**
Conversation in the Cathedral (Vargas Llosa) 282

Cooper, James Fenimore 109
   The Last of the Mohicans 122, **150**
   "Leatherstocking Tales" 122, 150, 188
   The Pioneers 122, 188
Corneille, Pierre 61
   Le Cid **103**
   Psyché 90
The Corrections (Franzen) 182, 295, **328–29**, 331
Cortázar, Julio, *Hopscotch* 249, **274–75**, 282
The Count of Monte Cristo (Dumas) 146, **152–53**
The Counterfeiters (Gide) **242**
The Country of the Pointed Firs (Jewett) 188
Crane, Stephen 191
   The Red Badge of Courage 190, **202**
Crash (Ballard) 313, **332**
Crime and Punishment (Dostoyevsky) 14, 156, **172–77**, 178
Crow (Hughes) **291**
Cry, the Beloved Country (Paton) **286**, 322
The Crying of Lot 49 (Pynchon) 276, **290**, 296
Cullen, Countee, "The Ballad of the Brown Girl" 235

D

The Da Vinci Code (Brown) 261
"Daffodils" (Wordsworth) 192
Dahl, Roald, *Charlie and the Chocolate Factory* 171
d'Alembert, Rond, *Encyclopédie* 61, 96
A Dance of the Forests (Soyinka) 266
Dance of the Happy Shades (Munro) 337
The Dancing Girl (Ōgais) 209
Daniel Deronda (Eliot) **200**
Dante Alighieri **65**, 71
   The Divine Comedy 41, 60, **62–65**, 312
Danticat, Edwidge, *The Farming of Bones* 306
Dao De Jing (Laozi) **54**
A Dark Night's Passing (Naoya) 209
Dark Romanticism **140–45**, 152
Darwin, Charles, *On the Origin of Species* 156, 190
David Copperfield (Dickens) 94, **153**, 225, 226
Davies, Robertson, *Fifth Business* 326
The Day of the Locust (West) 276
"The Dead" (Brooke) 212
Dead Souls (Gogol) **152**
The Death of Artemio Cruz (Fuentes) 282, **290**
Death of a Naturalist (Heaney) **277**
Death in Venice (Mann) 194, 207, 224–25, **240**
The Decameron (Boccaccio) 60, 68, 72, **102**

Defoe, Daniel 14, **94**, 156
   Robinson Crusoe 61, **94–95**, 196
DeLillo, Don 328, **335**
   Falling Man 331
   Underworld 296, 335
   White Noise **335–36**
Demirkan, Renan, *Schwarzer Tee mit drei Stuck Zucker* 324
Desai, Kiran, *The Inheritance of Loss* 314, 317
detective fiction 207, **208**
The Devil to Pay in the Backlands (Guimarães Rosa) **288**
Dhu al-Rummah 44
Diamond Sutra 19
The Diary of a Superfluous Man (Turgenev) 124
Dias, Gonçalves, *I-Juca-Pirama* 164
Díaz, Junot, *Drown* 306
Dickens, Charles 135–36, 137, **147**, 157, 166, 168, 182, 185
   A Tale of Two Cities **198**
   Bleak House 109, 134, **146–49**, 166, 195, 208
   David Copperfield 94, **153**, 225, 226
   Great Expectations **198**
   Little Dorrit 109, 166
   Martin Chuzzlewit 186
   The Old Curiosity Shop 146
   Oliver Twist 134, **151**
   Our Mutual Friend 166
   The Pickwick Papers 146, 147
Dickinson, Emily 125, 131, 213
A Dictionary of Maqiao (Han) 310
Diderot, Denis
   Encyclopédie 61, 96
   Jacques the Fatalist 96, **105**
Digenis Akritas **56**
"Digging" (Heaney) 277
The Discomfort Zone (Franzen) 329
Discourse on the Arts and Sciences (Rousseau) 98
Disgrace (Coetzee) 295, **322–23**
Disraeli, Benjamin, *Sybil* 166
The Divine Comedy (Dante) 41, 60, **62–65**, 312
Döblin, Alfred, *Berlin Alexanderplatz* 207, **234**
Doctor Faustus (Marlowe) 60, **75**
Doctor Zhivago (Pasternak) **288**
A Doll's House (Ibsen) **200**
Don Juan (Byron) 110
Don Quixote (Cervantes) 51, 61, 67, **76–81**, 274, 298, 320
Doña Bárbara (Gallegos) **242**
Donne, John, "A Nocturnal Upon St Lucy's Day" 91
Dos Passos, John, *U.S.A.* trilogy 230
Dostoyevsky, Fyodor **174**, 211
   The Brothers Karamazov 149, 178, **200–01**, 210
   Crime and Punishment 14, 156, **172–77**, 178
   The Idiot **199**
Double Indemnity (Cain) 236
Douglass, Frederick **127**
   Narrative of the Life of Frederick Douglass 109, **126–27**

Dracula (Stoker) 157, **195**
Dream of the Red Chamber (Cao) 66
"The Dream of the Road" 42
Dream Story (Schnitzler) 194
Dreiser, Theodore 191
   Sister Carrie **203**
Drown (Díaz) 306
A Dry White Season (Brink) **333–34**
Du Fu 19, **46**
Dubliners (Joyce) 216
The Duchess of Malfi (Webster) 75
Dujardin, Édouard, *Les Lauriers sont coupés* 216
"Dulce et Decorum Est" (Owen) 206, **212**
Dumas, Alexandre **123**
   The Count of Monte Cristo 146, **152–53**
   The Three Musketeers 109, **122–23**
Duras, Marguerite, *The Lover* **335**
dysfunction in the modern family 295, **328–29**
dystopian literature **250–55**

E

Early Gothic **120–21**
Eça de Queirós **202**
   The Maias **202**
Eddur 52
Edgeworth, Maria, *Castle Rackrent* 122
The Edible Woman (Atwood) 327
Effi Briest (Fontane) **202**
Egyptian Book of the Dead 20, **54**
Ekwensi, Cyprian, *People of the City* 266
El Cantar de mio Cid 48
Eliot, George 109, **183**
   Daniel Deronda **200**
   Middlemarch 130–31, 156, 174, **182–83**
   The Mill on the Floss 128
Eliot, T S 65
   "The Love Song of J. Alfred Prufrock" 213
   The Waste Land 192, 206, **213**, 216, 230, 232
Ellis, Bret Easton, *American Psycho* 261, 270, **313**
Ellison, Ralph 249
   Invisible Man 145, **259**, 306, 309
Emerson, Ralph Waldo 13, 108–09, 125
Empire of the Sun (Ballard) 332
Enamels and Cameos (Gautier) 165
encyclopedic novel **296–97**
Encyclopédie (d'Alembert/Diderot) 61, 96
The English Patient (Ondaatje) **336**
English Romantic poets **110**
Enheduanna 20
Ennius, Quintus, *Annals* 40
The Epic of Gilgamesh 13, 18, **20**, 28
epistolary novel 15, **100–01**, 104, 105, 174
Ethan Frome (Wharton) **240**

Eugene Onegin (Pushkin) 109, **124**
Eugenides, Jeffrey, *The Virgin Suicides* 328
Euripides 18, 37
   Medea **55**
Evenings on a Farm near the Dikanka (Gogol) 178
Exeter Book 42
existentialism **210–11**
Extremely Loud and Incredibly Close (Safran Foer) 295, **331**

F

Fables (La Fontaine) 90
The Faerie Queene (Spenser) 63, **103**
Fahrenheit 451 (Bradbury) 252, **287**
Fairy Tales (Andersen) 45, **151**, 169
Falling Man (DeLillo) 331
The Family (Ba) 222
The Famished Road (Okri) 269
Far From the Madding Crowd (Hardy) 190, **200**
The Farming of Bones (Danticat) 306
Faulkner, William **243**
   The Sound and the Fury 188, 216, **242–43**, 271
Faust (Goethe) 98, 108, 109, **112–15**
Fear and Loathing in Las Vegas (Thompson) **332**
Fernando de Rojas, *La Celestina* 78
Ficciones (Borges) **245**, 282, 298, 299
fictional autobiography **94–95**
Fielding, Henry 61, 81, 156
   Tom Jones 94, **104**, 182
Fifth Business (Davies) 326
Fight Club (Palahniuk) 313
Findley, Timothy, *The Last of the Crazy People* 326
Finnegans Wake (Joyce) 206, 216
Fires on the Plain (Ōoka) 263
First Folio (Shakespeare) 14, 61, **82–89**
Fitzgerald, F Scott **230**, 256, 319
   The Beautiful and Damned 230
   "Bernice Bobs Her Hair" 230
   The Great Gatsby 145, 207, **228–33**
   Tender is the Night 233
   This Side of Paradise 230
Five Classics 18, **21**
Five Weeks in a Balloon (Verne) 184
Flaubert, Gustave 14, **160**
   Madame Bovary 81, 146, 156, **158–63**, 190
   Sentimental Education 163, **199**, 225
   The Temptation of Saint Anthony 161
folklore collections **116–17**
Fontane, Theodore, *Effi Briest* **202**
Forster, E M, *A Passage to India* 196, **241–42**
The Fountainhead (Rand) **245**
Fowles, John, *The French Lieutenant's Woman* **291**
Frame, Janet, *The Lagoon and Other Stories* **286**

frame narrative 23, **68–71**, 102, 203
Frankenstein (Shelley) 108, **120–21**, 184, 192
Franz Sternbald's Wanderings (Tieck) 224
Franzen, Jonathan **329**
   The Corrections 182, 295, **328–29**, 331
   The Discomfort Zone 329
The French Lieutenant's Woman (Fowles) **291**
French neoclassicism **90**, 103–04
French realism 156, **158–63**
French Symbolists **165**
Fuentes, Carlos, *The Death of Artemio Cruz* 282, **290**
Fujiwara no Shunzei, *Senzaishū (Collection of a Thousand Years)* 47
Fuller, Margaret 125
Futon (Katai) 209

G

Gaddis, William, *The Recognitions* 328
Galgut, Damon, *The Good Doctor* 322
Galland, Antoine 45
Gallegos, Rómulo, *Doña Barbara* **242**
Gao Xingjian 310
García Márquez, Gabriel 15, **284**, 287
   The General in His Labyrinth 122
   Love in the Time of Cholera **335**
   One Hundred Years of Solitude 249, **280–85**, 302
Garcilaso Inca de la Vega 78, 164
Gargantua and Pantagruel (Rabelais) 60, 61, **72–73**, 260
Gaskell, Elizabeth **153**
   Mary Barton 153, 166
   North and South **153**
The Gaucho Martín Fierro (Hernandez) **199**
Gautier, Théophile, *Enamels and Cameos* 165
The General in His Labyrinth (García Márquez) 122
Genet, Jean, *Les Nègres* 262
Geneva Bible 84
German Romanticism 99, **111**, 115
Germinal (Zola) 157, 163, 166, **190–91**
Ghosh, Amitav, *The Glass Palace* 314, 317
Gibran, Khalil, *The Prophet* **223**
Gibson, William, *Neuromancer* **334–35**
Gide, André, *The Counterfeiters* **242**
Gilbert, Sandra M, *The Madwoman in the Attic* 131
Gilman, Charlotte Perkins, "The Yellow Wallpaper" 128, 131
Ginsberg, Allen 265
   Howl and Other Poems 248, 261, 264, **288**

Gissing, George, *New Grub Street* 190
The Glass Bead Game (Hesse) 234
The Glass Palace (Ghosh) 314, 317
Glenarvon (Lamb) 185
Go (Holmes) 264
Go Set a Watchman (Lee) 273
Go Tell It on the Mountain (Baldwin) 259, 306
The God of Small Things (Roy) 314, 317
Godwin, William, *The Adventures of Caleb Williams* 166
Goethe, Johann Wolfgang von 99, **115**, 183
   Faust 98, 108, 109, **112–15**
   The Sorrows of Young Werther 98, **105**, 256
   Wilhelm Meister's Apprenticeship 224–25
Gogol, Nikolai **152**
   Dead Souls **152**
   Evenings on a Farm near the Dikanka 178
Golden Age of Latin literature **40–41**
The Golden Ass (Apuleius) 40, **56**
The Goldfinch (Tartt) 328
Golding, William **287**
   Lord of the Flies **287**
Goldsmith, Oliver 90
The Good Doctor (Galgut) 322
Goodbye, Columbus (Roth) 276
Goodison, Lorna, *To Us, All Flowers Are Roses: Poems* 312
Gordimer, Nadine 322
   July's People 261
The Grapes of Wrath (Steinbeck) 188, 189, **244**
Grass, Günter **271**
   The Tin Drum 249, **270–71**, 302
Gravity's Rainbow (Pynchon) 294, 295, **296–97**
Great American Novel **145**
Great Expectations (Dickens) **198**
The Great Gatsby (Fitzgerald) 145, 207, **228–33**
Greek epic **26–33**
Green Grass, Running Water (King) **337**
Green Henry (Keller) 224
Grimm, Jacob and Wilhelm **117**
   Children's and Household Tales 45, 108, **116–17**, 168–69
The Groves of Academe (McCarthy) 318
The Guarani (Alencar) **164**
Gubar, Susan, *The Madwoman in the Attic* 131
The Guest (Hwang) 295, **330**
Guillaume de Lorris, *Romance of the Rose* **57**
Guilleragues, Gabriel-Joseph de, *Letters of a Portuguese Nun* 100
Guimarães Rosa, João, *The Devil to Pay in the Backlands* **288**
Gulliver's Travels (Swift) 61, 94, 95, **104**, 270, 321
Gustavus Vassa, the African 126

H

Habila, Helon, *Waiting for an Angel* 266
haiku and haibun **92**, 209
Haley, Alex 307
    Roots 306, **333**
Half of a Yellow Sun (Adichie) 266, **339**
Ham on Rye (Bukowski) 256
Hamid, Mohsin, *The Reluctant Fundamentalist* 331, **339**
Hamlet (Shakespeare) 85, 87, **88**, 144, 174, 221
Hammett, Dashiell
    The Maltese Falcon 236
    Red Harvest 236
Hamsun, Knut, *Hunger* **202**
Han Shaogong, *A Dictionary of Maqiao* 310
The Handmaid's Tale (Atwood) 252, 327, **335**
hard-boiled detective fiction 207, **236–37**, 336
Hardy, Thomas **193**
    Far From the Madding Crowd 190, **200**
    Jude the Obscure **202**
    Tess of the d'Urbervilles 157, **192–93**
Harlem Renaissance **235**
Harmonium (Stevens) 213
Harry Potter (Rowling) **170**, 261
The Hawk in the Rain (Hughes) 277
Hawthorne, Nathaniel 141
    The House of the Seven Gables 140
    The Scarlet Letter 140, **153**
Heaney, Seamus
    Death of a Naturalist **277**
    "Digging" 277
Heart of Darkness (Conrad) 157, **196–97**, 267, 271
The Heart Is a Lonely Hunter (McCullers) 272
The Heart of Redness (Mda) 322
The Heartless (Yi) **241**
Heian court, Japan 19, **47**
Heidi (Spyri) 169
Heine, Heinrich, *The Book of Songs* 111
Heller, Joseph, *Catch-22* 249, **276**
Hemingway, Ernest 188–89, **286**
    The Old Man and the Sea **287**
    The Sun Also Rises 186, 230, 264, 286
Henry IV (Shakespeare) 75, 88, 89
The Heptameron (Marguerite de Navarre) 68
Herbert, George, "The Agony" 91
Herder, Gottfried 112, 113
Hernandez, José, *The Gaucho Martín Fierro* **199**
A Hero of Our Time (Lermontov) 124, **151–52**
Herrick, Robert, *Hesperides* 91
Hesiod, *Theogony* 28, **54**

Hesperides (Herrick) 91
Hesse, Hermann
    The Glass Bead Game 234
    Siddhartha **241**
Hildebrandslied **56**
Hilsenrath, Edgar, *The Nazi and the Barber* 258
historical novel **122–23**
History (Morante) **332**
The Hobbit (Tolkien) 171, 287
Hoffmann, E T A 109
    Nachtstücke **111**, 120
    "The Sandman" 111, 120
Hölderlin, Friedrich, *Hyperion* 111
Holmes, John Clellon, *Go* 264
Holocaust **258**
Homer **28**
    Iliad 18, **26–33**, 41, 54, 62, 294, 312
    Odyssey 18, 28, 33, 41, **54**, 62, 220–21, 312
Hopscotch (Cortázar) 249, **274–75**, 282
Horace 28, 40, 74
Hosseini, Khaled, *The Kite Runner* **338**
The Hound of the Baskervilles (Conan Doyle) 206, **208**
A House For Mr Biswas (Naipaul) **289**
The House of Mirth (Wharton) 118
The House of the Seven Gables (Hawthorne) 140
The House of The Spirits (Allende) 302, **334**
Howl and Other Poems (Ginsberg) 248, 261, 264, **288**
Hughes, Langston, *The Ways of White Folks* 235
Hughes, Ted
    Crow **291**
    The Hawk in the Rain 277
Hughes, Thomas, *Tom Brown's School Days* 169
Hugo, Victor 122, 157, **167**, 181, 182
    Les Miserables 156, **166–67**, 182
The Human Stain (Roth) 318
Hunger (Hamsun) **202**
The Hunger Games (Collins) 320
Hurston, Zora Neale, *Their Eyes Were Watching God* 207, **235**
Hussein, Taha, *A Man of Letters* 223
Huxley, Aldous, *Brave New World* **243**, 252, 261
Huysmans, Joris-Karl, *Against Nature* 194
Hwang Sok-yong
    The Guest 295, **330**
    The Shadow of Arms 330
Hymns (Ronsard) 74
Hyperion (Hölderlin) 111

IJ

I Am a Cat (Sōseki) **209**
I Ching **21**
I Know Why the Caged Bird Sings (Angelou) 259, **291**

I-Juca-Pirama (Dias) 164
I-novel **209**
Ibsen, Henrik **200**
    A Doll's House **200**
Icelandic sagas 19, **52–53**
The Idiot (Dostoyevsky) **199**
If This is a Man (Levi) 258
If on a Winter's Night a Traveller (Calvino) 69, 294, **298–99**
Iliad (Homer) 18, **26–33**, 41, 54, 62, 294, 312
Imperial Chinese poetry **46**
Imuzo, Takedo, *Chūshingura* 93
"In the Apartments of Death" (Sachs) 258
In the Castle of My Skin (Lamming) 312
In Cold Blood (Capote) 249, 273, **278–79**
In the Miso Soup (Murakami) 319
In Search of Lost Time (Proust) 216, **240–41**
In the Skin of a Lion (Ondaatje) 324
Incidents in the Life of a Slave Girl (Jacobs) 126
Indian English writing 294, 295, **314–17**
Indianism/Indianismo **164**
Infinite Jest (Wallace) 296, **337**
The Inheritance of Loss (Desai) 314, 317
Interpreter of Maladies (Lahiri) **338**
invention of childhood **168–71**
Invisible Man (Ellison) 145, **259**, 306, 309
Ionesco, Eugène, *Rhinocéros* 262
Irving, Washington, *The Sketch Book* **150**
Islamic Golden Age 19, 44–45
Issa, Kobayashi, *The Spring of My Life* 92
Ivanhoe (Scott) 122, **150**
Jacobethan theatre **75**
Jacobs, Harriet 109
    Incidents in the Life of a Slave Girl 126
Jacques the Fatalist (Diderot) 96, **105**
James, Henry 177, 183, **187**, 217
    The Portrait of a Lady 157, 174, **186–87**
    The Turn of the Screw **203**, 271
Jane Eyre (Brontë) 109, 118, **128–31**, 137
Jean de Meun, *Romance of the Rose* **57**
Jewett, Sarah Orne, *The Country of the Pointed Firs* 188
Jewish Holocaust **258**
Johannes von Tepl, *Ploughman of Bohemia* 72
Johnson, Samuel 91
Jonson, Ben 61, 84
    The Alchemist 75
    Works 84, 85–86
Journey to the Centre of the Earth (Verne) 184
Journey to the End of The Night (Céline) **243**

Journey to the West (Wu) 66
Joyce, James **216**
    Dubliners 216
    Finnegans Wake 206, 216
    A Portrait of the Artist as a Young Man 217, 225, **241**, 256
    Ulysses 206, **214–21**, 241, 260
Jude the Obscure (Hardy) **202**
Julie, or the New Heloise (Rousseau) 100
Julius Caesar (Shakespeare) 87, 88, 89
July's People (Gordimer) 261
The Jungle Book (Kipling) 157, 168, **202**
The Jungle (Sinclair) 166

K

Kabuki and Bunraku theatre **93**
Kafka, Franz **211**
    The Castle 211
    Letter to His father 211
    Metamorphosis 206, **210–11**, 234
    The Trial 211, **242**
Kafka on the Shore (Murakami) 302, 319
Kalevala (Lönnrot) 116, **151**
Kalidasa 19
Karlamagnús saga 48
Katai, Tayama, *Futon* 209
Kawabata, Yasunari, *Snow Country* **286**
Keats, John 256
    "Ode to a Nightingale" 110
Keller, Gottfried, *Green Henry* 224
Kemal, Yasar **288**
    Memed, My Hawk **288**
Keneally, Thomas, *Schindler's Ark* 311
Kerouac, Jack **265**
    On the Road 185, 248, **264–65**
Kesey, Ken, *One Flew Over the Cuckoo's Nest* 271, **289**
Kindred (Butler) 126
King Lear (Shakespeare) **88**, 144
King, Thomas, *Green Grass, Running Water* **337**
The Kingdom of this World (Carpentier) 312
Kingsley, Charles, *The Water Babies* 168
Kipling, Rudyard 196
    The Jungle Book 157, 168, **202**
Kitchen (Yashimoto) 319
The Kite Runner (Hosseini) **338**
Kivi, Aleksis, *Seven Brothers* **199**
Klinger, Friedrich Maximilian von, *Sturm und Drang* 98
Kokinshū poetry collection 47
Konjaku monogatari 47
Kundera, Milan **334**
    The Unbearable Lightness of Being **334**
Kyd, Thomas, *The Spanish Tragedy* 75

L

La Celestina (Fernando de Rojas) 78
La Comédie humaine (Balzac) 156, 160
La Fayette, Madame de, *The Princess of Cleves* **104**
La Fontaine, Jean de, *Fables* 90
La Jalousie (Robbe-Grillet) **288–89**
La Regenta (Alas) **201**
Laclos, Pierre Choderlos de **101**
    Les Liaisons dangereuses 13, **100–01**
Lady Chatterley's Lover (Lawrence) 260
The Lagoon and Other Stories (Frame) **286**
Lahiri, Jhumpa 317, **338**
    Interpreter of Maladies **338**
Lamb, Lady Caroline, *Glenarvon* 185
Lamming, George, *In the Castle of My Skin* 312
Lancelot, the Knight of the Cart (Chrétien de Troyes) 19, **50–51**
Lancelot-Grail cycle (Vulgate Cycle) 50
The Land (Park) 330
Laozi, *Dao De Jing* **54**
Larkin, Philip, *Whitsun Weddings* 277
L'Assommoir (Zola) 166
The Last of the Crazy People (Findley) 326
The Last of the Mohicans (Cooper) 122, **150**
Latin American Boom **282–85**
Lawrence, D H **241**
    Lady Chatterley's Lover 260
    Sons and Lovers 192, **240**
Lazarillo de Tormes 78
Le Cid (Corneille) **103**
Le Morte d'Arthur (Malory) 50, 51, **102**
"Leatherstocking Tales" (Cooper) 122, 150, 188
Leaves of Grass (Whitman) 109, **125**
Lee, Harper **273**, 278
    Go Set a Watchman 273
    To Kill a Mockingbird 249, 271, **272–73**
Lermontov, Mikhail 108
    A Hero of Our Time 124, **151–52**
Leroux, Gaston, *The Phantom of the Opera* 195
Les Amours de Cassandre (Ronsard) **74**
Les Fleurs du mal (Baudelaire) **165**
Les Lauriers sont coupés (Dujardin) 216
Les Liaisons dangereuses (Laclos) 13, **100–01**
Les Miserables, (Hugo) 156, **166–67**, 182
Les Nègres (Genet) 262
Lessing, Gotthold Ephraim, *Nathan the Wise* 96
Letters Concerning the English Nation (Voltaire) 97
Letters of a Portuguese Nun (Guilleragues) 100
Levi, Primo, *If This is a Man* 258
Levy, Andrea, *Small Island* 324
Lewis, C S, *Narnia* series 171
Lewis, Matthew, *The Monk* 121
L'homme rapaillé (Miron) **332**
Li Bai 19, **46**
Life is a Dream (Calderón de la Barca) 78
The Life of Lazarillo de Tormes 78
Life of Pi (Martel) 270, **338**
Life A User's Manual (Perec) **333**
literature
    definition and literary canon 12–13
    global explosion 15
    story of 13–14
    vocabulary, expanded 15
Little Dorrit (Dickens) 109, 166
The Little Prince (Saint-Exupéry) 207, **238–39**
Little Women (Alcott) 169, **199**
Lolita (Nabokov) 186, 248, **260–61**, 270
London, Jack 191
    The Call of the Wild **240**
Lönnrot, Elias, *Kalevala* 116, **151**
Lope de Vega, *New Rules for Writing Plays at this Time* 78
Lord of the Flies (Golding) **287**
Lord Jim (Conrad) **203**
The Lord of the Rings (Tolkien) **287**
Lost Generation literature 207, **228–33**
The Lost World (Conan Doyle) 184
"The Love Song of J. Alfred Prufrock" (Eliot) 213
The Love Suicides at Sonezaki (Monzaemon) **93**
Love in the Time of Cholera (García Márquez) **335**
The Lover (Duras) **335**
Love's Labour's Lost (Shakespeare) 87, 88
Lu Xun
    Call to Arms 207, **222**
    Old Tales Retold 222
Lucky Jim (Amis) 318
Luo Guanzhong **66**
    Romance of the Three Kingdoms 60, **66–67**
The Lusiads (Camões) 62, **103**
lyric poetry **49**
Lyrical Ballads (Wordsworth/Coleridge) 108, **110**

M

Maalouf, Amin, *The Rock of Tanios* **337**
Mabinogion **56**, 116
Macbeth (Shakespeare) 85, 87, 88, 144
McCabe, Patrick, *The Butcher Boy* 313
McCarthy, Mary, *The Groves of Academe* 318
McCullers, Carson, *The Heart Is a Lonely Hunter* 272
McEwan, Ian 331
McInerney, Jay, *Bright Lights, Big City* 313
Madame Bovary (Flaubert) 81, 146, 156, **158–63**, 190
Madame de Treymes (Wharton) 186
The Madwoman in the Attic (Gilbert and Gubar) 131
Magalhães, Gonçalves de, *A Confederação dos Tamoios* 164
The Magic Mountain (Mann) 206–07, **224–27**
magic realism 15, 234, 294, 295, **302–05**
Mahabharata (Vyasa) 13, 18, **22–25**, 28
Mahfouz, Naguib, *The Cairo Trilogy* 223
The Maias (Eça de Queirós) **202**
Mailer, Norman **291**
    The Armies of the Night **291**
Mallarmé, Stéphane 157
    "The Afternoon of a Faun" 165
Malory, Sir Thomas, *Le Morte d'Arthur* 50, 51, **102**
The Maltese Falcon (Hammett) 236
A Man of Letters (Hussein) 223
The Man Without Qualities (Musil) 234, **243**
Mann, Thomas **227**
    Buddenbrooks 194, 227
    Death in Venice 194, 207, 224–25, **240**
    The Magic Mountain 206–07, **224–27**
Marguerite de Navarre, *The Heptameron* 68
Marlowe, Christopher 61, 89, 114
    Doctor Faustus **75**
Martel, Yann, *Life of Pi* 270, **338**
Martin Chuzzlewit (Dickens) 186
Marvell, Andrew, *Miscellaneous Poems* **91**
Mary Barton (Gaskell) 153, 166
The Master and Margarita (Bulgakov) **290–91**
Maupassant, Guy de, *Bel Ami* 160
Mda, NoZakes, *The Heart of Redness* 322
Measure for Measure (Shakespeare) 87, 88
Medea (Euripides) **55**
Melville, Herman **140**
    Bartleby, the Scrivener 140
    Moby-Dick 109, **138–45**, 296
Memed, My Hawk (Kemal) **288**
Men of Maize (Asturias) 282
metafiction 295, **298–99**, 302–03
Metamorphoses (Ovid) 40, **55–56**, 84
Metamorphosis (Kafka) 206, **210–11**, 234
Metaphysical Poets **91**
Middlemarch (Eliot) 130–31, 156, 174, **182–83**
Midnight's Children (Rushdie) 227, 271, 294, **300–05**, 314, 315
A Midsummer Night's Dream (Shakespeare) 85, 87, **88–89**
The Mill on the Floss (Eliot) 128
Miller, Henry, *Tropic of Cancer* **243**, 260
Milton, John 61, **103**
    Paradise Lost 62, **103**, 144
Mimes, Lessons, and Proverbs (Baif) 74
Miron, Gaston, *L'homme rapaillé* **332**
The Misanthrope (Molière) 90
Miscellaneous Poems (Marvell) **91**
Mishima, Yukio, *The Temple of the Golden Pavilion* **263**
Mitchell, David, *Cloud Atlas* 69
Mo Yan, *Red Sorghum* **310**
Moby-Dick (Melville) 109, **138–45**, 296
Modern Arabic voices **223**
Modernism 15, 69, 200, **206–07**, 224, 235
Modernist poetry **213**, 232
Moe, Jørgen, *Norwegian Folktales* 116
Molière 13, 61
    The Misanthrope **90**
    Psyché 90
The Monk (Lewis) 121
Montalvo, Garci Rodríguez de, *Amadis of Gaul* **102–03**
Montesquieu, *Persian Letters* 96
Monzaemon, Chikamatsu, *The Love Suicides at Sonezaki* **93**
The Moonstone (Collins) 146, 149, **198–99**, 208, 271
Morante, Elsa, *History* **332**
More, Thomas, *Utopia* 252
Morrison, Toni 295, **309**
    Beloved 145, 294, **306–09**
    The Bluest Eye 307, 309
    Song of Solomon 307, 309
    Sula 307
Moses Ascending (Selvon) 324
Mother Courage and Her Children (Brecht) 238, **244–45**
Mr President (Asturias) 282
Mrs Dalloway (Woolf) 182, 217, **242**
multiculturalism 294–95, **324–25**
Munro, Alice **337**
    Dance of the Happy Shades 337
    Selected Stories **337**
    Too Much Happiness 326
Murakami, Haruki
    Kafka on the Shore 302, 319
    Norwegian Wood 319
    The Wind-Up Bird Chronicle **319**
Murakami, Ryu, *In the Miso Soup* 319
Murasaki Shikibu, *The Tale of Genji* 19, **47**, 61, 174
The Murders in the Rue Morgue (Poe) 208
Musäus, Johann Karl August 116
Musil, Robert, *The Man Without Qualities* 234, **243**
My Name is Red (Pamuk) **338**
The Mysteries of Udolpho (Radcliffe) 120
The Mysterious Affair at Styles (Christie) 208

NO

Nabokov, Vladimir **261**
 Lolita 186, 248, **260–61**, 270
Nachtstücke (Hoffmann) **111**, 120
Naevius, Gnaeus 40
Naipaul, V S 294
 A House For Mr Biswas **289**
Naked Lunch (Burroughs) 260, 264
Naoya, Shiga, *A Dark Night's Passing* 209
Narayan, R K 315
Narnia series (Lewis) 171
Narrative of the Life of Frederick Douglass (Douglass) 109, **126–27**
The Narrow Road to the Interior (Bashō) 61, **92**
Nathan the Wise (Lessing) 96
Native Son (Wright) 259
Naturalism **190–91**, 219
Nausea (Sartre) 210, **244**
The Nazi and the Barber (Hilsenrath) 258
Négritude literary movement 196
Negro literature **235**
Neuromancer (Gibson) **334–35**
New Grub Street (Gissing) 190
New Journalism **278–79**
New Rules for Writing Plays at this Time (Lope de Vega) 78
The New York Trilogy (Auster) 298, **336**
Ngugi wa Thiong'o, *Wizard of the Crow* **339**
Nibelungenlied **57**
Nietzsche, Friedrich, *Thus Spoke Zarathustra* 210
Nigerian voices **266–69**
Nights at the Circus (Carter) 302
Nineteen Eighty-Four (Orwell) 248, **250–55**, 261
Njal's Saga **52–53**
"A Nocturnal Upon St Lucy's Day" (Donne) 91
Nordic sagas **52–53**
North and South (Gaskell) **153**
Northup, Solomon 109
 Twelve Years a Slave 127
Norwegian Folktales (Asbjørnsen/ Moe) 116
Norwegian Wood (Murakami) 319
Nostromo (Conrad) **240**
Notes from the Underground (Dostoyevsky) 219
novel of manners **118–19**
O'Brien, Flann, *At Swim-Two-Birds* 274
"Ode to a Nightingale" (Keats) 110
Odyssey (Homer) 18, 33, 38, 41, **54**, 62, 220–21, 312
Oedipus the King (Sophocles) **34–39**
Of Mice and Men (Steinbeck) **244**
Ōgais, Mori, *The Dancing Girl* 209
Okri, Ben, *The Famished Road* 269
The Old Curiosity Shop (Dickens) 146

Old English poetry **42–43**
Old French **48**, 51
Old Goriot (Balzac) **151**
The Old Man and the Sea (Hemingway) **287**
Old Tales Retold (Lu) 222
Oliver Twist (Dickens) 134, **151**
Omeros (Walcott) 294, **312**
omniscient narrator **182–83**
On the Origin of Species (Darwin) 156, 190
On the Road (Kerouac) 185, 248, **264–65**
Ondaatje, Michael
 The English Patient **336**
 In the Skin of a Lion 324
One Day in the Life of Ivan Denisovich (Solzhenitsyn) **289**
One Flew Over the Cuckoo's Nest (Kesey) 271, **289**
One Hundred Years of Solitude (García Márquez) 249, **280–85**, 302
One Thousand and One Nights 14, 19, **44–45**, 68
Ōoka, Shōhei, *Fires on the Plain* 263
Oresteia (Aeschylus) **54–55**
Orlando Furioso (Ariosto) 63
Orwell, George **252**
 Animal Farm **245**, 248, 252, 253, 320
 Nineteen Eighty-Four 248, **250–55**, 261
Oscar and Lucinda (Carey) **311**
Other Voices, Other Rooms (Capote) 279
Oulipo group 299, 333
Our Mutual Friend (Dickens) 166
The Outsider (Camus) 211, **245**, 262
Ovid 28, 71
 Ars Amatoria (Art of Love) 57
 Metamorphoses 40, **55–56**, 84
Owen, Wilfred
 "Dulce et Decorum Est" 206, **212**
 Poems 206, 207, **212**
"Ozymandias" (Shelley) 110

P

Palahniuk, Chuck, *Fight Club* 313
The Palm-Wine Drinkard (Tutuola) 266
Pamela (Richardson) 94, 100, 104, 118, 174, 217
Pamuk, Orhan, *My Name is Red* **338**
Paradise Lost (Milton) 62, **103**, 144
Park Kyong-ni, *The Land* 330
Paroles (Prévert) **286**
A Passage to India (Forster) 196, **241–42**
Pasternak, Boris, *Doctor Zhivago* **288**
pathetic fallacy **192–93**
Paton, Alan, *Cry, the Beloved Country* **286**, 322
Pedro Páramo (Rulfo) **287–88**
People of the City (Ekwensi) 266

Perdita (Scharper) 326
Perec, Georges, *Life A User's Manual* **333**
Perfume (Süskind) 227
Perrault, Charles
 "Cendrillon" 117
 Tales of Mother Goose 116
Persian Letters (Montesquieu) 96
Pessoa, Fernando, *The Book of Disquiet* 216, **244**
Peter Pan (Barrie) 169
Petrarch 72, 74
The Phantom of the Opera (Leroux) 195
Phèdre (Racine) 90, **103–04**
philosophes **96–97**
picaresque novel 78, 127
The Pickwick Papers (Dickens) 146, 147
The Picture of Dorian Gray (Wilde) 157, **194**, 195
"Pierre Menard, Author of the Quixote" (Borges) 81
The Pilgrim's Progress (Bunyan) 330
The Pillow Book (Sei Shōnagon) 19, 47, **56**
Pinter, Harold, *The Caretaker* 262
The Pioneers (Cooper) 122, 188
Plath, Sylvia
 Ariel 276
 The Bell Jar 185, 256, **290**
Playing for Thrills (Wang) **336**
The Pléiade **74**
Ploughman of Bohemia (Johannes von Tepl) 72
The Plum in the Golden Vase 66
Poe, Edgar Allan 109, 134, 141, 207, 327
 The Murders in the Rue Morgue 208
 "The Raven" 140
 Tales of the Grotesque and Arabesque **152**
Poems (Owen) 206, 207, **212**
Poetics (Aristotle) **39**, 90
Poppy and Memory (Celan) 238, **258**
A Portrait of the Artist as a Young Man (Joyce) 217, 225, **241**, 256
The Portrait of a Lady (James) 157, 174, **186–87**
Possession: A Romance (Byatt) 318
post 9/11 America **331**
post-classical epic poetry **62–63**
post-war Japanese writing **263**
post-war poetry **277**
The Postman Always Rings Twice (Cain) 236
Pound, Ezra 206, 216, 230
 Cantos 213
The Prelude (Wordsworth) 168
Prévert, Jacques, *Paroles* **286**
Pride and Prejudice (Austen) 12, 108, **118–19**
The Prince of Homburg (von Kleist) 111
The Princess of Cleves (La Fayette) **104**
The Prophet (Gibran) **223**

Prose Edda (Sturluson) 52
protest novel **259**
Proust, Marcel 217
 In Search of Lost Time 216, **240–41**
Psyché (Molière/Corneille/Quinault) 90
psychological realism **172–77**
Puranas (Hindu texts) 22
Purple Hibiscus (Adichie) 269, 339
Pushkin, Alexander 108
 Eugene Onegin 109, **124**
 Tales of Belkin 178
Pynchon, Thomas **296**
 Bleeding Edge 296, 331
 The Crying of Lot 49 276, **290**, 296
 Gravity's Rainbow 294, 295, **296–97**
 V. 296

QR

Qu Yuan, *Songs of Chu* 46, **55**
Quan Tangshi **46**
Quinault, Philippe
 Psyché 90
 The Rivals 90
Qur'an ("Recitation") 44
"Rabbit" series (Updike) 328
Rabelais, François **73**, 219
 Gargantua and Pantagruel 60, 61, **72–73**, 260
Racine, Jean 61
 Phèdre 90, **103–04**
Radcliffe, Ann, *The Mysteries of Udolpho* 120
The Radetzky March (Roth) 238
Radical Chic and Mau-Mauing the Flak Catchers (Wolfe) 278
Ramayana (Valmiki) 18, 22, 23, 25, **55**
Rand, Ayn, *The Fountainhead* **245**
"The Raven" (Poe) 140
"Recitation" (Qur'an) 44
The Recognitions (Gaddis) 328
The Red Badge of Courage (Crane) 190, **202**
The Red and the Black (Stendhal) **150–51**, 160, 174
Red Harvest (Hammett) 236
The Red Room (Strindberg) **185**
Red Sorghum (Mo) **310**
The Reluctant Fundamentalist (Hamid) 331, **339**
Renaissance humanism 14, **72–73**
René (Chateaubriand) **150**
Return to My Native Land (Césaire) 312
Rhinocéros (Ionesco) 262
Rhys, Jean, *Wide Sargasso Sea* 131, **290**
Richard III (Shakespeare) 87, 88, **89**
Richardson, John, *Wacousta* 326
Richardson, Samuel **104**
 Clarissa 100, **104**
 Pamela 94, 100, 104, 118, 174, 217
Rimbaud, Arthur, *A Season in Hell* 165, **199–200**

The Rime of the Ancient Mariner (Coleridge) 144
The Rivals (Quinault) 90
Rob Roy (Scott) 122
Robbe-Grillet, Alain, *La Jalousie* **288–89**
The Robbers (Schiller) 61, **98–99**
Robinson Crusoe (Defoe) 61, **94–95**, 196
The Rock of Tanios (Maalouf) **337**
roman à clef **185**
Roman literature **40–41**
Romance of the Rose (Guillaume de Lorris/Jean de Meun) **57**
Romance of the Three Kingdoms (Luo) 60, **66–67**
Romances of the Landscape (Ah Cheng) 310
Ronsard, Pierre de
Hymns 74
Les Amours de Cassandre **74**
Sonnets for Hélène 74
Roots (Haley) 306, **333**
"roots-seeking" (*xungen*) movement **310**
Rossetti, Christina 131
Roth, Joseph, *The Radetzky March* 238
Roth, Philip 328
Goodbye, Columbus 276
The Human Stain 318
Rousseau, Jean-Jacques 96
Discourse on the Arts and Sciences 98
Émile 168
Julie, or the New Heloise 100
Rowe, Nicholas, *Shakespeare's Complete Works* 84
Rowling, J K, *Harry Potter* series **170**, 261
Roy, Arundhati, *The God of Small Things* 314, 317
The Royal Game (Zweig) 238
Rulfo, Juan, *Pedro Páramo* **287–88**
Rushdie, Salman 294, **302**, 317, 325
Midnight's Children 227, 271, 294, **300–05**, 314, 315
The Satanic Verses 260, 261, 302, **336**
Ruskin, John 137, 171, 192
Russia's Golden Age **178–81**

S

Sachs, Nelly, "In the Apartments of Death" 258
Safran Foer, Jonathan, *Extremely Loud and Incredibly Close* 295, **331**
Saint-Exupéry, Antoine de **239**
The Little Prince 207, **238–39**
Sakurajima (Umezaki) 263
Salinger, J D **257**
The Catcher in the Rye 248, **256–57**, 271, 328
The Sand Child (Ben Jelloun) 223
"The Sandman" (Hoffmann) 111, 120
Sanskrit epics 18, 19, **22–25**

Saramago, José 287, 295, **321**
Blindness 295, **320–21**
Sartre, Jean-Paul 177, 211, 249, 274
Nausea 210, **244**
Sassoon, Siegfried 212
The Satanic Verses (Rushdie) 260, 261, 302, **336**
The Scarlet Letter (Hawthorne) 140, **153**
Scharper, Hilary, *Perdita* 326
Schiller, Friedrich **99**, 112, 113–14, 115
The Robbers 61, **98–99**
Wallenstein 112
Schindler's Ark (Keneally) 311
Schnitzler, Arthur, *Dream Story* 194
Schreiner, Olive, *The Story of an African Farm* **201**, 322
Schwarzer Tee mit drei Stück Zucker (Demirkan) 324
scientific romance **184**
Scott, Sir Walter 53, 109, **150**, 162
Ivanhoe 122, **150**
Rob Roy 122
Waverley 122, 150
Scudéry, Madeleine de, *Clelia* 185
A Season in Hell (Rimbaud) 165, **199–200**
Sebald, W G, *Austerlitz* **338**
"The Second Coming" (Yeats) 266
The Secret History (Tartt) **318**
Sei Shōnagon **56**
The Pillow Book 19, 47, **56**
Selected Stories (Munro) **337**
Selvon, Sam, *Moses Ascending* 324
Senghor, L-S 196
Sentimental Education (Flaubert) 163, **199**, 225
Senzaishū (Collection of a Thousand Years) (Fujiwara) 47
serial novel **146–49**
Seth, Vikram 294, **315**
A Suitable Boy 295, **314–17**
Seven Brothers (Kivi) **199**
The Shadow of Arms (Hwang) 330
Shakespeare, William **82–89**, 125
A Midsummer Night's Dream 85, 87, **88–89**
Antony and Cleopatra 87, 89
As You Like It 85, 88, 89
authorship debate 89
The Comedy of Errors 88, 89
First Folio 14, 61, **82–89**
Hamlet 85, 87, **88**, 144, 174, 221
Henry IV 75, 88, 89
Julius Caesar 87, 88, 89
King Lear 88, 144
Love's Labour's Lost 87, 88
Macbeth 85, 87, 88, 144
Measure for Measure 87, 88
recurring motifs 88
Richard III 87, 88, **89**
The Tempest 84, 87, 88, 89, 196, 243
Twelfth Night 84, 85, 87, 88, 89
Shelley, Mary **121**, 131
Frankenstein 108, **120–21**, 184, 192
Shelley, Percy Bysshe 120, 121
"Ozymandias" 110

Sheridan, Richard Brinsley 90
Sherlock Holmes stories (Doyle) 149
Shi Nai'an, *The Water Margin* 60, 66
shi tradition 46
Shika, Masaoka 92
Shimazaki, Tōson, *The Broken Commandment* 209
Shoraku, Miyoshi, *Chūshingura* 93
Shriver, Lionel, *We Need to Talk about Kevin* 328
Siddhartha (Hesse) **241**
Sinclair, Upton 191
The Jungle 166
Sir Gawain and the Green Knight 71, **102**
Sister Carrie (Dreiser) **203**
The Sketch Book (Irving) **150**
Slaughterhouse-Five (Vonnegut) 276, **291**
slave narratives **126–27**
The Sleepwalkers (Broch) 234
Small Island (Levy) 324
Smith, Zadie **325**
White Teeth 295, **324–25**
Snow Country (Kawabata) **286**
So Long a Letter (Bâ) **334**
social protest novel **166–67**
Solzhenitsyn, Aleksandr, *One Day in the Life of Ivan Denisovich* **289**
The Song of Roland (Turold) **49**
Song of Solomon (Morrison) 307, 309
Songs of Chu (Qu Yuan) 46, **55**
Songs of Innocence and Experience (Blake) **105**, 110
Songs without Words (Verlaine) 165
Sonnets for Hélène (Ronsard) 74
Sons and Lovers (Lawrence) 192, **240**
Sophocles 18, **36**
Oedipus the King **34–39**
The Sorrows of Young Werther (Goethe) 98, **105**, 256
Sōseki, Natsume, *I Am a Cat* **209**
Sosuke, Namiki, *Chūshingura* 93
The Sound and the Fury (Faulkner) 188, 216, **242–43**, 271
South African literature 295, **322–23**
South Korea, 38th parallel **330**
Southern Gothic **272–73**
Southern Ontario Gothic **326–27**
Soyinka, Wole, *A Dance of the Forests* 266
Spain's Golden Century **78–81**
The Spanish Tragedy (Kyd) 75
Spenser, Edmund 61
The Faerie Queene 63, **103**
The Spring of My Life (Issa) 92
Spyri, Johanna, *Heidi* 169
Stein, Gertrude 230
Steinbeck, John 12, **244**
The Grapes of Wrath 188, 189, **244**
Of Mice and Men **244**
Stendhal
The Charterhouse of Parma 160
The Red and the Black **150–51**, 160, 174
Sterne, Laurence 12
Tristram Shandy 61, **104–05**, 221, 271, 298

Stevens, Wallace, *Harmonium* 213
Stevenson, Robert Louis **201**
The Strange Case of Dr Jekyll and Mr Hyde 157, 195, **201–02**
Treasure Island **201**
Stoker, Bram, *Dracula* 157, **195**
The Story of an African Farm (Schreiner) **201**, 322
The Story of Bayad and Riyad 44
Stowe, Harriet Beecher 15
Uncle Tom's Cabin 145, **153**, 166, 188, 261
The Strange Case of Dr Jekyll and Mr Hyde (Stevenson) 157, 195, **201–02**
stream of consciousness 15, 105, 206, **216–21**, 282
Strindberg, August, *The Red Room* **185**
Sturlunga Saga 52
Sturluson, Snorri, *Prose Edda* 52
Sturm und Drang (Klinger) 98
Sturm und Drang movement 14, **98–99**, 105, 108, 113
A Suitable Boy (Seth) 295, **314–17**
Sula (Morrison) 307
The Sun Also Rises (Hemingway) 186, 230, 264, 286
superfluous man 108, **124**
Süskind, Patrick, *Perfume* 227
Swift, Jonathan, *Gulliver's Travels* 61, 94, 95, **104**, 270, 321
Swiss Family Robinson (Wyss) 168
Sybil (Disraeli) 166

T

The Tale of Genji (Murasaki) 19, **47**, 61, 174
The Tale of Igor's Campaign **57**
The Tale of the Lady Ochikubo 46
A Tale of Two Cities (Dickens) **198**
Tales of Belkin (Pushkin) 178
Tales of the Grotesque and Arabesque (Poe) **152**
Tales of Mother Goose (Perrault) 116
Talese, Gay 278
Tanpinar, Ahmet Hamdi, *The Time Regulation Institute* **289**
Tartt, Donna
The Goldfinch 328
The Secret History **318**
teenager, birth of the **256–57**
The Tempest (Shakespeare) 84, 87, 88, 89, 196, 243
The Temple of the Golden Pavilion (Mishima) **263**
The Temptation of Saint Anthony (Flaubert) 161
Tender is the Night (Fitzgerald) 233
Tess of the d'Urbervilles (Hardy) 157, **192–93**
Texaco (Chamoiseau) **336–37**
Thackeray, William Makepeace, *Vanity Fair* 118, **153**
Theatre of the Absurd **262**

Their Eyes Were Watching God (Hurston) 207, **235**
Theogony (Hesiod) 28, **54**
Thérèse Raquin (Zola) **198**
Things Fall Apart (Achebe) 248, **266–69**
This Side of Paradise (Fitzgerald) 230
Thomas of Britain, *Tristan* 50
Thompson, Hunter S, *Fear and Loathing in Las Vegas* **332**
Thoreau, Henry David 108–09
Walden 125
Three Hundred Tang Poems (Tang shisanbai shou) 46
The Three Musketeers (Dumas) 109, **122–23**
Thus Spoke Zarathustra (Nietzsche) 210
Tibet (Zhaxi [Tashi] Dawa) 310
Tieck, Ludwig, *Franz Sternbald's Wanderings* 224
The Time of the Hero (Vargas Llosa) **290**
The Time Machine (Wells) 184
The Time Regulation Institute (Tanpinar) **289**
The Tin Drum (Grass) 249, **270–71**, 302
To Kill a Mockingbird (Lee) 249, 271, **272–73**
To the Lighthouse (Woolf) 216, 217
To Us, All Flowers Are Roses: Poems (Goodison) 312
Tolkien, J R R 43, 53
The Hobbit 171, 287
The Lord of the Rings **287**
Tolstoy, Leo **181**, 182
Anna Karenina 149, 178, **200**
War and Peace 109, 156, **178–81**, 182
Tom Brown's School Days (Hughes) 169
Tom Jones (Fielding) 94, **104**, 182
Too Much Happiness (Munro) 326
Toole, John Kennedy, *A Confederacy of Dunces* 272
Toomer, Jean, *Cane* 235
transatlantic fiction **186–87**
Transcendentalism 14, **125**, 140, 141
transgressive fiction **313**
Treasure Island (Stevenson) **201**
The Trial (Kafka) 211, **242**
Tristan (Thomas of Britain) 50
Tristram Shandy (Sterne) 61, **104–05**, 221, 271, 298
Troilus and Criseyde (Chaucer) 69
Trollope, Anthony, *The Way We Live Now* 186
Tropic of Cancer (Miller) **243**, 260
troubadours and minnesingers 19, **49**, 50–51
The True History of the Kelly Gang (Carey) 311
Turgenev, Ivan 108
The Diary of a Superfluous Man 124
The Turn of the Screw (James) **203**, 271

Turold, *The Song of Roland* **49**
Tutuola, Amos, *The Palm-Wine Drinkard* 266
Twain, Mark 15, **189**
The Adventures of Huckleberry Finn 145, 157, **188–89**, 270
Twelfth Night (Shakespeare) 84, 85, 87, 88, 89
Twelve Years a Slave (Northup) 127
Twenty Thousand Leagues Under the Sea (Verne) **184**

UV

Ulysses (Joyce) 206, **214–21**, 241, 260
Umezaki, Haruo, *Sakurajima* 263
The Unbearable Lightness of Being (Kundera) **334**
Uncle Tom's Cabin (Stowe) 145, **153**, 166, 188, 261
Uncle Vanya, (Chekhov) **203**
"Under the Linden Tree" (Walther) **49**
Underworld (DeLillo) 296, 335
A Universal History of Infamy (Borges) 302
universal (world) writing **319**
unreliable narrator **270–71**
Up From Slavery (Washington) 306
Updike, John, "Rabbit" series 328
Urban Gothic 157, **195**
U.S.A. trilogy (Dos Passos) 230
Utopia (More) 252
V. (Pynchon) 296
Valmiki **55**
Ramayana 22, 23, 25, **55**
Vanity Fair (Thackeray) 118, **153**
Vargas Llosa, Mario
Conversation in the Cathedral 282
The Time of the Hero **290**
Vaughan, Henry, "The World" 91
Vedas 20, 22–23
Verlaine, Paul, *Songs without Words* 165
Verne, Jules 157
Five Weeks in a Balloon 184
Journey to the Centre of the Earth 184
Twenty Thousand Leagues Under the Sea **184**
Vestiges of the Natural History of Creation 184
Vicente, Gil, *Barcas* trilogy **103**
Victorian feminism **128–31**
Victorian Gothic **134–37**
Villa-Matas, Enrique, *Bartleby & Co.* 274
Villette (Brontë) 128
Virgil 28, **40**, 64
Aeneid 19, **40–41**, 62
Voltaire **97**
Candide 61, **96–97**, 260
Letters Concerning the English Nation 97
Von Kleist, Heinrich, *The Prince of Homburg* 111

Vonnegut, Kurt, *Slaughterhouse-Five* 276, **291**
Voss (White) 311
Vulgate Cycle (Lancelot-Grail) 50
Vyasa
Bhagavad Gita 24, **25**
Mahabharata 13, 18, **22–25**, 28

W

Wacousta (Richardson) 326
Waiting for an Angel (Habila) 266
Waiting for Godot (Beckett) 210, 248, **262**
Walcott, Derek 294
Omeros 294, **312**
Walden (Thoreau) 125
Waldere 42
Walker, Alice 307
The Color Purple 306
Wallace, David Foster, *Infinite Jest* 296, **337**
Wallenstein, (Schiller) 112
Walpole, Horace, *The Castle of Otranto* 120
Walther von der Vogelweide, "Under the Linden Tree" **49**
Wang Anyi, *Bao Town* 310
Wang Shuo, *Playing for Thrills* **336**
Wang Wei 19, **46**
War and Peace (Tolstoy) 109, 156, **178–81**, 182
Washington, Booker T, *Up From Slavery* 306
Wasps (Aristophanes) **55**
The Waste Land (Eliot) 192, 206, **213**, 216, 230, 232
The Water Babies (Kingsley) 168
The Water Margin (Shi) 60, 66
Waverley (Scott) 122, 150
The Way We Live Now (Trollope) 186
The Ways of White Folks (Hughes) 235
We (Zamyatin) 252, 253
We Need New Names (Bulawayo) **339**
We Need to Talk about Kevin (Shriver) 328
Wealth (Aristophanes) 39
Webster, John, *The Duchess of Malfi* 75
Weimar Classicism 99, 108, 111, **112–15**
Weimar-era experimentalism 207, **234**
Weiss, Peter, *The Aesthetics of Resistance* **333**
The Well Cradle (Izutsu) (Zeami Motokiyo) **102**
Wells, H G, *The Time Machine* 184
Wen of Zhou, King 18, **21**
West, Nathanael, *The Day of the Locust* 276
Wharton, Edith 187
Ethan Frome **240**
The House of Mirth 118
Madame de Treymes 186

White Noise (DeLillo) **335–36**
White, Patrick, *Voss* 311
White Teeth (Smith) 295, **324–25**
Whitman, Walt 108–09
Leaves of Grass 109, **125**
Whitsun Weddings (Larkin) 277
Wide Sargasso Sea (Rhys) 131, **290**
Wieland, Christoph Martin 113
Wilde, Oscar 90
The Picture of Dorian Gray 157, **194**, 195
Wilhelm Meister's Apprenticeship (Goethe) 224–25
Williams, Tennessee, *Cat on a Hot Tin Roof* 272
The Wind-Up Bird Chronicle (Murakami) **319**
Wizard of the Crow (Ngugi wa Thiong'o) **339**
Wolfe, Tom
Radical Chic and Mau-Mauing the Flak Catchers 278
The Bonfire of the Vanities 149
Wollstonecraft, Mary 121
The Woman in the Dunes (Abe) 263
Woolf, Virginia 135, **242**
Mrs Dalloway 182, 217, **242**
To the Lighthouse 216, 217
Wordsworth, William
"Daffodils" 192
Lyrical Ballads 108, **110**
The Prelude 168
Works (Jonson) 84, 85–86
"The World" (Vaughan) 91
World War I poets 206, 207, **212**
world (universal) writing **319**
Wright, Alexis, *Carpentaria* 311
Wright, Richard, *Native Son* 259
writers in exile **238–39**
Wu Cheng'en, *Journey to the West* 66
Wuthering Heights (Brontë) 69, 109, 128, 132, **134–37**, 192, 271
Wyss, Johann David, *Swiss Family Robinson* 168

XYZ

xungen ("roots-seeking") movement **310**
Yashimoto, Banana, *Kitchen* 319
Yeats, W B, "The Second Coming" 266
"The Yellow Wallpaper" (Gilman) 128, 131
Yi Kwang-su, *The Heartless* **241**
Zamyatin, Yevgeny, *We* 252, 253
Zeami Motokiyo, *The Well Cradle (Izutsu)* **102**
Zhaxi (Tashi) Dawa, *Tibet* 310
Zola, Émile **191**, 218–19
Claude's Confession 191
Germinal 157, 163, 166, **190–91**
L'Assommoir 166
Thérèse Raquin **198**
Zweig, Stefan, *The Royal Game* 238

ACKNOWLEDGMENTS

Dorling Kindersley would like to thank: Margaret McCormack for providing the index; Christopher Westhorp for proofreading the book; Alexandra Beeden, Sam Kennedy, and Georgina Palffy for editorial assistance; and Gadi Farfour and Phil Gamble for design assistance.

Quotations on page 212 are taken from *Wilfred Owen: The War Poems* (Chatto & Windus, 1994), edited by Jon Stallworthy.

Quotations on page 223 taken from *The Prophet* by Kahlil Gibran (Penguin Books, 2002) Introduction © Robin Waterfield, 1998.

PICTURE CREDITS

The publisher would like to thank the following for their kind permission to reproduce their photographs:

(Key: a-above; b-below; c-centre; l-left; r-right; t-top)

23 akg-images: Roland and Sabrina Michaud (br). **25 akg-images:** British Library (tl). **28 Alamy Images:** Peter Horree (bl). **29 Dreamstime.com:** Nikolai Sorokin (br). **30 Corbis:** Alfredo Dagli Orti/The Art Archive (tr). **32 Getty Images:** Universal History Archive/Contributor (b). **33 Alamy Images:** ACTIVE MUSEUM (tr). **36 Corbis:** (bl). **Dreamstime.com:** Emicristea (tr). **38 Getty Images:** De Agostini Picture Library (bl). **39 Alamy Images:** epa european pressphoto agency b.v. (tl). **51 Alamy Images:** World History Archive (tl). **64 Corbis:** David Lees (tl). **65 Corbis:** Hulton-Deutsch/Hulton-Deutsch Collection (tr). **67 The Art Archive:** Ashmolean Museum (br). **69 The Bridgeman Art Library:** Private Collection/

Bridgeman Images (tl). **70 Alamy Images:** Pictorial Press Ltd. (bl). **71 Corbis:** (tr). **73 Corbis:** Michael Nicholson (tr). **78 Corbis:** (bl). **81 Dreamstime.com:** Typhoonski (bl). **84 Corbis:** (bl). **85 Corbis:** Steven Vidler/Eurasia Press (tr). **87 Corbis:** Lebrecht Authors/Lebrecht Music & Arts (tl). **Alamy Images:** Lebrecht Music and Arts Photo Library (br). **88 Corbis:** John Springer Collection (br). **89 Alamy Images:** AF archive (tl). **97 Corbis:** The Art Archive (tr). **99 Corbis:** (bl). **101 Corbis:** Leemage (tr). **114 Corbis:** Robbie Jack (tl). **115 Topfoto:** The Granger Collection (bl). **Corbis:** Leemage (tr). **117 Getty Images:** DEA PICTURE LIBRARY (tr). **119 Corbis:** Hulton-Deutsch/Hulton-Deutsch Collection (tr). **121 Corbis:** (tr). **123 Corbis:** Hulton-Deutsch Collection (tr). **127 Corbis:** (bl). **129 Getty Images:** Stock Montage/Contributor (bl). **134 Getty Images:** Hulton Archive/Stringer (bl). **136 Alamy Images:** Daniel J. Rao (t). **137 Corbis:** (tr). **140 Corbis:** (bl). **142 Corbis:** John Springer Collection (tr). **143 Corbis:** (br). **144 Alamy Images:** North Wind Picture Archives (tl). **145 Alamy Images:** United Archives GmbH (tl). **147 Corbis:** Chris Hellier (tr). **Alamy Images:** Classic Image (bc). **148 Corbis:** Geoffrey Clements (tl). **160 Corbis:** Hulton-Deutsch Collection (tl). **161 Corbis:** Leemage (tr). **162 Topfoto:** The Granger Collection (tr). **163 The Bridgeman Art Library:** Archives Charmet (br). **167 Corbis:** Hulton-Deutsch Collection (tr). **170 Corbis:** (tl). **Alamy Images:** ITAR-TASS Photo Agency (bl). **171 Getty Images:** Oscar G. Rejlander/Contributor (tr). **Corbis:** Derek Bayes/Lebrecht Music & Arts/Lebrecht Music & Arts (bc). **174 Corbis:** (bl). **175 Getty Images:** Imagno (tr). **176 Corbis:** David Scharf (tl). Hulton-Deutsch Collection (tr). **180 Alamy Images:** Heritage Image Partnership Ltd. (tl). **181 Corbis:** Leemage (bl). **Alamy Images:** GL Archive (tr). **183 Corbis:** The Print Collector (bl). **187 Corbis:** (bl). **189 Corbis:** (tr). **191 Corbis:** Hulton-Deutsch

Collection (tr). **193 Corbis:** (tr). **197 Corbis:** Hulton-Deutsch Collection (tr). **211 Corbis:** (tr). **216 Getty Images:** Culture Club/Contributor (bl). **217 Getty Images:** Apic/Contributor (tr). **219 Alamy Images:** Gabriela Insuratelu (tl). **220 Corbis:** Leemage (br). **225 akg-images:** ullstein bild (t). **227 akg-images:** (bc). **Corbis:** Hulton-Deutsch Collection (tr). **230 Corbis:** (bl). **231 Getty Images:** Paramount Pictures/Handout (tr). **239 Corbis:** Bettmann (tr). **252 Getty Images:** Hulton Archive/Stringer (bl). **255 Getty Images:** Heritage Images/Contributor (br). **257 Dreamstime.com:** Nicolarenna (tr). **Corbis:** Bettmann (tr). **261 Alamy Images:** Everett Collection Historical (bl). **265 Corbis:** Bettmann (bl). CHARLES PLATIAU/Reuters (tr). **267 Alamy Images:** Eye Ubiquitous (tl). **268 Topfoto:** Charles Walker (bl). **269 Alamy Images:** ZUMA Press, Inc. (tr). **271 Corbis:** Marc Brasz (tr). **273 Getty Images:** Donald Uhrbrock/Contributor (bl). **274 Getty Images:** Keystone-France/Contributor (b). **275 Corbis:** Sophie Bassouls/Sygma (tr). **279 Corbis:** Hulton-Deutsch Collection (tr). **282 Corbis:** Karl-Heinz Eiferle/dpa (br). **284 Getty Images:** Philippe Le Tellier/Contributor (bl). **285 Alamy Images:** Jan Sochor (tr). **297 Corbis:** Bettmann (br). **299 Corbis:** Sophie Bassouls/Sygma (tr). **302 Corbis:** Walter McBride (tr). **303 Alamy Images:** Dinodia Photos (br). **304 Getty Images:** Dinodia Photos/Contributor (tl). **305 Alamy Images:** FotoFlirt (br). **307 Corbis:** (tr). **309 Corbis:** Nigel Pavitt/JAI (bl). Colin McPherson (tr). **315 Corbis:** Destinations (bl). Eric Fougere/VIP Images (tr). **317 Corbis:** Jihan Abdalla/Blend Images (tl). **321 Alamy Images:** PPFC Collection (tr). **Corbis:** Sophie Bassouls/Sygma (bl). **323 Corbis:** James Andanson/Sygma (tr). **325 Corbis:** Colin McPherson (bl). **327 Corbis:** Rune Hellestad (tr). **329 Alamy Images:** dpa picture alliance (tr).

All other images © Dorling Kindersley. For more information see: **www.dkimages.com**